THE

Periplus Maris Erythraei

THE
Periplus Maris Erythraei

TEXT WITH INTRODUCTION,
TRANSLATION, AND COMMENTARY

BY

LIONEL CASSON

PRINCETON
UNIVERSITY PRESS

Library of Congress Cataloging-in-Publication Data

Casson, Lionel, 1914-
The Periplus maris Erythraei.

Bibliography: p.   Includes index.
1. Rome—Commerce—History. 2. Commerce—History—
To 500. I. Periplus maris Erythraei. English. II. Title.
HF377.C27 1989   382'.0937   88-15178
ISBN 0-691-04060-5 (alk. paper)

This book has been composed in Linotron Bembo

Designed by Laury A. Egan

To Bluma, Blanche, and Annalina:
the "Greek Readers"

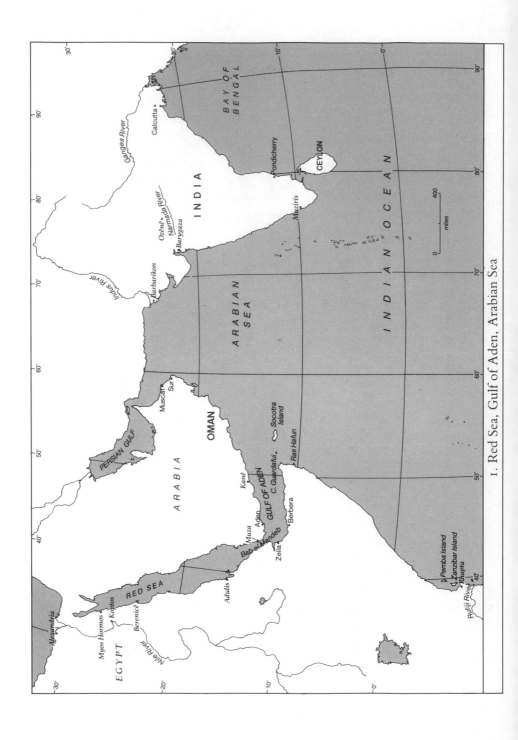

1. Red Sea, Gulf of Aden, Arabian Sea

CONTENTS

LIST OF MAPS

PREFACE

The *Periplus Maris Erythraei*, a handbook for merchants trading between Roman Egypt and eastern Africa, southern Arabia, and India, is a unique and precious document—unique because nothing else like it has survived from the writings of the ancient world; precious because it provides precise and detailed information about a subject otherwise little known. Yet no proper edition of it is available.

The sole modern text, that published by H. Frisk in 1927, has long been out of print. There is no satisfactory translation in any language. Because of the nature of the work, with its plethora of technical terms and obscure place names, a comprehensive commentary is essential; the latest available, W. Schoff's, appeared in 1912 and is hopelessly out of date.

The present edition seeks to fill all these needs. It reproduces Frisk's text with whatever improvements have been suggested since publication. This updated text is accompanied by a translation that attempts to be as literal as possible consonant with the requirements of good English. There are two commentaries—a full general commentary for all readers and a short one dealing with textual matters, grammar, vocabulary, and the like for readers competent in Greek—and five appendixes on matters that required more lengthy treatment.

The understanding of a work like the *Periplus* requires much specialized knowledge; experts in a wide variety of fields have most generously assisted me. To N. Lewis's intimate knowledge of the language of the Greek papyri I owe the explication of many a textual crux, and to John Scarborough's encyclopedic knowledge of ancient pharmacy the explication of many a puzzling drug name. A.F.L. Beeston, authority on the language and history of pre-Islamic southern Arabia, gave invaluable aid with the sections dealing with that region. Sir Laurance Kirwan, Honorable Life President of the British Institute in Eastern Africa, sent me a prepublication copy of a vitally important paper on the identification of Leukê Kômê. Bluma Trell, specialist in numismatic studies, provided invaluable bibliography for problems involving coinages. Robert Fowkes, the linguist, clarified several passages involving Sanskrit. The maps were prepared by Paul J. Pugliese. To my wife I owe, as always, a deep debt

for her encouragement, her critical review of the manuscript that unerr-
ingly identified obscurities and repetitions, and her patient retyping of
draft upon draft.

ABBREVIATIONS

AJA: *American Journal of Archaeology*

ANRW: *Aufstieg und Niedergang der römischen Welt*

Beeston: A. Beeston, review of Huntingford, *BSOAS* 44 (1981): 353–58

BGU: *Berliner griechische Urkunden* (Berlin, 1895–)

BSOAS: *Bulletin of the School of Oriental and African Studies*, London University

Bunbury: E. Bunbury, *A History of Ancient Geography* (London, 1879)

CAH: *Cambridge Ancient History*

Casson 1980: L. Casson, "*Periplus Maris Erythraei*: Three Notes on the Text," *CQ* 30 (1980): 495–97

Casson 1980a: L. Casson, "Rome's Trade with the East: The Sea Voyage to Africa and India," *Transactions of the American Philological Association* 110 (1980): 21–36 = Casson 1984.182–98

Casson 1981: L. Casson, "The Location of Adulis," L. Casson and M. Price, eds., *Coins, Culture and History in the Ancient World: Numismatic and Other Studies in Honor of Bluma L. Trell* (Detroit, 1981), 113–22 = Casson 1984.199–210

Casson 1982: L. Casson, "*Periplus Maris Erythraei*: Notes on the Text," *JHS* 102 (1982): 204–6

Casson 1982a: L. Casson, "*Periplus Maris Erythraei* 36: Teak, not Sandalwood," *CQ* 32 (1982): 181–83

Casson 1983: L. Casson, "Greek and Roman Clothing: Some Technical Terms," *Glotta* 61 (1983): 193–207

Casson 1983a: L. Casson, "Sakas versus Andhras in the *Periplus Maris Erythraei*," *JESHO* 26 (1983): 164–77

Casson 1984: L. Casson, *Ancient Trade and Society* (Detroit, 1984)

Casson 1984a: L. Casson, "Egypt, Africa, Arabia, and India: Patterns of Seaborne Trade in the First Century A.D.," *Bulletin of the American Society of Papyrologists* 21 (1984): 39–47

Casson 1984b: L. Casson, "The Sea Route to India: *Periplus Maris Erythraei* 57," *CQ* 34 (1984): 473–79

Casson 1986: L. Casson, "The Location of Tabai (*Periplus Maris Erythraei* 12–13)," *JHS* 106 (1986): 179–82

Casson 1986a: L. Casson, "P. Vindob. G 40822 and the Shipping of Goods from India," *Bulletin of the American Society of Papyrologists* 23 (1986): 73–79

Casson 1987: L. Casson, "*Periplus Maris Erythraei* 60," *CQ* 37 (1987): 233–35

CHA: *Cambridge History of Africa*

CHI: *Cambridge History of Iran*

Conti Rossini: C. Conti Rossini, *Storia d'Etiopia*, "Africa italiana," Collezione di monografie a cura del Ministero delle Colonie 3 (Milan, 1928)

CQ: *Classical Quarterly*

Desanges: J. Desanges, *Recherches sur l'activité des Méditerranéens aux confins de l'Afrique*, Collection de l'École Française de Rome 38 (Rome, 1978)

Drakonaki-Kazantzaki: E. Drakonaki-Kazantzaki, "Textual Problems in the '*Periplus Maris Erythraei*,' " *Corolla Londiniensis* 2 (1982): 47–55

Ed. Diocl.: *Edictum Diocletiani*, ed. S. Lauffer, *Diokletians Preisedikt*, Texte und Kommentare 5 (Berlin, 1971)

ESAR: T. Frank, ed., *An Economic Survey of Ancient Rome* (Baltimore, 1933–40)

Fabricius: B. Fabricius, *Der Periplus des Erythräischen Meeres von einem Unbekannten* (Leipzig, 1883)

Frisk: H. Frisk, *Le Périple de la mer Érythrée*, Göteborgs Högskolas Årsskrift 33 (Göteborg, 1927)

GGM: *Geographi Graeci Minores*

Giangrande 1975: G. Giangrande, "On the Text of the *Periplus Maris Erythraei*," *Mnemosyne* 28 (1975): 293–96

Giangrande 1976: G. Giangrande, "Textual Problems in the *Periplus Maris Erythraei*," *JHS* 96 (1976): 154–57

GJ: *Geographical Journal*

Glaser: E. Glaser, *Skizze der Geschichte und Geographie Arabiens* ii (Berlin, 1890)

Gloss.: G. Loewe, G. Goetz, and F. Schoell, eds., *Corpus Glossariorum Latinorum* (Leipzig, 1888–1924)

Guillain: C. Guillain, *Documents sur l'histoire, la géographie et le commerce de l'Afrique Orientale* i (Paris, 1856)

Harrauer-Sijpesteijn: H. Harrauer and P. Sijpesteijn, "Ein neues Dokument zu Roms Indienhandel, P. Vindob. G 40822," *Anzeiger der Österreichischen Akademie der Wissenschaften*, phil.-hist. Kl. 122 (1985): 124–55

Hobson-Jobson: H. Yule and A. Burnell, *Hobson-Jobson* (London, 1903²)

Huntingford: G. Huntingford, *The Periplus of the Erythraean Sea*, Hakluyt Society, 2d series 151 (London, 1980)

IGRR: R. Cagnat, ed., *Inscriptiones Graecae ad Res Romanas Pertinentes* (Paris, 1911–27)

IJNA: *International Journal of Nautical Archaeology*

JA: *Journal Asiatique*

JAOS: *Journal of the American Oriental Society*

JEA: *Journal of Egyptian Archaeology*

JESHO: *Journal of the Economic and Social History of the Orient*

JHS: *Journal of Hellenic Studies*

JRAS: *Journal of the Royal Asiatic Society*

Lassen: C. Lassen, *Indische Alterthumskunde* (Leipzig, 1858–74)

Löw: I. Löw, *Die Flora der Juden* (Vienna and Leipzig), 1924–34

LSJ: H. Liddell, R. Scott, and H. Jones, eds., *A Greek-English Lexicon* (Oxford, 1940⁹)

McCrindle: J. McCrindle, *The Commerce and Navigation of the Erythraean Sea* (Calcutta, 1879)

Meile: P. Meile, "Les Yavanas dans l'Inde tamoule," *JA* 232 (1940): 85–123

Miller: J. Miller, *The Spice Trade of the Roman Empire* (Oxford, 1969)

Mokhtar: G. Mokhtar, ed., *General History of Africa*. ii, *Ancient Civilizations of Africa* (Berkeley, 1981)

Müller: C. Müller's edition of the *Periplus* in *Geographi Graeci Minores* i (Paris, 1855), 257–305

O. Tait: J. Tait and others, *Greek Ostraca in the Bodleian Library at Oxford and Various Other Collections* (London, 1930–64)

P. Aberd.: E. Turner, *Catalogue of Greek and Latin Papyri and Ostraca in the Possession of the University of Aberdeen* (Aberdeen, 1939)

P. Amh.: B. Grenfell and A. Hunt, *The Amherst Papyri* (London, 1900–1901)

P. Ant.: C. Roberts and others, The Antinoopolis Papyri (London, 1950–67)

P. Cairo Zen.: C. Edgar, *Zenon Papyri* (Cairo, 1925–40)

P.Col.: W. Westermann and others, *Columbia Papyri* (New York, 1929–79)

P. Coll. Youtie: A. Hanson, *Collectanea Papyrologica: Texts Published in Honor of H. C. Youtie* (Bonn, 1976)

P. Corn.: W. Westermann and C. Kraemer, *Greek Papyri in the Library of Cornell University* (New York, 1926)

P. Genova: M. Amelotti and L. Zingale Migliardi, *Papiri dell' Università di Genova*, 2 vols. (Genoa, 1974; Florence, 1980)

P. Giss.: O. Eger, E. Kornemann, and P. Meyer, *Griechische Papyri im*

Museum des oberhessischen Geschichtsverein zu Giessen (Leipzig and Berlin, 1910–22)

P. Hamb.: P. Meyer, *Griechische Papyrusurkunden der Hamburger Staats- und Universitätsbibliothek* (Leipzig and Berlin, 1911–24)

P. Hib.: B. Grenfell and others, *The Hibeh Papyri*, 2 vols. (London, 1906, 1955)

P. Holm.: O. Lagercrantz, *Papyrus Graecus Holmiensis* (Uppsala and Leipzig, 1913)

P. Laur.: R. Pintaudi, *Dai Papiri della Biblioteca Medicea Laurenziana* (Florence, 1976)

P. Lond.: F. Kenyon and others, *Greek Papyri in the British Museum* (London, 1893–1974)

P. Merton: H. Bell and others, *A Descriptive Catalogue of the Greek Papyri in the Collection of Wilfred Merton* (London, 1948–67)

P. Micha.: D. Crawford, *Papyri Michaelidae* (Aberdeen, 1955)

P. Mich. Zen.: C. Edgar, *Zenon Papyri*, University of Michigan Studies, Humanistic Series 24 (Ann Arbor, 1931)

P. Oxy.: B. Grenfell and others, *The Oxrhynchus Papyri* (London 1898–)

Preisigke, *WB*: F. Preisigke and others, *Wörterbuch der griechischen Papyrusurkunden* (Berlin, 1925–)

P. Ross. Georg.: G. Zereteli and others, *Papyri russischer und georgischer Sammlungen* (Tiflis, 1925–35)

P. Ryl.: A. Hunt and others, *Catalogue of the Greek Papyri in the John Rylands Library, Manchester* (Manchester, 1911–52)

PSI: G. Vitelli and others, *Papiri greci e latini* (Florence, 1912–)

P. Teb.: B. Grenfell and others, *The Tebtunis Papyri* (London, 1902–76)

P. Vindob. Worp: K. Worp, *Einige Wiener Papyri* (Amsterdam, 1972)

Raschke: M. Raschke, "New Studies in Roman Commerce with the East," *ANRW* ii 9.2 (Berlin, 1978): 604–1361

RE: *Paulys Real-Encyclopädie der classischen Altertumswissenschaft*

RSP: *Red Sea and Gulf of Aden Pilot* (published by the Hydrographer of the [British] Navy, 1980[12])

Salt: H. Salt, *Voyage to Abyssinia* (London, 1814)

SB: *Sammelbuch griechischer Urkunden aus Aegypten*

Schoff: W. Schoff, *The Periplus of the Erythraean Sea* (London, 1912)

SDA: *Sailing Directions for the Southeast Coast of Africa* (published by the [USA] Defense Mapping Agency, Hydrographic Center 1968[5], revised 1975)

SDRS: *Sailing Directions for the Red Sea and the Persian Gulf* (published by the [USA] Defense Mapping Agency, Hydrographic/Topographic Center, 1983[2])

Sel. Pap.: A. Hunt and C. Edgar, *Select Papyri* i–ii (Loeb Classical Library, London, 1932, 1934)

Sidebotham: S. Sidebotham, *Roman Economic Policy in the Erythra Thalassa, 30 B.C.–A.D. 217* (Leiden, 1986)

Smith: V. Smith, *The Early History of India* (Oxford, 1924[4])

Sprenger: A. Spenger, *Die alte Geographie Arabiens* (Bern, 1875)

SSAW: L. Casson, *Ships and Seamanship in the Ancient World* (Princeton, 1986[2])

Stud. Pal.: C. Wessely, ed., *Studien zur Palaeographie und Papyruskunde* (Leipzig, 1901–24)

Tarn: W. Tarn, *The Greeks in Bactria and India* (Cambridge, 1951[2])

UPZ: U. Wilcken, ed., *Urkunden der Ptolemäerzeit* (Berlin, 1927–57)

Vincent: W. Vincent, *The Commerce and Navigation of the Ancients in the Indian Ocean*. ii, *The Periplus of the Erythrean Sea* (London, 1807)

Warmington: E. Warmington, *The Commerce between the Roman Empire and India* (Cambridge, 1974[2])

Watt: G. Watt, *A Dictionary of the Economic Products of India* (Calcutta, 1889–96)

WChrest: L. Mitteis and U. Wilcken, *Grundzüge und Chrestomathie der Papyruskunde*, i.2, *Chrestomathie* (Leipzig, 1912)

WCIP: *West Coast of India Pilot* (published by the Hydrographer of the [British] Navy, 1975[11])

Wellsted: J. Wellsted, *Travels in Arabia* (London, 1838)

Wheeler: M. Wheeler, *Rome Beyond the Imperial Frontiers* (London, 1954)

W. Müller: W. Müller, "Weihrauch," *RE* Suppl. 15.700–777 (1978)

Yule-Cordier: *Marco Polo*, ed. by H. Yule and revised and augmented by H. Cordier (London, 1903)

NOTES TO THE READER

References to the text of the *Periplus* are by chapter number followed by the page and line number(s) in Frisk's edition. Thus '57:19.1' = chapter 57, line 1 on Frisk's page 19.

References to Ptolemy are to the *Geography*.

Modern place names are spelled as in *SDA, SDRS*, and the *Official Standard Names Gazetteer*.

THE

Periplus Maris Erythraei

INTRODUCTION

3

I. TEXT AND AUTHOR

The *Periplus* is preserved in a single manuscript, Codex Palatinus Graecus 398, fols. 40v–54v, in the Universitäts Bibliothek, Heidelberg. It dates from the beginning of the tenth century.

The scribe wrote the text in minuscules, added marginal headings in small uncials, and made a number of corrections. The text is replete with errors, as a glance at the apparatus criticus will show. To begin with, the scribe worked from an exemplar that he recognized was faulty. In two places (2:1.11, 58:19.14) he left a blank space, indicating a gap in the manuscript he had before him. In quite a few places,[1] he put a tick in the margin to flag passages with manifest errors in them, and in these and others he would often leave the misspelled or incomprehensible words unaccented.[2] To the mistakes in the exemplar he no doubt added a good number of his own. Some of the mistakes, whether his own or copied from the exemplar, he corrected by adding replacements for missing letters above the line or by placing dots over erroneous letters (Frisk 27–30). Subsequently a second hand made further corrections, noting erroneous letters by underdotting them or deleting them with a stroke and adding still more superimposed letters. Here and there this hand contributed mistakes instead of improvements (Frisk 30–31). The corrections of both hands derived solely from a rereading of the manuscript and not from collation against another copy.

The plethora of mistakes in the manuscript is not hard to explain. The *Periplus*, dealing as it does with remote areas and their products, contains an abundance of rare words and obscure place names, which are fertile sources of error.

There is a manuscript of the *Periplus* in the British Museum (B.M. Add. 19391, fols. 9r–12r, 14th–15th century). It is merely a copy of the Palatine manuscript, errors and all, and has no independent authority.

The first printed edition of the *Periplus* appeared in 1533, and numerous

---

[1] Listed in Frisk 33, n. 2.
[2] See, e.g., under B 10:4.11, B 15:5.25–26a, B 53:17.23–24.

5

others came out in the succeeding centuries.[3] Unfortunately, the editors had little knowledge of the Greek it was written in, the *koinê* (see below), and they made matters worse by indulging in liberal emendation, as was the practice when they wrote. To top it all, the best of these texts, Müller's in the *Geographi Graeci Minores*, was overshadowed by Fabricius's second edition,[4] in which he displays a total disregard for the readings of the manuscript. In 1927 Hjalmar Frisk finally made available a proper modern edition. Since then a few minor adjustments have been contributed, notably by G. Giangrande, his student E. Drakonaki-Kazantzaki, and me.

Yet even Frisk's text with the emendations that have been added since it appeared still has passages whose meaning eludes us[5] and words and phrases whose translation is in doubt.[6] This is inevitable in a work that is preserved in but a single manuscript and that, to compound the difficulty, is so full of unfamiliar words and names. One common source of error was the attempt of the scribes—whether the writer of the Palatine codex or of those that preceded it—to give these unfamiliar terms a familiar look. Some of the resultant aberrations are easy to detect: "Ibêria" in 41:14.4 is surely a transformation of the Indian place name Abêria, "Arabikê" in 41:14.2 of the Indian place name Ariakê, "*lykon*" (wolf) in 39:13.10 of *lykion* (the name of a drug), etc. But that still leaves a good number that are beyond convincing emendation, that we can only translate with a query or leave untranslated.

THE DATE

There has been a long-standing debate over when the *Periplus* was written, one that has spawned a voluminous literature.[7] The work has been dated as early as A.D. 30 to as late as 230 and to various times in between.

There is no need to review the arguments put forth by the adherents of the various datings. Recent studies in Nabataean history have determined

---

[3] Schoff 17–19 lists the various editions.

[4] E.g., Schoff (20) refers to Fabricius's text as one "which has been revised with extreme care . . . and leaves little to be desired."

[5] See under B 15:5.19, B 15:5.25–26a, B 47:16.6, B 59:20.1a, B 61:20.16–18, B 65:21.22–23, and cf. Frisk 35.

[6] See under B 6:2.27, B 6:3.2 and 3.3, B 48:16.17, B 53:17.23–24, B 58:19.18.

[7] For the literature, see Raschke 979–81, nn. 1342–46. For a critical review of the arguments, see W. Raunig, "Die Versuche einer Datierung des *Periplus maris Erythraei*," *Mitteilungen der anthropologischen Gesellschaft in Wien* 100 (1970): 231–42, and Rodinson's studies cited under 5:2.19–20 and 22:7.25–26. Raschke states (n. 1342) that Raunig "concludes that a date cannot be convincingly established." On the contrary, Raunig (240) concludes that "Allerdings scheint . . . das Schwergewicht der Argumente eine Datierung der Schrift in die zweite Hälfte des 1. Jhdts n. Chr. zu rechtfertigen."

the sequence of the Nabataean kings,[8] and this enables us to assign the *Periplus* without any doubt to the middle of the first century A.D. In 19:6.28–29, the author speaks of going "to Petra, to Malichus, king of the Nabataeans." The word "Nabataeans" is a restoration, but that is of little import: a king in Petra can only be a king of the Nabataeans, and the list of their kings includes certainly two and possible three named Malichus. Malichus I belongs to the first century B.C. and hence can be eliminated. Malichus II ruled from A.D. 40 to 70.[9] He was succeeded by his son, Rabbel II, who held the throne right up to the Roman annexation in 106.[10] It has been argued that Rabbel had a son named Malichus who, on his father's death, became either a king in exile or, more probably, a Roman client-king holding sway over the sparsely populated desert area to the south of the country, around Hegra.[11] If there were such a Malichus, he was in any event not at Petra. Thus the Malichus mentioned in the *Periplus* can only be Malichus II, and the work must be dated to his reign, that is, between A.D. 40 and 70.

There are still some who cling to a date in the third century A.D. They must, of course, somehow exorcize the mention of Malichus, and this they do by asserting that the *Periplus* was not all written at one time but is a compilation garnered from works that date from the time of Malichus to the particular time in the third century that they favor.[12] This is simply scholarly legerdemain, for the *Periplus* is beyond question the work of one man; there is not the slightest trace in it either of different hands or of different times.[13]

THE AUTHOR AND HIS WORK

The author must have been an Egyptian Greek, for he refers at one point (29:9.27) to "the trees we have in Egypt" and he consistently gives the

[8] See G. Bowersock in *Journal of Roman Studies* 61 (1972): 223.

[9] Cf. A. Negev in *Palestine Exploration Quarterly* 114 (1982): 122.

[10] The annexation took place in 106 (Dio Cassius 68.14.5), and a Nabataean graffito attests to a "36th year of Rabbel" (*Revue Biblique* n.s. 8 [1911]: 273–77).

[11] Cf. J. Eadie in J. Eadie and J. Ober, eds., *The Craft of the Ancient Historian: Essays in Honor of Chester G. Starr* (Lanham, Md., 1985): 412–15. The evidence offered is debatable; see G. Bowersock in *Classical Review* 38 (1988): 104.

[12] So J. Palmer in *CQ* 41 (1974): 140; H. von Wissmann in *ANRW* ii 9.1 434–35 (1976); M. Rodinson in J. Chelhod et al. (op. cit. under 23:7.27–29) 67–68. J. Pirenne, one of the most vocal of the advocates of a date in the third century, used a miscellany of arguments to eliminate the mention of Malichus and to support a late date, all of which were convincingly refuted by A. Dihle, *Umstrittene Daten: Untersuchungen zum Auftreten der Griechen am Roten Meer* (Cologne, 1965), 9–35; see also P. Lévêque's summary in *Revue des études grecques* 79 (1966): 730–32.

[13] Cf. Fraser (op. cit. under 19:6.31) ii 294, n. 328.

Egyptian equivalents of the Roman months (6:3.6, 14:5.8, 24:8.12, 39:13.13, 49:16.32, 56:18.29). He writes from personal experience, as is evident not only from the nature of his reporting, direct and detailed, but from a passage in which he reveals that he himself plied the route under discussion ("we set a course . . . we put on extra speed," 20:7.14–15). His personal experience included the African route down to Rhapta[14] and the Arabian-Indian at least down to Cape Comorin at India's southern tip.[15] Many authorities[16] hold that he did not himself travel the next leg, up the east coast of India to the mouth of the Ganges, since his report on it lacks the detail found elsewhere, but this is arguable.[17]

He seems to have been a merchant who, after sailing the routes the *Periplus* describes and trading in the products it lists, decided to write a handbook on the subject.[18] The title, *Periplus Maris Erythraei*, is misleading, for the work is not at all like the other *periploi* that have come down to us, such as those of Scylax, Arrian, Marcian of Heraclea, and so on. These were first and foremost guides for seamen, whereas the *Periplus Maris Erythraei* is first and foremost a guide for merchants; it supplies some sailing information, mostly the general direction of the courses and their length, but the emphasis is overwhelmingly on trading information, the products that could be bought or sold in each port. A related service that it provides is the noting of the rank and, when possible, the name of the local ruler of each port and of the supreme ruler, if the two are not the same (see below, Political Geography). This information, invaluable for people doing business in a foreign land, had an economic dimension as

[14] Many argue that, since his description of the East African coast is so summary, he did not himself sail down it; see Müller 268 (bottom of first col.), Bunbury ii 452, McCrindle 66, Schoff 16, Freeman-Grenville (op. cit. under 15:5.17–16:6.13) 24. But, as Datoo (op. cit. under 16:6.4, 74) points out, his description seems summary only because a large part of the area was commercially unimportant and hence given minimal treatment; the rest is handled with as much detail as elsewhere.

[15] One good indication that he spent time in India is the accuracy with which he transcribes Indian names and words into Greek; see J. Bloch, "Sur quelques transcriptions de noms indiens dans le Périple de la mer Érythrée," *Mélanges d'Indianisme offerts par ses élèves à M. M. Sylvain Lévi* (Paris, 1911), 1–16 at 4.

[16] Lassen iii 5; Thomson (op. cit. under 15:5.17–16:6.13) 304; M. Charlesworth in P. Coleman-Norton, ed., *Studies in Roman Economic and Social History in Honor of Allen Chester Johnson* (Princeton, 1951), 135–36; Wheeler 144; K. Nilakanta Sastri, *The Cōlas* (Madras, 1955²), 22.

[17] Their conclusion is based on the summary fashion in which the author deals with this coast. This could well be because most of its trade was outside his range of interest; see below, Trade in the Indian Ocean: The Trade with India.

[18] G. Mathew in Chittick-Rotberg (op. cit. under 15:5.17–16:6.13) 153–54 holds that the author was an official of the Roman government and that the *Periplus* was a report submitted to the prefect of Egypt; this is pure fantasy.

8

well: where relevant, the author itemizes what goods can be sold to the ruler or to members of his court (see under 24:8.7–9). Yet another useful service is the identifying of those places where a merchant has to be on his guard against the locals (7:3.21–22, 9:4.4–5, 20:7.7–9, 34:11.23–24) and those where they are peaceful (8:3.25–26, 20:7.16–17).

But the author by no means sticks to the straight and narrow of his avowed topic; a lively curiosity leads him into other fields. Although he was presumably writing about the trade conducted by the merchants from Roman Egypt, he paints a complete picture by including all the trade that went on in the region he deals with, that of the merchants from Arabia, India, and Africa as well as from Roman Egypt (see below, Trade in the Indian Ocean: The Lines and Objects of Trade). Moreover, throughout he adds bits of information that have nothing to do with trade but rather with anthropology and natural history. He is particularly interested in unusual features of the local populations one meets in the ports or passes en route, their special appearance (the big men of Rhapta [16:6.6–7]; the big, dark-skinned men of Syrastrênê [41:14.6–8]; the flat-faced tribes of northeast India [62:20.24–28]), homes (the mean huts of the Ichthyophagoi [2:1.7–8], the cave dwellings along the south Arabian coast [32:10.28]), language (the bilingual inhabitants of western Arabia [20:7.8], the Arabic-speaking inhabitants of the Isle of Sarapis [33:11.15–17]), eating habits (the eating of lizards and the use of their fat for oil on Dioscuridês [30:10.5–6]), dress (the loincloths of palm leaves on the Isle of Sarapis [33:11.17]). He notes the use of convict labor for gathering frankincense (29:9.29) or diving for pearls (59:19.22–23). He is equally interested in unusual features of the animal population, remarking on the lack of any animals except big and harmless "crocodiles" on Menuthias (15:5.29), the curious fauna of Dioscuridês (30:10.4–5), the multitude of wild animals in Dachinabadês (50:17.3–7). As a man who spent much time on the sea, he is understandably interested in unusual marine matters—boats whose planks are sewn together (15:5.30, 16:6.5, 36:12.8), rafts supported by inflated skins (27:9.9–10), dugouts (15:5.30), catamarans and other unfamiliar Indian craft (60:20.6–9), a special way of catching turtles (15:6.1–2).

He has some interest in history. He explains (3:1.14–15) how Ptolemais Thêrôn got its name from the hunting parties sent out from it by the Ptolemies, he remarks (41:14.9–11) that remains of buildings and wells around Barygaza or Minnagara go back to the time of Alexander, and he informs us (47:16.7) that Alexander reached the Ganges (he did not; see under 47:16.7); he recounts (57:19.2–12) the discovery of the direct route over open water to India; he notes (26:8.31–32) the recent destruction of Eudaimôn Arabia at the hands of the Romans.

Curiously, one subject he gives short shrift to is religion. Although he came from Egypt, the land par excellence of religious memorabilia, and his chief trade contacts were with India where, in his day as in ours, religion was of great moment,[19] he mentions but a single religious monument, the shrine of Durga near Cape Comorin (58:19.18–21 and see note ad loc.).

He was a businessman, not a man of letters. He uses the Greek of his day, the *koinê*, but writes a businessman's version of it,[20] purely functional, flat, and styleless, replete with repetitions[21] and studded with technical language[22] and trade terms,[23] much like the writing we meet in the business documents among the Greek papyri found in Egypt. Yet he can, when he wants, rise to a higher level. His description (46:15.22–16.2) of the mighty tides along India's northwestern coast conveys excitement, his words have drive and color. And every now and then he attempts to break out of the businessman's unvarnished style by deliberately avoiding a repetition[24] or by a conscious touch of literary elegance.[25]

[19] Strabo describes at great length (15.712–19) India's multifarious forms of worship as reported by Megasthenes, the ambassador of Seleucus Nicator (r. 311–281 B.C.), to the court of Chandragupta, and by Onesicritus and Nearchus, both of whom accompanied Alexander.

[20] Cf. Frisk 102, Giangrande 1975.293.

[21] Cf. Frisk 92, n. 1.

[22] See Frisk 92 for a list of *hapax legomena* in the *Periplus*; the majority are technical terms.

[23] See under B 6:2.23, B 6:2.24–25, B 6:2.34–35.

[24] A good example is λεγόμενος and καλούμενος. The author uses the first some sixty-five times throughout, but in three places (30:9.33, 30:10.3, 58:19.16) substitutes the second. Cf. Frisk 117–18; Drakonaki-Kazantzaki 48, n. 11 (variations in spelling). And, in noting the best time of year to set sail for a given destination, he rarely uses the same words (14:5.7–8, 24:8.11–12, 28:9.20–21, 39:13.12–13, 49:16.31–32, 56:18.28–29).

[25] Cf. Frisk 102, Giangrande 1976.155 (use of the dual in 40:13.29), Drakonaki-Kazantzaki 47–48 (the poetic form κλειομένη in 63:21.9). The literary touches are particularly noticeable in connection with the sea: in 33:11.12 he uses ὕψος "height" in the sense of "high sea," in 57:19.11 ὑψηλός "high" in the sense of "high on the open sea," in 20:7.13 ἀκάθαρτος "uncleansed" to describe the dangerous and reef-strewn east coast of the Red Sea. None of these marine figurative senses are noted in *LSJ*. And, in referring (46:15.29) to the power of the sea, he uses the plural βίαι, just as Homer (Il. 16.213) does for the power of the winds.

II. TRADE IN

THE INDIAN OCEAN

THE SETTING

From at least the beginning of the second millennium B.C. traders were using the seaways of the Indian Ocean. Mesopotamian ships went from ports at the head of the Persian Gulf along the southern coast of what is today Iran and Pakistan to Indian ports at the mouth of the Indus; Indian ships did the journey in reverse.[1] Further west, the Old Kingdom pharaohs sent vessels to the Straits of Bab el Mandeb at the mouth of the Red Sea and possibly as far as Cape Guardafui.[2]

During the subsequent ages such voyaging was continued by Phoenician, Arab, Indian, and perhaps other seaman, continued by them for centuries before Greek vessels appeared in these waters.[3] In the course of these centuries the Arabs and Indians unquestionably learned to exploit the monsoons, those seasonal winds that, in the western Indian Ocean, Gulf of Aden, and Arabian Sea, blow from the southwest during the summer and from the northeast during the winter, thereby ensuring a favorable voyage both ways (App. 3). Somehow they were able to keep this knowledge from Greek seamen so that, when these do start taking part in the trade with Arabia and India, they sailed, as the *Periplus* specifically informs us (26:8.28–29), no further east than Eudaimôn Arabia, where Aden now stands, less than one hundred nautical miles from the mouth of the Red Sea. Here they unloaded whatever cargoes they were carrying and took on what Indian vessels had brought from their home ports (26:8.27–31); Eudaimôn Arabia was truly an entrepôt.

Then came the moment when Greek seamen no longer stopped short

---

[1] See S. Ratnagar, *Encounters: The Westerly Trade of the Harappa Civilization* (Delhi, 1981).

[2] As early as ca. 2400 B.C., Egypt dispatched expeditions to a land called Punt to bring back myrrh or frankincense (*CAH* i.2 183 [1971³]). Punt is usually taken to be Somalia, although an argument has been offered that it was much nearer, the Ethiopian shore of the Red Sea (K. Kitchen, "Punt and How to Get There," *Orientalia* 40 [1971]: 184–207).

[3] Cf. Solomon's use of Phoenicians for trading down the Red Sea (*CAH* ii.2 594 [1975³]).

at Eudaimôn Arabia but continued all the way to India, when, in other words, they had learned to exploit the monsoons. The *Periplus* attributes the discovery to a certain captain or pilot named Hippalos, without mentioning his date (57:19.2–7). Strabo, on the other hand, mentions a pioneering voyage made by Eudoxus of Cyzicus around 116 B.C. that almost certainly marked the Greeks' first use of the monsoons for getting to India and back. The resolution of the discrepancy is a minor point; what is significant is that, from then on, Greek ships sailed regularly to India (see under 57:19.5–7).

But they did so only in limited numbers, and this remained the case until Augustus made Egypt part of the Roman Empire. That ushered in a new era: from the Augustan Age on, the ships of Roman Egypt plied the route to Arabia and India in greatly increased numbers; we not only have Strabo's word for it[4] but the tangible evidence of quantities of Roman coins and Roman pottery found in India.[5] Within half a century trade in the Indian Ocean had grown so, that the author of the *Periplus* was moved to draw up a handbook for the use of merchants and skippers involved in it.

He begins his work with a short section—about a quarter of the whole; Arabia takes about another quarter and India half—on the African trade route. This too had long been known to other seamen before the Greeks took part in it. Indeed, according to Herodotus (4.42), around 600 B.C. a Phoenician expedition succeeded in circumnavigating the whole continent. At this time the pharaohs were still sending their ships down to the Straits of Bab el Mandeb or beyond.[6] By about 200 B.C. Greek merchants were on the scene, seeking to purchase myrrh in the ports on the southern shore of the Gulf of Aden.[7] They may even have reached Cape Guardafui; certainly by the end of the second century B.C., Greek geographers knew the coast of Africa that far.[8] It was inevitable that Greek seamen sooner or later would become aware that the same monsoons that took voyagers so conveniently to India and back would perform the identical service for them down the east coast of Africa and back. By the time the *Periplus* was written, they had extended their range of trade as far south as Rhapta, somewhere in the vicinity of Dar es Salaam (see under 16:6.4).

---

[4] He points out (2.118) that in his day 120 vessels sailed, presumably annually, to Arabia and India. Previously less than twenty had (17.798).

[5] Wheeler 137–39 and C. Rodewald, *Money in the Age of Tiberius* (Manchester, 1976), 48–51 (coins); V. Begley in *AJA* 87 (1983): 475 (Arretine were dating from the first quarter of the first century A.D. found at Arikamedu).

[6] Desanges 228–29.

[7] Desanges 299–301.

[8] Strabo 16.774, citing Artemidorus, who wrote ca. 100 B.C.

BETWEEN ALEXANDRIA AND THE RED SEA

In the days of the *Periplus*, the ships plying the seaways from Egypt to
Africa and India left from, and returned to, the ports of Myos Hormos
and Berenicê on the Red Sea (see under 1:1.2-4)—but not their cargoes;
these had an additional leg at the beginning and end. Some of what was
exported in these vessels came from outside Egypt.[9] This merchandise
arrived at Alexandria and from there went up the Nile in river craft which
stopped at various ports en route to take on export items that Egypt itself
produced. The final destination was Koptos, a port set at the point where
a great eastward bend of the river brings it closest to the shore of the Red
Sea.[10] From Koptos the goods went by camel over the desert to Myos
Hormos or Berenicê. What was imported made the trip in reverse—by
camel from Myos Hormos or Berenicê over the desert to Koptos and
from there down the Nile to Alexandria. Myos Hormos had the advantage of offering a shorter desert crossing—six to seven days as against
eleven to twelve from Berenicê. But Berenicê, in turn, had a signal advantage of its own to offer: it lay 230 nautical miles south of Myos Hormos, and this saved homebound vessels that much relief from beating
against consistently foul winds. Until the time of the *Periplus*, both ports
seem to have been used equally. The records of a transport company that
hauled provisions for the use of the merchants and their agents residing
at these ports, for example, show the deliveries going to both places, and,
in addition, reveal that a few of the shipping companies maintained offices at both places.[11] Strabo's remarks seem to indicate that in his day

---

[9] E.g., Italian and Laodicean wine (6:2.32–33, 49:16.20–21), tin (7:3.18, 28:9.15, 49:16.21,
56:18.19), saffron (see under 24:8.3a), storax (see under 28:9.16a), coral (see under 28:9.16),
orpiment (see under 56:18.21).

[10] Koptos was serving the Red Sea trade at least as early as ca. 2000 B.C. (*CAH* i.2 491
[1971³]).

[11] For the roads from Koptos to Myos Hormos and Berenicê, see under 1:1.2–4. The
transport company records, the so-called archive of Nicanor, consists of a group of almost
ninety ostraca found at Koptos, dating from 18 B.C. to A.D. 69 (*O. Tait* i P220–304, ii 1968–
71; *Chronique d'Égypte* 31 [1956]: 356). In them various signatories at Myos Hormos and
Berenicê acknowledge receipt, on behalf of themselves or their employers, of goods delivered to them from Koptos by a company belonging to a certain Nicanor and his family. For
discussion of the archive, see M. Rostovtzeff in *Gnomon* (1931): 23–25, A. Fuks in *Journal of
Juristic Papyrology* 5 (1951): 207–16, Sidebotham 83–92. For recipients with offices in both
ports, see Fuks 211. The transport was done by camel (cf. P225 and Fuks 208; transport by
camel is also attested in the Vienna papyrus mentioned below [Harrauer-Sijpesteijn 130, line
2]), but transport by donkey as well cannot be entirely ruled out; see R. Bagnall in *Bulletin
of the American Society of Papyrologists* 22 (1985): 4.

What was delivered was primarily food and drink, in particular, wheat (38 instances) and
wine (18 instances); barley also occurs (5 instances), as does bread (2 instances). The other

Myos Hormos was the more important, whereas statements in the *Periplus* point to the balance having tipped in favor of Berenicê. A third port, Leukos Limên, saw some use in the course of time but apparently never attained the status of the other two.[12]

Once a cargo from overseas was unloaded, there was transport and supervision to arrange and paperwork to go through. The goods were all costly and consequently had to be kept constantly under guard. They were subject to an import duty of twenty-five percent, and this involved much red tape, including delivery to government customs houses. A recently published papyrus from the Vienna collection,[13] dating to the mid-second century A.D., supplies illuminating detail. It contains the text of an agreement between two shippers, whereby one contracts to serve as agent for a cargo belonging to the other that, having originated in Muziris, had apparently just arrived in some Red Sea port. He promises the following:

> I will give to your camel driver 170 talents, 50 drachmas, for use of the road to Koptos, and
>
> I will convey [sc. your goods] inland through the desert under guard and under security to the public warehouses for receiving revenues at Koptos, and
>
> I will place [them] under your ownership and seal, or of your representatives or of whoever of them is present, until loading aboard at the river, and
>
> I will load [them] aboard at the required time on a seaworthy boat on the river, and
>
> I will convey [them] downstream to the warehouse that receives the duty of one-fourth at Alexandria, and I will similarly place [them] under the ownership of you or your representatives.

items are a total miscellany: there are five instances of delivery of some drug (called simply *pharmakon*), four of rush mats, two of chaff, and one each of almost a dozen various things (e.g., hides, wallets, tow, rope, tin, clothing). The amounts of food and drink listed are modest. Those of wheat, for example, in 27 of the 38 instances are under 10 artabs, with over half being 4 or less, including one of a single artab; in 6 instances they are between 10 and 16 artabs; there was one delivery of 24 artabs, one or perhaps two of 36, one of 37, and a lone large delivery of 132. Some assume that the deliveries involve trade goods (Fuks 212–13, Sidebotham 86), but the scant quantities and the fact that arrival took place all year round (Fuks 213), not just before the time that ships usually departed, make it far more likely that they were for consumption or use by the local population (cf. Rostovtzeff 23–24; J. Schwartz in *Annales: économies, sociétés, civilisations* 15 [1960]: 29).

[12] For the literature on these ports, see under 1:1.2–4. Presumably they had extensive facilities for shipbuilding as well as ship maintenance and repair.

[13] First published in Harrauer-Sijpesteijn; reprinted with emendations and detailed commentary by G. Thür in *Tyche* 2 (1987): 229–45; partially reprinted with emendations and revised interpretation in Casson 1986a.

The Lines and Objects of Trade

The prime purpose of the *Periplus* is to describe two major lines of trade, both of which started from the Red Sea ports of Egypt. Upon leaving the Red Sea, the first followed the coast of Africa, while the second went eastward as far as India (App. 3). However, through remarks that the author drops here and there, we are able to discern certain other lines originating from different places and carried on by different casts of characters.

What chiefly interests the author, the raison d'être for his handbook, is the trade in luxury goods for the Mediterranean world that was carried on by the merchants of Roman Egypt. That these were, indeed, the merchants involved follows from the fact that the handbook was written in Greek. That they began from, and ended at, the Red Sea ports is made evident by a series of remarks that the author carefully inserts at appropriate points, advising the proper time to depart for the key destinations; these times make sense only if we assume he has a round trip in mind.

REFERENCE	DESTINATION	DEPARTURE TIME
6:3.6–7	Adulis	between January and September, September the best
14:5.7–8	"far-side" ports	around July
24:8.11–12	Muza	around September or even earlier
28:9.20–21	Kanê	a little earlier than for Muza
39:13.12–13	Barbarikon	around July
49:16.31–32	Barygaza	around July
56:18.28–29	Muziris/Nelkynda	around July

In most instances Egypt is specifically mentioned as the point of departure (6:3.5, 14:5.7, 49:16.31, 56:18.28–29), in the others clearly implied. The dates were based on the prevailing winds that vessels leaving from and returning to Egypt would encounter (App. 3). They reveal that some traders went the whole length of a route, all the way down the east coast of Africa to Rhapta or all the way across to India, but that some stopped short, at Adulis or Muza or Kanê (App. 3, note 15). Very likely those that went all the way included stops en route; vessels heading for India put in at Muza or Kanê or both before starting the long run over open water.[14] However, only a handful actually tramped and then only along the coast

---

[14] The Arabic wine delivered to Barygaza was very likely picked up at Muza and the incense delivered to Barbarikon at Kanê; see below. The author mentions (57:19.7) that Kanê was one of the departure points for the run to India.

of Somalia which lent itself to such trading (14:5.13–14). The rest went out to pick up cargoes for transport back to Egypt.

And they wasted no space in their holds on cheap mundane staples. The shippers for whom the author wrote were, first and foremost, dealers in luxuries. This is patently clear from the items he lists as being available to them in the various regions:

Ethiopian shore of the Red Sea (Ptolemais Thêrôn [3:1.15–16], Adulis [6:3.4]): ivory, tortoise shell, rhinoceros horn

Ethiopian shore of Bab el Mandeb (Avalitês [7:3.20]): a little ivory, tortoise shell, aromatics, a very little myrrh (cf. under 7:3.20)

northern Somalia (Malaô [8:3.30–32], Mundu [9:4.3–5], Mosyllon [10:4.10–12], Spice Port [12:4.27–28], Opônê [13:5.4–5]): myrrh (cf. under 10:4.13), frankincense (cf. under 8:3.30a), cassia, aromatics, drugs, slaves, ivory, tortoise shell

east coast of Africa (principally Rhapta [17:6.18–20]): ivory, tortoise shell, rhinoceros horn, nautilus shell

Arabia

    Straits of Bab el Mandeb (Muza [24:8.9–10]): myrrh, white marble

    southern shore (Kanê [28:9.19]): aloe, frankincense (Kanê was by government policy [27:9.8–10] the sole port of export for frankincense; some was shipped out of Moscha Limên, but only in exceptional circumstances and by special dispensation of the royal agents [see under 32:11.1–3])

India

    northwest (Barbarikon [39:13.10–12], Barygaza [48:16.14–19, 49:16.28–31]): costus, bdellium, *lykion*, nard, Indian myrrh (? see under B 49:16.29), indigo, turquoise, lapis lazuli, onyx, agate (? see under 48:16.15), ivory, cotton cloth, fine cotton garments, silk cloth and yarn, Chinese pelts, pepper

    southwest and southern (Muziris/Nelkynda [56:18.22–28], Argaru [59:20.2–3]): nard, malabathron, pepper, pearls, ivory, tortoise shell, transparent gems (see under 56:18.26), diamonds, sapphires, silk cloth, fine cotton garments

    northeast (Masalia [62:20.21–22], Dêsarênê [62:20.23–24], Gangês [63:21.4–6]): nard, malabathron, pearls, ivory, fine cotton garments (all or most of which was probably picked up by western merchants at Muziris/Nelkynda[15])

[15] Although Greek vessels unquestionably sailed as far as the mouth of the Ganges (Strabo 15:686), the *Periplus* gives the impression that they did not regularly put in at the Bay of Bengal ports, preferring to pick up east coast products at Muziris/Nelkynda, which maintained constant trade relations with that area; see below under "The Trade with India."

In sum the African trade route, from the Red Sea down to Rhapta, yielded basically ivory, tortoise shell, frankincense, myrrh, and various grades of cassia (this last was actually of Southeast Asian origin, but its sale to the merchants of Roman Egypt took place in certain of the "farside" ports; see under 8:3.30–13:5.4). Arabia yielded basically frankincense, myrrh, and aloe. The widest spread of goods was furnished by India: native spices and drugs and aromatics (costus, bdellium, *lykion*, nard, malabathron, pepper), gems (turquoise, lapis lazuli, onyx, diamonds, sapphires, "transparent gems"), textiles (cotton cloth and garments as well as silk cloth and yarn from China), ivory, pearls, and tortoise shell. The last item was particularly sought after, for all the major ports traded in it (see under 3:1.15–16). The finest quality was brought to Muziris/Nelkynda all the way from Malay to be made available to Western merchants (56:18.26–28 and note ad loc.; 63:21.9–10).

These are the items a shipper from Roman Egypt concentrated on, these are what he loaded aboard to carry back to Myos Hormos and Berenicê. None of them appears among the imports listed for any of the intermediate ports; clearly none were dropped off, all stayed aboard until the last stop to be put on the market there, some no doubt for consumption in Egypt itself but by far the greater part for distribution all around the Mediterranean. Unlike bulky commodities, such items took up scant space in the hold; thus ships used on the run, which were probably quite large (App. 3), could accommodate cargoes of enormous value,[16] thereby ensuring substantial profits at the end of a voyage—even after the Roman government creamed off its twenty-five percent import duty. One item, shipped out of Barygaza, the author calls "ordinary cotton cloth" (48:16.15–16, 51:17.13; cf. 49:16.29, where it is very likely included under "cotton cloth of all kinds"); it was "ordinary" only in a relative sense, in contrast to the finer textiles with which it is coupled.

The goods imported from southern India were so costly that they far outpriced what Western goods were sold there. The result was a steady flow of cash out of Rome into India; Tiberius grumbled (Tac., *Ann.* 3.53) that "the ladies and their baubles are transferring our money to foreigners," and Pliny (6.101, 12.84) reviews the figures for the vast amount of coin that the East, but especially India, drained from Rome. As it happens, Rome was merely the first of a long line to fall into this imbalance.

---

[16] E.g., the Vienna papyrus described above records a shipment from Muziris in India that was probably worth no less than 131 talents and yet represented but a fraction of what the ship it traveled on could have carried; see below under "The Traders: Africa versus India."

It was inherent in the nature of the products reciprocally offered, and the great trading states of later Europe were to suffer the same fate.[17]

Granted that the author's chief interest is in this line of trade in high-priced goods for the Western world, there is yet apparent in his account a second line that was in every respect the opposite: it was not in luxuries but in commodities, and the merchants of Roman Egypt had no part, or very little part, in it. We are aware of it only indirectly, through examination of the imports, and their sources, that he lists for the various ports. From this it emerges that India was a supplier of textiles, foods, and raw materials to the Persian coast, southern Arabia, and East Africa:

Persian coast (Apologos, Omana [36:12.6–7]): copper, wood (teak, sissoo, ebony)

Socotra (31:10.21–22): grain, rice, cotton cloth, female slaves

southern Arabia (Moscha Limên [32:11.3]): grain, sesame oil, cotton cloth

northern Somalia ("far-side" ports [14:5.10–13]): grain, rice, sesame oil, ghee, cane sugar, cotton cloth, girdles

Ethiopian coast (Adulis [6:3.1–3]): iron, steel, lac, cotton cloth, girdles, cloaks, fine cotton garments

Aside from the textiles, all the items above are conspicuously absent from the lists of exports that the author gives for the various Indian ports, lists that were intended for the use of merchants from Roman Egypt; the best explanation for their omission is that they were of no interest to these merchants and hence trading in them was handled by Arabs or Indians.[18] The author of the *Periplus* is witness at many points to the wide-ranging activities of the ships from these lands. He reports, for example, that Socotra's imports, a handful of staples, were brought by "shippers from Muza and also by those sailing out of Limyrikê and Barygaza who by chance put in" (31:10.21–22). He further reports that at the moment Socotra was "leased out"; it could well have been to Arab traders (see under 31:10.24–25). In describing Muza, he remarks on the throng of Arab shippers there and the trade they carried on with African ports and Ba-

---

[17] Cf. J. Needham, *Science and Civilisation in China* iv.3 (Cambridge, 1971), 518–19; F. Braudel, *Civilization and Capitalism, 15th–18th Century*. iii, *The Perspective of the World* (New York, 1984), 490.

[18] Warmington (257, 259) correctly inferred that iron, ghee, sugar, and certain other products were handled by merchants from India and Arabia but saw in this an attempt on their part to keep the handling a trade secret, to shut traders from Roman Egypt out. This was certainly true of costly items such as cassia (see under 8:3.30–13:5.4), but hardly of commodities. For merchants making the long voyage from Egypt, the profit was to be found in ivory, tortoise shell, spices, and the like, not iron or ghee.

rygaza (21:7.21–23). Muza was an entrepôt as well, offering for export what it had imported from Adulis (24:8.10–11). So too was Kanê, exchanging goods with the ports in Africa, Omana on the southern coast of Iran, and the northwestern ports of India (28:9.10–12).

The cotton cloth exported to Adulis and northern Somalia were cheap grades (see under B 14:5.11–12) and that exported to Socotra and southern Arabia, in view of the items it is coupled with, almost certainly so. Adulis also took in some finer cotton cloth and a small number of deluxe cotton garments (6:3.3); these could well have been for the foreign colony resident there (6:2.32).

Why does the author bother to include such information? For one, as we shall see in a moment, he aims at a certain comprehensiveness, at giving a total picture. But he may have another reason as well, namely the possible incidental interest of some of the items noted above to skippers from Roman Egypt. If one of these happened to leave India with space still left in his hold, presumably he could, if he chose, fill it with cargo of this cheaper nature to be dropped off en route home.

However, the author reports on certain lines of trade that could have been of no interest whatsoever to a merchant from Roman Egypt. They must have been included simply to round off his account, to present to the reader all forms of maritime traffic that went on in the area. The trade of the Persian Gulf is a case in point. The merchants of Roman Egypt must have been indifferent to it, for the author carries his readers right past the mouth of the gulf: he merely notes the landmarks around the entrance and its width (35:11.27–30), names a port at the head of the gulf (35:11.32–12.1), and then, with the words "after sailing by the mouth of the gulf" (36:12.3), moves on to the coast beyond, where he names another port. Yet he lists the exports of the two ports—low-quality pearls, purple and local garments, wine, dates, gold, slaves—and informs us that these go to Arabia and Barygaza (36:12.9–12). He notes Arabia's trade with African ports (Malaô [8:3.31–32], the "far-side" ports [21:7.23, 27:9.10–12], Rhapta [16:6.10–11]), and the Nabataean port of Leukê Kômê (19:6.30–31). He has a few words on India's trade with the Malay Peninsula (60:20.9–10, 63:21.8–10), an area outside the sphere of interest of the traders from Roman Egypt, and he lists Ceylon's products, although Ceylon was equally outside it (see under 61:20.15–19). He even makes mention of small-scale local trade: between Avalitês and the ports across the Straits of Bab el Mandeb (7:3.18–20), carried on by Barbaroi using rafts and small craft (7:3.15); local deliveries to Kanê by means of buoyed rafts as well as ships (27:9.9–10); trade between the Isle of Sarapis and Kanê in small craft (33:11.18–19); between India's east and west coast (60:20.6–8), some of which went in large canoes.

Did foreign vessels come to the ports of Roman Egypt? In earlier days they did not, to judge from the author's remark, discussed above, that Indian ships used to stop short of the mouth of the Red Sea, putting in at Eudaimôn Arabia, where they exchanged cargoes with ships from Egypt that had ventured to this point. But by the time he was writing, Western vessels were voyaging as far as India, eliminating that exchange and causing the decline of Eudaimôn Arabia to a mere harbor of refuge and watering station (26:8.23–31). Very likely the reverse was also true, that Indian vessels voyaged as far as Roman Egypt; the author does not mention this but he had no need to since it was something his readers could see for themselves. From at least the early second century A.D. on, there was at Koptos an association of "Palmyrene Red Sea Shipowners" (see below under "The Traders"). Their vessels certainly must have docked at Berenicê or Myos Hormos or other Red Sea ports that Koptos was linked with, and presumably other foreign bottoms did too.

Let us return to the prime line of trade, that carried on by the merchants of Roman Egypt, and review its other side, not the items they came back with but those they took from Egypt to sell abroad. These were a mix of staples and luxuries, the nature of the mix varying according to the region it was intended for.

On the African route the first major stop was Adulis (6:2.23–3.3), which imported not only to satisfy its own needs—these could not have been great, since it was but a modest village (4:2.6)—but also those of the court. Thus it took in some staples, such as tools (axes, adzes, knives), iron, cheap clothing, but in addition a good many items of greater worth: brass for making into personal adornments, bronze vessels both for use and for cutting up into personal adornments, ornamental glass. The only foodstuffs imported were olive oil and Italian and Laodicean wine, probably for the resident foreign colony (6:2.32). The court must have been relatively humble (cf. under 6:2.33–35) for its needs were few and simple: silverware and goldware fashioned in the local manner and inexpensive cloaks. After Adulis came Avalitês and the "far-side" ports, a homogeneous region to judge from the way the author treats it as a whole, listing most of the imports for the first port and referring to that list when he comes to the others (7:3.16–18, 8:3.26–28, 9:4.3, 10:4.8–9, 12:4.26–27, 13:5.3). Here staples were predominant (cheap clothing including some secondhand, grain, wine, iron, ironware, tin), but there were some imports that were more costly (silverware, glassware, drinking vessels). There was no overall monarch in these regions, each port being under a local chief (14:5.14–16), and these chiefs, it would appear, could not afford many expensive purchases.

Arabia too took in staples: clothing, textiles, grain, oil, wine, copper, tin (24:8.2–6, 28:9.13–15). But it was also a market for a wide selection of drugs or cosmetics: saffron, *cyperus*, fragrant ointments, storax (24:8.3–5, 28:9.16). And in Arabia there were not only royal courts to supply but the courts of the local governors; together they took in a whole range of high-priced items: horses, pack mules, silverware, goldware, bronze-ware, deluxe clothing, statuary (24:8.7–9, 28:9.16–18).

For India the mix tilted decidedly toward the expensive side. Shippers bound there from Egypt loaded only a few staples, such as metals (lead, tin, copper [49:16.21, 56:18.19, 60:20.10–11]), but a whole range of ex-pensive items: drugs and cosmetics (antimony, realgar, orpiment, storax [39:13.8, 49:16.23, 56:18.19–21, 60:20.10–11]), silverware, glassware, coral, multicolored textiles (39:13.8–9, 49:16.21–23, 56:18.19). And the courts of the rulers required fine ointments, vintage wine, deluxe cloth-ing, handsome slave girls for the harem and slave boys trained in music (49:16.25–28). All the exports to India were loaded aboard at Egypt with two exceptions: the incense imported by Barbarikon (39:13.8) and the Arabian wine by Barygaza (49:16.20–21). The wine could have been picked up at Muza, an area that produced a good deal of it (24:8.6), and the incense at Kanê (see under 27:9.8–9).

To sum up. The *Periplus*, on careful analysis, reveals several lines of trade over and above the well-known movement of Eastern luxuries to the ports of Egypt. That was, to be sure, the most important and received the most attention. But alongside it we can clearly distinguish a trade in commodities from India to the coasts of Persia, Arabia, and Africa that had nothing to do with the West; some of it may on occasion have trav-eled in ships from Roman Egypt but the bulk was handled by Arabs and Indians.[19] We can even distinguish certain local forms of trade, so local that the means of transport was small craft and rafts. From its end, Egypt sent out to Africa, Arabia, and India a mix that ranged from everyday tools and cheap clothing to the costliest of luxuries for the courts of re-gional rulers.

THE TRADE WITH INDIA

Roman Egypt's trade with India was so much more important than that with Africa or Arabia that the author devoted almost half his book to it.

---

[19] Inscriptions reveal a line of trade that ran from the head of the Persian Gulf to the mouth of the Indus and back carried on by merchants and shippers of Charax Spasinu and other cities in the area; cf. J. Matthews in *Journal of Roman Studies* 74 (1984): 166. The author of the *Periplus* fails to mention it, although he does mention the line to Barygaza (36:12.9–10).

The picture he presents is consequently more detailed, enough so to enable us to identify various sides of India's trade and to discern differences in nature and function of the major ports.

To begin with, he makes abundantly clear that, for the merchants of Roman Egypt, India's west coast was the prime trading area, and the east coast played a distinctly secondary role. And his account reveals that the west coast fell into two spheres, in each of which were two major ports: the northwest with the ports of Barbarikon and Barygaza, the southwest with Muziris and Nelkynda.

Turning first to the northwest coast, we find that its two ports, though they handled a number of the same objects of trade (coral, peridots, storax, and multicolored textiles as imports; costus, bdellium, *lykion*, and silk cloth as exports), were basically dissimilar. Barbarikon was merely a port: all the merchandise that arrived there was forwarded to the royal capital at Minnagar upriver (39:13.5–6). Barygaza, on the other hand, was not only a port but an industrial center as well. This emerges from a comparison of certain of the imports and exports handled by the two places, particularly glass, an item imported at all four of the west coast ports (see under 48:16.15): Barbarikon imported only glassware (39:13.9), Barygaza only raw glass (49:16.23). Barygaza imported such raw materials as copper, tin, and lead (49:16.21); none of these or any other basic raw materials were imported by Barbarikon. In textiles, Barbarikon exported only silk cloth, which had come there from China (see under B 39:13.11), whereas Barygaza exported cotton cloth of all kinds in addition to silk (49:16.29–30); some kinds were supplied by Ozênê (Ujjain) inland (48:16.14–16) but some surely must have been manufactured right in town.[20]

Barygaza seems to have been a somewhat more sophisticated place, to judge from the greater number of luxuries it required. Both it and Barbarikon/Minnagar imported clothing, but the latter was content with merely an adequate number of undecorated garments and a limited number of prints (39:13.7–8), whereas Barygaza received "all kinds of clothing with no adornment or of printed fabric" as well as specially wide girdles (49:16.22–23). Barygaza, but not Barbarikon, imported eye shadow and perfume (49:16.23, 25). And the court at Minnagara, where Barygaza's overlord resided, must have been vastly more luxurious than that at Minnagar, the seat of Barbarikon's. The latter was the recipient of

[20] In later centuries Gujarat was famed for its textiles (M. Pearson, *Merchants and Rulers in Gujarat* [Berkeley, 1976], 11–12; I. Watson in *Indian Economic and Social History Review* 13 [1976]:377), enough of which were manufactured at Broach (Barygaza) to induce the British to set up a "factory" or trading post there (Watson 386). Braudel (op. cit. n. 17 above, 511), in his treatment of India in the fifteenth to eighteenth centuries, talks of "the 'industrial bloc' of Gujarat, the most impressive in the Far East."

all the items unloaded on Barbarikon's docks, but these included nothing to match what used to go to Barygaza's ruler—precious silverware, slave musicians, beautiful slave girls for the harem, fine wine, expensive clothing, choice perfume (49:16.25–28 and see under 49:16.25a).

Turning now to the southwest coast, we find that, unlike the northwest, its two major ports were so similar that the author lumps them together and treats them as one (56:18.16-29). What these exported was almost totally different from the exports of the northwest—as one would expect, since the regions involved were dissimilar. There are only two items that appear among the exports of both Muziris/Nelkynda and Barygaza, ivory (49:16.29, 56:18.24) and silk cloth (49:16.29–30, 56:18.24). Nard appears in both, but the nard shipped out of Barygaza was the variety that came from Kashmir and its neighboring regions (see under 48:16.16–18), while at Muziris/Nelkynda it was the Gangetic (56:18.25). Both shipped out pepper, but at Barygaza it was long pepper (49:16.30), while at Muziris/Nelkynda it was black pepper (56:18.22) and the quantities were far greater, for pepper was the export par excellence of the Malabar coast (cf. 56:18.16–17). All their other exports were totally different.

The imports reveal that, like Barygaza, Muziris/Nelkynda were industrial centers as well as commercial: they too were importers of such raw materials as copper, tin, lead, and raw glass (56:18.19). They were less sophisticated places than Barygaza, or at least did not live in so high a style,[21] to judge from the reduced emphasis they gave to luxuries. Wine, including varieties from three different areas, stands at the head of the list of Barygaza's imports (49:16.20–21), but is low on the list at Muziris/Nelkynda; there is no indication of the import of different varieties (56:18.20). Barygaza took in all sorts of clothing, Muziris/Nelkynda only undecorated and not much of that (56:18.18–19). Barygaza took in at least some perfume (49:16.25), Muziris/Nelkynda none at all. At Barygaza, as noted above, the author lists a number of highly expensive items "for the king." Muziris and Nelkynda were ruled by kings too, each by a different one as the author is careful to point out, citing what he takes to be their names (54:17.29 and note ad loc., 54:18.5–6 and note ad loc.). But he does not supply a list of special items for them, nor in his general list of imports are there any that seem intended for a court; even silverware, a standard court item elsewhere (see under 39:13.7–9), is lacking. The rulers, it would seem, lived as simply as their subjects.

[21] But nothing like the exaggerated difference that Raschke thinks he perceives, a difference between a "poorer, less socially and economically developed South" (671) and a North whose areas "with their wealth and high level of culture provided excellent markets for imported Roman manufactured items, particularly luxury goods" (632).

A key difference between the two areas lies in the nature of their commercial communities. At Barygaza it appears that import-export was handled by local merchants; at least there are no indications otherwise. At Muziris/Nelkynda there are unmistakable indications of a foreign colony.

The clearest evidence comes from the *Tabula Peutingeriana* (see under 51:17.15). Next to Muziris this map shows (section 5 of segment xi) a building identified as *Templ(um) Augusti*, "temple to Augustus"; such a building could only have been put up by Roman subjects living there.[22] Almost as clear evidence is provided by the papyrus from the Vienna collection (see above, "Between Alexandria and the Red Sea"). It contains a reference[23] to "loan agreements at Muziris," agreements between two merchants, one of whom very probably was resident at Muziris. And there is an indication in the *Periplus* itself that points in the same direction. The author states (56:18.21–22) that Muziris/Nelkynda imported grain "in sufficient amount for those involved with shipping, because the merchants do not use it." The explanation can only be that the merchants "do not use it" because they are natives of the area and hence eat the local rice,[24] whereas "those involved with shipping" are Westerners who prefer to eat what they have been accustomed to even though it means importing it from thousands of miles away.[25] These Westerners, permanently established, served as middlemen between their countrymen who arrived with the cargoes and the local merchants.

To the east coast the author gives short shrift. Indeed, at one point he clearly implies that Western ships went no further than the waters between India and Ceylon (see under 51:17.16). There was good reason for this. The ships that plied between Roman Egypt and Limyrikê (the Malabar coast) were of large size, big enough to brave the waters of the Arabian Sea when the southwest monsoon was blowing its hardest (cf. App. 3). They could not have negotiated the shallow channels between the southern tip of India and the northern tip of Ceylon; they would have had to make the time-consuming voyage all around the island (cf. under 60:20.7–8). Thus it was to the advantage of Western shippers to leave to local craft the forwarding of merchandise from the west coast of India to

[22] Cf. Smith 462; Warmington 18; M. Charlesworth in P. Coleman-Norton, ed., *Studies in Roman Economic and Social History in Honor of Allen Chester Johnson* (Princeton, 1951), 142.

[23] Harrauer-Sijpesteijn 130 (rect, col. ii. 12–13) and cf. Casson 1986a.

[24] Cf. Marco Polo 3.17: "No wheat grows in this province, but rice only."

[25] Grain, to be sure, was available in northern India. The province of Ariakê, for example, produced it (41:14.5) and shipped it overseas (14:5.9–10). However, it obviously did not ship to southern India, where the rice eaters would have no use for it. Westerners resident there must have found it easier to draw from home the small quantities they needed rather than attempt to redirect the normal flow of Indian commerce in grain.

the east coast. As for the goods the east coast had to offer, these regularly went by local craft to Limyrikê (60:20.6–7) and were available for purchase there. Gangetic nard is a good case in point: collected at and shipped out from a port at the mouth of the Ganges (63:21.3–5), it was picked up by the merchants of Roman Egypt at Muziris or Nelkynda (56:18.25). Malabathron followed the same route (63:21.3–5, 56:18.25), and it was a major item in the trade of Muziris and Nelkynda (56:18.17).

There was also some transport between the two coasts by land. Some goods, for example, went from the east coast to Tagara and from there to Barygaza (51:17.11-14 and cf. under 51:17.14).

In the light of the author's manifest secondary interest in the east coast, it is curious that, at Arikamedu some two miles south of Pondicherry, archaeology has brought to light convincing signs of a colony of Westerners, an abundance of Roman pottery, especially Arretine ware, which reveals that its members were active from the early years of the first century A.D. on (see under 60:20.6a). In addition, a passage in a Tamil poem attests to the presence of a colony of Westerners at a port on the mouth of the Kāveri River to the south of Arikamedu (see under 60:20.6).[26] It could well be that the Westerners resident in these places were chiefly engaged in forwarding goods not all the way to Egypt but only to associates stationed in Muziris/Nelkynda, who then sold them to the merchants from Roman Egypt.

Goods went from India's west coast to the east coast as well as in the other direction: the east coast craft that came to Limyrikê were sent back loaded down not only with products that had originated in Limyrikê but also with some that had come to it from overseas (60:20.10–11); thus cash the merchants of Roman Egypt had brought with them found its way to the east coast (60:20.11–12) as payment for east coast goods purchased in Limyrikê. The author mentions only here and there (59:20.2–3, 61:20.19–20) what these products are until he comes to the port of Gangês in the Ganges Delta, where he provides detail. Gangês was an entrepôt: it received goods from inland areas near and far (63:21.5–6: nard and mala-

---

[26] Contact with resident Westerners may well be responsible for the representations of armchairs in Buddhist reliefs of the second century A.D. found in Andhradesha, the coastal area from the Kistna River north to the Godavari; see *La vie publique et privée dans l'Inde ancienne*. fasc. ii, *Le mobilier (iiᵉ siècle av. J.-C.—viiiᵉ siècle environ)*, by I. Gobert, Publications du Musée Guimet, Recherches et documents d'art et d'archéologie, 6 (Paris, 1976), 126 and cf. pl. 29. There is evidence for the presence in eastern India not only of Western merchants but of their wives as well. A statue found at Dīdārganj (25°59′N, 82°46′E, i.e., a little northeast of Benares) portrays a young girl whose hairdo is strikingly similar to that on busts of Roman women of the Augustan period; see D. Schlumberger, "Coiffures féminines similaires à Rome et dans l'Inde," in R. Chevallier, ed., *Mélanges d'archéologie et d'histoire offerts à André Piganiol* i (Paris, 1966), 587–95.

bathron from far away, pearls and deluxe garments from nearby) as well as some by sea from areas further east (63:21.10: tortoise shell, almost certainly shipped to Gangês, although this is not stated in so many words) and forwarded these to the west coast.

Gangês also—again, this is not stated in so many words but is practically certain—handled silk, thereby making this one of the very few products[27] that could be acquired in all of the four major exporting regions of India. At Barbarikon in the Indus Delta, silk cloth and yarn were available (39:13.11 and see under B 39:13.11); at Barygaza on the northwest coast, silk cloth and yarn (49:16.30 and under B 49:16.30); at Muziris/Nelkynda on the southwest coast, silk cloth (56:18.24); in the Ganges Delta, silk cloth and yarn and floss[28] (64:21.13–14). And yet in this trade India was solely an intermediary, for the products all came from China.[29]

They made their way to India by a route that went "by land via Bactria to Barygaza" as well as "via the Ganges River back to Limyrikê" (64:21.14–15). The first, the one that went "via Bactria," was the famed Silk Route that ran from China clean across Asia; from it one or more branches turned off to go down to India. The route began at Loyang or Sian and traveled inside the Great Wall to An-hsi where, to bypass the grim Taklamakan Desert, it split into a northern and a southern loop. These came together at Kashgar, and from there the track snaked through the lofty Pamirs into Bactria. Shipments intended for the Mediterranean market continued westward, while those for the Indian followed a branch that took off perhaps near Balkh and headed southward. On reaching the upper Indus this route split: one branch followed the river down to Barbarikon, while another more to the east followed the well established road that passed through Sialkot and Mathura to Ujjain (cf. under 48:16.16–18) and from there to Barygaza (cf. under 48:16.12–13).[30] There was also a shorter but more difficult route that from Kashgar struck out southward through the Pamirs and, passing by Gilgit, ended in Kashmir.[31]

---

[27] There were but two, of which the other was nard; see 39:13.10 (Barbarikon), 49:16.28 (Barygaza), 56:18.25 (Muziris/Nelkynda), 63:21.5 (Gangês).

[28] On this term, see under 64:21.13–14.

[29] Barbarikon received shipments of Chinese furs as well as of silk products (39:13.11). Although India had a silk industry of its own (see L. Gopal in *JESHO* 4 [1961]: 61–64), the *Periplus's* references are all to the Chinese import (cf. 64:21.13–15).

[30] For the Silk Route, see J. Thomson, *History of Ancient Geography* (Cambridge, 1948), 177–81, 306–12; W. Watson in *CHI* iii 544–45 (map), 547–48 (1983); Needham (op. cit. n. 17 above) i 181–82 (1954), iv.3 17–18 (details of the routes around the Taklamakan Desert); Wheeler 156 (branch to India).

[31] See Moti Chandra, *Trade and Trade Routes in Ancient India* (Delhi, 1977), 177; Wheeler 155; and, for a detailed review of the various routes from Kashgar through the Pamirs, Sir

The route that went "via the Ganges River" very likely is the same as that described by Ptolemy (1.17.4) as going "to India by way of Palimbothra [Pātaliputra]." It probably followed the line of travel just described as far as Mathura and, from there, the main road that led eastward via Pātaliputra (Patna) to Tāmralipti (Tamluk) in the Ganges Delta.[32] From the delta coastal craft carried the shipments "back to Limyrikê," i.e., westward again to the Malabar coast.

There is always the possibility that some silk may have come to the Ganges Delta by sea. Against it, however, is the fact that, although at the time of the *Periplus* there was regular traffic across the Bay of Bengal (see under 63:21.1), for the next leg from Indonesia to China, the first good evidence for seaborne trade dates as late as the fifth century A.D.[33]

We have some indications of what merchants gave to China in exchange for her silk products. A Chinese account mentions that in "the ninth year of the Yen-hsi period, during the emperor Huan-ti's reign . . . the king of Ta-ts'in, An-tun, sent an embassy which, from the frontier of Jih-nan [Annam], offered ivory, rhinoceros horns, and tortoise shell."[34] Ta-ts'in is the Chinese name for the Roman Empire, and An-tun is Antoninus, the family name of Marcus Aurelius, and the date works out to A.D. 166. The embassy most likely was not an official body but a group of Western merchants trying to buy silk directly from the Chinese instead of through Indian middlemen.[35] What they offered in exchange—ivory, rhinoceros horn, and tortoise shell—were all available in India.

THE TRADE IN METALS

The information provided by the *Periplus* on metals presents difficulties. It lists certain places as importers of one or more of the following: iron,

---

Aurel Stein, "On Ancient Tracks Past the Pamirs," *The Himalayan Journal* 4 (1932): 1–24. K. Gardiner in S. Mukherjee, *India: History and Thought, Essays in Honour of A. L. Basham* (Subarnarekha, 1982), 53–54, cites evidence from the Chinese sources.

[32] See Chandra (op. cit. n. 31 above) 5 (the Mathura-Tāmralipti road) and under 63:21.4 (possible identification of Tāmralipti with Gangês). Needham (op. cit. n. 17 above, i 182) prefers to take it as a route that went over some Himalayan pass more or less directly to Pātaliputra. There was yet another route, much less important, from Szechuan through Yunnan to Burma to Assam (Needham i 173–74).

[33] So O. Wolters, *Early Indonesian Commerce* (Ithaca, 1967), 35. According to Needham (op. cit. n. 17 above, i 179), Indonesian ships were sailing to China by the second century A.D. and, by the fourth century A.D., Chinese ships to Indonesia, although in no great numbers.

[34] F. Hirth, *China and the Roman Orient* (Shanghai, 1885), 42 (reprinted in Schoff 276).

[35] Cf. Hirth (op. cit. n. 34 above) 173–78.

lead, tin, and copper. Yet, for some of these places, the metals they are said to import were available from sources in the near or at least not too distant vicinity.

Iron offers no problems. The merchants of Roman Egypt shipped it to Adulis (6:2.29) as well as to Malaô and the other "far-side" ports (8:3.28, and presumably included under the term "the aforementioned" in 9:4.3, 10:4.8, 12:4.27, 13:5.3). Adulis used this iron for the manufacture of points for hunting and war spears (6:2.29–30) and, in addition, imported Indian iron and steel, no doubt for purposes requiring the finer grades that India could furnish (6:3.1 and see under 6:3.1a).

Lead offers what at first sight seems to be a problem. The *Periplus's* lists of objects of trade reveal that the sole market for Western lead was India: shippers delivered it to Barygaza (49:16.21) on the northwest coast and to Muziris/Nelkynda on the southwest (56:18.19). Conformably, Pliny states categorically (34.163) that India has no lead. This is not so: she has ample deposits of it; as an authority cited by Watt (iv 602) puts it, "there is probably no metal of which the ores have been worked to so large an extent in ancient times, excepting those of iron." But there is a plausible explanation why Pliny thought otherwise and why we find India importing lead: the commonest lead-bearing ore there is galena, and, as Watt suggests, it may well have been worked solely for the silver it contained.

Tin presents a somewhat similar problem, but in this case there is no ready explanation. Tin was a commodity much in demand in ancient times for, alloyed with copper, it forms bronze. Western tin found a market in Avalitês (7:3.18) and the "far-side" ports (presumably included under the term "the aforementioned" in 8:3.26–27 and the passages noted above), in Kanê (28:9.15), and in two places in India, Barygaza (49:16.21) and Muziris/Nelkynda (56:18.19). It so happens that just across the Bay of Bengal, there are rich deposits in Burma, Thailand, and Malay (Watt vi 4 57–60), some of which recent archaeological discoveries indicate were exploited in very early times.[36] The *Periplus* makes it clear that India had trade contacts with these places (see under 63:21.1), and perhaps she did fill part of her requirements from them; if so, one wonders why she did not fill all her needs from so convenient a source.

The greatest puzzle is presented by copper. Western copper was shipped to Kanê (28:9.15) and, like tin and lead, to Barygaza (49:16.21) and Muziris/Nelkynda (56:18.19). Again there is a statement from Pliny

[36] See R. Smith and W. Watson, eds., *Early South East Asia* (New York, 1979), 25, where D. Bayard affirms that current evidence supports a date prior to 2000 B.C. for the first appearance of bronze in mainland Southeast Asia, and 37–38, where I. Selimkhanov argues not only for the use of local tin but for its exportation to the Near East. On India's scanty tin resources, cf. J. Muhly in *AJA* 89 (1985): 283.

(34.163) to support this: India lacked copper, he asserts, as well as lead. But India does have copper: there are deposits near Ajmer in Rajasthan that, if worked in ancient days, would have been convenient for transport to Barygaza, and deposits near Madras that would have been convenient for Muziris/Nelkynda (Watt ii 647).[37] What is more, there is clear evidence that either these or other deposits were worked: Strabo lists a series of objects that he characterizes as being made of "Indian copper."[38] Indeed, the *Periplus* itself reports that Barygaza—the very place that took in shipments of copper from the West—sent out shipments to Apologos at the head of the Persian Gulf and to Omana, a port passed en route there (36:12.6). Schoff asserts (151) that this was Western copper that was reshipped; possibly, but there is absolutely no way to prove it or to explain why Barygaza resorted to imported copper for this trade rather than native copper. In a word, our information about Indian copper is contradictory, and attempts to resolve the problem are mere guesswork.

BARTER AND PURCHASE

In his lists of imports for the various ports of trade, the author every now and then includes money.

In three instances he specifies "Roman money" (*dênarion*). The first is in connection with Adulis (6:2.32). He recommends "a small quantity" and adds the reason for its inclusion: "for [sc. dealings with] the resident foreigners," presumably the Greco-Roman traders settled there. The second instance is in connection with Malaô (8:3.28–29) and, by implication in the words "the aforementioned" (see the passages cited above), with the other African ports around to Opônê; again only a small quantity is involved and, although he vouchsafes no further information, it no doubt was for the same purpose, for dealings with the local foreign colony. The third instance is Barygaza, and here too there is a particular reason: Ro-

---

[37] Further east there are copper deposits at Chota Nagpur, a district west of Calcutta, and these seem to have been worked well before the Christian Era; see F. Allchin in *JESHO* 5 (1962): 196. Ptolemy (7.2.20) reports the existence of copper mines in more distant India, beyond the Ganges.

[38] 15.718 (tables, thrones, drinking cups, and bath basins of "Indian copper"). On the other hand, there is archaeological evidence that India imported bronzeware of this sort: at Brahmapuri (17°33′N, 75°34′E), some one hundred miles northeast of Goa, a group of Roman bronze items was found that included a jug and basin as well as a statuette of Poseidon; see K. Khandalavala in *Lalit Kala* 7 (1960): 56–62 and cf. Wheeler 151. Most of them date from the first half of the first century A.D. and were probably manufactured in Campania (R. De Puma in *AJA* 91 [1987]: 292).

man money "commands an exchange at some profit against the local currency" (49:16.23–24 and note ad loc.).

In three other instances he states merely "money" (*chrêma, chrêmata*): Barbarikon (39:13.9); Muza (24:8.5), where he recommends "a considerable amount"; and Muziris/Nelkynda (56:18.18), where he heads the list of imports with the words "mainly a great amount of money." Finally, for Kanê (28:9.17), money is included among the gifts to be given to the king of the land. In this passage, however, it may be the result of scribal error; see under B 28:9.17.

The inference to be drawn from all this is that the merchants whom the *Periplus* addresses must have bartered at times and at times purchased, depending upon the region.

In Africa they did some business with the resident foreign traders for which they had to have a small amount of Roman currency; perhaps the traders insisted on a certain number of sales in cash because they needed the money for buying in goods from the Arabian or Indian ships that called at their ports. Since these were the only sales in cash, it follows that all other trading was through barter, the merchants of Roman Egypt exchanging the tools, clothing, metals, etc., that they brought from home for the ivory, tortoise shell, aromatics, etc., that they took back. They dealt with the natives as well as resident foreign traders; indeed, in Azania they distributed gratis no small amount of wine and grain among them just to gain their favor (17:6.16–17).

In Arabia a certain amount of purchase was involved as well as barter. The author advises bringing "a considerable amount of money" to Muza; its chief product was myrrh and this, being expensive, must have required cash over and above the exchange of the clothing and textiles that were Muza's chief imports (24:8.2–6). One would expect to find the same situation at Kanê, where the merchants of Roman Egypt traded for frankincense, but the author does not list money there as he does at Muza. The explanation may lie in the relative cheapness of frankincense. Its price was almost half that of myrrh (see under 7:3.20 and 27:9.8–9), so Western trade goods alone might have sufficed to meet its cost.

India's exports, too, involved purchase as well as barter, particularly in the south. At Barbarikon the author recommends bringing money without stating any amount. In other words, some goods had to be paid for in cash, and these could well have been the Chinese furs and silks available there (39:13.11), items that surely cost a great deal. At Barygaza, however, he mentions money solely in connection with turning a profit on foreign exchange values, so the implication is that there barter was the order of the day. The one region where there was little bartering and much buying was the Malabar coast. The *Periplus* makes this absolutely clear. As noted a moment ago, the author recommends bringing there "mainly a great amount of money," and this ties in with a statement of his that manifestly implies that vessels arrived at the Malabar coast with cargoes far lighter than those they took away (see under 55:18.9–10). Other sources confirm that there was little bartering and much buying. A Tamil poem describes Western merchants as "arriving with gold and departing with pepper" (App. 5), and over 6000 silver denarii and gold aurei, mostly in the form of coin hoards, have been found in southern India.[39] A celebrated passage in Pliny[40] laments the vast amount of cash that India drained from Rome; the hoards are ample witness to what he was talking about.

On the other hand, the north of India has yielded but a mere handful of Roman coins.[41] One explanation offered is that in the north Roman coins were melted down and remade into native currency whereas in the south they circulated.[42] Another is that the coins gravitated from north to south, particularly to the Coimbatore region (in which by far the largest number of hoards have been found), because that was where geographical features permitted transpeninsular traffic and where brigandage and others factors favored the planting of hoards.[43] But the *Periplus's* statements strongly suggest that few coins have been found in the north because few were spent there, that the merchants from Roman Egypt got their Indian products from Barygaza in exchange for the goods they brought, whereas at Muziris/Nelkynda they had to pay cash.[44]

THE TRADERS

Who were the people involved in the trade that Roman Egypt carried on with Africa, Arabia, and India?

The most precise information we have dates from an earlier period, the first half of the second century B.C. A papyrus document drawn up probably at Alexandria contains the text of a loan agreement to finance a trading venture to the "spice-bearing land," most likely the coastal area of

[39] See Raschke 665; Rodewald (op. cit. n. 5 above) 48–51; the maps in Wheeler 138, 144.

[40] 6.101; cf. Warmington 274.

[41] See Raschke 665; Rodewald 48.

[42] Warmington 292.

[43] Wheeler 143–45.

[44] Cf. Raschke 671. The cash was reckoned by the value of its metal, not its face value. The locals treated it as bullion: a mass of coins of a given weight would be exchanged for a given amount of pepper or cotton or gems, etc.; see Wheeler 140–41 and, in greater detail, Wheeler in W. Grimes, ed., *Aspects of Archaeology in Britain and Beyond, Essays presented to O.G.S. Crawford* (London, 1951), 361–65.

Somalia where the *Periplus's* "far-side" ports lay (cf. under 7:3.10–11). A veritable international consortium was involved. The borrowers, five partners, all have Greek names; one came from Sparta, another from Massilia, ancient Marseilles. The lender's name is Greek. The banker who handled the funds was probably a Roman. Repayment was guaranteed by five sureties, of whom four were in the army and the fifth was a traveling merchant; the merchant was Carthaginian and, of the soldiers, one came from Massilia, another from Elia in southern Italy, a third from Thessalonica. As it happens, they were acting as private individuals; there is not the least hint of governmental connections.[45]

The Vienna papyrus mentioned above unfortunately provides no names, although it makes clear that the trading venture it deals with, a shipment of goods from Muziris to Alexandria, was a matter of private enterprise.[46] In a papyrus containing the poll-tax register of the town of Arsinoe for the year A.D. 72/73, one Arsinoite, a certain "Gaiôn, also called Diodôros," is reported as being away in India;[47] he could well have been resident there, as one of the parties in the Vienna papyrus probably was. The records mentioned above, of a transport company that hauled supplies from Koptos to Myos Hormos and Berenicê, reveal that wealthy families of various extractions resident in Egypt maintained agencies at these ports, almost certainly for handling the family interests in overseas trade. Thus a Gaius Norbanus, no doubt a member of the Norbani, a prominent Roman family with holdings in Egypt, had an agent at Myos Hormos, while Marcus Julius Alexander, very likely of the immensely rich Alexandria-based Jewish family to which the renowned Philo belonged (Marcus was probably his nephew and brother to the Tiberius Julius Alexander who became prefect of Egypt), had agents at both Myos Hormos and Berenicê.[48] And let us not forget the author of the *Periplus* himself; he was a Greek from Egypt who had personally made the voyage to the major ports of trade in Africa, Arabia, and India and must have been in the business of exporting to and importing from those places.[49] The funding for the merchants in this trade need not have been drawn

---

[45] U. Wilcken, "Punt-Fahrten in der Ptolemäerzeit," *Zeitschrift für ägyptische Sprache und Altertumskunde* 60 (1925): 86–102 at 90 (text = *SB* 7169), 91 (date), 92 (provenance), 92–93 and 96–98 (parties).

[46] Harrauer-Sijpesteijn and cf. Casson 1986a. There has been general agreement all along that Rome's trade with the East was a matter of private enterprise; cf. M. Rostovtzeff, *The Social and Economic History of the Roman Empire* (Oxford, 1957²), 576–77; Warmington 310–11.

[47] *P. Lond.* ii 260 = *Stud.Pal.* iv, pp. 72–79, p. 74, line 549.

[48] On Norbanus, see M. Rostovtzeff in *Gnomon* (1931): 24 and, on the Norbani, op. cit. (n. 46 above) 293; on Marcus Julius Alexander, see A. Fuks in *Journal of Juristic Papyrology* 5 (1951): 214–16.

[49] See above, Text and Author: The Author and His Work.

solely from investors living in Egypt; it could well have been supplemented by the local agents or representatives of wealthy individuals off in Rome or other great centers who were on the lookout for profitable ventures in which to place spare cash.[50]

Though these merchants were private individuals, in business for themselves or the investors behind them, the people they dealt with were very often government officials. The *Periplus* frequently lists goods recommended for sale to the local rulers (see under 24:8.7–9); such sales would have been negotiated with employees of the court. Adulis, the chief port on the African side of the Red Sea, was an *emporion nomimon*, i.e., a port where all commerce was handled through the government (App. 1). The same was true of Muza, the chief port on the Arabian side of the Red Sea and the sole place where Arabian myrrh could be purchased. Arabian frankincense was available only at Kanê and, being a monopoly of the temple and state, only through royal agents.[51] At Barbarikon in northwest India, all imports were forwarded upriver "to the king" (39:13.5–6); it follows that their sale would have been arranged with the king's agents.

The situation finally changes at India's west coast. At Barygaza, though there was a towing service furnished by the crown (44:15.4–7), trading, with the exception of course of the items destined for the court, seems to have been in private hands. This was almost certainly the case at Muziris/Nelkynda, where indeed there may well have been a resident colony of Westerners.[52]

---

[50] For investment in trade by high-level Romans through agents and representatives, see J. D'Arms, *Commerce and Social Standing in Ancient Rome* (Cambridge, Mass., 1981), 39–47 (late Republic), 152–53 and 158 (early Empire). For investment by wealthy members of the urban elite, see H. Pleket, "Urban elites and business in the Greek part of the Roman Empire," in P. Garnsey, K. Hopkins, C. Whittaker, eds., *Trade in the Ancient Economy* (Berkeley, 1983), 130–44, esp. 137. M. Crawford, "Economia imperiale e commercio estero," *Tecnologia economia e società nel mondo romano*, Atti del Convegno di Como 27/28/29 settembre 1979 (Como, 1980), 207–17 at 215–17, offers a provocative argument that some of the merchants who traded with southern India may have been financed by members of the imperial family. It has long been recognized (cf. Raschke 666) that the coin finds from southern India consist overwhelmingly of issues from Tiberius's reign and the last years of Augustus's, all in fine condition; the best explanation, argues Crawford, is that they came there through the mediation of people who had direct access to the mint at Rome, and that points to members of the imperial family.

[51] This is the natural inference from the author's statement (29:9.28–29) that the labor was supplied by royal slaves and convicts and from the fact that at Moscha Limên sales were handled by royal agents and no loading aboard ship could take place without royal permission (32:11.2–6). Moscha Limên was a port of export only in exceptional cases; see under 32:11.1–3.

[52] The Vienna papyrus (Harrauer-Sijpesteijn) involves a loan agreement drawn up at Muziris for a shipment from there. For the foreign colony, see above, "The Trade with India."

So much for the Roman subjects involved in the trade with Africa, Arabia, and India. What about foreigners? That they had a share is beyond question. At Koptos, the key port on the Nile for handling trade goods from the Red Sea, from at least the early second century A.D. on there was a foreign colony of Palmyrene businessmen—an association of Palmyrene merchants, an association of "Palmyrene Red Sea Shipowners" (i.e., who sailed the Red Sea, Gulf of Aden, and western Indian Ocean), and some Palmyrene organization that had its own clubhouse; one of the shipowners was sufficiently wealthy and sufficiently well disposed towards Koptos to pay for the erection of a number of public buildings. A merchant from Aden is attested at Koptos as well. Indians, some of whom were merchants, were to be seen at Alexandria.[53] These are but straws in the wind, yet enough to indicate that foreigners were by no means shut out of the trade.

THE TRADERS: AFRICA VERSUS INDIA

As noted at the outset, the *Periplus* treats two major trade routes, one that ran along the eastern coast of Africa and another that crossed the water to the western coast of India. These involved very different sailing conditions—and, as a consequence, very different kinds of traders.

Along the African route sailing conditions were excellent, the chances of meeting trials at sea minimal. Thus it could be traversed by small craft as well as big, even by craft indifferently maintained. This meant it was open to small-scale merchants, those whose funds extended only to buying in a very modest supply of trade goods and chartering space at bargain rates on some unprepossessing freighter. The route to India, on the other hand, was just the opposite: the outbound voyage took place when the southwest monsoon was blowing its hardest, always strong and fre-

[53] For the Palmyrenes, see Sidebotham 95 (clubhouse); *l'Année épigraphique* (1912) no. 171 = *ESAR* ii no. 235, improved text by J. Bingen in *Chronique d'Égypte* 59 (1984): 356 (dedication by an association of Palmyrene merchants, chartered by Hadrian, in honor of a fellow countryman, a member of the "Palmyrene Shipowners of the Red Sea," who had paid for a propylaeum and three stoas as well as other benefactions; there is no evidence for an organization of "Palmyrene shippers and merchants," as is often asserted [cf. Sidebotham 95; Schwartz (op. cit. n. 11 above) 32; H. Ingholt in *Mélanges de l'Université Saint-Joseph* 45 (1970): 198–99]). For the merchant from Aden, see the inscription published by G. Wagner in *Bulletin de l'Institut français d'archéologie orientale* 76 (1976): 278. For Indians, see Dio Chrys. 32.40 (Indians among the spectators at games in Alexandria), Xenophon Ephes. 3.11.2 (an Indian rajah in Alexandria "for sightseeing in the city and for the business of trade").

quently increasing to gale force. Skippers of later ages waited until it had lost its bite before venturing forth during its period, but not the Greeks or Romans, thanks to the nature of their ships. For these were built in the special fashion favored by ancient shipwrights, one that guaranteed a hull of massive strength, and they carried a rig that not only was conservative but allowed quick and efficient reefing.[54] No doubt the ships were big as well as safe.[55] To charter space on such vessels and fill it with the spices and other costly items that India exported called for amounts of capital that only large-scale merchants could come up with, men who, as suggested above, might have had the backing of wealthy Roman financiers, even of members of the royal family. The Vienna papyrus gives us an idea of the sums that were required. On the portion preserved (the document is incomplete) there is listed[56] a shipment that consisted of at least 700 to 1700 pounds of nard (see under 56:18.25), ca. 4700 pounds of ivory,[57] and ca. 790 of textiles,[58] in other words a total weight of at most 7190 pounds, little more than three and one-half tons. Yet the cost of this modest tonnage was just short of 131 talents.[59] If the ship it had been loaded on was, say, a 500-tonner—no very great size by Roman standards[60]—there could well have been over 150 times that amount aboard with an aggregate value of 20,000 talents, a great sum indeed.[61] Even though the cargo aboard any one vessel almost certainly consisted of dozens of consignments, each belonging to a different merchant, the funds each merchant had to command must have been considerable.

A ROMAN ECONOMIC POLICY?

We have reviewed the trade that the merchants of Roman Egypt carried on with Africa, Arabia, and India. Did the emperors take measures that affected it? In other words, was there an imperial economic policy?

[54] For details of the sailing conditions along the two routes, the ships used, and the construction and rig of Greco-Roman craft, see App. 3.

[55] Cf. App. 3, n. 22.

[56] Harrauer-Sijpesteijn 132, lines 1–21.

[57] Line 4: 78 tal., 54½ mnas.

[58] Line 16: 13 tal., 9¾ mnas.

[59] The nard was valued at 45 tal. (line 3), the ivory at 76 tal. 4500 dr. (line 10), the textiles at 8 tal. 4290 dr. (line 21). The total shipment had a value of over 1154 talents (lines 27–29).

[60] *SSAW* 172.

[61] It would be the equivalent of 30,000,000 denarii (20,000 talents = 120,000,000 drachmas, and the denarius was usually reckoned as the equivalent of a tetradrachm). This is, e.g., a third more than one of the distributions Augustus proudly proclaimed he gave to the populace of Rome (*Res Gestae* xv.iii.15–17: 60 denarii each to 320,000 people, a total of 19,200,000 denarii).

Under the Ptolemies it is clear that the government was very much concerned with what went on in the Red Sea and beyond and figured directly in its commerce. Ptolemy II and Ptolemy III founded the ports that lined the western shore of the Red Sea. Ptolemy VII organized and dispatched the pioneering voyage to India in which Eudoxus took part (Strabo 2.98; cf. under 57:19.5–7). And, though the trading itself was left in the hands of private individuals, the spices and aromatics they brought back became crown property, purchased at rates fixed by the government.[62]

When Egypt came under Roman rule, the number of ships that sailed from there to Arabia and India, as noted above, increased dramatically. They were still privately owned, carrying the goods of individual merchants (see above, "The Traders"). But, unlike Ptolemaic times, the government no longer exercised a direct control over these goods. As the Vienna papyrus cited earlier reveals, they remained in the names of their shippers even after entering the customs house at Alexandria. The government, however, was by no means left out in the cold: it took over, by way of customs duty, no less than a quarter of all that was brought in.

In the early part of this century there was a school of thought that attributed to the Roman emperors a much greater involvement in the trade of the Indian Ocean than the mere levying of a customs duty. It ascribed to them a far-reaching economic policy aimed at keeping such trade in Roman hands, even to the extent of securing control of key ports along the way.[63] This has since been shown to be little more than theorizing with nothing solid to support it;[64] indeed, it is doubtful if the emperors even conceived of their realm as an economic unit.[65] Yet there are some who still see the emperors' hands at work in the area. They are impressed by the numerous embassies that the rulers of the trading nations of Arabia and India dispatched to Rome.[66] They feel that these were connected with imperial policy, with measures the emperors had in mind to abet or protect Rome's trade.[67]

[62] M. Rostovtzeff, *The Social and Economic History of the Hellenistic World* (Oxford, 1941), 389; Desanges 300–301.

[63] Réumé by J. Anderson in *CAH* x 880–81 (1934).

[64] Cf. M. Charlesworth in *CQ* 22 (1928): 92; J. Anderson in *CAH* x 881–83; Desanges 321–23.

[65] Crawford (op. cit. n. 50 above) 208.

[66] Embassies from Arabia, see *Periplus* 23:7.29–30, Pliny 12.57. Embassies from India, see Raschke 1045, n. 1623; Charlesworth (op. cit. Text and Author, n. 16 above) 140, note 22; Sidebotham 129.

[67] Charlesworth (op. cit. n. 66 above, 141) confidently asserts that "they had the definite purpose of arranging for the protection and the safety of members of the nations involved," and this view has been repeated by B. Mukherjee, *An Agrippan Source* (Calcutta, 1969), 9, n. 38. W. Schmitthenner, in *Journal of Roman Studies* 69 (1979): 104, sees them as diplomatic

It is worthwhile to examine the evidence for embassies in some detail. To begin with, those from Arabia. The *Periplus* reports (23:7.29–30) that Charibaêl, ruler of the state that comprised the southwestern corner of the peninsula, sent them continuously in order to cement his friendship with the emperors. Pliny (12.57) mentions embassies that must have come from the kings of the neighboring state in the Hadramaut;[68] no doubt they had the same purpose. We must first bear in mind that the initiative came from Arabia, not Rome. Second, in 26 or 25 B.C.[69] Augustus had undertaken a full-scale invasion of Arabia that penetrated deeply before it was turned back[70] and either then or later an attack was mounted on the port of Eudaimôn Arabia that was successful, although its ultimate effects appear to have been of small consequence (see under 26:8.31–32). In the light of all this, there is manifest political motivation to explain Charibaêl's efforts to be the Roman emperors' friend: it was a way of lessening the likelihood of their repeating Augustus's attempt. He no doubt had the very considerable commercial consequences well in mind, but these were totally dependent upon the political developments.[71]

---

moves whose aim was "to serve the re-establishment and protection of the maritime connections with India." Charlesworth's argument that Rome and India sought to effect the necessary protection by creating "treaty ports" is based on a misunderstanding of the *Periplus's* terminology; see App. 1. Schmitthenner's views on Rome's military efforts to protect trade are pure speculation; cf. Rostovtzeff (op. cit. n. 46 above) 577, where he rightly points out that "after Augustus very little was done to protect it [sc. maritime trade with the East]. We see no serious attempts to occupy the Arabian coast or fight the growing kingdom of Axûm or even to maintain any military fleet in the Red Sea. The trade was carried on by the merchants at their own risk."

[68] See under 23:7.29–30. In a discussion of frankincense, Pliny refers to an embassy that had brought a gift of incense; it must have come from the "frankincense-bearing land," to use the *Periplus's* terminology.

[69] The campaign is usually dated 25–24 B.C. (Desanges 308); S. Jameson in *Journal of Roman Studies* 58 (1968): 77 argues for 26–25.

[70] Strabo 16.780–82; thoughtful résumé in G. Bowersock, *Roman Arabia* (Cambridge, Mass., 1983), 46–49.

[71] The Arabian expedition seems to have been part of a widespread program of territorial aggrandizement that Augustus had set in motion; see Jameson (op. cit. n. 69 above) 82; Bowersock (op. cit. n. 70 above) 46. But Augustus was well aware of the commercial advantages: as Strabo reports (16.780), he had heard the rumors of Arabia's lucrative sales of aromatics and gems and he hoped to end up "either treating with wealthy friends or holding sway over wealthy enemies." Just as the conquest of Egypt had put in Rome's lap an annual tribute of thousands of tons of grain, so the conquest of Arabia would add an annual tribute of precious myrrh and frankincense. Charibaêl, anxious to have his kingdom's yield of myrrh to sell rather than give up as tribute, had a good case to present: by maintaining friendship with him Rome received, at no expense whatsoever, one quarter, collected by way of customs duty, of all the myrrh and frankincense that crossed the frontiers of the empire, and the more the trade flourished, the greater would be Rome's take; tribute, to be

Next, the embassies from India. They are mentioned by Augustus in his own account of his reign (*Res Gestae* xxxi. v. 50–51), where he emphasizes their frequency and that he was the very first Roman commander to whom India had ever dispatched any. As it turned out, he was the first of many emperors to receive them.[72] Our sources dwell chiefly on the gifts that were brought,[73] but for one embassy sent to Augustus by Porus, probably a king in northwestern India, we have some indications of its purpose. Strabo (15.719) reports that the members brought a written communication from Porus in which he offered Rome the right of passage through his realm and his cooperation in "suitable ventures." Dio Cassius (54.9.8) states of the same embassy that the members, after negotiations at some earlier date, at this time concluded a treaty of friendship. It sounds as if Porus was trying to increase his diplomatic stature. In any case, there is not the slightest hint that commercial matters were discussed, and the same is true of all the subsequent embassies.

A recent study emphasizes the care the emperors lavished on maintaining and guarding the roads in Egypt's eastern desert that linked the Nile with the ports on the Red Sea, arguing that this reflects imperial interest in the trade that used those ports.[74] But there are other ways of explaining the concern for these roads. For one, they served the mines and quarries in the area, both of which belonged to the crown.[75] For another, the goods that moved over them paid customs duties, which were a lucrative source of income for the imperial treasury; the flow of that income depended upon the flow of goods, and this certainly was aided by well-maintained and safe roads.

---

sure, would produce a far higher take, but only at the cost of policing a remote people inhabiting a forbidding terrain. Cf. T. Frank in *ESAR* v 21, where he emphasizes Augustus's interest in port dues.

[72] From Claudius to Constantine; see Charlesworth (op. cit. n. 66 above) ibid.

[73] Either prized products, such as gems and pearls, or exotic curiosities, such as pythons and tigers; see Warmington 35–37.

[74] Sidebotham 48–68, 176. He connects the care for the roads with "direct imperial involvement in and profit from the Erythraean Sea trade. . . . A slave of Tiberius operated a business for his imperial master at Berenice for at least two and one-half years" (136; cf. 89). His basis for this statement is chiefly four ostraca (*O. Tait* i P237–39, P242) in the archive of Nicanor (see n. 11 above) that are receipts, signed by an imperial slave, acknowledging modest amounts of food and drink, such as four artabs (roughly four bushels) of wheat or six jars of wine. The signer, far from being director of an import-export company owned by the emperor, seems rather to be the commissary clerk of some local government office accepting supplies for the feeding of the staff, like those who, in other receipts in the archive (P280, P285, P288, P291), acknowledge receipt of modest amounts of barley "for the public granary"; cf. Rostovtzeff (op. cit. n. 11 above) 24. The emperors may well have had some stake in the Red Sea trade, but the evidence Sidebotham offers does not prove it.

[75] Cf. *ESAR* ii 241–42.

In short, the historical record reveals no measures taken by the emperors which unquestionably were part of a policy for promoting maritime trade with the East.[76]

Nature of the Objects of Trade
(Numbers = Chapters)

FOOD AND DRINK

From Roman Egypt to Overseas Ports
olive oil 6
unripe olives 7
grain 7, 17, 24, 28, 56
wine 6, 7, 17, 24, 28, 39, 49, 56; fine grade for the court 49

From Overseas Ports to Roman Egypt
none

From India to Ports Other than those in Roman Egypt
grain 14, 31, 32
rice 14, 31
sesame oil 14, 32
ghee 14
cane sugar 14

From Arabia, Persis, Gedrosia to Ports
Other than those in Roman Egypt
wine 36, 49
dates 36

TEXTILES, CLOTHING

From Roman Egypt to Overseas Ports
ORDINARY QUALITY
clothing 39, 49, 56
clothing: for the Barbaroi 6, 7
clothing: for the Arabs 24, 28
cloaks (*abollai*) 6, 24
cloaks (*kaunakai*) 6
cloaks (*sagoi*, used) 8
wraps (*stolai*, from Arsinoe) 6

---

[76] Sidebotham's long chapter, "The Genesis and Evolution of Roman Policy in the Erythra Thalassa" (113–74), offers argument and conjecture but no cogent proof.

tunics 8
girdles 24
girdles, multicolored 49
double-fringed items (*dikrossia*) 6
linens 6
purple cloth 24
(wool?) cloth 24
multicolored textiles (*polymita*) 39, 56
EXPENSIVE QUALITY
clothing for the court 24, 28, 49
purple cloth, fine quality, 24

From Overseas Ports to Roman Egypt
ORDINARY QUALITY
cotton garments 48, 51, 59
cotton cloth 48, 49, 51
garments of *molochinon* 48, 51
cloth of *molochinon* 49

EXPENSIVE
Chinese pelts 39
silk cloth 39, 49, 56
Gangetic cotton garments 63

From India to Ports Other than those in Roman Egypt
cotton garments 6
cotton cloth 6, 14, 31, 32
garments of *molochinon* 6
girdles 6, 14
cloaks (*kaunakai*) 6

From Arabia, Persis, Gedrosia to Ports Other than those in Roman Egypt
purple cloth 36
clothing 36

HOUSEHOLD ITEMS, TOOLS
From Roman Egypt to Overseas Ports
glassware 6, 7, 17, 39
copper honey pans (?) 6, 8
copper drinking vessels 6
drinking vessels 8

ironware 10
axes 6, 17
adzes 6
knives 6, 17
awls 17
blankets 24

EXPENSIVE
copperware for the court 24
silverware 10
silverware for the court 6, 24, 28, 39 (probably), 49
goldware for the court 6, 24
statuary for the court 28
slaves for the court 49
horses for the court 24, 28
pack mules for the court 24

From Overseas Ports to Roman Egypt
slaves 8, 13

From India to Ports Other
than those in Roman Egypt
slaves 31

From Arabia, Persis, Gedrosia to Ports
Other than those in Roman Egypt
slaves 36

RAW MATERIALS
From Roman Egypt to Overseas Ports
brass 6
iron 6, 8
tin 7, 28, 49, 56
lead 49, 56
copper 28, 49, 56
raw glass 49, 56

From Overseas Ports to Roman Egypt
white marble 24

From India to Ports Other
than those in Roman Egypt
iron and steel 6
copper 36
teak 36

sissoo 36
ebony 36

From Arabia, Persis, Gedrosia to Ports
Other than those in Roman Egypt
none

COSTLY MATERIALS, GEMS

From Roman Egypt to Overseas Ports
precious stones 10
coral 28, 39, 49, 56
peridot (?) 39, 49, 56

From Overseas Ports to Roman Egypt
tortoise shell 3, 6, 7, 10, 13, 17, 30, 56
ivory 3, 6, 7, 10, 17, 49, 56
rhinoceros horn 6, 17
nautilus shell 17
turquoise 39
lapis lazuli 39
onyx 48, 49, 51
agate (?) 48, 49
pearls 56, 63
transparent gems 56
diamonds 56
sapphires 56

From India to Ports
Other than those in Roman Egypt
none

From Arabia, Persis, Gedrosia to Ports
Other than those in Roman Egypt
pearls 36
gold 36
tortoise shell 31

SPICES, AROMATICS

From Roman Egypt to Overseas Ports
none

From Overseas Ports to Roman Egypt
aromatics 7, 10
myrrh 7, 8, 10, 24

frankincense 8, 10, 11, 12, 28
cassia 8, 10, 12, 13
duaka (gum resin?) 8
kankamon (gum resin?) 8
mokrotu (incense) 9, 10
bdellium 39, 49
pepper 49, 56

From India to Ports Other
than those in Roman Egypt

From Arabia, Persis, Gedrosia to Ports
Other than those in Roman Egypt

frankincense 32, 36, 39

DRUGS, DYES

From Roman Egypt to Overseas Ports

saffron 24
cyperus 24
unguent 24, 49; fine quality for the court 49
storax 28, 39
yellow clover 49
realgar 49, 56
sulphide of antimony 49, 56
orpiment 56

From Overseas Ports to Roman Egypt

makeir 8
aloe 28
cinnabar 30
costus 39, 49
nard 39, 49, 56, 63
indigo 39
lykion 39, 49
malabathron 56, 63

From India to Ports Other
than those in Roman Egypt

lac dye 6

From Arabia, Persis, Gedrosia to Ports
Other than those in Roman Egypt

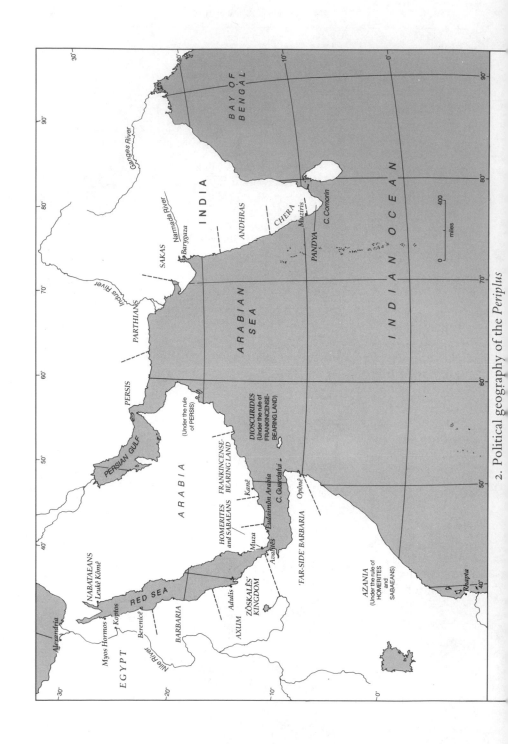

2. Political geography of the *Periplus*

III. POLITICAL GEOGRAPHY

The *Periplus* notes not only the names of ports and harbors but, like a modern coast pilot, the countries to which they belong and, wherever possible, the rulers. By collating this information we can draw up an almost complete political map of the part of the world the work embraces.

First Africa. Just below Berenicê was the southern boundary of Roman Egypt. Here began the land of Barbaria[1] (2:1.6–7), which extended to a point just north of Ptolemais Thêrôn (see under 5:2.19–20). Populated by primitive peoples (see under 2:1.7–10), it had no single sovereign but was ruled by local chieftains (see under B 2:1.9–10). The coastal area from just north of Ptolemais Thêrôn south to the Straits of Bab el Mandeb formed a nation with its capital at Adulis; it was ruled by a king, Zôskalês, who was so Hellenized that he was at home in the Greek language (5:2.19–22 and see under 5:2.19–20). At the straits began the "rest of Barbaria" (5:2.20). It included the African side of the Straits of Bab el Mandeb (cf. 7:3.19, 25:8.14–15), the northern coast of Somalia right up to Cape Guardafui (12:4.21), and a short stretch south of the cape as far as Ras Hafun; strung along its shore were the so-called "far-side" ports (7:3.10–11), from Avalitês on the strait (7:3.13) to Opônê on Ras Hafun (see under 13:5.3). Like the part of Barbaria just below Roman Egypt, it had no central authority but was ruled by local chieftains (14:5.14–16). South of Opônê began what the author calls Azania (15:5.17–18, 16:6.3), the coast of Africa down to Rhapta in the vicinity of Dar es Salaam. At this time it was under Arab rule, a possession of the kingdom of the Sabaeans and Homerites (see under 23:7.27–29) in the southwest part of the Arabian peninsula, more or less modern Yemen. Azania was administered directly by the governor of Mapharitis (31:10.19–20), a province of the kingdom concentrated in the southwestern tip of the peninsula whose port of Muza[2] was the foremost in the kingdom's trade with Africa (cf. 17:6.14–15). Azania ended at Rhapta; below was terra incognita (17:6.21–23). Rhapta, Azania's largest and most active port, was administered, like the

---

[1] On the use of *barbaros* and its derivatives as geographical terms, see H. Ingholt in *Palmyre: Bilan et Perspectives, Colloque de Strasbourg, 18–20 Octobre 1973* (Strasbourg, 1976), 107.

[2] That Mapharitis included Muza is implicit in the administrative arrangements for Rhapta described below.

rest of the region, by the governor of Mapharitis, but its taxes were handled in a special fashion: the crown farmed them out to the shippers of the port of Muza (16:6.10–13).

Next Arabia. The northeast coast of the Red Sea, with its port of Leukê Kômê, was controlled by the Nabataeans; the king at this time was Malichus II, with his capital at Petra, its traditional location (19:6.28–29 and see above, Text and Author: The Date). South of Leukê Kômê began what the author considers Arabia proper (20:7.3). Most of the Arabian Red Sea coast, from where Nabataean jurisdiction ended to a point north of Muza where that of the kingdom of the Sabaeans and Homerites began (cf. under 20:7.16–17), had no central authority, being inhabited by primitive fisher folk and herdsmen; the latter eked out their meager livelihood with the profitable returns from piracy (20:7.6–11). The southwest corner of the peninsula, from north of Muza on the Red Sea around to at least Eudaimôn Arabia on the site of modern Aden (26:8.23–24), was the kingdom of the Sabaeans and Homerites to which Azania was subject; it was ruled by Charibaêl, with his capital at Saphar (23:7.27–29 and note ad loc.). The southwestern tip of the peninsula, site of the ports of Okêlis (25:8.19) as well as Muza, made up the province of Mapharitis under Charibaêl's governor, Cholaibos; the provincial capital was at Sauê (22:7.24–26). Charibaêl's realm ended somewhere east of Eudaimôn Arabia. Then came a stretch of coast inhabited by primitive fisher folk that extended to just short of Kanê (27:9.1–4). Kanê was the major port of the "frankincense-bearing land," ruled at this time by Eleazos, with his capital at Sabautha (27:9.4–8). This kingdom, corresponding roughly to the Hadramaut of today, reached eastward to a point on the coast opposite the Isles of Zênobios (33:11.10–12) or Kuria Muria Islands (see under 33:11.10–11). The "frankincense-bearing land" had its own overseas possession, the island of Socotra (31:10.19–20). The coast eastward of this point, an area the author characterizes as primitive (33:11.11), was at this time under the control of the kingdom of Persis (33:11.12 and note ad loc.).

And Persis held the coast east of the Persian Gulf at least as far as Omana, six days sail from its mouth (36:12.3–4). Beyond this began the rule of the Indo-Parthian kings. First came a district inhabited by a people called the Parsidai (37:12.13–14 and note ad loc.) and then Skythia, more or less modern Sind (38:12.23 and note ad loc.); here was the area's major port, Barbarikon at the mouth of the Indus. The author names no king presumably because, as he drily comments, the rulers were "constantly chasing each other off" the throne (38:13.3–4). The capital was at Minnagar, upriver from Barbarikon (39:13.3, 6).

What the author calls India proper began at the Little Rann and the Gulf of Kutch (see under 41:14.2–3), where at this time the Sakas ruled. Formerly their kingdom had included northwest India from the Indus Delta eastward to Ujjain but, by the time of the *Periplus*, invading Parthians had driven them out of the delta (see under 38:12.23, 38:13.3–4). This still left them with a sizable realm, the southern border of which they managed to extend as far as Bombay (see under 41:14.2) by pushing back the Andhran kingdom below them. The Saka kingdom boasted India's chief port, Barygaza. The throne at the moment was held by Manbanos (41:14.2), probably a Hellenization of Nahapāna, one of the greatest Saka rulers. The capital was at Minnagara (41:14.8), northeast of Barygaza; it had formerly been at Ozênê (48:16.12–13) , modern Ujjain, in the same general area. North of the Sakas were the Kushans (Bactrians in the author's terminology, 47:16.6). South of the Sakas were the powerful Andhras, to whom the *Periplus* refers only obliquely, with a by-the-way mention of one of their earlier rulers (52:17.18 and see under 52:17.18a). The two nations were constantly at war with each other, and at the moment the Sakas had succeeded in taking some major Andhran ports (see under 52:17.19–21). This would explain why the author makes no direct reference to the Andhran kingdom; when he was writing, it did not figure in trade with the West.

South of the Andhras lay the three great kingdoms of southern India, the Chera, Pandya, and Chola (see under 54:17.29). Ships sailing down the coast came first to the Chera kingdom, whose northern border was just above Tyndis (54:17.29) and whose southern was somewhere between Muziris and Nelkynda (54:18.4–6), in modern terms, north of Ponnāni and south of Cranganore (App. 5). The author calls the ruler Kêprobotos, following the Indian practice of naming a king after his country (see under 54:17.29). Below the "kingdom of Kêprobotos" was the "kingdom of. . . Pandion" (54:18.5–6), i.e., the Pandya kingdom. It embraced the whole southern tip of the peninsula, extending along the western coast from Nelkynda down to Cape Comorin and along the eastern from the cape up to at least Kolchoi on the Gulf of Mannar (59:19.22–24 and see under 59:19.22–23). At this point the author's political information stops. The next ports named—Argaru, Kamara, Podukê, and Sôpatma (59:20.1, 60:20.6)—must have belonged to the Chola kingdom, but there is no mention of this fact (cf. under 59:19.25–20.1). The ports beyond, listed right up to the delta of the Ganges, similarly lack any indication of countries or rulers.

47

TEXT AND TRANSLATION

Since Frisk's text has stood the test of time and requires relatively few changes, and since it has become common practice to refer to the *Periplus* by the line(s) and page(s) in his edition, I have reproduced his text with whatever adjustments proved necessary.

In the text, ⟨ ⟩ enclose letters or words to be added; [ ] enclose letters or words to be deleted;. . . . indicates a lacuna left by the scribe; ⟨**⟩ indicates a lacuna according to the editor.

The changes from Frisk's text, indicated by being set in smaller type, or by blank space, or both occur in the following lines:

4:2.2	30:10.5–6	55:18.11
7:3.16–17	30:10.14–16	56:18.16
7:3.19	32:11.4–7	56:18.20
10:4.11	36:12.6	57:18.30–19.12
12:4.22	36:12.7	58:19.18
15:5.25–26a	37:12.15	58:19.19–20
16:6.7	40:13.19–20	60:20.8
19:6.31–7.1	40:13.29	61:20.14
20:7.14–15	42:14.14	62:20.25
26:8.25	46:15.23–24	63:21.9
26:8.26	46:15.29	65:21.22–23
26:8.28	47:16.3	65:21.24–25

For explanation of the changes, see the notes to the above lines in Commentary B. See also notes to B 30:10.11 and B 65:22.4.

257 M.   Τῶν ἀποδεδειγμένων ὅρμων τῆς Ἐρυθρᾶς θαλάσσης καὶ τῶν περὶ 1
αὐτὴν ἐμπορίων πρῶτός ἐστιν λιμὴν τῆς Αἰγύπτου Μυὸς ὅρμος, μετὰ
3 δὲ αὐτὸν εἰσπλεόντων ἀπὸ χιλίων ὀκτακοσίων σταδίων ἐν δεξιᾷ ἡ Βερ-
νίκη· ἀμφοτέρων ⟨δὲ⟩ οἱ λιμένες ἐν τῷ ἐσχάτῳ τῆς Αἰγύπτου κόλποι
[δὲ] τῆς Ἐρυθρᾶς θαλάσσης κεῖνται.

258 M.   6   Τούτων ἐκ μὲν τῶν δεξιῶν ἀπὸ Βερνίκης συναφὴς ἡ Βαρβαρικὴ 2
χώρα ἐστίν· τὰ μὲν παρὰ θάλασσαν Ἰχθυοφάγων μάνδραις οἰκοδομημέ-
ναις ἐν στενώμασιν καὶ σποράδην δὲ οἰκοῦνται, τὰ δὲ μεσόγεια Βαρβά-
9 ρων καὶ τῶν μετ᾽ αὐτοὺς Ἀγριοφάγων καὶ Μοσχοφάγων κατὰ τυραν-
νίδα νεμομένων, οἷς ἐπίκειται κατὰ νώτου μεσόγειος ἀπὸ τῶν πρὸς
δύσιν μερῶν ⟨μητρόπολις λεγομένη Μερόη⟩.

12   Μετὰ δὲ τοὺς Μοσχοφάγους ἐπὶ θαλάσσης μικρὸν ἐμπόριόν ἐστιν, 3
ἀπέχον † τὸ πέρας τῆς ἀνακομιδῆς † σταδίους περὶ τετρακισχιλίους,
Πτολεμαῒς ἡ τῶν θηρῶν λεγομένη, ἀφ᾽ ἧς οἱ ἐπὶ Πτολε⟨μαί⟩ων τῷ
259 M.   15 βασιλεῖ θηρεύοντες ἀνέβησαν. Ἔχει δὲ τὸ ἐμπόριον χελώνην ἀληθινὴν
καὶ χερσαίαν ὀλίγην καὶ λευκὴν μικροτέραν τοῖς ὀστράκοις· εὑρίσκεται
δὲ ἐν αὐτῇ ποτὲ μὲν ἐλέφας ὀλίγος, ὅμοιος τῷ Ἀδουλιτικῷ. Ὁ δὲ
18 τόπος ἀλίμενος καὶ σκάφαις μόνον τὴν ἀποδρομὴν ἔχων.

Μετὰ δὲ τὴν Πτολεμαΐδα τὴν τῶν θηρῶν ἀπὸ σταδίων ὡς τρισχι- 4
λίων ἐμπόριόν ἐστιν νόμιμον ἡ Ἄδουλι, κείμενον ἐν κόλπῳ βαθεῖ κατ᾽
21 αὐτὸν τὸν νότον, οὗ πρό[σ]κειται νῆσος Ὀρεινὴ λεγομένη, τοῦ μὲν
260 M. ἐσωτάτου κόλπου σταδίους ὡς εἰς πέλαγος ἔχουσα διακοσίους, ἐξ ἀμφοτέρων ⟨δὲ⟩ τῶν μερῶν παρακειμένην ἔχουσα τὴν ἤπειρον, ἐν ᾗ νῦν

In tit. ante Περίπλους habet Ἀρριανοῦ
4 δὲ huc revocavit Müller   6 Βαρβαρικὴ Müller: ¡τισηβαρικὴ   11 ⟨μητρό-
πολις λεγομένη Μερόη⟩ Schwanbeck, Müller: post μερῶν spatium 8—9 litterarum,
dein σης μικρὸν   14 Πτολε⟨μαί⟩ων Bernhardy   15 θηρεύοντες Müller in comm:
θηρευθέντες   ἀνέβ- Müller: ἐνέβ-   17 ἀοιδοτικῶι corr. edd.   18 ἐπιδρο-
μὴν Stuck   20 ἀδουλεί (sic ubique) correxi   21 πρό[σ]κειται m. alt.
23 ⟨δὲ⟩ Müller

THE *PERIPLUS* OF

THE ERYTHRAEAN SEA

1. Of the designated harbors of the Erythraean Sea and the ports of trade on it, first comes Egypt's port of Myos Hormos and, beyond it, after a sail of 1800 stades to the right, Berenicê. The ports of both are bays of the Red Sea on the edge of Egypt.

2. To the right of these places, immediately beyond Berenicê, comes the country of the Barbaroi. The coastal parts are inhabited by Ichthyophagoi ["fish eaters"] living in mean huts built in narrow areas, hence in scattered groups, while the inland parts are inhabited by Barbaroi and the people beyond them, Agriophagoi ["wild animal eaters"] and Moschophagoi ["shoot eaters"], organized in chiefdoms. In the interior behind them, in the parts toward the west is [? a metropolis called Meroe].

3. Beyond the Moschophagoi, about 4000 stades distant . . . on the sea is a small port of trade called Ptolemais Thêrôn ["Ptolemais of the Hunts"]; from it, in the days of the Ptolemies, the royal huntsmen made their way inland. The port of trade offers genuine tortoise shell, a little land tortoise, and a light-colored variety with rather small shields. On occasion, even a little ivory is to be found there, similar to that from Adulis. The place has no harbor and offers refuge only to small craft.

4. About 3000 stades beyond Ptolemais Thêrôn is a legally limited port of trade, Adulis. It is on a deep bay extending due south, in front of which lies an island called Oreinê ["hilly"] that is situated about 200 stades from the innermost part of the bay towards the open sea and, on both sides, lies parallel to the coast; here at the present time

ὁρμεῖ τὰ καταγόμενα πλοῖα διὰ τὰς ἐκ τῆς γῆς καταδρομάς. Πρῶτον μὲν γὰρ ὥρμει κατ᾽ αὐτὸν τὸν ἐξώτατον κόλπον ἐν τῇ Διδώρου λεγομένη νήσῳ παρ᾽ αὐτὴν τὴν ἤπειρον, ἐχούσῃ πεζῇ τὴν διάβασιν, δι᾽ ἧς 3 οἱ κατοικοῦντες Βάρβαροι κατέτρεχον τὴν νῆσον. Καὶ κατ᾽ αὐτὴν τὴν ἐν τῇ Ὀρεινῇ ἤπειρον ἀπὸ σταδίων εἴκοσι τῆς θαλάσσης ἐστὶν ἡ Ἄδουλι, κώμη σύμμετρος, ἀφ᾽ ἧς εἰς μὲν Κολόην μεσόγειον πόλιν καὶ πρῶτον 6 ἐμπόριον τοῦ ἐλέφαντος ὁδός ἐστιν ἡμερῶν τριῶν· ἀπὸ δὲ ταύτης εἰς αὐτὴν τὴν μητρόπολιν τὸν Ἀξωμίτην λεγόμενον ἄλλων ἡμερῶν πέντε, εἰς ὃν ὁ πᾶς ἐλέφας ἀπὸ τοῦ πέρα⟨ν⟩ τοῦ Νείλου φέρεται διὰ τοῦ 9 λεγομένου Κυηνείου, ἐκεῖθεν δὲ εἰς Ἄδουλι. Τὸ μὲν οὖν ὅλον πλῆθος τῶν φονευομένων ἐλεφάντων καὶ ῥινοκερώτων περὶ τοὺς ἄνω νέμεται τόπους, σπανίως δέ ποτε καὶ ἐν τῷ παρὰ θάλασσαν περὶ αὐτὴν τὴν 12 Ἄδουλι θεωροῦνται. Πρόκεινται δὲ τοῦ ἐμπορίου καὶ κατὰ πέλαγος ἐκ 261 M. δεξιῶν ἄλλαι νῆσοι μικραὶ ἄμμιναι πλείονες, Ἀλαλαίου λεγόμεναι, χελώνην ἔχουσαι τὴν εἰς τὸ ἐμπόριον φερομένην ἀπὸ τῶν Ἰχθυοφάγων. 15

5   Καὶ ἀπὸ σταδίων ὡσεὶ ὀκτακοσίων κόλπος ἕτερος βαθύτατος, οὗ κατὰ τὴν εἰσβολὴν ἐν δεξιοῖς ἄμμος ἐστὶν πολλὴ κεχυμένη, καθ᾽ ἧς ἐν βάθει κεχωσμένος εὑρίσκεται ὁ ὀψιανὸς λίθος, ἐν ἐκείνῃ μόνῃ τοπικῶς 18 γεννώμενος. Βασιλεύει δὲ τῶν τόπων τούτων ἀπὸ τῶν Μοσχοφάγων μέχρι τῆς ἄλλης Βαρβαρίας Ζωσκάλης, ἀκριβὴς μὲν τοῦ βίου καὶ τοῦ πλείονος ἐξεχόμενος, γενναῖος δὲ περὶ τὰ λοιπὰ καὶ γραμμάτων Ἑλλη- 21 νικῶν ἔμπειρος.

6   Προχωρεῖ δὲ εἰς τοὺς τόπους τούτους ἱμάτια Βαρβαρικὰ ἄγναφα τὰ ἐν Αἰγύπτῳ γινόμενα, Ἀρσινοϊτικαὶ στολαὶ καὶ ἀβόλλαι νόθοι χρω- 24 μάτινοι καὶ λέντια καὶ δικρόσσια καὶ λιθίας ὑ⟨α⟩λῆς πλείονα γένη καὶ ἄλλης μορρίνης τῆς γινομένης ἐν Διοσπόλει, καὶ ὠρόχαλκος, ᾧ χρῶνται 262 M. πρὸς κόσμον καὶ εἰς συγκοπὴν ἀντὶ νομίσματος, καὶ μελίεφθα χαλκᾶ εἴς 27 τε ἕψησιν καὶ εἰς συγκοπὴν ψελίων καὶ περισκελίδων τισὶν τῶν γυναικῶν καὶ σίδηρος ὁ δαπανώμενος εἴς τε λόγχας πρὸς τοὺς ἐλέφαντας καὶ τὰ ἄλλα θηρία καὶ τοὺς πολέμους. Ὁμοίως δὲ καὶ πελύκια προχωρεῖ 30 καὶ σκέπαρνα καὶ μάχαιραι καὶ ποτήρια χαλκᾶ στρογγύλα μεγάλα καὶ δηνάριον ὀλίγον πρὸς τοὺς ἐπιδημοῦντας καὶ οἶνος Λαδικηνὸς καὶ Ἰταλικὸς οὐ πολὺς καὶ ἔλαιον οὐ πολύ· τῷ δὲ βασιλεῖ ἀργυρώματα καὶ 33 χρυσώματα τοπικῷ ῥυθμῷ κατεσκευασμένα καὶ ἱματίων ἀβόλλαι καὶ γαννάκαι ἁπλοῖ, οὐ πολλοῦ δὲ ταῦτα. Ὁμοίως δὲ καὶ ἀπὸ τῶν ἔσω

---

5 εἴκοσι: κ̄   9 τοὔπερα corr. Stuck   11 καὶ Müller in comm: ἢ   14 αμμειναι (sine spir. et acc.): corr. Müller ad Ptol. 4,7,3.   20 τῶν πλείονος corr. Bernhardy   24 Ἀρσι- Stuck: ἀρσε-   ἄβολοι corr. Müller   25 ὑαλῆς Stuck: ὕλης

arriving vessels moor because of raids from the mainland. Formerly they used to moor at the very outermost part of the bay at the island, called Didôros Island, right by this part of the coast; there is a ford crossing to it by which the Barbaroi dwelling roundabout used to overrun the island. On this part of the coast, opposite Oreinê, 20 stades in from the sea is Adulis, a fair-sized village. From Adulis it is a journey of three days to Koloê, an inland city that is the first trading post for ivory, and from there another five days to the metropolis itself, which is called Axômitês [Axum]; into it is brought all the ivory from beyond the Nile through what is called Kyêneion, and from there down to Adulis. The mass of elephants and rhinoceroses that are slaughtered all inhabit the upland regions, although on rare occasions they are also seen along the shore around Adulis itself. In front of the port of trade, that is, towards the open sea, on the right are a number of other islands, small and sandy, called Alalaiu; these furnish the tortoise shell that is brought to the port of trade by the Ichthyophagoi.

5. After about 800 stades comes another, very deep, bay near whose mouth, on the right, a great amount of sand has accumulated; under this, deeply buried, obsidian is found, a natural local creation in that spot alone. The ruler of these regions, from the Moschophagoi to the rest of Barbaria, is Zôskalês, a stickler about his possessions and always holding out for getting more, but in other respects a fine person and well versed in reading and writing Greek.

6. In this area there is a market for: articles of clothing for the Barbaroi, unused, the kind produced in Egypt; wraps from Arsinoe; colored *abollai* [cloaks] of printed fabric; linens; double-fringed items; numerous types of glass stones and also of millefiori glass of the kind produced in Diospolis; brass, which they use for ornaments as well as cutting up for coins; copper honey pans (?) for cooking and for cutting up into armlets and anklets for certain of the women; iron which is expended on spears for elephants and the other wild animals as well as for war. Likewise there is also a market for: axes, adzes, knives; large round copper drinking vessels; a little Roman money for the resident foreigners; wine of Laodicea and Italy, limited quantity; olive oil, limited quantity. For the king, silverware and goldware fashioned in the local manner; in clothing, *abollai* and *kaunakai* [heavy cloaks], with no adornment and modest in price. Likewise also, from the interior

53

τόπων τῆς Ἀριακῆς σίδηρος Ἰνδικὸς καὶ στόμωμα καὶ ὀθόνιον Ἰνδικὸν
263 M. τὸ πλατύτερον ἡ λεγομένη μοναχὴ καὶ σαγματογῆναι καὶ περιζώματα
3 καὶ γαυνάκαι καὶ μολόχινα καὶ σινδόναι ὀλίγαι καὶ λάκκος χρωμάτινος.
Φέρεται δὲ ἀπὸ τῶν τόπων ἐλέφας καὶ χελώνη καὶ ῥινόκερως. Τὰ δὲ
πλεῖστα ἐκ τῆς Αἰγύπτου φέρεται εἰς τὸ ἐμπόριον τοῦτο ἀπὸ μηνὸς
6 Ἰανουαρίου μέχρι τοῦ Σεπτεμβρίου, ὅ ἐστιν ἀπὸ Τῦβι ἕως Θῶθ· εὐκαίρως δὲ ἀπὸ Αἰγύπτου ἀνάγονται περὶ τὸν Σεπτέμβριον μῆνα.

Ἤδη ἐπ' ἀνατολὴν ὁ Ἀραβικὸς κόλπος διατείνει καὶ κατὰ τὸν 7
9 Ἀυαλίτην μάλιστα στενοῦται. Μετὰ δὲ σταδίους ὡσεὶ τετρακισχιλίους,
κατὰ τὴν αὐτὴν ἤπειρον εἰς ἀνατολὴν πλεόντων, ἐστὶν ἄλλα ἐμπόρια
Βαρβαρικά, τὰ πέρα⟨ν⟩ λεγόμενα, κείμενα μὲν κατὰ τὸ ἑξῆς, ἀγκυρο-
12 βολίοις δὲ καὶ σάλοις ἔχοντα τοὺς ὅρμους κατὰ καιροὺς ἐπιτηδείους.
Πρῶτος μὲν ὁ λεγόμενος Ἀυαλίτης, καθ' ὃν καὶ στενότατός ἐστιν ἀπὸ τῆς
264 M. Ἀραβικῆς εἰς τὸ πέραν διάπλους. Κατὰ τοῦτον τὸν τόπον μικρὸν ἐμ-
15 πόριόν ἐστιν ὁ Ἀυαλίτης, σχεδίαις καὶ σκάφαις εἰς τὸ αὐτὸ προσερχο-
μένων. Προχωρεῖ δὲ εἰς αὐτὴν ὑαλῆ λιθία σύμμικτος καὶ   Διοπολιτικῆς ὄμφακος καὶ ἱμάτια Βαρβαρικὰ σύμμικτα γεγναμμένα καὶ σῖτος
18 καὶ οἶνος καὶ κασσίτερος ὀλίγος. Φέρεται δ' ἐξ αὐτῆς, ποτὲ καὶ τῶν
Βαρβάρων ἐπὶ σχεδίαις διαφερόντων   εἰς τὴν ἄντικρυς ⟨Ὅ⟩κηλιν καὶ
Μούζα, ἀρώματα καὶ ἐλέφας ὀλίγος καὶ χελώνη καὶ σμύρνα ἐλαχίστη,
21 διαφέρουσα δὲ τῆς ἄλλης. Ἀτακτότεροι δὲ οἱ κατοικοῦντες τὸν τόπον
Βάρβαροι.

Μετὰ δὲ τὸν Ἀυαλίτην ἕτερον ἐμπόριόν ἐστιν τούτου διαφέρον ἡ λε- 8
24 γομένη Μαλαώ, πλοῦν ἀπέχουσα σταδίων ὡς ὀκτακοσίων· ὁ δὲ ὅρμος
ἐπίσαλος ⟨* *⟩ σκεπόμενος ἀκρωτηρίῳ τῷ ἐξ ἀνατολῆς ἀνατείνοντι· οἱ
δὲ κατοικοῦντες εἰρηνικώτεροι. Προχωρεῖ δὲ εἰς τοῦτον τὸν τόπον τὰ
27 προειρημένα καὶ πλείονες χιτῶνες, σάγοι Ἀρσινοϊτικοὶ γεγναμμένοι καὶ
βεβαμμένοι, καὶ ποτήρια καὶ μελίεφθα ὀλίγα καὶ σίδηρος καὶ δηνάριον
οὐ πολύ, καὶ χρυσοῦν δὲ καὶ ἀργυροῦν. Ἐκφέρεται δὲ ἀπὸ τῶν τόπων
30 τούτων καὶ σμύρνα καὶ λίβανος ὁ περατικὸς ὀλίγος καὶ κασ[σ]ία σκλη-
265 M. ροτέρα καὶ δουακα καὶ κάγκαμον καὶ μάκειρ, τὰ εἰς Ἀραβίαν προχωροῦντα, καὶ σώματα σπανίως.

1 ἀραβικῆς corr. Müller in Add. et Corr.   ἐνδι-(bis): corr. L, Gelenius
2 μονοχη (sine acc.) corr. Blancard   ἡ σαγματογήνη Müller in comm. cl. 5,11
3 σινδόνες Stuck   μολόχιναι σινδόνες (pro μ. καὶ σ.) Müller in Add.
et Corr.   6 τυβὶ correxi   11 τὰ πέραν Schwanbeck: τάπαρα   16 ⟨χυλὸς⟩
Müller   19 διαπερώντων scripsi: διαφερόντων   κῆλιν corr. Stuck   25 lacunam suscipatus est Müller; an ἐπὶ σάλῳ σκεπ-?   27 Ἀρσι- Stuck: ἀρσε-   29
εἰσφέ- corr. Stuck   30 κασ[σ]ία: alt. σ delevi   κάνκαμον corr. edd.

of Ariakê: Indian iron and steel; cotton cloth of the broader make, the so-called *monachê* and *sagmatogênê*; girdles; *kaunakai*; garments of *molochinon*; garments of cotton in limited number; lac dye. Exports from this area are: ivory, tortoise shell, rhinoceros horn. Most exporting from Egypt to this port of trade is from January to September, that is, from Tybi to Thoth; the best time for departure from Egypt is around the month of September.

7. By now the Arabian Gulf [Red Sea] trends eastward and at Avalitês is at its narrowest. After about 4000 stades on an eastward heading along the same coast, come the rest of the ports of trade of the Barbaroi, those called "far-side," lying in a row and offering, by way of anchorages and roadsteads, suitable mooring when the occasion calls. The first is called Avalitês; at it the crossing from Arabia to the other side is shortest. At this place there is a small port of trade, namely Avalitês, where rafts and small craft put in. It offers a market for: assorted glass stones; some of the unripe olives that come from Diospolis; assorted articles of clothing for the Barbaroi, cleaned by fulling; grain; wine; a little tin. Exports from here, with the transport across to Okêlis and Muza on the opposite shore at times carried out by the Barbaroi on rafts, are: aromatics; a little ivory; tortoise shell; a minimal amount of myrrh but finer than any other. The Barbaroi who inhabit the place are rather unruly.

8. After Avalitês, about an 800-stade sail distant, comes another, better, port of trade called Malaô. Its harbor is an open roadstead sheltered by a promontory extending from the east. Its inhabitants are rather peaceable. This place offers a market for the aforementioned as well as for: tunics in quantity; cloaks from Arsinoe, cleaned and dyed; drinking vessels; honey pans (?), in limited number; iron; Roman money, in limited quantity, both gold and silver. Exports from this area are: myrrh, a little "far-side" incense; a rather harsh cassia, *duaka, kankamon, makeir*, which items are exported to Arabia; on rare occasions slaves.

9   Ἀπὸ δὲ Μαλαὼ δύο δρόμοις ἐστὶν ἐμπόριον ἡ Μούνδου, ἐν ᾧ καὶ ἀσφαλέστερον ὁρμεῖ τὰ πλοῖα εἰς τὴν προκειμένην ἔγγιστα τῆς γῆς νῆσον. Προχωρεῖ δὲ εἰς αὐτὴν τὰ προειρημένα καὶ ἐκεῖθεν ὁμοίως ἐκφέρεται τὰ 3 προειρημένα φορτία ⟨καὶ⟩ θυμίαμα τὸ λεγόμενον μοκροτου. Οἱ δὲ κατοικοῦντες ἔμποροι σκληρότεροι.

10   Ἀπὸ δὲ τῆς Μούνδου, πλεόντων εἰς τὴν ἀνατολήν, ὁμοίως μετὰ 6 δύο δρόμους ἢ τρεῖς πλησίον ⟨* *⟩ κεῖται τὸ Μόσυλλον ἐν αἰγιαλῷ δυσόρμῳ. Προχωρεῖ δὲ εἰς αὐτὴν τὰ προειρημένα γένη καὶ σκεύη ἀργυρᾶ, σιδηρᾶ δὲ ἐλάσσω, καὶ λιθία. Ἐξάγεται δὲ ἀπὸ τῶν τόπων 9 κασίας χύμα πλεῖστον — ⟨δι⟩ὸ καὶ μειζόνων πλοίων χρῄζει τὸ ἐμπόριον — καὶ   ἄλλα εὐοδία   καὶ ἀρώματα καὶ χελωνάρια ὀλίγα καὶ θυμίαμα μοκροτου, ἧττον τοῦ Μουνδιτικοῦ, καὶ λίβανος ὁ περατικός, ἐλέφας δὲ 12 καὶ σμύρνα σπανίως.

11   Ἀπὸ δὲ τοῦ Μοσύλλου † παραπλεύσαντα μετὰ δύο δρόμους τὸ λεγόμενον Νειλοπτολεμαίου καὶ Ταπατηγη καὶ δαφνῶνα μικρὸν [καὶ] ἀκρω- 15 266 Μ τήριον Ἐλέφας· [ἀπὸ Ὀπώνης εἰς νότον προχωρεῖ εἶτα εἰς λίβα ἡ χώρα] ποταμὸν ἔχει τὸν λεγόμενον Ἐλέφαντα καὶ δαφνῶνα μέγαν λεγόμενον Ἀκάνναι, ἐν ᾗ μονογενῶς λίβανος ὁ περατικὸς πλεῖστος καὶ διάφορος 18 γίνεται.

12   Καὶ μετὰ ταύτην, τῆς γῆς ὑποχωρούσης εἰς τὸν νότον ἤδη, τὸ τῶν Ἀρωμάτων ἐμπόριον καὶ ἀκρωτήριον τελευταῖον τῆς Βαρβαρικῆς ἠπείρου 21 πρὸς ἀνατολὴν ἀπόκοπον· ὁ δὲ ὅρμος ἐπίσαλος κατὰ καιροὺς ἐπικίνδυνος διὰ τὸ προσεχῆ τὸν τόπον εἶναι τῷ βορέᾳ. Σημεῖον δὲ τοῦ μέλλοντος χειμῶνος τοπικὸν τὸ τὸν βυθὸν θολερώτερον γίνεσθαι καὶ τὴν χρόαν 24 ἀλ⟨λ⟩άσσειν. Τούτου δὲ γενομένου πάντες ἀποφεύγουσιν εἰς τὸ μέγα ἀκρωτήριον, τόπον καὶ σκέπην, τὸ λεγόμενον Τάβαι. Προχωρεῖ δὲ εἰς 267 Μ. τὸ ἐμπόριον ὁμοίως τὰ προειρημένα· γίνεται δὲ τὰ ἐν αὐτῷ κασία καὶ 27 γίζειρ καὶ ἄσυφη καὶ ἄρωμα καὶ μαγλα καὶ μοτὼ καὶ λίβανος.

---

1 ⟨μετὰ⟩ δύο δρόμους malim cum Fabr.   4 ⟨καὶ⟩ Fabr.   7 lacunam sic explere velim ⟨ἀκρωτηρίου ἐμπόριον⟩   10 διὸ Hudson, Müller: δ   11 ἄλλη εὐωδία Müller: ἄλλα εὐοδια (sine acc.)   14 † παραπλεύσαντα μετὰ δύο δρόμους: μ. δ. δρ. παραπλεύσαντι Müller, παραπλεύσαντι ἀπαντᾷ μ. δ. δρ. Stuck, Fabr.   15 [καὶ] Letronne, Fragmens des Poëmes géograph. 314.   16 [ἀπὸ Ὀπ. — χώρα] marg. notam, ad 5, 17 pertinentem, esse vid. Vincent, Müller   17 ποταμὸν Müller: -μοὺς   22 ἐπὶ σάλῳ scripsi: ἐπὶ σαλε sine acc. m. pr., acc. add. et ος supra ε scr. (i. e. ἐπὶ σάλοις) m. alt., ἐστὶ σάλοις Müller in Add. et Corr.   25 ἀλ⟨λ⟩άσσειν m. alt.   26 τόπον καὶ σκέπην suspectum   28 ἄρωμα : ἀρηβὼ maluit Müller in comm. cl. Galeno 14, 72, 18 Kühn

9. From Malaô it is two runs to the port of trade of Mundu, where vessels moor fairly safely at the island that lies very near the shore. This place offers a market for the aforementioned and, similarly, from it is exported the aforementioned merchandise plus the incense called *mokrotu*. The traders who live here are rather hard bargainers.

10. From Mundu, with the course heading eastward, similarly after two, perhaps three, runs near [? a promontory] lies Mosyllon on a beach with a poor harbor. Here there is a market for the aforementioned goods plus silverware; ironware, but in lesser quantity; precious stones. Exports from this area are: a great quantity of cassia (for this reason the port requires bigger ships); other spices and aromatics; a little low-quality tortoise shell; *mokrotu* incense, poorer than that from Mundu; "far-side" frankincense; ivory and myrrh but only on rare occasions.

11. Beyond Mosyllon, after a two-run voyage come the so-called Neiloptolemaiu, Tapatêgê, a small laurel grove, Cape Elephas, . . . it has a river called Elephas and a large laurel grove called Akannai, the one place that produces most "far-side" incense, of fine quality to boot.

12. Beyond this, with the coast by now trending to the south, is the Spice Port and a promontory, the last along the coast of the country of the Barbaroi towards the east, a precipitous one. The harbor, an open roadstead, is dangerous at times, because the site is exposed to the north. A local indication of a coming storm is when the depths become rather turbid and change color; when this happens, all take refuge at the big promontory, a site that offers shelter, called Tabai. The port of trade [sc. the Spice Port] likewise offers a market for the aforementioned. Its products are: cassia, *gizeir, asyphê, arôma, magla, motô*, frankincense.

Ἀπὸ δὲ Τάβαι μετὰ σταδίους τετρακοσίους παραπλεύσαντι χερσό- 13
νησον, καθ᾽ ὃν τόπον [εἰς ἣν] καὶ ὁ ῥοῦς ἕλκει, ἕτερόν ἐστιν ἐμπόριον
3 Ὀπώνη, εἰς ἣν καὶ αὐτὴν προχωρεῖ μὲν τὰ προειρημένα· τὸ δὲ πλεῖστον
ἐν αὐτῇ γεννᾶται κασία καὶ ἄρωμα καὶ μοτὼ καὶ δουλικὰ κρείσσονα, ἃ
εἰς Αἴγυπτον προχωρεῖ[ν] μᾶλλον, καὶ χελώνη πλείστη καὶ διαφορωτέρα
6 τῆς ἄλλης.

Πλέεται δὲ εἰς πάντα ταῦτα τοῦ πέραν ἐμπόρια ἀπὸ μὲν Αἰγύπτου 14
περὶ τὸν Ἰούλιον μῆνα, ὅ ἐστιν Ἐπῖφι. Ἐξαρτίζεται δὲ συνήθως καὶ
9 ἀπὸ τῶν ἔσω τόπων τῆς Ἀριακῆς καὶ Βαρυγάζων εἰς τὰ αὐτὰ τὰ τοῦ
πέρα⟨ν⟩ ἐμπόρια γένη προχωροῦντα ἀπὸ τῶν τόπων, σῖτος καὶ ὄρυζα
καὶ βούτυρον καὶ ἔλαιον σησάμινον καὶ ὀθόνιον, ἥ τε μοναχὴ[ν] καὶ ἡ
12 σαγματογήνη, καὶ περιζώματα καὶ μέλι τὸ καλάμινον τὸ λεγόμενον
σάκχαρι. Καὶ οἱ μὲν προηγουμένως εἰς ταῦτα τὰ ἐμπόρια πλέου-
σιν, οἱ δὲ ⟨κατὰ⟩ τὸν παράπλουν ἀντιφορτίζονται τὰ ἐμπεσόντα. Οὐ
15 βασιλεύεται δὲ ὁ τόπος, ἀλλὰ τυράννοις ἰδίοις καθ᾽ ἕκαστον ἐμπόριον
διοικεῖται.

Ἀπὸ δὲ Ὀπώνης, τῆς ἀκτῆς εἰς τὸν νότον ὑποχωρούσης ἐπὶ πλεῖον, 15
268 M. 18 πρῶτα μέν ἐστιν τὰ λεγόμενα μικρὰ Ἀπόκοπα καὶ μεγάλα τῆς Ἀζανίας
† διὰ ἀγκυροβολίων ποταμοὶ † ἐπὶ δρόμους ἓξ παρ᾽ αὐτὸν ἤδη τὸν λίβα·
269 M. εἶτα Αἰγιαλὸς καὶ μικρὸς καὶ μέγας ἐπ᾽ ἄλλους δρόμους ἓξ καὶ μετ᾽
21 αὐτὸν κατὰ τὸ ἑξῆς οἱ τῆς Ἀζανίας δρόμοι, πρῶτον μὲν ὁ λεγόμενος
Σαραπίωνος, εἶθ᾽ ὁ Νίκωνος, μεθ᾽ ὃν ποταμοὶ πλείονες καὶ ἄλλοι συνεχεῖς
ὅρμοι, διῃρημένοι κατὰ σταθμοὺς καὶ δρόμους ἡμερησίους πλείους, τοὺς
24 πάντας ἑπτά, μέχρι Πυραλάων νήσων καὶ τῆς λεγομένης Διώρυχος, ἀφ᾽
270 M. ἧς μικρὸν ἐπάνω τοῦ λιβὸς μετὰ δύο δρόμους νυχθημέρους παρ᾽ αὐτὴν
τὴν   δύσιν ειτενηδιων   Μενουθ[εσ]ιὰς ἀπαντᾷ νῆσος ἀπὸ σταδίων τῆς
27 γῆς ὡσεὶ τριακοσίων, ταπεινὴ καὶ κατάδενδρος, ἐν ᾗ καὶ ποταμοὶ
καὶ ὀρνέων γένη πλεῖστα καὶ χελώνη ὀρεινή. Θηρίων δὲ οὐδὲν ὅλως
ἔχει πλὴν κορκοδείλων· οὐδένα δὲ ἄνθρωπον ἀδικοῦσι. Ἔστιν δὲ ἐν
30 αὐτῇ πλοιάρια ῥαπτὰ καὶ μονόξυλα, οἷς χρῶνται πρὸς ἁλείαν καὶ ἄγραν

---

1 ταβαι acc. add. edd.   τετρακοσίους: aut ὀκτακοσίους legendum aut post hanc
vocem lacunam statuendam censuit Müller in Add. et Corr., quam sic explere
voluit: ⟨Πανὼν κώμη · ἐντεῦθεν δὲ μετὰ σταδίους τετρακοσίους⟩   2 [εἰς ἣν] m. alt.
3 αὐτὴι corr. Stuck   4 ἀρηβὼ (pro ἄρωμα) Fabr.   ἃ Fabr.: καὶ   5 προχωρεῖ[ν]
edd.   7 τόὐπεραν et 9 τούπερα corr. Müller   8 ἐπιφί (sic ubique) correxi
11 μοναχην (sine acc.) corr. edd.   14 ⟨κατὰ⟩ Stuck   23 [πλείους]
Müller   24 καὶ τῆς Fabr. et Schwanbeck: κανῆς   26 Αὐσινείτην ἠιόνα Müller
G. G. M. II, 506: δύσιν ειτενηδιων (sine spir. et acc.)   μενουθ[εσ]ιὰς edd.

13. Beyond Tabai, after a 400-stade sail along a peninsula towards which, moreover, the current sets, comes another port of trade, Opônê, and it too offers a market for the aforementioned. Its products for the most part are: cassia; *arôma; motô*; better-quality slaves, the greater number of which go to Egypt; tortoise shell in great quantity and finer than any other.

14. Departure from Egypt for all these "far-side" ports of trade is around the month of July, that is Epeiph. To these "far-side" ports of trade it is also common to ship in from the inner regions of Ariakê and Barygaza goods from those places that find a market: grain; rice; ghee; sesame oil; cotton cloth, the *monachê* and the *sagmatogênê*; girdles; cane sugar. Some ships sail principally to these ports of trade but some follow the coast and take on whatever cargoes come their way. The area is not ruled by a king but each port of trade is administered by its own chief.

15. Beyond Opônê, with the coast trending more to the south, first come what are called the Small and Great Bluffs of Azania . . . , six runs by now due southwest, then the Small and Great Beaches for another six, and beyond that, in a row, the runs of Azania: first the so-called Sarapiôn run; then the Nikôn; after that numerous rivers and also harbors, one after the other, numbers of them separated by daily stops and runs, seven in all, up to the Pyralaoi Islands and what is called the Canal; from here a little more towards the west, after two night and day runs, lying due west . . . comes Menuthias Island, about 300 stades from the mainland. It is low and wooded and has rivers, a wide variety of birds, and mountain tortoise. There are no wild animals at all except crocodiles; these, however, are not harmful to humans. The island has sewn boats and dugout canoes that are used for fishing and for catching

χελώνης. Ἐν δὲ ταύτῃ τῇ νήσῳ καὶ γυργάθοις αὐτὰς ἰδίως λινεύουσιν, ἀντὶ δικτύων καθιέντες αὐτοὺς περὶ τὰ στόματα τῶν † προραχων †.

16   Ἀφ᾽ ἧς μετὰ δύο δρόμους τῆς ἠπείρου τὸ τελευταιότατον τῆς Ἀζανίας 3 ἐμπόριον κεῖται, τὰ Ῥάπτα [τὰ] λεγόμενα, ταύτην ἔχον τὴν προσωνυμίαν 271 M. ἀπὸ τῶν προειρημένων ῥαπτῶν πλοιαρίων, ἐν ᾧ καὶ πλεῖστός ἐστιν ἐλέφας καὶ χελώνη. Μέγιστοι δὲ ἐν σώμασιν περὶ ταύτην τὴν χώραν ἄνθρωποι 6 ὁρατοὶ   κατοικοῦσιν καὶ κατὰ τὸν τόπον ἕκαστος ὁμοίως τιθέμενοι τυράννοις. Νέμεται δὲ αὐτήν, κατά τι δίκαιον ἀρχαῖον ὑποπίπτουσαν τῇ βασιλείᾳ τῆς πρώτης γενομένης Ἀραβίας, ὁ Μοφαρίτης τύραννος. 9 Παρὰ δὲ τοῦ βασιλέως ὑπόφορον αὐτὴν ἔχουσιν οἱ ἀπὸ Μούζα καὶ πέμπουσιν εἰς αὐτὴν ἐφόλκια, τὰ πλείονα κυβερνήταις καὶ χρειακοῖς [καὶ] Ἄραψιν χρώμενοι τοῖς κατὰ συνήθειαν καὶ ἐπιγαμβρείαν ἔχουσιν ἐμπείροις 12 τε οὖσιν τῶν τόπων καὶ τῆς φωνῆς αὐτῶν.

17   Εἰσφέρεται δὲ εἰς τὰ ἐμπόρια ταῦτα προηγουμένως ἡ τοπικῶς ἐν Μούζα κατασκευαζομένη λόγχη καὶ πελύκια καὶ μαχαίρια καὶ ὀπήτια καὶ λιθίας 15 ὑαλῆς πλείονα γένη, εἰς δέ τινας τόπους οἶνός τε καὶ σῖτος οὐκ ὀλίγος, οὐ πρὸς ἐργασίαν ἀλλὰ δαπάνης χάριν εἰς φιλανθρωπίαν τῶν Βαρβάρων. Ἐκφέρεται δὲ ἀπὸ τῶν τόπων ἐλέφας πλεῖστος, ἥσσων δὲ τοῦ Ἀδουλι[ν]- 18 272. τικοῦ, καὶ ῥινόκερως καὶ χελώνη διάφορος μετὰ τὴν Ἰνδικὴν καὶ ναύπλιος ὀλίγος.

18   Καὶ σχεδὸν τελευταιότατά ἐστιν ταῦτα τὰ ἐμπόρια τῆς Ἀζανίας 21 τῆς ἐν δεξιοῖς ἀπὸ Βερνίκης ἠπείρου· ὁ γὰρ μετὰ τούτους τοὺς τόπους ὠκεανὸς ἀνερεύνητος ὢν εἰς τὴν δύσιν ἀνακάμπτει καὶ τοῖς ἀπεστραμμένοις μέρεσιν τῆς Αἰθιοπίας καὶ Λιβύης καὶ Ἀφρικῆς κατὰ τὸν νότον παρεκ- 24 τείνων εἰς τὴν ἑσπέριον συμμίσγει θάλασσαν.

19   Ἐκ δὲ τῶν εὐωνύμων Βερνίκης ἀπὸ Μυὸς ὅρμου δυσὶν δρόμοις ἢ τρισὶν εἰς τὴν ἀνατολὴν διαπλεύσαντι τὸν παρακείμενον κόλπον ὅρμος 27 ἐστὶν ἕτερος καὶ φρούριον, ὃ λέγεται Λευκὴ κώμη, δι᾽ ἧς ἐστιν εἰς Πέτραν πρὸς Μαλίχαν, βασιλέα Ναβαταίων, ⟨ἀνάβασις⟩. Ἔχει δὲ 273 M. ἐμπορίου τινὰ καὶ αὐτὴ τάξιν τοῖς ἀπὸ τῆς Ἀραβίας ἐξαρτιζομένοις εἰς 30 αὐτὴν πλοίοις οὐ μεγάλοις. Διὸ καὶ   παραφυλακῆς χάριν καὶ   εἰς αὐτὴν

<hr>

2 τῶν † προραχων † (sine acc.): an τῶν ⟨ποταμῶν⟩ πρὸ ⟨τῶν⟩ ῥαχ⟨ι>ῶν? 4 ῥαπτὰ corr. Müller ad Ptol. 1, 1, 22.   [τὰ] L, Stuck   7 πειραταὶ Müller in comm.: ὁρατοὶ (spir. pos. m. alt.)   8 ὑποπίπτουσιν corr. m. alt.   9 γε- νομένης Fabr: γιν-   11 [καὶ] m. alt.   12 κατὰ: malim καὶ cum Fabr. 18 ἧσσον corr. Fabr.   ἀδουλε[ν]τικοῦ edd.   20 ναύπλιος: ναργίλιος Müller in Proll. p. CVIII   21 τελευταιότατος (supra o punctum pos. m. pr.) corr. m. alt.   29 Ναβαταίων m. alt.: ἀναβαταιως (sine acc.)   ⟨ἀνάβασις⟩ Müller in Add. et Corr.   30 αὐτὸ corr. Fabr.

turtles. The inhabitants of this island also have their own way of going after these with baskets, which they lower instead of nets around the mouths of [? rocky inlets].

16. Two runs beyond this island comes the very last port of trade on the coast of Azania, called Rhapta ["sewn"], a name derived from the aforementioned sewn boats, where there are great quantities of ivory and tortoise shell. Very big-bodied men, tillers of the soil, inhabit the region; these behave, each in his own place, just like chiefs. The region is under the rule of the governor of Mapharitis, since by some ancient right it is subject to the kingdom of Arabia as first constituted. The merchants of Muza hold it through a grant from the king and collect taxes from it. They send out to it merchant craft that they staff mostly with Arab skippers and agents who, through continual intercourse and intermarriage, are familiar with the area and its language.

17. The principal imports into these ports of trade are: spears from Muza of local workmanship; axes; knives; small awls; numerous types of glass stones. Also, to certain places, wine and grain in considerable quantity, not for trade but as an expenditure for the good will of the Barbaroi. The area exports: a great amount of ivory but inferior to that from Adulis; rhinoceros horn; best-quality tortoise shell after the Indian; a little nautilus shell.

18. These are just about the very last ports of trade on the coast of Azania to the right of Berenicê. For, beyond this area lies unexplored ocean that bends to the west and, extending on the south along the parts of Ethiopia and Libya and Africa that turn away, joins the western sea.

19. To the left of Berenicê, after a voyage of two or three runs eastward from Myos Hormos past the gulf lying alongside, there is another harbor with a fort called Leukê Kômê ["white village"], through which there is a way inland up to Petra, to Malichus, king of the Nabataeans. This harbor also serves in a way the function of a port of trade for the craft, none large, that come to it loaded with freight from Arabia. For that reason, as a safeguard

παραλήπτης τῆς τετάρτης τῶν εἰσφερομένων φορτίων καὶ ἑκατοντάρχης μετὰ στρατεύματος ἀποστέλλεται.

3   Μετὰ δὲ ταύτην εὐθέως ἐστὶν συναφὴς Ἀραβικὴ χώρα, κατὰ μῆκος 20 ἐπὶ πολὺ παρατείνουσα τῇ Ἐρυθρᾷ θαλάσσῃ. Διάφορα δὲ ἐν αὐτῇ ἔθνη κατοικεῖ[ται], τινὰ μὲν ἐπὶ ποσόν, τινὰ δὲ καὶ τελείως τῇ γλώσσῃ διαλ-
6 λάσσοντα. Τούτων ⟨τὰ⟩ παρὰ θάλασσαν ὁμοίως Ἰχθυοφάγων μάνδραις διείληπται, τὰ δὲ ἐπάνω κατὰ κώμας καὶ νομαδίας οἰκεῖται πονηροῖς ἀνθρώποις διφώνοις, οἷς παραπίπτοντες ἀπὸ τοῦ μέσου πλοὸς ὁτὲ μὲν
9 διαρπάζονται, οἱ δὲ καὶ ἀπὸ ναυαγίων σωθέντες ἀνδραποδίζονται. Διὸ καὶ συνεχῶς ἀπὸ τῶν τυράννων καὶ βασιλέων τῆς Ἀραβίας αἰχμαλωτί- ζονται· λέγονται δὲ Κανραῖται. Καθόλου μὲν οὗτος ὁ τῆς Ἀραβικῆς
12 χώρας ἠπείρου παράπλους ἐστὶν ἐπισφαλής, καὶ ἀλίμενος ἡ χώρα καὶ δύσορμος καὶ ἀκάθαρτος ῥαχίαις καὶ σπίλοις ἀπρόσιτος καὶ κατὰ πάντα φοβερά. Διὸ καὶ εἰσπλεόντων ⟨τὸν⟩ μέσον πλοῦν κατέχομεν εἰς τὴν
15 Ἀραβικὴν χώραν ⟨καὶ⟩ μᾶλλον παροξύνομεν ἄχρι τῆς Κατακεκαυμένης νήσου, μεθ᾽ ἣν εὐθέως ἡμέρων ἀνθρώπων καὶ νομαδιαίων θρεμμάτων καὶ καμήλων συνεχεῖς ⟨χῶραι⟩.

18   Καὶ μετὰ ταύτας ἐν κόλπῳ τῷ τελευταιοτάτῳ τῶν εὐωνύμων τούτου 21 τοῦ πελάγους ἐμπόριόν ἐστιν νόμιμον παραθαλάσσιον Μούζα, σταδίους
274 Μ. ἀπέχον τοὺς πάντας ἀπὸ Βερνίκης, παρ᾽ αὐτὸν τὸν νότον πλεόντων, ὡς
21 εἰς μυρίους δισχιλίους. Τὸ μὲν ὅλον Ἀράβων, ναυκληρικῶν ἀνθρώπων καὶ ναυτικῶν, πλεονάζον [δὲ] καὶ τοῖς ἀπὸ ἐμπορίας πράγμασι κινεῖται· συγχρῶνται γὰρ τῇ τοῦ πέραν ἐργασίᾳ καὶ Βαρυγάζων ἰδίοις ἐξαρτισμοῖς.
24   Ὑπέρκειται δὲ αὐτῆς ἀπὸ τριῶν ἡμερῶν πόλις Σαυὴ τῆς περὶ αὐτὴν 22 Μαφαρ⟨ί⟩τιδος λεγομένης χώρας· ἔστιν δὲ τύραννος καὶ κατοικῶν αὐτὴν Χόλαιβος.
27   Καὶ μετ᾽ ἄλλας ἐννέα ἡμέρας ⟨Σ⟩αφὰρ μητρόπολις, ἐν ᾗ Χαριβαὴλ[α], 23 ἔνθεσμος βασιλεὺς ἐθνῶν δύο, τοῦ τε Ὁμηρίτου καὶ τοῦ παρακειμένου λεγομένου Σαβαίτου, συνεχέσι πρεσβείαις καὶ δώροις φίλος [δὲ] τῶν
30 αὐτοκρατόρων.
    Τὸ δὲ ἐμπόριον ἡ Μούζα ἀλίμενον μὲν εὔσαλον δὲ καὶ εὔορμον διὰ 24

---

1 verba καὶ παραφυλακῆς χάριν quae habet post διὸ huc revocavit Fabr. deleto καὶ ante ἑκατοντάρχης   5 κατοικεῖ[ται] Fabr.   6 ⟨τὰ⟩ Gelenius   8 ἀπό τε corr. Gelenius   11 Καρναεῖται Glaser, Skizze d. Gesch. u. Geogr. Arabiens 165 sq.   14 ⟨τὸν⟩ Fabr.   [εἰς — χῶραν] ut glossema delevi   15 ⟨καὶ⟩ Gelenius   17 ⟨χῶραι⟩ Stuck, ⟨οἰκήσεις⟩ Müller in comm.   22 [δὲ] Fabr. πράγματα corr. Fabr.   25 Μαφαρ⟨ί⟩τιδος Salmasius   27 ⟨Σ⟩αφὰρ Stuck   χαριβαὴλ[α] m. pr.   29 [δὲ] m. alt.

there is dispatched for duty in it a customs officer to deal with the (duty of a) fourth on incoming merchandise as well as a centurion with a detachment of soldiers.

20. Immediately after this harbor begins the country of Arabia, extending lengthwise far down the Erythraean Sea. It is inhabited by a variety of tribes speaking languages that differ, some to a certain extent, some totally. The coastal area is, similarly, marked by clusters of the mean huts of the Ichthyophagoi, while the area inland has villages and pasturages inhabited by people, speaking two languages, who are vicious: they plunder any who stray from a course down the middle and fall among them, and they enslave any who are rescued by them from shipwreck. For this reason they are constantly being taken prisoner by the governors and kings of Arabia. Kanraitai is their name. In fact, to set a course along the coast of Arabia is altogether risky, since the region with its lack of harbors offers poor anchorage, is foul with rocky stretches, cannot be approached because of cliffs, and is fearsome in every respect. This is why, when sailing down this sea, we set a course for Arabia down the middle and put on extra speed as far as Katakekaumenê ["burnt"] Island, immediately beyond which there is a succession of shores with peaceful inhabitants, animals at pasture, and camels.

21. Beyond these regions, on the very last bay on the lefthand shore of this sea, is Muza, a legally limited port of trade on the coast, about 12,000 stades in all from Berenicê if you follow a course due south. The whole place teems with Arabs—shipowners or charterers and sailors—and is astir with commercial activity. For they share in the trade across the water and with Barygaza, using their own outfits.

22. A three-day journey inland from Muza lies Sauê, the city of the province, called Mapharitis, that surrounds it. The governor, Cholaibos, has his residence there.

23. Nine days further inland is Saphar, the metropolis, residence of Charibaêl, legitimate king of the two nations, the Homerite and the one, lying next to it, called the Sabaean; he is a friend of the emperors, thanks to continuous embassies and gifts.

24. The port of trade of Muza, though without a harbor, offers a good roadstead for mooring

τὰ περὶ αὐτὴν ἀμμόγεια ἀγκυροβόλια. Φορτία δὲ εἰς αὐτὴν προχωρεῖ
πορφύρα διάφορος καὶ χυδαία καὶ ἱματισμὸς Ἀραβικὸς χειριδωτός, ὅ τε 275 M.
ἁπλοῦς καὶ ὁ κοινὸς καὶ σκοτουλᾶτος καὶ διάχρυσος, καὶ κρόκος καὶ 3
κύπερος καὶ ὀθόνιον καὶ ἀβόλλαι καὶ λώδικες οὐ πολλαί, ἁπλοῖ τε καὶ
ἐντόπιοι, ζῶναι σκιωταὶ καὶ μύρον μέτριον καὶ χρῆμα ἱκανόν, οἶνός τε καὶ
σῖτος οὐ πολύς· φέρει γὰρ καὶ ἡ χώρα πυρὸν μετρίως καὶ οἶνον πλείονα. 6
Τῷ τε βασιλεῖ καὶ τῷ τυράννῳ δίδονται ἵπποι τε καὶ ἡμίονοι νωτηγοὶ
καὶ χρυσώματα καὶ τορ[ν]ευτὰ ἀργυρώματα καὶ ἱματισμὸς πολυτελὴς καὶ
χαλκουργήματα. Ἐξάγεται δὲ ἐξ αὐτῆς, ἐντόπια μέν, σμύρνα ἐκλεκτὴ 9
καὶ στακτή, Ἀβειρ⟨αία καὶ⟩ Μιναία, λύγδος καὶ τὰ ἀπὸ τῆς πέραν
Ἄδουλι προειρημένα φορτία πάντα. Πλέεται δὲ εἰς τὴν αὐτὴν εὐκαίρως
περὶ τὸν Σεπτέμβριον μῆνα, ὅς ἐστι Θώθ· οὐδὲν δὲ κωλύει κἂν τάχιον. 12

25   Μετὰ δὲ ταύτην ὡσεὶ τριακοσίους παραπλεύσαντες σταδίους, ἤδη
συνερχομένης τε τῆς Ἀραβικῆς ἠπείρου καὶ τῆς πέραν κατὰ τὸν Αὐαλίτην
Βαρβαρικῆς χώρας, αὐλών ἐστιν οὐ μακρός, ὁ συνάγων καὶ εἰ⟨ς⟩ στενὸν 15
ἀποκλείων τὸ πέλαγος, οὗ τὸν μεταξὺ πόρον ἑξήκοντα σταδίων μεσολαβεῖ
νῆσος ἡ Διοδώρου. Διὸ καὶ ῥοώδης, καταπνεόμενος ἀπὸ τῶν παρακειμέ-
νων ὀρῶν, ἐστὶν ὁ κατ' αὐτὴν διάπλους. Κατὰ τοῦτον τὸν ἰσθμὸν πα- 18
ραθαλάσσιός ἐστιν Ἀράβων κώμη τῆς αὐτῆς τυραννίδος Ὀκηλις, οὐχ οὕτως 276 M.
ἐμπόριον ὡς ὅρμος καὶ ὕδρευμα καὶ πρώτη καταγωγὴ τοῖς ἔσω διαίρουσιν.

26   Μετὰ δὲ Ὀκηλιν, ἀνοιγομένης πάλιν τῆς θαλάσσης εἰς ἀνατολὴν 21
καὶ κατὰ μικρὸν εἰς πέλαγος ἀποφαινομένης, ἀπὸ σταδίων ὡς χιλίων
διακοσίων ἐστὶν Εὐδαίμων Ἀραβία, κώμη παραθαλάσσιος, βασιλείας τῆς
αὐτῆς Χαριβαήλ, τοὺς ὅρμους μὲν ἐπιτηδείους καὶ ὑδρεύματα γλυκύτερα 24 277
κρεῖσσον   τῆς Ὀκήλεως ἔχουσα, ἤδη δὲ ἐν ἀρχῇ κόλπου κειμένη
τῷ τὴν χώραν ὑποφεύγειν. Εὐδαίμων Ἀραβία   εὐδαίμων δὲ ἐπεκλήθη,
πρότερον οὖσα πόλις, ὅτε, μήπω ἀπὸ τῆς Ἰνδικῆς εἰς τὴν Αἴγυπτον 27
ἐρχομένων μηδὲ ἀπὸ Αἰγύπτου τολμώντων εἰς τοὺς ἔσω τόπους διαίρειν
ἀλλ' ἄχρι ταύτης παραγινομένων, τοὺς παρ' ἀμφοτέρων φόρτους ἀπεδέ-
χετο, ὥσπερ Ἀλεξάνδρεια καὶ τῶν ἔξωθεν καὶ τῶν ἀπὸ τῆς Αἰγύπτου 30
φερομένων ἀποδέχεται. Νῦν δὲ οὐ πρὸ πολλοῦ τῶν ἡμετέρων χρόνων
Καῖσαρ αὐτὴν κατεστρέψατο.

---

6 φέρεται corr. edd.   7 Τῷ δὲ malim cum edd.   8 τορ[ν]ευτὰ L, Fabr.
10 Γαβειρ<αία καὶ> Müller in comm. Ἀβ - Sprenger, Alt. Geogr. Arab. 167
τῆς πέραν Fabr.: τουπεραν (sine acc.)   13 -πλεύσαντι malim cum Schwanbeck
     15 εἰ<ς> Gelenius   24 χαριβαήλτος (supra o punctum pos. m. pr.) ὅρμους
corr. Salmasius, Hudson   25 <καὶ> Blancard   κρείσσον<α> Fabr.   26 [εὐδαίμων
ἀραβία] m. alt.   28 ἔξω Fabr.: ἔσω

because of the anchorages with sandy bottom all around. Merchandise for which it offers a market are: purple cloth, fine and ordinary quality; Arab sleeved clothing, either with no adornment or with the common adornment or with checks or interwoven with gold thread; saffron; *cyperus*; cloth; *abollai*; blankets, in limited number, with no adornment as well as with traditional local adornment; girdles with shaded stripes; unguent, moderate amount; money, considerable amount; wine and grain, limited quantity because the region produces wheat in moderate quantity and wine in greater. To the king and the governor are given (?): horses and pack mules; goldware; embossed silverware; expensive clothing; copperware. Its exports consist of local products—myrrh, the select grade and *stactê*, the Abeirian (?) and Minaean; white marble—as well as all the aforementioned merchandise from Adulis across the water. The best time for sailing to this place is around the month of September, that is Thoth, though there is nothing to prevent leaving even earlier.

25. About a 300-stade sail past this port, the Arabian mainland and the country of Barbaria across the water in the vicinity of Avalitês converge to form a strait, not very long, that contracts the waters and closes them off into a narrow passage; here in the middle of the channel, 60 stades wide, stands Diodôros Island. For this reason, and because a wind blows down from the mountains that lie alongside, the sail through along the island meets strong currents. Along this strait is Okêlis, an Arab village on the coast that belongs to the same province; it is not so much a port of trade as a harbor, watering station, and the first place to put in for those sailing on.

26. Beyond Okêlis, with the waters again opening out towards the east and little by little being revealed to be open sea, about 1200 stades distant is Eudaimôn Arabia, a village on the coast belonging to the same kingdom, Charibaêl's. It has suitable harbors and sources of water much sweeter than at Okêlis. It stands at the beginning of a gulf formed by the receding of the shore. Eudaimôn Arabia ["prosperous Arabia"], a full-fledged city in earlier days, was called Eudaimôn when, since vessels from India did not go on to Egypt and those from Egypt did not dare sail to the places further on but came only this far, it used to receive the cargoes of both, just as Alexandria receives cargoes from overseas as well as from Egypt. And now, not long before our time, Caesar sacked it.

Ἀπὸ δὲ τῆς Εὐδαίμονος Ἀραβικῆς ἐκδέχεται συναφὴς αἰγιαλὸς ἐπι- **27**
μήκης καὶ κόλπος ἐπὶ δισχιλίους ἢ πλείονας παρήκων σταδίους, Νομάδων
3 τε καὶ Ἰχθυοφάγων κώμαις παροικούμενος, οὗ μετὰ τὴν προέχουσαν ἄκραν
ἐμπόριόν ἐστιν ἕτερον παραθαλάσσιον Κανή, βασιλείας Ἐλεάζου, χώρας
278 M. Λιβανωτοφόρου, καὶ κατ᾽ αὐτὴν ἔρημοι νῆσοι δύο, μία μὲν ἡ τῶν Ὀρνέων,
6 ἡ δ᾽ ἑτέρα λεγομένη Τρουλλάς, ἀπὸ σταδίων ἑκατὸν εἴκοσι τῆς Κανῆς.
Ὑπέρκειται δὲ αὐτῆς μεσόγειος ἡ μητρόπολις Σαυβαθά, ἐν ᾗ καὶ ὁ βασιλεὺς
κατοικεῖ· πᾶς δ᾽ ὁ γεννώμενος ἐν τῇ χώρᾳ λίβανος εἰς αὐτὴν ὥσπερ ἐκ-
9 δοχεῖον εἰσάγεται καμήλοις τε καὶ σχεδίαις ἐντοπίαις δερματίναις ἐξ
279 M. ἀσκῶν καὶ πλοίοις. Ἔχει δὲ καὶ αὐτὴ[ν] σύγχρησιν τῶν τοῦ πέραν ἐμπορίων, Βαρυγάζων καὶ Σκυθίας καὶ Ὀμάνω⟨ν⟩ καὶ τῆς παρακειμένης
12 Περσίδος.

Εἰσάγεται δὲ εἰς αὐτὴν ἀπ᾽ Αἰγύπτου μὲν ὁμοίως πυρὸς ὀλίγος καὶ **28**
οἶνος ὥσπερ καὶ εἰς Μούζα, ἱματισμὸς Ἀραβικός, [καὶ] ὁμοίως καὶ
15 κοινὸς καὶ ἁπλοῦς καὶ ὁ νόθος περισσότερος, καὶ χαλκὸς καὶ κασσίτερος
καὶ κοράλλιον καὶ στύραξ καὶ τὰ λοιπὰ ὅσα εἰς Μούζα· τὰ πλείονα δὲ
ἀργυρώματα τετορευμένα καὶ χρήματα τῷ βασιλεῖ, ἵπποι τε καὶ ἀνδριάντες
18 καὶ ἱματισμὸς διάφορος ἁπλοῦς. Ἐξάγεται δὲ ἐξ αὐτῆς ἐντόπια μὲν
φορτία, λίβανος καὶ ἀλόη, τὰ δὲ λοιπὰ κατὰ μετοχὴν τῶν ἄλλων ἐμπορίων.
Πλεῖ[σ]ται δὲ εἰς αὐτὴν περὶ τὸν αὐτὸν καιρὸν ὃν ἂν καὶ εἰς Μούζα,
21 προϊμώτερον δέ.

Μετὰ δὲ Κανή, τῆς ⟨γῆς⟩ ἐπὶ πλεῖον ὑποχωρούσης, ἄλλος ἐκδέχεται **29**
βαθύτατος κόλπος, ἐπὶ πολὺ παρεκτείνων, ὁ λεγόμενος Σαχαλίτης, καὶ
280 M. 24 χώρα Λιβανωτοφόρος, ὀρεινή τε καὶ δύσβατος, ἀέρα παχὺν ἔχουσα καὶ
ὁμιχλώδη ⟨καὶ⟩ κατὰ τῶν δένδρων φερόμενον τὸν λίβανον. Ἔστιν δὲ τὰ
δένδρα τὰ λιβανοφόρα οὐ μεγάλα λίαν οὐδὲ ὑψηλά, φέρει δὲ ἐπὶ τῷ φλοιῷ
27 πησσόμενον τὸν λίβανον, ὥς τινα καὶ τῶν παρ᾽ ἡμῖν ἐν Αἰγύπτῳ δένδρων
δακρύει τὸ κόμμι. Μεταχειρίζεται δὲ ὁ λίβανος ὑπὸ δούλων βασιλικῶν
καὶ τῶν ὑπὸ τιμωρίαν πεμπομένων. Ἐπίνοσοι δὲ δεινῶς οἱ τόποι καὶ
30 τοῖς μὲν παραπλέουσι λοιμικοὶ τοῖς δὲ ἐργαζομένοις πάντοτε θανατώδεις,
ἔτι δὲ καὶ διὰ τὴν ἔνδειαν τῆς τροφῆς εὐχερῶς ἀπολλύμενοι.

Τοῦτο⟨ν⟩ δ᾽ ἐστὶν ἀκρωτήριον τοῦ κόλπου μέγιστον, ἀποβλέπον εἰς **30**
33 ἀνατολήν, ὁ καλούμενος Σύαγρος, ἐφ᾽ οὗ φρούριόν ἐστι τῆς χώρας καὶ

---

3 παροικουμέναις corr. Müller   10 αὐτὴ[ν] m. pr.   11 ὁμάνω⟨ν⟩ m. alt.
14 [καὶ] L, Stuck   16 κορδάλιον (δ exp. m. pr.) corr. Müller   17 τε
καὶ Müller in comm.: δὲ καὶ   20 πλεῖ[σ]ται m. alt.   ὃν s. scr. m. pr.
22 ⟨γῆς⟩ edd.   24 τε καὶ Salmasius: δὲ καὶ   25 ⟨καὶ⟩ Müller
31 ἀπολλυμένοις Müller   32 τοῦτο corr. Salmasius   κόλπου Mannert, Alt. Geogr.
VI, 1, 120: κόσμου

27. Immediately after Eudaimôn Arabia come a long coast and bay, populated by the villages of Nomads and Ichthyophagoi, that stretch for 2000 stades or more, at which point, beyond the projecting headland, is another port of trade on the coast, Kanê, belonging to the kingdom of Eleazos, the frankincense-bearing land; near it are two barren islands, one called Orneôn ["of the birds"] and the other Trullas, 120 stades offshore from Kanê. Above it inland lies the metropolis of Saubatha, which is also the residence of the king. All the frankincense grown in the land is brought into Kanê, as if to a warehouse, by camel as well as by rafts of a local type made of leathern bags, and by boats. It also carries on trade with the ports across the water—Barygaza, Skythia, Omana—and with its neighbor, Persis.

28. Its imports from Egypt are: wheat, limited quantity, and wine, just as to Muza; also as to Muza, Arab clothing, either with common adornment or no adornment or of printed fabric, in rather large quantities; copper; tin; coral; storax; and the rest of the items that go to Muza. Also, for the king, embossed silverware and money (?), rather large quantities, plus horses and statuary and fine-quality clothing with no adornment. It exports local wares, namely frankincense and aloe; the rest of its exports are through its connections with the other ports of trade. The time to set sail for this place is about the same as for Muza, but earlier.

29. After Kanê, with the shoreline receding further, there next come another bay, very deep, called Sachalitês, which extends for a considerable distance, and the frankincense-bearing land; this is mountainous, has a difficult terrain, an atmosphere close and misty, and trees that yield frankincense. The frankincense-bearing trees are neither very large nor tall; they give off frankincense in congealed form on the bark, just as some of the trees we have in Egypt exude gum. The frankincense is handled by royal slaves and convicts. For the districts are terribly unhealthy, harmful to those sailing by and absolutely fatal to those working there—who, moreover, die off easily because of the lack of nourishment.

30. On this bay is a mighty headland, facing the east, called Syagros, at which there are a fortress to guard the region,

λιμὴν καὶ ἀποθήκη τοῦ συναγομένου λιβάνου· καὶ κατὰ τοῦτον ἐν τῷ
πελάγει νῆσος, ἀνὰ μέσον τούτου καὶ τοῦ πέραν ἀκρωτηρίου τῶν Ἀρωμάτων, τῷ Συάγρῳ συνο[υ]ρίζουσα μᾶλλον, ἢ Διοσκουρίδου καλουμένη, 3
μεγίστη μὲν ἔρημος δὲ καὶ κάθυγρος, ἔχουσα ποταμοὺς ἐν αὐτῇ καὶ 281 M.
κροκοδείλους καὶ ἐχίδνας πλείστας καὶ σαύρας ὑπερμεγέθεις, ὡς τὸ κρέας
τῶν σαυρῶν ἐσθίουσι τὸ δὲ λίπος τήκουσι καὶ ἀντ᾽ ἐλαίου χρῶνται· 6
καρπὸν δὲ οὔτε ἀμπελ⟨ικ⟩ὸν οὔτε σιτικὸν ἡ νῆσος φέρει. Οἱ δὲ ἐνοι-
κοῦντες αὐτὴν ὀλίγοι κατὰ μίαν πλευρὰν τῆς νήσου τὴν πρὸς ἀπαρκίαν
οἰκοῦσι, καθ᾽ ὃ μέρος ἀποβλέπει τὴν ἤπειρον· εἰσὶν δὲ ἐπίξενοι καὶ ἐπί- 9
μικτοι Ἀράβων τε καὶ Ἰνδῶν καί τινα μὲν Ἑλλήνων τῶν πρὸς ἐργασίαν
ἐκπλεόντων. Φέρει δὲ ἡ νῆσος χελώνην τήν τε ἀληθινὴν καὶ χερσαίαν
καὶ τὴν λευκήν, πλείστην τε καὶ διάφορον τοῖς ὀστράκοις μείζοσιν, τήν 12
τε ὀρεινὴν ὑπερμεγέθη καὶ παχύτατον ὄστρακον ἔχουσαν, οὗ τὰ παρὰ τὴν
κοιλίαν μέρη μὲν τὰ ἐγχρήζοντα τομὴν οὐκ ἐπιδέχεται, καὶ πυρρότερα
ὄντα· ὁλοτελῶς δὲ τὰ εἰς γλωσσόκομα καὶ πινακίδια καὶ μαγίδια 15
ἐγχρήζοντα καὶ τοιαύτην τινὰ γρύτην κατατέμνεται. Γίνεται δὲ ἐν αὐτῇ
καὶ κιννάβαρι τὸ λεγόμενον Ἰνδικόν, ἀπὸ τῶν δένδρων ὡς δάκρυ συναγό-
μενον.   18

31 Ὑποπίπτει μὲν οὖν, ὥσπερ ἡ Ἀζανία Χαριβαὴλ καὶ τῷ Μαφαρίτῃ
τυράννῳ, καὶ ἡ νῆσος αὐτῷ τῷ βασιλεῖ τῆς Λιβανωτοφόρου. Συνεχρήσαντο
δὲ αὐτῇ καὶ ἀπὸ Μούζα τινὲς καὶ τῶν ἐκπλεόντων ἀπὸ Λιμυρικῆς καὶ 21
Βαρυγάζων ὅσοι κατὰ τύχην εἰς αὐτὴν ἐπιβάλλοντες ὄρυζάν τε καὶ σῖτον
καὶ ὀθόνιον Ἰνδικὸν ἀντικαταλλασσόμενοι καὶ σώματα θηλυκὰ διὰ σπάνιν 282 M.
ἐκεῖ προχωροῦντα χελώνην ἀντεφορτίζοντο πλείστην· νῦν δὲ ὑπὸ τῶν 24
βασιλέων ἡ νῆσος ἐκμεμίσθωται καὶ παραφυλάσσεται.

32 Μετὰ δὲ τὸν Σύαγρον κόλπος ἐστὶν συναφής, ἐπὶ βάθος ἐνδύνων
εἰς τὴν ἤπειρον, Ὄμανα, σταδίους ἔχων ἑξακοσίους τὸ διαπέραμα, καὶ 27
μετ᾽ αὐτὸν ὑψηλὰ ὄρη πετρώδη καὶ ἀπόκοπα, ἀνθρώπων ἐν σπηλαίοις
κατοικούντων, ἐπὶ σταδίους ἄλλους πεντακοσίους, καὶ μετ᾽ αὐτοὺς ὅρμος
ἀποδεδειγμένος τοῦ Σαχαλίτου λιβάνου πρὸς ἐμβολήν, Μόσχα λιμὴν λεγό- 30

---

3 συνο[υ]ρίζουσα m. pr. 4 αὐτῇ Fabr. 5 ὧν Stuck: ὡς 6 [τῶν σαυρῶν]
Stuck 7 ἀμπελ⟨ικ⟩ὸν scripsi: ἄμπελον; ἀμπέλου Stuck 8 τῆς πρὸς corr.
Fabr. 10 ⟨ἐξ⟩ Ἀράβων Müller in comm. 12 πλείστην δὲ διάφορον καὶ corr.
edd. 14 [τὰ ἐγχρήζοντα] Bernhardy aut καὶ delendum aut lacuna statuenda
στερρότερα Bernhardy: πυρρότερα 15 ⟨νῶτα⟩ Bernhardy 16 [ἐγχρήζοντα]
ut glossema ad γρύτην pertinens delevi 21 διὰ λιμυρ- corr. Müller 22 εἰς
αὐτὰς corr. Stuck 23 ὀθόνιον scripsi: ὀθόνην 24 τοῦ βασιλέως Müller in
comm. 28 ἀνθρώποις (supra οις punctum pos. m. pr.) corr. Gelenius

a harbor, and a storehouse for the collection of frankincense. In the open sea off it is an island, between it and the Promontory of Spices across the water but nearer to Syagros, called Dioscuridês; though very large, it is barren and also damp, with rivers, crocodiles, a great many vipers, and huge lizards, so huge that people eat the flesh and melt down the fat to use in place of oil. The island bears no farm products, neither vines nor grain. The inhabitants, few in number, live on one side of the island, that to the north, the part facing the mainland; they are settlers, a mixture of Arabs and Indians and even some Greeks, who sail out of there to trade. The island yields tortoise shell, the genuine, the land, and the light-colored, in great quantity and distinguished by rather large shields, and also the oversize mountain variety with an extremely thick shell, of which the parts over the belly, whichever are useful, do not take [sc. regular] cutting; besides, they are rather tawny. On the other hand, whatever can be used for small boxes, small plaques, small disks, and similar items gets cut up completely. The so-called Indian cinnabar is found there; it is collected as an exudation from the trees.

31. The island is subject to the aforementioned king of the frankincense-bearing land, just as Azania is to Charibaêl and the governor of Mapharitis. Trade with it used to be carried on by some of the shippers from Muza and also by those sailing out of Limyrikê and Barygaza who by chance put in at it; these would exchange rice, grain, cotton cloth, and female slaves, which found a market because of a shortage there, for big cargoes of tortoise shell. At the present time the kings have leased out the island, and it is under guard.

32. Immediately after Syagros is a bay indenting deeply into the coast, Omana, 600 stades across the mouth; after it, high mountains, rocky and sheer, where men live in caves, for another 500; and, after these, a designated harbor for loading the Sachalite frankincense, called Moscha Limên ["Moscha Harbor"].

μενος, εἰς ἣν ἀπὸ Κανὴ συνήθως πλοῖα πέμπεταί τινα καὶ παραπλέοντα
ἀπὸ Λιμυρικῆς ἢ Βαρυγάζων, ὀψινοῖς καιροῖς παραχειμάσαντα, παρὰ
3 τῶν βασιλικῶν πρὸς ὀθόνιον καὶ σῖτον καὶ ἔλαιον λίβανον ἀντιφορτίζουσιν
παρ᾽ ὅλον δὲ τὸν Σαχαλίτην   χώματι κειμένῳ καὶ ἀφυλάκτῳ   δυνάμει
θεῶν τινὶ τοῦτον τὸν τόπον ἐπιτηρούντων· οὔτε γὰρ λάθρα οὔτε φανερῶς
6 χωρὶς βασιλικῆς δόσεως εἰς πλοῖον ἐμβληθῆναι δύναται· κἂν χόνδρον τις
ἄρῃ, οὐ δύναται πλεῦσαι τὸ πλοῖον ἀπὸ δαίμονος δίχα·

283 M.   ⟨Ἀπὸ δὲ Μόσχα⟩ λιμένος ἐπ᾽ ἄλλους σταδίους ὡς χιλίους πεντα- 33
9 κοσίους ἕως Ἀσίχωνος ἄχρι ⟨ὄρος⟩ τῇ γῇ παρατείνει καὶ κατὰ τὸ ἀπο-
λῆγον αὐτοῦ μέρος ἑπτὰ νῆσοι πρόκεινται κατὰ τὸ ἑξῆς, αἱ Ζηνοβίου
λεγόμεναι, μεθ᾽ ἃς ἄλλη παράκειται χώρα βάρβαρος οὐκέτι τῆς αὐτῆς
12 βασιλείας ἀλλ᾽ ἤδη τῆς Περσίδος, ἣν ἀφ᾽ ὕψους παραπλέοντι ὡς σταδίους
δισχιλίους ἀπὸ τῶν Ζηνοβίου συναντᾷ νῆσος Σαράπιδος λεγομένη, ἀπὸ
σταδίων τῆς γῆς ὡσεὶ ἑκατὸν εἴκοσι. Ταύτης τὸ μὲν πλάτος ἐστὶν ὡσεὶ
15 σταδίων διακοσίων, τὸ δὲ μῆκος ἑξακοσίων, οἰκεῖται δὲ κώμαις τρισὶν
καὶ ἀνθρώποις ἱεροῖς Ἰχθυοφάγων· γλώσσῃ δὲ Ἀραβικῇ χρῶνται [δὲ] καὶ
περιζώμασι φύλλων κουκίνων. Ἔχει δὲ ἡ νῆσος χελώνην ἱκανὴν καὶ διά-
18 φορον. Ἐξαρτίζουσι δὲ εἰς αὐτὴν συνήθως οἱ ἀπὸ Κανῆς σκάφας καὶ
ἐφόλκια.

284 M.   Περικολπίζοντι δὲ τὴν ἐχομένην ἤπειρον εἰς αὐτὴν τὴν ἄρκτον ἤδη 34
21 περὶ τὴν εἰσβολὴν τῆς Περσικῆς θαλάσσης κεῖνται νῆσοι πλείονες, αἱ
Καλαίου λεγόμεναι νῆσοι, σχεδὸν ἐπὶ σταδίους δισχιλίους παρατεταμέναι
τῇ χώρᾳ· πονηροὶ δὲ οἱ κατοικοῦντες αὐτὰς ἄνθρωποι καὶ ἡμέρας οὐ
24 πολύ τι βλέποντες.

Περὶ δὲ τὴν ἐσχάτην κεφαλὴν τῶν Καλαίου νήσων καὶ τὸ λεγόμενον 35
Καλὸν ὄρος ἐκδέχεται μετ᾽ οὐ πολὺ τὸ στόμα τῆς Περσικῆς καὶ πλεῖσται
27 κολυμβήσεις εἰσὶν τοῦ πινικίου κόγχου. Τούτου δὲ τοῦ στόματος ἐκ τῶν
εὐωνύμων ἐστὶν ὄρη μέγιστα λεγόμενα ⟨Ἀ⟩σαβῶ⟨ν⟩, ἐκ δὲ τῶν δεξιῶν
ἄντικρυς ἀφορώμενον ἄλλο στρογγύλον ὑψηλόν, τὸ Σεμιράμεως λεγόμενον,
30 καὶ μέσος αὐτὸς ὁ διάπλους τοῦ στόματος ὡς σταδίους ἑξακοσίους, δι᾽
οὗ μέγιστος καὶ πλατύτατος εἰς τοὺς ἐσωτάτους τόπους ὁ Περσικὸς κόλπος
ἀναχεῖται, καθ᾽ ὃν ἐν τοῖς ἐσχάτοις αὐτοῦ μέρεσιν ἐμπόριόν ἐστιν νόμιμον,

---

4 [δὲ] Fabr.   χώματι κειμένῳ καὶ ἀφυλάκτῳ corr. Fabr.   7 [ἀπὸ δαίμονος
δίχα] Müller in comm.   8 ⟨Ἀπὸ δὲ Μόσχα⟩ Müller   9 ⟨ὄρος⟩ τῇ γῇ Müller:
τῆς γῆς   16 [δὲ] m. alt.   21 πλείονες αἱ Stuck, Schwanbeck: πλεόμεναι
     22 [νῆσοι] Müller   παρεσταμέναι corr. L, Vincent   25 Καλαίου Fabr.:
παπίου   28 ⟨Ἀ⟩σαβῶ⟨ν⟩ Stuck

Some vessels are customarily sent to it from Kanê; in addition, those sailing by from Limyrikê or Barygaza that passed the winter [sc. at Moscha] because of the season being late, by arrangement with the royal agents take on, in exchange for cotton cloth and grain and oil, a return cargo of frankincense, the Sachalite variety throughout, at a mole that stands there unguarded, thanks to some power of the gods who watch over this place. For, neither covertly nor overtly can frankincense be loaded aboard a ship without royal permission; if even a grain is lifted aboard, the ship cannot sail, since it is against the god's will.

33. Beyond Moscha Limên, for about another 1500 stades a mountain range (?) stretches along the shore up to Asichôn, and off the very end of this lie seven islands in a row called the Isles of Zênobios, beyond which stretches another country, inhabited by an indigenous people, which is no longer in the same kingdom but already in that of Persis. After sailing along it over open water for about 2000 stades from the Isles of Zênobios, you come to the Isle of Sarapis, as it is called, about 120 stades offshore. It is some 200 stades wide and 600 long and is populated by three villages and by holy men of the Ichthyophagoi. They use the Arabic tongue and wear loincloths of palm leaves. The island has good supplies of fine-quality tortoise shell. The merchants of Kanê customarily fit out small sailing vessels to trade with it.

34. After coasting due north along the next stretch of the shore, in the vicinity by now of the entrance to the Persian Gulf, you meet numerous islands, called the Isles of Kalaios, strung out along the coast for almost 2000 stades. The men who populate them are rascals who do not do much looking during the daytime.

35. In the vicinity of the furthest tip of the Isles of Kalaios and of Kalon Oros ["fair mountain"], as it is called, a little further on is the mouth of the Persian Gulf, where there is much diving for pearl oysters. On the left side of the mouth is a mighty range of mountains called the Asabô; on the right side, visible directly across, is another mountain, round and high, called Mt. Semiramis. The sail across the mouth between them is about 600 stades; beyond, the Persian Gulf, a vast expanse, spreads up to places deep within it. At its very head is a legally limited port of trade

λεγόμενον ἡ Ἀπολόγου, κειμένη κατὰ Πασίνου Χάρακα καὶ ποταμὸν 285 M. Εὐφράτην.

36   Παραπλεύσαντι δὲ τοῦτο τὸ στόμα τοῦ κόλπου μετὰ δρόμους ἐξ ἕτερον 3 ἐμπόριόν ἐστιν τῆς Περσίδος, ἡ λεγομένη Ὄμμανα. Ἐξαρτίζεται δὲ εἰς αὐτὴν συνήθως ἀπὸ μὲν Βαρυγάζων εἰς ἀμφότερα ταῦτα τῆς Περσίδος ἐμπόρια πλοῖα μεγάλα χαλκοῦ καὶ ξύλων   σαγαλίνων   καὶ δοκῶν καὶ κεράτων 6 καὶ φαλάγγων   σασαμίνων   καὶ ἐβενίνων, εἰς δὲ τὴν Ὄμανα καὶ ἀπὸ Κανὴ λίβανος καὶ ἀπὸ Ὀμάνων εἰς τὴν Ἀραβίαν ἐντόπια ῥαπτὰ πλοιάρια, τὰ λεγόμενα μαδαράτε. Εἰσφέρεται δὲ ἀπὸ ἑκατέρων τῶν ἐμπορίων εἴς 9 τε Βαρύγαζαν καὶ εἰς Ἀραβίαν πινικὸν πολὺ μὲν χεῖρον δὲ τοῦ Ἰνδικοῦ 286 M. καὶ πορφύρα καὶ ἱματισμὸς ἐντόπιος καὶ οἶνος καὶ φοῖνιξ πολὺς καὶ χρυσὸς καὶ σώματα.

12

37   Μετὰ δὲ τὴν Ὀμανιτικὴν χώραν ὁμοίως ἡ Παρσιδῶν παράκειται, βασιλείας ἑτέρας, καὶ κόλπος τῶν Τεράβδων λεγόμενος, οὗ κατὰ μέσον εἰς τὸν κόλπον · παρανατείνει. Καὶ παρ᾽ αὐτὸν ποταμός ἐστιν, ἔχων 15 εἰσαγωγὴν πλοίοις, καὶ μικρὸν ἐπὶ τοῦ στόματος ἐμπόριον Ὡραία λεγόμενον καὶ κατὰ νώτου μεσόγειος πόλις, ἔχουσα ὁδὸν ἡμερῶν ἑπτὰ ἀπὸ θαλάσσης, ἐν ᾗ καὶ βασίλεια, ἡ λεγομένη ⟨**⟩. Φέρει δὲ ἡ χώρα σῖτον 18 πολὺν καὶ οἶνον καὶ ὄρυζαν καὶ φοίνικα, πρὸς δὲ τὴν ἤπειρον οὐδὲν ἕτερον ἢ βδέλλα⟨ν⟩.

38   Μετὰ δὲ ταύτην τὴν χώραν, ἤδη τῆς ἠπείρου διὰ τὸ βάθος τῶν 21 κόλπων ἐκ τῆς ἀνατολῆς ὑπερκερώσης, ἐκδέχεται ⟨τὰ⟩ παραθαλάσσια μέρη τῆς Σκυθίας παρ᾽ αὐτὸν κειμένης τὸν βορέαν, ταπεινὰ λίαν, ἐξ ὧν ποταμὸς Σίνθος, μέγιστος τῶν κατὰ τὴν Ἐρυθρὰν θάλασσαν ποταμῶν 24 καὶ πλεῖστον ὕδωρ ἐς θάλασσαν ἐκβάλλων, ὥστε ἄχρι πολλοῦ, καὶ πρὶν ἢ συμβάλῃ τῇ χώρᾳ, εἰς τὸ πέλαγος ἀπαντᾶν ἀπ᾽ αὐτοῦ λευκὸν 287 M. ὕδωρ. Σημεῖον δὲ ἤδη τῆς περὶ αὐτὸν χώρας ἐπιβολῆς τοῖς ἐκ πελάγους 27 ἐρχομένοις οἱ προαπαντῶντες ὄφεις ἐκ τοῦ βάθους· τῶν γὰρ ἐπάνω καὶ περὶ τὴν Περσίδα τόπων σημεῖόν ἐστιν αἱ λεγόμεναι γράαι. Ἑπτὰ δὲ οὗτος ὁ ποταμὸς ἔχει στόματα, λεπτὰ δὲ ταῦτα καὶ τεναγώδη, καὶ τὰ μὲν 30

---

1 Χάρακα καὶ Müller: χώρα κακα: (sine acc.)   6 σανταλίνων καὶ δοκῶν Salmasius: σαγαλινοκαιδοκῶν   κεράτων suspectum   7 σησαμ- Stuck: σασαμ- (supra pr. a punctum pos. m. pr.)   9 μαδάρατα Müller in comm.   Ἐκφέρ- malim cum Fabr. 13 Παρσιδῶν Müller: παρ᾽ ὁδὸν   14 κόλπον (ν s. scr. m. pr.) corr. m. alt. Τεραβαίων coni. Müller in Proll. CII, Γεδρωσῶν in comm.   εἰς τὸν κόλπον delere malim cum Müller   15 ⟨ἄκρα⟩ Müller [παρ]ανατ. malim cum Müller 17 κατὰ νώτου Müller: κατ᾽ αὐτὸν   18 ⟨τὰ⟩ βασ. Fabr.   ⟨Ῥαμβακία⟩ Mannert, Alt. Geogr. V, 2, 19; ⟨Πάρσις⟩ Müller in Proll. CII.   20 βδέλλα⟨ν⟩ Fabr.   22 ⟨τὰ⟩ Müller   23 κείμενον corr. Müller   27 περὶ αὐτὴν correxi

called Apologos, lying near Charax Spasinu and the Euphrates River.

36. After sailing by the mouth of the gulf, six runs further on you come to another port of trade of Persis called Omana. Customarily the merchants of Barygaza deal with it, sending out big vessels to both of Persis's ports of trade [sc. Apologos and Omana], with supplies of copper, teakwood, and beams, saplings, and logs of sissoo and ebony; Omana also takes in frankincense from Kanê and sends out to Arabia its local sewn boats, the kind called *madarate*. Both ports of trade export to Barygaza and Arabia pearls in quantity but inferior to the Indian; purple cloth; native clothing; wine; dates in quantity; gold; slaves.

37. After the country to which Omana belongs comes the country of the Parsidai, part of another kingdom, and the gulf called the Gulf of the Terabdoi, around the middle of which . . . bulges into the gulf. And washing into it is a river that boats can enter; at the mouth is a small port of trade called Hôraia and behind it, a seven-day journey from the sea, is an inland city, which is also the site of a royal palace, called. . . . The region produces grain in quantity, wine, rice, and dates, but along the coast nothing except bdellium.

38. After this region, with the coast by now curving like a horn because of the deep indentations to the east made by the bays, there next comes the seaboard of Skythia, which lies directly to the north; it is very flat and through it flows the Sinthos River, mightiest of the rivers along the Erythraean Sea and emptying so great an amount of water into the sea that far off, before you reach land, its light-colored water meets you out at sea. An indication to those coming from the sea that they are already approaching land in the river's vicinity are the snakes that emerge from the depths to meet them; there is an indication as well in the places around Persis mentioned above, the snakes called *graai*. The river has seven mouths, narrow and full of shallows;

ἄλλα διάπλουν οὐκ ἔχει, μόνον δὲ τὸ μέσον, ἐφ' οὗ καὶ τὸ παραθαλάσσιον ἐμπόριόν ἐστιν Βαρβαρικόν. Πρόκειται δὲ αὐτοῦ νησίον μικρόν, καὶ
3 κατὰ νώτου μεσόγειος ἡ μητρόπολις αὐτῆς τῆς Σκυθίας Μινναγάρ· βασιλεύεται δὲ ὑπὸ Πάρθων, συνεχῶς ἀλλήλους ἐκδιωκόντων.

Τὰ μὲν οὖν πλοῖα κατὰ τὴν Βαρβαρικὴν διορμίζονται, τὰ δὲ φορτία 39
6 πάντα εἰς τὴν μητρόπολιν ἀναφέρεται διὰ τοῦ ποταμοῦ τῷ βασιλεῖ.
Προχωρεῖ δὲ εἰς τὸ ἐμπόριον ἱματισμὸς ἁπλοῦς ἱκανὸς καὶ νόθος οὐ πολύς, πολύμιτα καὶ χρυσόλιθον καὶ κοράλλιον καὶ στύραξ καὶ λίβανος
9 καὶ ὑαλᾶ σκεύη καὶ ἀργυρώματα καὶ χρῆμα, οἶνος δὲ οὐ πολύς. Ἀντι-
288 M. φορτίζεται δὲ κόστος, βδέλλα, λύκ⟨ι⟩ον, νάρδος καὶ καλλεανὸς λίθος καὶ σάπφειρος καὶ Σιρικὰ δέρματα καὶ ὀθόνιον καὶ νῆμα Σιρικὸν καὶ Ἰνδι-
12 κὸν μέλαν. ⟨Ἀν⟩άγονται δὲ καὶ αὐτοὶ οἱ πλέοντες μετὰ τῶν Ἰνδικῶν περὶ τὸν Ἰούλιον μῆνα, ὅς ἐστιν Ἐπῖφι· δυσεπίβολος μὲν ἐπιφορώτατος δὲ ἐκείνων καὶ συντομώτερος ὁ πλοῦς.

15 Μετὰ δὲ τὸν Σίνθον ποταμὸν ἕτερός ἐστιν κόλπος ἀθεώρητος παρὰ 40 τὸν βορέαν· ὀνομάζεται δὲ Εἰρινόν, ἐπιλέγεται δέ ὁ μὲν μικρὸν ὁ δὲ μέγα. Πελάγη δέ ἐστιν ἀμφότερα τεναγώδη καὶ δίνας ἐλαφρὰς ἔχοντα
18 καὶ συνεχεῖς καὶ μακρὰς ἀπὸ τῆς γῆς, ὡς πολλάκις, τῆς ἠπείρου μηδὲ βλεπομένης, ἐποκέλλειν τὰ πλοῖα, ἐνδοτέρω δὲ προληφθέντα καὶ ἀπόλλύμενα. Τούτου δὲ ὑπερήκει τοῦ κόλπου ἀκρωτήριον, ἐπικαμπὲς ἀπὸ
289 M. 21 τοῦ Εἰρινοῦ μετὰ τὴν ἀνατολὴν καὶ τὸν νότον ὡς εἰς τὴν δύσιν, ἐμπεριλαμβάνον αὐτὸν τὸν κόλπον λεγόμενον Βαράκην, νήσους ἑπτὰ ἐμπεριειλημμένον, οὗ περὶ μὲν τὰς ἀρχὰς οἱ περιπεσόντες ὀλίγον ὀπίσω καὶ εἰς
24 τὸ πέλαγος ἀναδραμόντες ἐκφεύγουσιν, οἱ δὲ εἰς αὐτὴν κατακλεισθέντες τὴν τοῦ Βαράκου κοιλίαν ἀπόλλυνται· τό τε γὰρ κῦμα μέγα καὶ βαρὺ λίαν, ἡ δὲ θάλασσα ταραχώδης καὶ θολερὰ καὶ δίνας ἔχουσα καὶ ῥοώδεις
27 εἰλίγγους. Ὁ δὲ βυθὸς ἔν τισι μὲν ἀπόκοπος ἔν τισιν δὲ πετρώδης καὶ ἀπόξυρος, ὥστε τέμνεσθαι τὰς παρακειμένας ἀγκύρας ἀντέχειν ἀποκοντουμένας, ἃς δὲ καὶ συντριβομένας ἐν τῷ βυθῷ. Σημεῖον δ' αὐτοῖν τοῖς ἀπὸ
30 πελάγους ἐρχομένοις οἱ προαπαντῶντες ὄφεις ὑπερμεγέθεις καὶ μέλανες· ἐν γὰρ τοῖς μετὰ ταῦτα τόποις καὶ τοῖς περὶ Βαρύγαζαν μικρότεροι καὶ τῷ χρώματι χλωροὶ καὶ χρυσίζοντες ὑπαντῶσι.

---

3 Μινναγάρ<a> malim cum Fabr.   5 τὸ Βαρβαρικὸν malim cum Fabr.
8 πολύμπα corr. Stuck   10 λύκ<ι>ον Gelenius   11 Σηρ- edd.
12 <'Αν>άγονται Stuck   'Ινδικῶν <ἐτησίων> Müller in comm.   19 ἐποκέλλειν
(pr. λ exp. m. pr.)   19 ἀπόλλυσθαι Fabr.: ἀπολλύμενα   21 Εἰρινοῦ Müller
ὅρμου   21—22 ἐμπεριλαμβάνων (supra ω punctum pos. m. pr.) .... λεγόμενος
Βαράκης .... ἐμπεριειλημμένος corr. Hudson, Fabr.   29 συντρίβεσθαι scripsi:
συντριβομένας   αὐτοῖν corr. Hudson

none are navigable except the one in the middle. At it, on the coast, stands the port of trade of Barbarikon. There is a small islet in front of it; and behind it, inland, is the metropolis of Skythia itself, Minnagar. The throne is in the hands of Parthians, who are constantly chasing each other off it.

39. Vessels moor at Barbarikon, but all the cargoes are taken up the river to the king at the metropolis. In this port of trade there is a market for: clothing, with no adornment in good quantity, of printed fabric in limited quantity; multicolored textiles; peridot (?); coral; storax; frankincense; glassware; silverware; money; wine, limited quantity. As return cargo it offers: costus; bdellium; *lykion*; nard; turquoise; lapis lazuli; Chinese pelts, cloth, and yarn; indigo. Those who sail with the Indian [sc. winds] leave around July, that is, Epeiph. The crossing with these is hard going but absolutely favorable and shorter.

40. After the Sinthos River there is another bay, hidden from view, to the north. It is named Eirinon, with the additional names Little and Big. Both are bodies of water with shoals and a succession of shallow eddies reaching a long way from land so that frequently, with the shore nowhere in sight, vessels will run aground and, if caught and thrust further in, be destroyed. Beyond this bay a promontory juts out, curving from Eirinon first east and south and then west; it embraces the gulf called Barakê, which itself embraces seven islands. Ships around its entrance that blunder in and then pull back the short distance into open water, escape; those that get closed inside the basin of Barakê are destroyed. For not only are the waves there very big and oppressive, but the sea is choppy and turbid, with eddies and violent whirlpools. The bottom in some places has sheer drops, in others is rocky and sharp, so that the anchors lying parallel [i.e., dropped from the bows], thrust out to withstand [sc. the difficult waters], get cut loose and some even get smashed on the sea floor. An indication of these [sc. dangers] to vessels coming from the sea are the snakes, huge and black, that emerge to meet them. In the areas beyond, and around Barygaza, snakes that are smaller and yellow and golden in color are met with.

41   Μετὰ δὲ τὸν Βαράκην εὐθύς ἐστιν ὁ Βαρυγάζων κόλπος καὶ ἡ ⟨ἤ⟩π⟨ει⟩ρος τῆς Ἀριακῆς χώρας, τῆς τε Μανβάνου βασιλείας ἀρχὴ καὶ τῆς ὅλης Ἰνδικῆς οὖσα. Ταύτης τὰ μὲν μεσόγεια τῇ Σκυθίᾳ συνορίζοντα 3 Ἀβηρία καλεῖται, τὰ δὲ παραθαλάσσια Συ[ν]ραστρήνη. Πολυφόρος δὲ 290 Μ. ἡ χώρα σίτου καὶ ὀρύζης καὶ ἐλαίου σησαμίνου καὶ βουτύρου καὶ καρπάσου καὶ τῶν ἐξ αὐτῆς Ἰνδικῶν ὀθονίων τῶν χυδαίων. Βουκόλια 6 δὲ ἐν αὐτῇ πλεῖστα καὶ ἄνδρες ὑπερμεγέθεις τῷ σώματι καὶ μέλανες τῇ χροιᾷ. Μητρόπολις δὲ τῆς χώρας Μινναγάρα, ἀφ᾽ ἧς καὶ πλεῖστον ὀθόνιον εἰς Βαρύγαζαν κατάγεται. Σῴζεται δὲ ἔτι καὶ νῦν τῆς Ἀλεξάν- 9 δρου στρατιᾶς σημεῖα περὶ τοὺς τόπους, ἱερά τε ἀρχαῖα καὶ θεμέλιοι παρεμβολῶν καὶ φρέατα μέγιστα. Ὁ δὲ παράπλους ταύτης τῆς χώρας ἀπὸ τοῦ Βαρβαρικοῦ μέχρι τοῦ κατὰ Ἀστακάπρα πέραν Βαρυγάζων 12 ἀκρωτηρίου τῆς λεγομένης Παπικῆς ἐστιν [δὲ] σταδίων τρισχιλίων.

42   Μεθ᾽ ἧς ἕτερός ἐστι κόλπος ἔσω κυμάτων εἰς αὐτὸν ἐνδύνων τὸν βορέαν, οὗ κατὰ μὲν τὸ στόμα νῆσός ἐστιν ἡ λεγομένη Βαιώνης, ἐν δὲ 15 τοῖς ἐσωτάτοις τόποις μέγιστος ποταμὸς ὁ λεγόμενος Μάϊς. Τοῦτον τὸν 291 Μ. κόλπον, τὸ πλάτος ὡς σταδίων τριακοσίων, οἱ πλέοντες εἰς Βαρύγαζαν διαπερῶντες, ἐξ εὐωνύμων ἀκροφανῆ καταλιπόντες τὴν νῆσον, καὶ εἰς 18 αὐτὴν ⟨τὴν⟩ ἀνατολὴν ἐπ᾽ αὐτὸ τὸ στόμα τοῦ ποταμοῦ Βαρυγάζων· λέγεται δὲ αὐτὸς ὁ ποταμὸς Λαμναῖος.

43   Ὁ δὲ κόλπος αὐτὸς ὁ κατὰ Βαρύγαζαν στενὸς ὢν τοῖς ἐκ πελάγους 21 ἐρχομένοις ἐστὶν δυσεπίβολος· ἡ γὰρ εἰς τὰ δεξιὰ ἢ εἰς τὰ εὐώνυμα παραπίπτουσιν, ἥ τε ἐπιβολὴ κρεί⟨σ⟩σων ἐστὶν τῆς ἑτέρας. Ἀλλ᾽ ἐκ μὲν τῶν δεξιῶν κατ᾽ αὐτὸ τὸ στόμα τοῦ κόλπου παράκειται ταιν⟨ί⟩α τραχεῖα 24 καὶ διάσπιλος, Ἡρώνη λεγομένη, κατὰ Καμμωνὶ κώμην· ἐκ δὲ τῶν εὐωνύμων ἀπέναντι ταύτης τὸ πρὸ Ἀστακά[ν]ρων ἀκρωτήριον, ἡ Πα- πικὴ λεγομένη, δύσορμος οὖσα διά τε τὸν ῥοῦν τὸν περὶ αὐτὴν καὶ διὰ 27 τὸ ἀποκόπτειν τὰς ἀγκύρας τραχὺν ὄντα καὶ πετρώδη τὸν βυθόν. Κἂν κατ᾽ αὐτὸν δέ τις ἐπιβάλῃ τὸν κόλπον, αὐτὸ τὸ στόμα τοῦ κατὰ Βαρύγαζαν

---

2 πρὸς τῆς corr. Schwanbeck   Ἀραβικῆς corr. Stuck   3 τῆς σκυθίας συνο- ρίζοντα ἰβηρία καλεῖται δὲ τὰ παρ. συνραστρήνη corr. Mannert, Alt. Geogr. V, 1, 171 nisi quod retinuit Ἰβηρία, quod corr. Lassen, Ind. Alt. 1, 539.   5 σασαμ- (supra pr. a punctum pos. m. pr.) corr. Gelenius   12 Ἀστακάπρα πέραν Schwan- beck: ἄστα καὶ τραπεραν (sine acc.)   13 [δὲ] edd.   14 κόλπος Mannert, Alt. Geogr. V, 1, 165: τόπος   ἔξω Müller in comm.: ἔσω   17 πλάτος Müller: πέ- λαγος   18 malim διαπερῶσιν   19 ⟨τὴν⟩ Fabr.   20 Ναμνάδιος Müller; Νάμ(μ)αδος Schwanbeck   21 ὅ τε corr. Fabr.   23 κρεῖσσον (pr. σ inser. m. alt.) corr. Stuck   24 ταινία Stuck: τενα (sine acc. m. pr.) ί s. scr. m. alt. 26 Ἀστακά[ν]ρων edd.   27 διὰ δὲ corr. m. alt.

41. Immediately after the gulf of Barakê is the gulf of Barygaza and the coast of the region of Ariakê, the beginning both of Manbanos's realm and of all of India. The part inland, which borders on Skythia, is called Abêria, the part along the coast Syrastrênê. The region, very fertile, produces grain, rice, sesame oil, ghee, cotton, and the Indian cloths made from it, those of ordinary quality. There are a great many herds of cattle, and the men are of very great size and dark skin color. The metropolis of the region is Minnagara, from which great quantities of cloth are brought to Barygaza. In the area there are still preserved to this very day signs of Alexander's expedition, ancient shrines and the foundations of encampments and huge wells. The voyage along the coast of this region, from Barbarikon to the promontory near Astakapra across from Barygaza called Papikê, is 3000 stades.

42. Beyond it is another gulf, on the inside of the waves, that forms an inlet directly to the north. Near the mouth is an island called Baiônês, and, at the very head, a mighty river called the Mais. Vessels whose destination is Barygaza cross the gulf, which is about 300 stades wide, leaving the island, whose highest point is visible, to the left and heading due east toward the mouth of Barygaza's river. This river is called the Lamnaios.

43. This gulf which leads to Barygaza, since it is narrow, is hard for vessels coming from seaward to manage. For they arrive at either its right-hand side or its left-hand, and attempting it by the left-hand side is better than the other. For, on the right-hand side, at the very mouth of the gulf, there extends a rough and rock-strewn reef called Hêrônê, near the village of Kammôni. Opposite it, on the left-hand side, is the promontory in front of Astakapra called Papikê; mooring here is difficult because of the current around it and because the bottom, being rough and rocky, cuts the anchor cables. And, even if you manage the gulf itself, the very mouth of the river on which Barygaza stands

ποταμοῦ δυσεύρετόν ἐστιν διὰ τὸ τὴν χώραν ταπεινὴν εἶναι καὶ μηθὲν
ἐγγύτερον ἐνεχύρως θεωρεῖσθαι· κἂν εὑρεθῇ, δυσείσβολόν ἐστιν διὰ τὰ
3 περὶ αὐτὸ τενάγη τοῦ ποταμοῦ.

     Τούτου χάριν περὶ αὐτὸν τὸν εἴσπλουν βασιλικοὶ ἁλιεῖς ἐντόπιοι **44**
πληρώμασιν μακρῶν πλοίων, ἃ λέγεται τράππαγα καὶ κότυμβα, πρὸς
6 ἀπάντησιν ἐξέρχονται μέχρι τῆς Συραστρήνης, ἀφ᾽ ὧν ὁδηγεῖται τὰ πλοῖα
μέχρι Βαρυγάζων. Κλίνουσιν γὰρ εὐθὺς ἀπὸ τοῦ στόματος τοῦ κόλπου
διὰ τὰ τενάγη τοῖς πληρώμασιν καὶ ῥυμουλκοῦσιν αὐτὰ σταθμοῖς ἤδη
9 τεταγμένοις, ἀρχομένης δὲ τῆς πλήμης αἴροντες, ἱσταμένης δὲ διορμίζοντες
κατά τινας ὅρμους καὶ κυθρίνους. Οἱ δὲ κυθρῖνοι τόποι εἰσὶν τοῦ ποταμοῦ
βαθύτεροι μέχρι Βαρυγάζων· ἀπέχει γὰρ ἀπὸ τοῦ στόματος ἄνω παρὰ
12 ποταμὸν κειμένη ὡς σταδίων τριακοσίων.

292 M.   Πᾶσα μὲν ἡ Ἰνδικὴ χώρα ποταμοὺς ἔχει πλείστους, ἀμπώτεις τε **45**
καὶ πλήμας μεγίστας, συναπτομένας ὑπὸ τὴν ἀνατολὴν καὶ τὴν πανσέληνον
15 ἄχρι τριῶν ἡμερῶν καὶ τοῖς μεταξὺ καταστήμασιν τῆς σελήνης ἐλασσου-
μένας, πολὺ δὲ μᾶλλον ἢ κατὰ Βαρυγάζων, ὥστε αἰφνίδιον τόν τε βυθὸν
ὁρᾶσθαι καὶ ⟨******⟩ τινα μέρη τῆς ἠπείρου ποτὲ δὲ ξηρὰ τὰ πρὸ μικροῦ
18 πλοϊζόμενα, τούς τε ποταμοὺς ὑπὸ τὴν εἰσβολὴν τῆς πλήμ[μ]ης τοῦ
πελάγους ὅλου συνωθουμένου σφοδρότερον ἄνω φέρεσθαι τοῦ κατὰ φύσιν
ῥεύματος ἐπὶ πλείστους σταδίους.

21   Διὸ καὶ κινδυνώδεις εἰσὶν αἱ τῶν πλοίων προσαγωγαὶ καὶ ἐξαγωγαὶ **46**
τοῖς ἀπείροις καὶ πρώτως εἰσάγουσιν ἐς τὸ ἐμπόριον. Γινομένης γὰρ
ὁρμῆς ἤδη περὶ τὴν πλήμην οὐδὲν   παραμένουσιν   αἱ κατέχουσαι
24 ἄγκυραι· διὸ καὶ τὰ προληφθέντα πλοῖα τῇ ἰναίᾳ, πλαγιασθέντα ὑπὸ τῆς
ὀξύτητος τοῦ ῥοός, ἐποκέλλει τοῖς τενάγεσι καὶ ἀνακλᾶται, τὰ δὲ μικρότερα
καὶ περιτρέπεται, τινὰ δὲ καὶ περὶ τὰς διώρυχας ἀποκεκλικότα διὰ τὸ
27 περὶ τὴν ἄμπωτιν, ὅταν μὴ διερ⟨ε⟩ίσῃ, τῆς πλήμης αἰφνίδιον ἀπελθούσης,
ὑπὸ τῆς πρώτης κεφαλῆς τοῦ ῥοὸς ἐμπίμπλαται. Τοσαῦται γὰρ περὶ
τὴν ἐσβολὴν τῆς θαλάσσης γίνονται βίαι κατὰ τὰς συμμηνίας ὑπὸ τὴν
30 νυκτερινὴν μάλιστα πλήμην, ὥστε ἀρχομένης ἤδη τῆς εἰσαγωγῆς, ὅταν
ἠρεμῇ τὸ πέλαγος, ὑπ᾽ αὐτοῦ φέρεσθαι τοῖς ἀπὸ τοῦ στόματος παραπλήσιόν

2, 3 δυσείσβολος . . . . αὐτὸν corr. Fabr.   6 συραστρήνης corr. Blancard
8 αὐτὸ corr. Stuck   9 μὲν τῆς malim cum edd.   ἰσταμένης: εσταυμενης (sine
spir. et acc.) corr. Gelenius, Fabr.   17 ⟨ποτὲ μὲν πέλαγος εἶναι⟩ e. gr.
Müller   18 πλήμ[μ]ης edd.   23 οὐκ ἀντέχουσιν αἱ ἄγκ. Müller: αἱ κατέχουσιν
ἄγκ.   24 ἰναίᾳ Müller ex Hesych. ᾽ἰναίαν᾽ δύναμιν᾽: ἰνδίᾳ   25 ἐποκέλλει
(pr. λ exp. m. pr.)   27 διερ⟨ε⟩ίσῃ Müller, qui tamen praeter rationem -σῃς
scr.   ἐπελθ- Müller   29 συμμηνίας corr. Müller   31 τοῖς (ς s. scr.
m. pr.)   ἐπὶ τοῦ Müller

is hard to find because the land is low and nothing is clearly visible even from nearby. And, even if you find the mouth, it is hard to negotiate because of the shoals in the river around it.

44. For this reason local fishermen in the king's service come out with crews [sc. of rowers] and long ships, the kind called *trappaga* and *kotymba*, to the entrance as far as Syrastrênê to meet vessels and guide them up to Barygaza. Through the crew's efforts, they maneuver them right from the mouth of the gulf through the shoals and tow them to predetermined stopping places; they get them under way when the tide comes in and, when it goes out, bring them to anchor in certain harbors and basins. The basins are rather deep spots along the river up to Barygaza. For this lies on the river about 300 stades upstream from the mouth.

45. All over India there are large numbers of rivers with extreme ebb-and-flood tides that at the time of the new moon and the full moon last for up to three days, diminishing during the intervals. They are much more extreme in the area around Barygaza than elsewhere. Here suddenly the sea floor becomes visible, and certain parts along the coast, which a short while ago had ships sailing over them, at times become dry land, and the rivers, because of the inrush at flood tide of a whole concentrated mass of seawater, are driven headlong upstream against the natural direction of their flow for a good many stades.

46. Thus the navigating of ships in and out is dangerous for those who are inexperienced and are entering this port of trade for the first time. For, once the thrust of the flood tide is under way, restraining anchors do not stay in place. Consequently, the ships, carried along by its force and driven sideways by the swiftness of the current, run aground on the shoals and break up, while smaller craft even capsize. Even in the channels some craft, if not propped up, will tilt over on their sides during the ebb and, when the flood suddenly returns, get swamped by the first wave of the flow. So much power is generated at the inrush of the sea even during the dark of the moon, particularly if the flood arrives at night, that when the tide is just beginning to come in and the sea is still at rest, there is carried from it to people at the mouth

⟨τι⟩ βοῆς στρατοπέδου μακρόθεν ἀκονομένης, καὶ μετ᾽ ὀλίγον αὐτὴν
ἐπιτρέχειν τοῖς τενάγεσι ῥοίζῳ τὴν θάλασσαν.

47   Ἐπίκειται δὲ κατὰ ⟨νώ⟩του τῆς Βαρυγάζης μεσογείας πλείονα ἔθνη, 3
τό τε τῶν Ἀρατρίων καὶ ⟨Ἀ⟩ραχουσ⟨ί⟩ων καὶ Γανδαραίων καὶ τῆς
Προκλ⟨α⟩ΐδος, ἐν οἷς ἡ Βουκέφαλος Ἀλεξάνδρεια. Καὶ τούτων ἐπάνω 293 M.
μαχιμώτατον ἔθνος Βακτριανῶν, ὑπὸ βασιλέα ὄντων ἴδιον [τόπον]. Καὶ 6
Ἀλέξανδρος ὁρμηθεὶς ἀπὸ τῶν μερῶν τούτων ἄχρι τοῦ Γάγγου διῆλθε,
καταλιπὼν τήν τε Λιμυρικὴν καὶ τὰ νότια τῆς Ἰνδικῆς, ἀφ᾽ οὗ μέχρι
νῦν ἐν Βαρυγάζοις παλαιαὶ προχωροῦσιν δραχμαί, γράμμασιν Ἑλληνικοῖς 9
ἐγκεχαραγμέναι ἐπίσημα τῶν μετὰ Ἀλέξανδρον βεβασιλευκότων Ἀπολλο-
δότου καὶ Μενάνδρου.

48   Ἔνι δὲ αὐτῆς καὶ ἐξ ἀνατολῆς πόλις λεγομένη Ὀζήνη, ἐν ᾗ καὶ 12
τὰ βασίλεια πρότερον ἦν, ἀφ᾽ ἧς πάντα τὰ πρὸς εὐθηνίαν τῆς χώρας εἰς
Βαρύγαζαν καταφέρεται καὶ τὰ πρὸς ἐμπορίαν τὴν ἡμετέραν, ὀνυχίνη
λιθία καὶ μουρρίνη καὶ σινδόνες Ἰνδικαὶ καὶ μολόχιναι καὶ ἱκανὸν χυδαῖον 15
ὀθόνιον. Κατάγεται δὲ δι᾽ αὐτῆς καὶ ἀπὸ τῶν ἄνω τόπων ἡ διὰ Προκλαΐδος καταφερομένη νάρδος ἡ Καττυβουρίνη καὶ ἡ Πατροπαπίγη καὶ
ἡ Καβαλίτη καὶ ἡ διὰ τῆς παρακειμένης Σκυθίας, ὅ τε κόστος καὶ ἡ 18
βδέλλα.

49   Προχωρεῖ δὲ εἰς τὸ ἐμπόριον οἶνος προηγουμένως Ἰταλικὸς καὶ Λαοδι-
κηνὸς καὶ Ἀραβικὸς καὶ χαλκὸς καὶ κασσίτερος καὶ μόλυβος, κοράλλιον καὶ 21
χρυσόλιθον, ἱματισμὸς ἁπλοῦς καὶ νόθος παντοῖος, πολύμιται ζῶναι πη-
χυαῖαι, στύραξ, μελίλωτον, ὕελος ἀργή, σανδαράκη, στῖμι, δηνάριον χρυσοῦν
καὶ ἀργυροῦν, ἔχον ἀλλαγὴν καὶ ἐπικέρδειάν τινα πρὸς τὸ ἐντόπιον νόμισμα, 24
μύρον οὐ βαρύτιμον οὐδὲ πολύ. Τῷ δὲ βασιλεῖ κατ᾽ ἐκείνους τοὺς καιροὺς
εἰσφερόμενα βαρύτιμα ἀργυρώματα καὶ μουσικὰ καὶ παρθένοι εὐειδεῖς
πρὸς παλλακείαν καὶ διάφορος οἶνος καὶ ἱματισμὸς ἁπλοῦς πολυτελὴς καὶ 27
μύρον ἔξοχον. Φέρεται δὲ ἀπὸ τῶν τόπων νάρδος, κόστος, βδέλλα,
ἐλέφας, ὀνυχίνη λιθία καὶ σμύρνα καὶ λύκιον καὶ ὀθόνιον παντοῖον καὶ
Σηρικὸν καὶ μολόχινον καὶ νῆμα καὶ πέπερ⟨ι⟩ μακρὸν καὶ τὰ ἀπὸ τῶν 30
ἐμπορίων φερόμενα. Ἀποπλέουσιν δὲ κατὰ καιρὸν οἱ ἀπὸ τῆς Αἰγύπτου
εἰς τὸ ἐμπόριον ἀναγόμενοι περὶ τὸν Ἰούλιον μῆνα, ὅς ἐστιν Ἐπῖφι.

---

1 ⟨τι⟩ e. gr. Müller   3 δὲ Fabr.: γὰρ   κατὰ του (sine acc. m. pr.) τῇ βαρυγάζῃ
μεσογείᾳ correxi   4 τό τε edd.: ἤ τε   ῥαχούσων corr. Stuck   τανθαράγων
corr. Salmasius, Fabr.   5 Προκλ⟨α⟩ΐδος Müller   6 ὄντων Müller: οὖσαν
[τόπον] Stuck   12 αὐτῇ malim cum Fabr.   16 προκλαΐδος (a exp. m. pr.)
v. supra l. 5   17 ἡ Κασπαπυρηνὴ καὶ ἡ Παροπανισηνὴ Müller in Proll. CIV
22 πολύμιτοι Stuck   29 σμύρνα: μουρρίνη Müller   30 πέπερ⟨ι⟩ edd.

something like the rumble of an army heard from afar, and after a short while the sea itself races over the shoals with a hiss.

47. Inland behind Barygaza there are numerous peoples: the Aratrioi, Arachusioi, Gandaraioi, and the peoples of Proklais, in whose area Bukephalos Alexandreia is located. And beyond these is a very warlike people, the Bactrians, under a king. . . . Alexander, setting out from these parts, penetrated as far as the Ganges but did not get to Limyrikê and the south of India. Because of this, there are to be found on the market in Barygaza even today old drachmas engraved with the inscriptions, in Greek letters, of Apollodotus and Menander, rulers who came after Alexander.

48. There is in this region [sc. of Barygaza] towards the east a city called Ozênê, the former seat of the royal court, from which everything that contributes to the region's prosperity, including what contributes to trade with us, is brought down to Barygaza: onyx; agate (?); Indian garments of cotton; garments of *molochinon*; and a considerable amount of cloth of ordinary quality. Through this region there is also brought down from the upper areas the nard that comes by way of Proklais (the Kattyburinê, Patropapigê, and Kabalitê), the nard that comes through the adjacent part of Skythia, and costus and bdellium.

49. In this port of trade there is a market for: wine, principally Italian but also Laodicean and Arabian; copper, tin, and lead; coral and peridot (?); all kinds of clothing with no adornment or of printed fabric; multicolored girdles, eighteen inches wide; storax; yellow sweet clover (?); raw glass; realgar; sulphide of antimony; Roman money, gold and silver, which commands an exchange at some profit against the local currency; unguent, inexpensive and in limited quantity. For the king there was imported in those times precious silverware, slave musicians, beautiful girls for concubinage, fine wine, expensive clothing with no adornment, and choice unguent. This area exports: nard; costus; bdellium; ivory; onyx; agate (?); *lykion*; cotton cloth of all kinds; Chinese [sc. silk] cloth; *molochinon* cloth; [sc. silk] yarn; long pepper; and items brought here from the [sc. nearby] ports of trade. For those sailing to this port from Egypt, the right time to set out is around the month of July, that is Epeiph.

294 M.　Μετὰ δὲ Βαρύγαζαν εὐθέως ἡ συναφὴς ἤπειρος ἐκ τοῦ βορέου εἰς 50
τὸν νότον παρεκτείνει· διὸ καὶ Δαχιναβάδης καλεῖται ἡ χώρα· δάχανος
3 γὰρ καλεῖται ὁ νότος τῇ αὐτῶν γλώσσῃ. Ταύτης ἡ μὲν ὑπερκειμένη
πρὸς ἀνατολὰς μεσόγειος ἐμπεριέχει χώρας τε πολλὰς καὶ ἐρήμους καὶ
ὄρη μεγάλα καὶ θηρίων γένη παντοίων, παρδάλεις τε καὶ τίγρεις καὶ
6 ἐλέφαντας καὶ δράκοντας ὑπερμεγέθεις καὶ κροκόττας καὶ κυνοκεφάλων
πλεῖστα γένη, ἔθνη τε πλεῖστα καὶ πολυάνθρωπα τὰ μέχρι τοῦ Γάγγου.
Τῶν δὲ ἐν αὐτῇ τῇ Δαχιναβάδει δύο ἐστὶν τὰ διασημότατα ἐμπόρια, 51
9 Παίθανα μὲν ἀπὸ Βαρυγάζων ἔχουσα ὁδὸν ἡμερῶν εἴκοσι πρὸς νότον,
ἀπὸ ⟨δὲ⟩ ταύτης ὡς ἡμερῶν δέκα πρὸς ἀνατολὴν ἑτέρα πόλις μεγίστη
Ταγάρα. Κατάγεται δὲ ἐξ αὐτῶν πορείαις ἁμαξῶν καὶ ἀνοδίαις μεγίσταις
12 εἰς τὴν Βαρύγαζαν ἀπὸ μὲν Παιθάνων ὀνυχίνη λιθία πλείστη, ἀπὸ δὲ
Ταγάρων ὀθόνιον πολὺ[ν] χυδαῖον καὶ σινδόνων παντοῖα καὶ μολόχινα καί
τινα ἄλλα τοπικῶς ἐκεῖ προχωροῦντα φορτία τῶν παραθαλασσίων μερῶν.
15 Ὁ δ' ὅλος παράπλους μέχρι τῆς Λιμυρικῆς ἐστὶν σταδίων ἑπτακισχιλίων,
πλεῖστοι δὲ εἰς Αἰγιαλόν.

295 M.　Τοπικὰ δὲ ἐμπόρια κατὰ τὸ ἑξῆς κείμενα Ἀκαβαρου Σούππαρα 52
18 καὶ Καλλίενα πόλις, ἡ ἐπὶ τῶν Σαραγάνου τοῦ πρεσβυτέρου χρόνων
ἐμπόριον ἔνθεσμον γενομένη· μετὰ γὰρ τὸ κατασχεῖν αὐτὴν Σανδάνην
ἐκωλύθη ἐπὶ πολύ· καὶ γὰρ τὰ ἐκ τύχης εἰς τούτους τοὺς τόπους ἐσ-
21 βάλλοντα πλοῖα Ἑλληνικὰ μετὰ φυλακῆς εἰς Βαρύγαζαν εἰσάγεται.
Μετὰ δὲ Καλλίεναν ἄλλα ἐμπόρια τοπικὰ Σήμυλλα καὶ Μανδαγόρα 53
296 M. καὶ Παλαιπάτμαι καὶ Μελιζειγάρα καὶ Βυζάντιον † τοπαρον καὶ τύραννος
24 βοας †. Εἶτα Σησεκρείεναι λεγόμεναι νῆσοι καὶ ἡ τῶν Αἰγιδίων καὶ ἡ
τῶν Καινειτῶν κατὰ τὴν λεγομένην Χερσόνησον, καθ' οὓς τόπους εἰσὶν
πειραταί, καὶ μετὰ ταύτην Λευκὴ νῆσος. Εἶτα Νάουρα καὶ Τύνδις, τὰ
27 πρῶτα ἐμπόρια τῆς Λιμυρικῆς, καὶ μετὰ ταύτας Μούζιρις καὶ Νελκύνδα,
αἱ νῦν πράσσουσαι.

297 M.　Βασιλείας ἐστὶν ἡ μὲν Τύνδις Κηπροβότου, κώμη παραθαλάσσιος 54
30 ἔνσημος· ἡ δὲ Μούζιρις βασιλείας μὲν τῆς αὐτῆς, ἀκμάζουσα δὲ τοῖς ἀπὸ

---

7 Γάγγου Stuck, Fabr.: σύνεγγυς　　9 Παίθανα μὲν Schwanbeck: ἐπιφαινόμενα
10 <δὲ> edd.　　ταγάρα μεγίστη transp. Fabr.　　11 πορείαις (ult. ι s. scr. m.
pr.)　　12 πλιθάνων corr. Schwanbeck　　13 πολὺ[ν] edd.　　17 ἀκαβαρους
(sine acc.) οὔππαρα corr. edd.　Pro ἀκαβαρου Müller in comm. ἀπὸ Βαρυ<γάζων>
19 ἐμπορίω (sine acc.) corr. Gelenius　　γενόμενον corr. Fabr.　　μετὰ δὲ
malim cum Müller　　αὐτὸν corr. Fabr.　　23 βυζαντίω corr. Stuck
τὸ πάρος καὶ T. Müller in comm.　　26 τύνδις τὰ m. alt.: τύμπεστα
29 τυνδίσκη προβότου corr. m. alt.　Κηροβότρου Lassen, Ind. Alt. 3, 193

50. Immediately beyond Barygaza the coast runs from north to south. Thus the region is called Dachinabadês, for the word for south in their language is *dachanos*. The hinterland that lies beyond towards the east contains many barren areas, great mountains, and wild animals of all kinds—leopards, tigers, elephants, enormous serpents, hyenas, and a great many kinds of monkeys, as well as a great many populous nations up to the Ganges.

51. Of the trading centers in the region of Dachinabadês, two are the most outstanding: Paithana, twenty days' travel to the south from Barygaza; and, from Paithana, about ten days to the east, another very large city, Tagara. From these there is brought to Barygaza, by conveyance in wagons over very great roadless stretches, from Paithana large quantities of onyx, and from Tagara large quantities of cloth of ordinary quality, all kinds of cotton garments, garments of *molochinon*, and certain other merchandise from the coastal parts that finds a market locally there. The voyage as far as Limyrikê is 7000 stades in all, but most vessels continue on to the Strand.

52. The local ports [sc. of Dachinabadês], lying in a row, are Akabaru, Suppara, and the city of Kalliena; the last, in the time of the elder Saraganos, was a port of trade where everything went according to law. [Sc. It is so no longer] for, after Sandanês occupied it, there has been much hindrance [sc. to trade]. For the Greek ships that by chance come into these places are brought under guard to Barygaza.

53. Beyond Kalliena other local ports of trade are: Sêmylla, Mandagora, Palaipatmai, Melizeigara, Byzantion, Toparon, Tyrannosboas. Then come the Sêsekreienai Islands as they are called, the Isle of the Aigidioi, the Isle of the Kaineitoi near what is called the Peninsula, around which places there are pirates, and next White Island. Then come Naura and Tyndis, the first ports of trade of Limyrikê, and, after these, Muziris and Nelkynda, which are now the active ones.

54. Tyndis, a well-known village on the coast, is in the kingdom of Kêprobotos. Muziris, in the same kingdom, owes its prosperity to the shipping from

τῆς Ἀριακῆς εἰς αὐτὴν ἐρχομένοις πλοίοις καὶ τοῖς Ἑλληνικοῖς· κεῖται δὲ παρὰ ποταμὸν ἀπέχουσα ἀπὸ μὲν Τύνδεως διὰ τοῦ ποταμοῦ καὶ διὰ θαλάσσης σταδίους πεντακοσίους, ἀπὸ δὲ τοῦ ⟨**⟩ κατ᾽ αὐτὴν εἴκοσι. 3 Ἡ δὲ Νελκύνδα σταδίους μὲν ἀπὸ Μουζίρεως ἀπέχει[ν] σχεδὸν πεντακοσίους, ὁμοίως διά τε ποταμοῦ [καὶ πεζῇ] καὶ διὰ θαλάσσης, βασιλείας δέ ἐστιν ἑτέρας, τῆς Πανδίονος· κεῖται δὲ καὶ αὐτὴ παρὰ ποταμὸν ὡσεὶ ἀπὸ 6 σταδίων ἑκατὸν εἴκοσι τῆς θαλάσσης.

55   Ἑτέρα δὲ κατ᾽ αὐτὸ τὸ στόμα τοῦ ποταμοῦ πρόκειται κώμη Βακαρή, εἰς ἣν ἀπὸ Νελκύνδων ἐπὶ τῆς ἀναγωγῆς προκαταβαίνουσι τὰ πλοῖα· 9   298 ἐπὶ σάλῳ διορμίζεται πρὸς ἀνάληψιν τῶν φορτίων διὰ τὸ τὸν ποταμὸν ἅλματα καὶ διάπλους ἔχει⟨ν⟩ ἐλαφρούς. Αὐτοὶ δὲ οἱ βασιλεῖς ἀμφοτέρων τῶν ἐμπορίων ἐν τῇ μεσογαίῳ κατοικοῦσιν. Καὶ περὶ τούσδε τοὺς τόπους 12 τοῖς ἐκ πελάγους σημεῖον ἐπιβολῆς εἰσὶν οἱ προαπαντῶντες ὄφεις, μέλανες μὲν καὶ αὐτοὶ τὴν χρόαν, βραχύτεροι δὲ καὶ δρακοντοειδεῖς τὴν κεφαλὴν καὶ τοῖς ὄμμασιν αἱματώδεις.   15

56   Πλεῖ δὲ εἰς τὰ ἐμπόρια ταῦτα μεστὰ πλοῖα διὰ τὸν ὄγκον καὶ τὸ πλῆθος τοῦ πιπέρεως καὶ τοῦ μαλαβάθρου. Προχωρεῖ δὲ εἰς αὐτὴν προηγουμένως [δὲ] χρήματα πλεῖστα, χρυσόλιθα, ἱματισμὸς ἁπλοῦς οὐ 18 πολύς, πολύμιτα, στῖμι, κοράλλιον, ὕελος ἀργή, χαλκός, κασσίτερος, μόλιβος, οἶνος δὲ οὐ πολύς, σώζει δὲ τοσοῦτον, ὅσον ἐν Βαρυγάζοις, σανδαράκη, ἀρσενικόν, σῖτος δὲ ὅσος ἀρκέσει τοῖς περὶ τὸ ναυκλήριον διὰ τὸ μὴ τοὺς 21 ἐμπόρους αὐτῷ χρῆσθαι. Φέρεται δὲ πέπερι, μονογενῶς ἐν ἑνὶ τόπῳ τούτων τῶν ἐμπορίων γεννώμενον πολύ, λεγομένη Κοτταναρικῇ. Φέρεται δὲ καὶ μαργαρίτης ἱκανὸς καὶ διάφορος καὶ ἐλέφας καὶ ὀθόνια Σηρικὰ 24 καὶ νάρδος ἡ Γαγγιτικὴ καὶ μαλάβαθρον ἐκ τῶν ἔσω τόπων εἰς αὐτὴν καὶ λιθία διαφανὴς παντοία καὶ ἀδάμας καὶ ὑάκινθος καὶ χελώνη ἥ τε Χρυσονησιωτικὴ καὶ ἡ περὶ τὰς νήσους θηρευομένη τὰς προκειμένας αὐτῆς 27 τῆς Λιμυρικῆς. Πλέουσι δὲ εἰς αὐτὴν οἱ κατὰ καιρὸν ἀναγόμενοι ἀπ᾽ Αἰγύπτου περὶ τὸν Ἰούλιον μῆνα, ὅ ἐστιν Ἐπῖφι.

57   Τοῦτον δὲ ὅλον τὸν εἰρημένον περίπλουν ἀπὸ Κανῆς καὶ τῆς Εὐδαί- 30

---

3 ⟨στόματος τοῦ ποταμοῦ τοῦ⟩ e. gr. Müller in comm.   4 μουνδίρεως corr. m. alt. ἀπέχει[ν] m. alt.   5 [καὶ πεζῇ] Müller   8 βαραρή corr. Schwanbeck   10 ἐπεὶ (pro ἐπὶ) corr. edd.   διὰ δὲ τὸν correxi   11 ἕρματα Müller: ἅλματα   ἔχει⟨ν⟩ Schwanbeck   13 πελάγους ⟨ἐρχομένοις⟩ Schwanbeck   ση- μείοις corr. Stuck   16 μεγάλα Stuck: μεστὰ   18 [δὲ] Stuck   19 ὕελος Stuck: τέλος   20 ὡσεὶ Schwanbeck: σώζει   τοσοῦτος ὅσος εἰς Βαρύγαζαν Fabr. 23 τούτῳ τῷ ἐμπορίῳ corr. Müller   λεγομένη Κοττανακικῇ corr. Müller 25 γαπανικὴ corr. Stuck, Vincent   27 Χρυσονησιωτικὴ Stuck

Ariakê that comes there as well as to Greek shipping. It lies on a river 500 stades distant from Tyndis by river and sea, and from [? the river mouth] to it is 20 stades. Nelkynda is just about 500 stades from Muziris, likewise by river and sea, but it is in another kingdom, Pandiôn's. It too lies on a river, about 120 stades from the sea.

55. Another settlement lies at the very mouth of the river, Bakarê, to which vessels drop downriver from Nelkynda for the outbound voyage; they anchor in the open roads to take on their cargoes because the river has sandbanks and channels that are shoal. The kings themselves of both ports of trade dwell in the interior. Vessels coming from the open sea in the vicinity of these places get an indication that they are approaching land from the snakes that emerge to meet them; these are also black in color but shorter and with dragon-shaped head and blood-red eyes.

56. Ships in these ports of trade carry full loads because of the volume and quantity of pepper and malabathron. They offer a market for: mainly a great amount of money; peridot (?); clothing with no adornment, in limited quantity; multicolored textiles; sulphide of antimony; coral; raw glass; copper, tin, lead; wine, in limited quantity, as much as goes to Barygaza; realgar; orpiment; grain in sufficient amount for those involved with shipping, because the [sc. local] merchants do not use it. They export pepper, grown for the most part in only one place connected with these ports of trade, that called Kottanarikê. They also export: good supplies of fine-quality pearls; ivory; Chinese [i.e., silk] cloth; Gangetic nard; malabathron, brought here from the interior; all kinds of transparent gems; diamonds; sapphires; tortoise shell, both the kind from Chrysê Island and the kind caught around the islands lying off Limyrikê itself. For those sailing here from Egypt, the right time to set out is around the month of July, that is, Epeiph.

57. The whole coastal route just described, from Kanê and

μονος Ἀραβίας οἱ μὲν ⟨πρότεροι⟩ μικροτέροις πλοίοις περικολπίζοντες
299 M. ἔπλεον, πρῶτος δὲ Ἵππαλος κυβερνήτης, κατανοήσας τὴν θέσιν τῶν ἐμπο-
3 ρίων καὶ τὸ σχῆμα τῆς θαλάσσης, τὸν διὰ πελάγους ἐξεῦρε πλοῦν. [ἀφ'
οὗ] καὶ τοπικῶς ἐκ τοῦ ὠκεανοῦ φυσώντων [τῶν] κατὰ καιρὸν τῶν παρ'
ἡμῖν ἐτησίων, ἐν τῷ Ἰνδικῷ πελάγει λιβόνοτος φαίνεται ⟨Ἵππαλος⟩
6 προσονομάζεται δὲ ἀπὸ τῆς προσηγορίας τοῦ πρώτως ἐξευρηκότος τὸν
διάπλουν· Ἀφ' οὗ μέχρι καὶ νῦν τινὲς μὲν εὐθὺς ἀπὸ Κανή, τινὲς δὲ
ἀπὸ τῶν Ἀρωμάτων ἀφιέντες, οἱ μὲν εἰς Λιμυρικὴν πλέοντες ἐπὶ πλεῖον
9 τραχηλίζοντες, οἱ δὲ εἰς Βαρύγαζαν οἵ τε εἰς Σκυθίαν οὐ πλεῖον ἢ τρεῖς
ἡμέρας ἀντέχουσι καὶ τὸ λοιπὸν † παρεπιφέρον πρὸς ἴδιον δρόμον
ἐκ τῆς χώρας ὑψηλοὶ διὰ τοῦ ἔξωθεν γῆς παραπλέουσι τοὺς προειρη-
12 μένους κόλπους.

Ἀπὸ δὲ Βακαρὴ τὸ λεγόμενον Πυρρὸν ὄρος ⟨καὶ⟩ ἄλλη παρῆκε⟨ι⟩ 58
χώρα τη.............κης ἡ Παραλία λεγομένη, πρὸς αὐτὸν τὸν νότον,
15 [ἐν ᾗ καὶ κολύμβησίς ἐστιν ὑπὸ τὸν βασιλέα Πανδίονα πινικοῦ καὶ πόλις
ἡ λεγομένη Κόλχοι]. Πρῶτος τόπος Βαλίτα καλούμενος ὅρμον καλὸν
300 M. ἔχων καὶ κώμην παραθαλάσσιον. Ἀπὸ δὲ ταύτης ἐστὶν ἕτερος τόπος τὸ
18 Κομὰρ λεγόμενος, ἐν ᾧ τόπῳ βριάριον ἐστιν καὶ λιμήν, εἰς ὃν οἱ βουλό-
μενοι τὸν μέλλοντα αὐτοῖς χρόνον ἱεροὶ γενέσθαι χῆροι μένουσιν αὐτοῦ, ἐκεῖ
ἐρχόμενοι ἀπολούονται· τὸ δ' αὐτὸ καὶ γυναῖκες. Ἱστορεῖται γὰρ
21 τὴν θεὸν ἐκεῖ ἐπιμεῖναι κατά τινα χρόνον καὶ ἀπολελοῦσθαι.

Ἀπὸ δὲ τοῦ Κομαρεὶ ἐκτείνουσα χώρα μέχρι Κόλχων, ἐν ᾗ κολύμ- 59
βησις τοῦ πινικοῦ ἐστίν, ἀπὸ δὲ κατακρισίμων κατεργάζεται [πρὸς τὸν
24 νότον]· ὑπὸ τὸν βασιλέα Πανδίονά ἐστιν. Μετὰ δὲ Κόλχους ἐκδέχεται
† πρότερος † Αἰγιαλὸς ἐν κόλπῳ κείμενος, ἔχων χώραν μεσόγειον, λεγομέ-

---

1 ⟨πρότεροι⟩ e. gr. Müller　　4 [τῶν] L, edd.　　5 ⟨Ἵππαλος⟩ Müller　　6 προσονομάζεται δὲ corr. Salmasius　　[ἀπὸ — διάπλουν] ut glossema del. Müller　　ἐξευρηκέναι
corr. Gelenius　　9 οἵ τε Müller: οἱ δὲ　　10 παρεπίφορον πρὸς ἴδιον δρόμον
⟨ἔχοντες ἄνεμον⟩ Müller in comm.; pro παρεπίφορον malim ἐπίφορον　　11 ἐκ τῆς
χώρας suspectum　　διὰ τῆς corr. Müller　　[γῆς] delevi　　13 ἀπ' ἐλαβακαρὴ
corr. Stuck　　⟨καὶ⟩ Müller in comm.; in textu habet ἄλλη παρῆκει χώρα; in Add.
et Corr. proponit ⟨ᾧ vel ὅθεν⟩ ἄλλη κτλ.　　παρῆκε corr. edd.　　14 τῆς⟨ς ὑπὸ Πανδίονι
Ἰνδι⟩κῆς Müller in Add. et Corr.　　15 [ἐν ᾗ κτλ.] ut ex. 19, 22 illata del. Müller
18 Κομαρεὶ malim cum Müller in comm.　　φρούριον Stuck: βριάριον
19 γενέσθαι χῆροι μένουσιν αὐτοῦ, ἐκεῖ ἐρχόμενοι ἀπολούονται· τὸ δ'αὐτὸ transp. Fabr.
addito καὶ deletoque ἐκεῖ　　21 ἐπιμεῖναι Schwanbeck: ἐπὶ μῆνας　　καὶ Schwanbeck: ἐκεῖ　　τὴν θεὸν ⟨Κομαρεὶ⟩ μείνασαν κατά τινα χρόνον ἐκεῖ ἀπολελοῦσθαι Müller in
comm.　　23 [πρὸς τὸν νότον] ut ex 19, 14 illata delevi　　25 † πρότερος †:
ἕτερος Müller in comm.　　λεγόμενον corr. Müller in comm.

Eudaimôn Arabia, men formerly used to sail over in smaller vessels, following the curves of the bays. The ship captain Hippalos, by plotting the location of the ports of trade and the configuration of the sea, was the first to discover the route over open water. . . . In this locale the winds we call "etesian" blow seasonally from the direction of the ocean, and so a southwesterly makes its appearance in the Indian Sea, but it is called after the name of the one who first discovered the way across. Because of this, right up to the present, some leave directly from Kanê and some from the Promontory of Spices, and whoever are bound for Limyrikê hold out with the wind on the quarter for most of the way, but whoever are bound for Barygaza and whoever for Skythia only three days and no more, and, carried along (?) the rest of the run on their own proper course, away from the shore on the high seas, over the [? ocean] off the land, they bypass the aforementioned bays.

58. After Bakarê comes Red Mountain, as it is called, and another region extends . . . called the Seaboard, directly to the south. Its first stopping place, called Balita, is a village on the coast with a good harbor. After this comes another stopping place called Komar, where there is a little settlement and a port; in it men who wish to lead a holy life for the rest of their days remain there celibate; they come there and they perform ablutions. Women, too, do the same. For it is said that at one time the goddess remained there and performed ablutions.

59. Beyond Komar the region extends as far as Kolchoi, where diving for pearls goes on; it is carried out by convicts. The region is under King Pandiôn. After Kolchoi . . . comes the Strand, bordering a bay with, inland, a region named

νην Ἀργάλου· ἐν ἑνὶ τόπῳ † τερονειτε παρ᾿ αὐτὴν τῆς ἠπιοδώρου † συλλεγόμενον πινικόν. Φέρονται δὲ ἐξ αὐτῆς σινδόνες αἱ Ἀργαρίτιδες 301 M. λεγόμεναι.   3

60   Τῶν δὲ κατὰ τοῦτον ἐμπορίων τε καὶ ὅρμων, ἐς οὓς οἵ τε ἀπὸ τῆς Λιμυρικῆς καὶ ἀπὸ ἄρκτου πλέοντες κατάγονται, ἐπισημότερα καὶ κατὰ τὸ ἑξῆς κείμενά ἐστιν ἐμπόρια Καμάρα καὶ Ποδούκη καὶ Σωπάτμα, ἐν 6 οἷς τοπικὰ μέν ἐστιν πλοῖα μέχρι Λιμυρικῆς παραλεγόμενα τὴν γῆν, ἕτερα δ᾿ ἐκ μο⟨ν⟩οξύλων πλοίων μεγίστων ἀφῆς· ἐζευγμένα, λεγόμενα σάνγαρα· τὰ δὲ εἰς τὴν Χρυσῆν καὶ εἰς τὸν Γάγγην διαίροντα κολανδιοφωντα τὰ 9 μέγιστα. Προχωρεῖ δὲ εἰς τοὺς τόπους τούτους πάντα τὰ εἰς τὴν Λιμυρικὴν ἐργαζόμενα, καὶ σχεδὸν εἰς αὐτοὺς καταντᾷ τό τε χρῆμα τὸ ἀπ᾿ Αἰγύπτου φερόμενον τῷ παντὶ χρόνῳ κα⟨ὶ⟩ τὰ πλεῖστα γένη πάντων τῶν ἀπὸ 12 Λιμυρικῆς φερομένων ⟨καὶ⟩ διὰ ταύτης τῆς παραλίας ἐπιχορηγουμένων.

61   Περὶ δὲ ·τῶν μετ᾿ αὐτὴν ·χωρῶν ἤδη πρὸς ἀνατολὴν τοῦ πλοὸς ἀπονεύοντος, εἰς πέλαγος ἔκκειται πρὸς αὐτὴν τὴν δύσιν νῆσος λεγομένη 15 Παλαισιμούνδου, παρὰ δὲ τοῖς † ἀρχαίοις αὐτῶν χαρηρις † ⟨Τα⟩προβάνη. 302 M. Ταύτης τὰ μὲν πρὸς βορέαν ἐστὶν ἥμερα καὶ διαπλεῖται τοῖς εἰς τὸν † πλιονακιστινει † καὶ σχεδὸν εἰς τὸ κατ᾿ αὐτῆς ἀντιπαρακείμενον Ἀζανίας 18 παρήκει. Γίνεται δὲ ἐν αὐτῇ πινικὸν καὶ λιθία διαφανὴς καὶ σινδόνες καὶ χελῶναι.

62   Περὶ δὲ τούτους τοὺς τόπους πολὺ τῆς μεσογείου παρήκουσα Μασαλία 21 παράκειται χώρα· γίνονται ἐν αὐτῇ σινδόνες πλεῖσται. Ἀπὸ δὲ ταύτης εἰς αὐτὴν τὴν ἀνατολὴν διαπεράσαντι τὸν παρακείμενον κόλπον ἡ Δησαρήνη χώρα, φέρουσα ἐλέφαντα, τὸν λεγόμενον βωσαρή, καὶ μετ᾿ αὐτήν, εἰς τὸν 24 βορέαν ἤδη   πλέοντος   τοῦ πλοός, βάρβαρα πολλὰ ἔθνη, ἐν οἷς οἱ Κιρράδαι, γένος ἀνθρώπων ἐκτεθλιμμένων τὴν ῥῖνα, ἀγρίων, καὶ Βαργύσων 303 M. ἕτερον ἔθνος καὶ τὸ τῶν Ἱππιοπροσώπων [Μακροπροσώπων], λεγομέ- 27 νων ἀνθρωποφάγων εἶναι.

63   Μετὰ δὲ ταῦτα εἰς τὴν ἀνατολὴν καὶ τὸν ὠκεανὸν ἐν δεξιοῖς ἐχόντων, εὐώνυμα δὲ τὰ λοιπὰ μέρη ἔξωθεν παραπλεόντων, ὁ Γάγγης ἀπαντᾷ καὶ 30

1 Ἀργάρου Fabr. ἐν ἐνὶ <τούτῳ τῷ> τόπῳ <ἐν οὐδενὶ δὲ ἑ>τέρῳ ὠνεῖται τὸ παρ᾿ αὐτὴν Müller in comm.   ἠπιοδώρου (ι in ras.)   2 δὲ ἐξ scripsi: γὰρ ἐξ   αἱ Ἀργαρίτιδες Müller in comm.: ἐβαργαρείτιδες   κατὰ τοῦτον scripsi: καὶ τούτων   8 ἀφῆς corr. Müller   11 τὸ δὲ corr. Bernhardy, Schwanbeck   12 καὶ τὰ Schwanbeck: κατὰ   13 <καὶ> διὰ Fabr.   14 τῶν . . χωρῶν corr. Müller 16 πάλαι σιμούνδου corr. edd.   voci χαρηρις diversam lectionem ἐπιχωρίοις subesse suspicatus est Müller in Add. et Corr.   τα in Ταπροβάνη e mg. add. m. alt. 23, 24 Δωσαρήνη. . . . δωσαρή Müller in comm.   αὐτόν corr. m. alt.   25 ἀπονεύοντος Stuck: πλέοντος   27 [Μακροπρ.] ut glossam delevi   λεγόμενον corr. Fabr.

Argaru. In one place . . . along it . . . pearls are gathered. It exports the cotton garments called Argaritides.

60. Of the ports of trade and harbors in these parts at which vessels sailing from both Limyrikê and the north call, the more important, lying in a row, are the ports of trade of Kamara, Podukê, and Sôpatma. They are the home ports for local boats that sail along the coast as far as Limyrikê and others, called *sangara*, that are very big dugout canoes held together by a yoke, as well as for the very big *kolandiophônta* that sail across to Chrysê and the Gangês region. There is a market in these places for all the [sc. Western] trade goods imported by Limyrikê, and, generally speaking, there come to them all year round both the cash originating from Egypt and most kinds of all the goods originating from Limyrikê and supplied along this coast.

61. As regards the regions beyond it [sc. the region of Argaru], with the course by now turning off towards the east, there projects due west into the ocean an island now called Palaisimundu, but by its ancient [? inhabitants] Taprobanê. The parts of it that lie towards the north are civilized. . . . It extends almost up to the part of Azania that lies opposite to it. It produces pearls, transparent gems, cotton garments, and tortoise shell.

62. Around this area lies the region of Masalia, extending far inland; a great many cotton garments are produced there. If you go due east from it across the bay that lies alongside, you come to the Dêsarênê region, the habitat of a kind of elephant called Bôsarê. Beyond it, with the course by now towards the north, are numerous barbaric peoples, among whom are the Kirradai, a race of wild men with flattened noses, and another people, the Bargysoi, and the Horse Faces, who are said to be cannibals.

63. After this, heading east with the ocean on the right and sailing outside past the remaining parts to the left, you reach the Gangês region and

ἡ περὶ αὐτὸν ἐσχάτη τῆς ἀνατολῆς ἤπειρος, ἡ Χρυσῆ. Ποταμὸς δέ
ἐστιν περὶ αὐτόν, ὁ Γάγγης λεγόμενος καὶ αὐτός, μέγιστος τῶν κατὰ τὴν
3 Ἰνδικήν, ἀπόβασίν τε καὶ ἀνάβασιν τὴν αὐτὴν ἔχων τῷ Νείλῳ, καθ᾽ ὃν
καὶ ἐμπόριόν ἐστιν ὁμώνυμον τῷ ποταμῷ, ὁ Γάγγης, δι᾽ οὗ φέρεται τό
τε μαλάβαθρον καὶ ἡ Γαγγι⟨τι⟩κὴ νάρδος καὶ πινικὸν καὶ σινδόνες αἱ
6 διαφορώταται, αἱ Γαγγιτικαὶ λεγόμεναι. Λέγεται δὲ καὶ χρυσωρύχια
περὶ τοὺς τόπους εἶναι, νόμισμά τε χρυσοῦ, ὁ λεγόμενος κάλτις. Κατ᾽
αὐτὸν δὲ τὸν ποταμὸν νῆσός ἐστιν ὠκεάνιος, ἐσχάτη τῶν πρὸς ἀνατολὴν
9 μερῶν τῆς οἰκουμένης, ὑπ᾽ αὐτὸν ἀνέχοντα τὸν ἥλιον, κλειομένη Χρυσῆ[ν], χελώνην ἔχουσα πάντων τῶν κατὰ τὴν Ἐρυθρὰν τόπων ἀρίστην.

Μετὰ δὲ ταύτην τὴν χώραν ὑπ᾽ αὐτὸν ἤδη τὸν βορέαν, ἔξωθεν εἰς 64
12 τινα τόπον ἀποληγούσης τῆς θαλάσσης, παράκειται [δὲ] ἐν αὐτῇ πόλις
μεσόγειος μεγίστη, λεγομένη Θῖνα, ἀφ᾽ ἧς τό τε ἔριον καὶ τὸ νῆμα καὶ
τὸ ὀθόνιον τὸ Σηρικὸν εἰς τὴν Βαρύγαζαν διὰ Βάκτρων πεζῇ φέρεται
304 M. 15 καὶ εἰς τὴν Λιμυρικὴν πάλιν διὰ τοῦ Γάγγου ποταμοῦ. Εἰς δὲ τὴν Θῖνα
ταύτην οὐκ ἔστιν εὐχερῶς ἀπελθεῖν· σπανίως γὰρ ἀπ᾽ αὐτῆς τινὲς οὐ
πολλοὶ ἔρχονται. Κεῖται δὲ ὁ τόπος ὑπ᾽ αὐτὴν τὴν μικρὰν ἄρκτον,
18 λέγεται δὲ συνορ[μ]ίζειν τοῖς ἀπεστραμμένοις μέρεσιν τοῦ Πόντου καὶ τῆς
Κασπίας θαλάσσης, καθ᾽ ἣν ἡ παρακειμένη λίμνη Μαιῶτις εἰς τὸν
ὠκεανὸν συναναστομοῦσα.

21 Κατ᾽ ἔτος δὲ παραγίνεται ἐπὶ τὴν συνορίαν τῆς Θινὸς ἔθνος τι, τῷ 65
μὲν σώματι κολοβοὶ καὶ σφόδρα πλατυπρόσωποι, † εν μοι εἰς τέλος † τε
αὐτοὺς λέγεσθαι Σησάτας, ፧ † : παρομοιοῦσιν ἡμέραις †   Παραγίνονται σὺν
24 γυναιξὶν καὶ τέκνοις, βαστάζοντες φορτία μεγάλα, ταρπόναις· ὠμαμπελίνων
παραπλήσια,   εἶτεν ἐπιμένουσιν ἐπί τινα τόπον τῆς συνορίας αὐτῶν καὶ
τῶν ἀπὸ τῆς Θινὸς καὶ ἑορτάζουσιν ἐπί τινας ἡμέρας, ὑποστρώσαντες
27 ἑαυτοῖς τὰς ταρπόνας, καὶ ἀπαίρουσιν εἰς τὰ ἴδια εἰς τοὺς ἐσωτέρους
τόπους. Οἱ ⟨**⟩ ταῦτα δοκοῦντες καὶ τότε παραγίνονται ἐπὶ τοὺς τόπους
καὶ συλλέγουσι τὰ ἐκείνων ὑποστρώματα καὶ ἐξινιάσαντες καλάμους τοὺς

---

5 γαγγι⟨τι⟩κὴ Stuck   6 χρυσορύχια (in mg. χρυσωρύχια) corr. L, Stuck   7 νο-
μίσματα χρυσοῦ corr. m. alt.   9 κλειομένη χρυσῆν corr. Salmasius   12 [δὲ]
m. pr.   17 ὑπ᾽ Müller: ἐπ᾽   18 συνορ[μ]ίζειν m. alt.   22 σφοδροὶ corr. Salmasius
† εν μοι εἰς τέλος † : coll. Ptol. 7, 2, 15 et 17, Per. 14,7 sic fere scribere pro-
posuerim: [σιμοὶ εἰς τέλος] ⟨λευκοὶ δὲ τῇ χροιᾷ· φασίν⟩   23 παρομοιοῦσιν ἡμέραις
corr. Salmasius   24, 27 ταρπόνας Salmasius: τέρπονας   25 παραπλήσια corr. Vossius ad Pomp. Melam 3, 7   εἶτ᾽ ἐνεπι- correxi   26 ἀπὸ scripsi: ὑπὸ
ἑορτάζουσιν Vossius l. c., Fabr.: ἁρπάζουσιν   28 lacunam statui   ⟨καρα⟩-
δοκοῦντες Salmasius; δοκεύοντες Müller

in its vicinity the furthest part of the mainland towards the east, Chrysê. There is a river near it that is itself called the Ganges, the greatest of all the rivers in India, which has a rise and fall like the Nile. On it is a port of trade with the same name as the river, Gangês, through which are shipped out malabathron, Gangetic nard, pearls, and cotton garments of the very finest quality, the so-called Gangetic. It is said that there are also gold mines in the area, and that there is a gold coin, the *kaltis*, as it is called. Near this river is an island in the ocean, the furthest extremity towards the east of the inhabited world, lying under the rising sun itself, called Chrysê. It supplies the finest tortoise shell of all the places on the Erythraean Sea.

64. Beyond this region, by now at the northernmost point, where the sea ends somewhere on the outer fringe, there is a very great inland city called Thina from which silk floss, yarn, and cloth are shipped by land via Bactria to Barygaza and via the Ganges River back to Limyrikê. It is not easy to get to this Thina; for rarely do people come from it, and only a few. The area lies right under Ursa Minor and, it is said, is contiguous with the parts of the Pontus and the Caspian Sea where these parts turn off, near where Lake Maeotis, which lies parallel, along with [sc. the Caspian] empties into the ocean.

65. Every year there turns up at the border of Thina a certain tribe, short in body and very flat-faced . . . called Sêsatai. . . . They come with their wives and children bearing great packs resembling mats of green leaves and then remain at some spot on the border between them and those on the Thina side, and they hold a festival for several days, spreading out their mats under them, and then take off for their own homes in the interior. The [? locals], counting on this, then turn up in the area, collect what the Sêsatai had spread out, extract the fibers from the reeds,

λεγομένους πέτρους, ἐπὶ λεπτὸν ἐπιδιπλώσαντες τὰ φύλλα καὶ σφαιροειδῆ
ποιοῦντες διείρουσιν ταῖς ἀπὸ τῶν καλάμων ἴναις. Γίνεται δὲ γένη τρία·
ἐκ μέν τοῦ μείζονος φύλλου τὸ ἀδρόσφαιρον μαλάβαθρον λεγόμενον, ἐκ 3
δὲ τοῦ ὑποδεεστέρου τὸ [ὑπο]μεσόσφαιρον, ἐκ δὲ τοῦ μικροτέρου τὸ μικρό- 305 M.
σφαιρον. Ἔνθεν τὰ τρία μέρη τοῦ μαλαβάθρου γίνεται καὶ τότε φέρεται
εἰς τὴν Ἰνδικὴν ὑπὸ τῶν κατεργαζομένων αὐτά.   6

66   Τὰ δὲ μετὰ τοὺς τόπους τούτους διά τε ὑπερβολὰς χειμώνων καὶ
πάγους μεγίστου δυσβάτων τε τόπων, εἶτα καὶ θείᾳ τινὶ δυνάμει θεῶν
ἀνερεύνητά ἐστιν.   9

---

2 διαίρουσιν corr. Salmasius   3—5 -σφερον (supra ε punctum pos. m. pr.)
corr. Stuck   ἐκ δὲ τοῦ Stuck: καὶ τοῦ   4 [ὑπο] μεσ. m. alt.   8 μεγίστους
(ult. ς s. scr. m. pr.)
De subscriptione scribae: διώρθωται οὐ πρὸς σπουδαῖον ἀντίγραφον, cf. p. 33.

which are called *petroi*, and lightly doubling over the leaves and rolling them into ball-like shapes, they string them on the fibers from the reeds. There are three grades: what is called big-ball malabathron from the bigger leaves; medium-ball from the lesser leaves; and small-ball from the smaller. Thus three grades of malabathron are produced, and then they are transported into India by the people who make them.

66. What lies beyond this area, because of extremes of storm, bitter cold, and difficult terrain and also because of some divine power of the gods, has not been explored.

GENERAL COMMENTARY

1:1.1   Erythraean Sea

Although the term means literally "red sea," the ancients used it not to refer to our Red Sea (which they called the "Arabian Gulf") but to a larger body of water; see Sidebotham 182–86, an exhaustive compilation of all occurrences. In the *Periplus* it embraces our Red Sea, Gulf of Aden, and western Indian Ocean. Sidebotham's statement (183) that in the *Periplus* "Erythra Thalassa = Red Sea, Indian Ocean, Persian Gulf throughout" is an error; the author calls the Persian Gulf precisely that (35:11.31).

1:1.2–4   Myos Hormos . . . Berenicê

For references and bibliography, see the entries in A. Calderini, *Dizionario dei nomi geografici e topografici dell'Egitto Greco-Romano* iii, fasc. 3, ed. S. Daris (Milan, 1982) and ii, fasc. 1, ed. S. Daris (1972); also D. Meredith in *JEA* 38 (1952): 102, n. 6 and 39 (1953): 99, n. 6.

Berenicê is securely located. Strabo describes it (16.769–70) as lying in a recess of the *Akathartos Kolpos*, "Foul Bay," just north of an island noted for its *topazia* or *topazos* (Strabo 16.770, Pliny 37.107). The bay is still called Foul Bay; the Cape of Ras Banas (23°54′N, 35°47′E), jutting out sixteen miles eastward, forms a deep recess; and St. John's Island (Jazirat Zabarjad), about thirty miles southeast (23°37′N, 36°12′E), is the world's richest source of peridots, which must be what in ancient writings is often called "topaz" (cf. A. Lucas and J. Harris, *Ancient Egyptian Materials and Industries* [London, 1962⁴] 402) and in the *Periplus chrysolithon* (see under 39:13.8a). See D. Meredith, "Berenice Troglodytica," *JEA* 43 (1957): 56–70, esp. 59; Desanges 271–72; and, on St. John's Island, F. Moon, *Preliminary Geological Report on St. John's Island* (Cairo, 1923) 2 (location), 8–9 (peridots). Berenicê was founded by Ptolemy Philadelphus (282–246 B.C.), who named it after his mother (Pliny 6.168). The extensive ruins, lying no more than a mile from the harbor (23°55′N; Meredith 58–59), may include some of Ptolemaic date. A temple there, for example, has at least one Ptolemaic inscription (of Ptolemy VII [145/144 B.C.]; Meredith 69), though all the others are Roman (60–69). There are the remains of

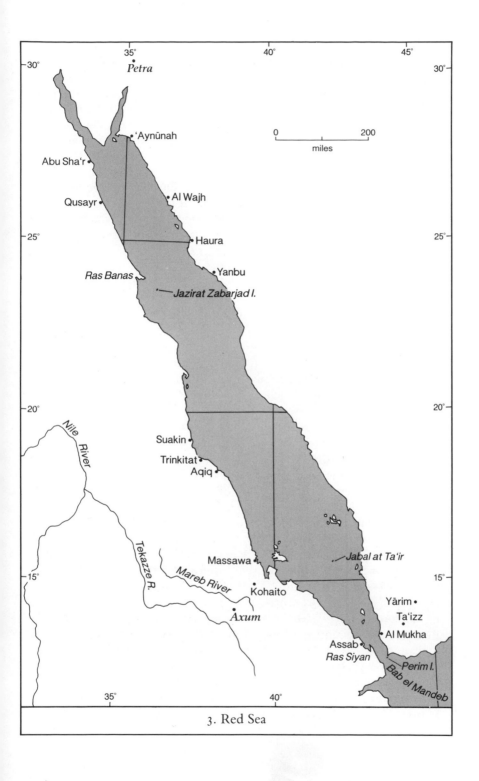

3. Red Sea

two Roman forts, of which one is among the biggest in the eastern desert (57).

Myos Hormos, "Mussel Harbor," so named for the rich beds there (cf. H. Kees, *RE* s.v. *Myos Hormos* 1081 [1933]; L. Kirwan, *GJ* 147 [1981]: 82), can also be considered more or less securely located, despite some lingering disagreement. Strabo (16.769) makes it clear that it lay north of Berenicê and gives a description, but it is Pliny's remark (6.168) that there was a spring nearby which provides a vital clue. In the region that qualifies for consideration, there is but one spot blessed with good water, namely Abu Sha'r (27°23'N, 33°35'E), and it boasts, moreover, the remains of a Roman fortified town; see Wellsted ii 123–25 (who noted that "the advantage of good water in the vicinity of its port rendered Myos Hormus a valuable station"), G. Murray in *JEA* 11 (1925): 141–42 and *GJ* 133 (1967): 32, Meredith in *JEA* 38 (1952): 102–4, Desanges 269–70. A number of commentators, including Müller and Schoff, place Myos Hormos further south at Abu Sawmah (26°51'N, 34°0'E), but there is no water there; cf. Kees 1082. Huntingford locates it at Qusayr (26°6'N, 34°17'E) but that—or rather Qusayr al-Qadim, just to the north—is surely the site of the port of Leukos Limên. In recent years this has been carefully excavated, revealing unmistakable evidence of contact with Arabia and India; see D. Whitcomb and J. Johnson, *Quseir al-Qadim 1978: Preliminary Report* (Cairo, 1979) and *Quseir al-Qadim 1980: Preliminary Report* (Malibu, 1982).

Strabo states (2.118) that in his day 120 vessels sailed, presumably annually, from Myos Hormos to Arabia and India. Previously as few as twenty had sailed from all Red Sea ports (17.798). The *Periplus* couples it with Berenicê as the only two ports serving this trade, and conformably, these two alone appear in the archive of Nicanor (see Introduction: Trade in the Indian Ocean, Between Alexandria and the Red Sea). From both Myos Hormos and Berenicê to Koptos there were well-marked routes fitted with watering stations for the caravans traversing this thirsty stretch and with forts and garrisons for their protection. See G. Murray, "The Roman Roads and Stations in the Eastern Desert of Egypt," *JEA* 11 (1925): 138–50; D. Meredith, "The Roman Remains in the Eastern Desert of Egypt," *JEA* 38 (1952): 94–111, 39 (1953): 95–106; R. Bagnall, *The Florida Ostraca: Documents from the Roman Army in Upper Egypt*, Greek, Roman, and Byzantine Monographs 7 (Durham, 1976) 34–39; Sidebotham 58–67. Myos Hormos to Koptos (ca. 130 miles) took six to seven days (Strabo 17.815), Berenicê to Koptos, a much longer route (ca. 270 miles), eleven to twelve (Pliny 6.103, and cf. Bagnall 37).

Leukos Limên must have flourished after the *Periplus* was written, for its first mention occurs in Ptolemy (4.5.8). In Strabo's day Myos Hormos apparently was the chief port for trade with Africa and India, for it is the only one he mentions (2.118, 16.781) in that connection. In the archive of Nicanor, Myos Hormos and Berenicê seem of equal rank. By the time the author of the *Periplus* was writing, Berenicê clearly took precedence: it is from here that he starts the trade routes to both Africa (18:6.21–22) and India (19:6.26), and from here that he reckons the length of the voyage down the Red Sea (21:7.19–20). Berenicê had one great advantage over Myos Hormos: it was some 230 nautical miles further south, and that spared homebound vessels days of beating against the northerlies that prevail in the Red Sea above latitude 20° (Wellsted ii 166; Murray 138–39; *SDRS*, sector 1–27). Merchants might have saved six to seven days in overland transport by sailing past Berenicê to discharge at Myos Hormos but they might well have lost a month in making the attempt (cf. Claire Préaux in *Chronique d'Égypte* 53 [1952]: 271; she was told by locals that from Qusayr to Suez, some 230 nautical miles, could take a month). These troublesome northerlies may well lie behind Strabo's remark (17.815) that Ptolemy II made Berenicê accessible by opening up a road to it "because the Red Sea is hard to sail, particularly for those who set sail from the innermost recess"; those who set sail from the innermost recess obviously had to get back there, and that, no question about it, involved hard sailing.

1:1.3   1800 stades

An underestimate, since the distance (Abu Sha'r to Foul Bay, ca. 230 nautical miles) is closer to 2300 stades.

2:1.7–10   Ichthyophagoi, Barbaroi, Agriophagoi, Moschophagoi

These were tribes that inhabited the lands between the coast of the Red Sea and the Nile Valley, the region the author calls Barbarikê. It is barren and hostile, which explains the names the Greeks gave to its dwellers: the coastal folk had to live off fish (Ichthyophagoi, "fish eaters"), those inland off game (Agriophagoi, "wild animal eaters") or edible shoots and stalks (Moschophagoi). The author is interested in anthropological pecularities; he notes them in a number of places (see Introduction: Text and Author, The Author and His Work).

The Ichthyophagoi of this area are also described by Diodorus and Strabo and others; see E. Jahn, *RE* s.v. *Trogodytai* 2498 (1948). Their information about the Red Sea and its environs derives largely from accounts by the geographer Agatharchides, whose *floruit* was about 120

97

B.C., and Artemidorus, who dates a few decades later. The Agriophagoi, save for irrelevant mentions in Pliny (6.195) and Solinus (30.6), occur only here and in a bilingual (Greek and Latin) inscription (*IGRR* i 1207) of Hadrian's time (A.D. 117–138) found at Thebes, a votive dedicated by a Roman officer who had fought in a successful engagement against the *Agriophagos nequissimos*, "the most evil Agriophagoi." The Moschophagoi are not attested elsewhere, but they could well be the same as the peoples the Greek geographers dubbed Rhizophagoi, "root eaters," or Spermatophagoi, "seed eaters" (Diodorus 3.23, 24).

The *Barbarikê chôra*, "country of the Barbaroi" (*Barbaria* in 5:2.20) of the *Periplus*, is called by these geographers *Trôgodytikê*, "country of the Trogodytes" (*Trôgodytai* or, less properly, *Trôglodytai*; cf. Warmington's foreword to the article by Murray in *GJ* 133 [1967]: 24), whom they describe as a primitive race of nomadic herders of cattle (Agatharchides in *GGM* i 153–56, cf. Diodorus 3.32–33; Artemidorus in Strabo 16.775–76). It would seem that "Trogodytes" was the general term for all the dwellers of the area and that these included Trogodytic Ichthyophagoi, Trogodytic Barbaroi, and so on (cf. Jahn 2498 and Pliny 6.176, where Ichthyophagoi are included among the Trogodytes). There were other Ichthyophagoi—i.e., non-Trogodytic—living along the east coast of the Red Sea (20:7.6) and the south coast of Arabia (27:9.3, 33:11.16), and there were other Barbaroi living along the west coast of the Straits of Bab el Mandeb (7:3.19, 22) and the east coast of Africa (17:6.17). No Moschophagoi other than the Trogodytic are mentioned and, as we learn in the next chapter (3:1.12), these reached only as far south as Ptolemais Thêrôn, whereas there were Trogodytic Barbaroi and Ichthyophagoi still further south around Adulis (4:2.4, 15).

The Barbaroi very likely were herders, like the Trogodytes of the geographers' descriptions, while the other three would be peoples who had not reached even that modest level of civilization. When Henry Salt visited the area at the beginning of the last century, this was precisely the situation he found. Around Baia d'Anfile (14°51′N, 40°46′E), he came across natives of whom he says (177–79):

> No people in the world is more straitened with respect to the necessaries of life; a little juwarry bread, a small quantity of fish, an inadequate supply of goats and camels milk, and a kid on very particular occasions constitutes the whole of their subsistence. In the interior they live a little better, and possess large droves of cattle. . . .
>
> Their huts are constructed in the shape of the wigwams of the American Indians, and are covered with mats formed out of the leaves of the doom-tree.

The Ichthyophagoi presumably ate more fish and drank less milk, the Agriophagoi more game, and the Moschophagoi more edible plants. Their "mean huts," however, could well have been just like those Salt describes. The geographers note that the Trogodytes were organized in groups under chiefs (*GGM* i 153, Diodorus 3.32, Strabo 16.775), just as were the peoples in the *Periplus*.

The geographers give the impression that the Trogodytes were a backward race utterly remote from the Greek world, and other reports are eloquent witness to their savagery. They were, for example, a menace to travelers passing through their territory; at the sanctuary of Pan at El-Kanaïs, a station on a major route connecting Berenicê with the Nile Valley, there has been found a series of Greek votives, dating from the third to the first century B.C., dedicated by individuals, probably mostly soldiers, who thank the deity for their "having been saved from the Trogodytes" (see A. Bernand, *Le Paneion d'El-Kanaïs: Les inscriptions grecques* [Leiden, 1972], 3, 8, 13, 18, 43, 47, 62, 82, 90). And the *Periplus* itself reports (4:2.1–4) that at Adulis, the most important port of trade on the west coast of the Red Sea, because of raids carried out by the local Barbaroi, the port had to be moved from its original location to an island a safe distance away. On the other hand, the Greek papyri from Egypt reveal that at least some Trogodytes were very much a part of the Greek world. For example, for two weeks in 257 B.C. a group of Trogodytes, along with an interpreter, received pay from Egypt's finance minister at a place a little north of Memphis, probably Heliopolis; see *P. Corn.* 1.149, 180, 228; *P. Col.* 3.5.27 and 32, 4.63.4; and, for the location, U. Wilcken in *Archiv für Papyrusforschung* 8 (1927): 69–72 and C. Edgar, *P. Mich. Zen.*, p. 21. In *UPZ* 227 (2d century B.C.), a certain Apollonios, "interpreter of the Trogodytes," receives pay from a royal bank; as Wilcken, the editor, points out, this would indicate that he held some official position. Another Trogodyte is attested serving as a shipper; see *PSI* 332.14 (257/256 B.C.) and Wilcken's comments in *Archiv* 8 (1927): 72. A Trogodyte slave appears in *P. Oxy.* 1102.25 (A.D. 142). Indeed, the Trogodytes had such well-established relations with Egypt that Cleopatra, an accomplished linguist who preferred to do without interpreters, spoke their language as well as Hebrew, Arabic, Syrian, and Persian (Plutarch, *Antony* 27.3–4).

That language was probably one of the Hamitic (Cushitic) family, the Trogodytes being forerunners of some of the Hamitic peoples who today inhabit the Red Sea littoral as well as parts of Ethiopia and Somalia; cf. R. Oliver and G. Mathew, eds., *History of East Africa* i (Oxford, 1963), 68–71. Indeed, A. Paul, *A History of the Beja Tribes of the Sudan* (Cambridge, 1954), 23, 35–37, 52–54, holds that the Beja of the Sudan are their direct descendants.

2:1.7–8 Ichthyophagoi living in mean huts built in narrow areas

On the Greek word translated "mean huts," see under B 2:1.7. Quite possibly they were similar to the primitive huts observed by travelers of the last century (see under 2:1.7–10) and still used by the Beja who inhabit the region today (cf. G. Murray, "Trogodytica: The Red Sea Littoral in Ptolemaic Times," *GJ* 133 [1967]: 24–33 at 24). The "narrow areas" could well mean that the huts were clustered along the wadis where these met the coast; as Murray (25) points out, "there is usually a slow seepage of fresh water down each wadi's bed, which may be tapped by a shallow well at the mouth. Such creeks and brackish wells sufficed for the needs of the Ichthyophagoi."

2:1.11 a metropolis called Meroe

The manuscript is defective at this point (there is even a blank space that would accommodate some eight to nine letters), and these words are a restoration that all recent editors and translators have approved. For a survey of the history of Meroe, see P. Shinnie in *CHA* ii 210–59 (1978). Located near the Sixth Cataract of the Nile, it was well suited as a center for trade between Central Africa and Egypt and, by the beginning of the Christian Era, had grown into a flourishing metropolis. It was gradually overtaken by the rising kingdom of Axum (see under 4:2.8). By the end of the fourth century A.D., it ceased to be of importance; cf. S. Burstein, "Axum and the Fall of Meroe," *Journal of the American Research Center in Egypt* 18 (1981): 47–49.

3:1.13 about 4000 stades

If Ptolemais Thêrôn is correctly located at Aqiq (see under 3:1.14), the distance is actually 350 nautical miles or so, i.e., 3500 stades (see App. 2). The author overestimates the next leg as well; see under 4:1.19–20.

3:1.14 Ptolemais Thêrôn

Strabo (16.770) reports that Ptolemais Thêrôn, "Ptolemais of the Hunts," was founded by Ptolemy Philadelphus (282–246 B.C.), and a description on the Pithom Stele of the expedition he sent out narrows the date to sometime between 270 and 264 and reveals that it was a full-scale colonial venture involving the cultivation of the surrounding fields and the raising of flocks; see C. Conti Rossini in *Aegyptus* 6 (1925): 6 and Desanges 273. Strabo further reports that the leader of the colonizing expedition successfully made friends with the natives; presumably these were Moschophagoi, since their territory at the time the *Periplus* was written lay just to the north (3:1.12–14). The colony's purpose was to provide not only a base for the parties dispatched to capture beasts for the army's elephant corps (cf. under 4:2.11), but also a port for the ships that transported them up the Red Sea; see H. Treidler, *RE* s.v. *Ptolemais Thêrôn* (1959). Commentators all agree on its general location—on the coast somewhere between latitude 19° and 18°—but not on the exact site. The choices offered are, from north to south: Suakin, 19°08′N, 37°21′E (Huntingford's second choice); Marsa Maqdam, 18°44′N, 37°40′E (Müller, *GGM* i 172; Bunbury i 578); Trinkitat, 18°41′N, 37°45′E (Treidler 1879–80); Aqiq, 18°12′N, 38°10′E (Fabricius; Murray in *GJ* 133 [1967]: 26; Huntingford's first choice and seemingly approved by N. Chittick in *Azania* 16 [1981]: 181); er Rih, 18°11′N, 38°28′E (McCrindle; Schoff). Treidler, on the basis of a study of the maps, argues for Trinkitat, though he admits (1879) the lack of any archaeological evidence. J. Crowfoot, on the basis of voyages under sail to the area as well as an extended visit in which he carried out some exploratory digging, makes a strong case for Aqiq; he claims to have found a piece of Greco-Roman molding embedded in a later structure, as well as extensive remains from the period of Axumite domination ("Some Red Sea Ports in the Anglo-Egyptian Sudan," *GJ* 37.5 [May 1911]: 523–50, esp. 531–34). I. Hofmann, who visited the region in 1970, also favors Aqiq (Desanges 274).

At the time of the *Periplus* the hunting parties had long been a thing of the past, and the port, with a mediocre harbor and its trade reduced to the export of tortoise shell and scant amounts of ivory, must have been but a shadow of what it had been under the early Ptolemies. Politically it seems to have been part of Zôskalês' kingdom (see under 5:2.19–20).

3:1.15–16   tortoise shell

Tortoise shell receives more mention in the *Periplus* than any other object of trade. It was exported by, or available at, ports in all the regions the author mentions: Red Sea (Ptolemais Thêrôn 3:1.15–16; Adulis 4:2.14–15, 6:3.4; Avalitês 7:3.20), the horn and east coast of Africa (Mosyllon 10:4.11; Opônê 13:5.5; Menuthias 15:5.28, 6.1; Rhapta 16:6.6, 17:6.19), Socotra (30:10.11–16), southern coast of Arabia (Isles of Zênobios 33:11.17–18), India (Muziris/Nelkynda 56:18.26–28), Ceylon (61:20.20), Malay or Sumatra (63:21.10). Commercial tortoise shell today comes from a single source, the handsome shields of the hawksbill turtle (*Eret-*

mochelys imbricata), a large sea turtle, and is used mostly for smaller objects: combs, brushes, and personal adornments such as rings, brooches, and the like. The Greeks and Romans, as is clear from this passage and others (15:5.28, 30:10.11–13) as well as from other authors (Pliny 9.39, 33.146; Martial 9.59.9), used the shell of several varieties, terrestrial as well as aquatic, and used it above all for large objects, for veneering beds, sideboards, dining couches, doors, etc.; see H. Blümner, *Technologie und Terminologie der Gewerbe und Künste bei Griechen und Römern* ii (Leipzig, 1879), 375–78. The "genuine" tortoise shell is no doubt that of the hawksbill turtle, which is found in many waters, including the Red Sea; see A. Loveridge and E. Williams, *Revision of the African Tortoises and Turtles of the Suborder Cryptodira*, Bulletin of the Museum of Comparative Zoology, Harvard College 115.6 (1957): 488–89. There are only three land turtles native to the area, *Kinixys belliana, Geochelone pardalis babcocki*, and *Geochelone sulcata* (Loveridge-Williams, table 2). The first is too small to furnish usable shell, the largest specimen noted being but eight inches or so long (Loveridge-Williams 391). The other two, however, are big creatures two feet or more in length (Loveridge-Williams 228, 233, 241–42). *Geochelone pardalis babcocki* is very likely what the author in a later passage refers to as "mountain" tortoise (see under 30:10.11–13), which leaves *Geochelone sulcata* for his "land" tortoise. It is lighter in color than the other (Loveridge-Williams 228) and the juvenile is lighter still (Loveridge-Williams 233). Thus the shell characterized as "a light-colored variety with rather small shields" might well be that of the juveniles.

3:1.17   ivory

See under 4:2.11.

4:1.19–20   About 3000 stades

If Ptolemais Thêrôn is correctly located at Aqiq (see under 3:1.14), the distance to Adulis (= Massawa; see under 4:1.19–2.15) is actually 180 nautical miles or so, i.e., 1800 stades (App. 2). Pliny (6.173) says that the run from Ptolemais Thêrôn took five days; assuming he means daytime runs, or 500 stades a day (App. 2), his estimate comes reasonably close to the *Periplus's* figure.

4:1.19–2.15   Adulis . . . by the Ichthyophagoi

The "deep bay" is Annesley Bay (or the Gulf of Zula, as it is also called), and Oreinê would be Dissei Island (15°28′N, 39°45′E), which lies at the mouth just about 20 nautical miles, or 200 stades, from the bottom of the bay. Early commentators did not hesitate to identify the fine harbor of Massawa (15°37'N, 39°28'E)—the only good natural harbor on the west coast of the Red Sea—which lies just before the bay, as the site of Adulis's port. The residential area was separate, since we are distinctly told that it lay 20 stades, some two miles, inland; if we assume that it was south of the port, in from Ras Amas (15°32'N, 39°35'E), everything fits: Didôrus Island would be what is today called Taulud; the modern causeway bearing water pipes and telephone lines that connects it with the mainland runs over shallows that could well have been the ford used by the raiders; Oreinê/Dissei Island, to which the port had been shifted because of the raiders, would lie opposite just six miles across the mouth of the bay, and the sandy islets lying in front towards the open sea would be Sheikh Said, Madote, Sciumma, and others around Dahlach Chebir.

In 1810 Henry Salt came upon ancient ruins some twenty-five miles south of Massawa, at a point halfway down the western shore of Annesley Bay. They lay along the bank of a stream four miles in from the coast, about three-quarters of a mile northwest of the modern town of Zula. The natives called the place "Azoole," and Salt concluded (451–53) that this was the site of Adulis. Subsequent archaeological exploration unearthed the remains of what had long been a modest settlement but, in the fourth to the sixth centuries A.D., had grown into a full-fledged center boasting impressive stone structures. Since this period was precisely when the kingdom of Axum was in its heyday (see under 4:2.8), and Adulis, being its sole access to the sea, was serving as its sole port, the identification seemed triumphantly confirmed and has since never been questioned (cf. E. Littmann, *RE* Suppl. 7.1–2 [1940]).

There is, however, one serious difficulty: the site of the ruins does not at all fit the description in the *Periplus*. There is no trace of an island and ford anywhere in the vicinity of the nearby coast; there is nothing in the way of a harbor there but merely a very gently shelving beach; this beach is not "on . . . the coast [i.e., the one being described, the west coast] opposite Oreinê" [Dissei Island] but a good twelve miles south of it; and there certainly are no sandy islets lying in front in the open sea. One solution is to assume that while, on the one hand, the port was always at Massawa, the natural place for it (save for the emergency when it had to be moved to nearby Dissei Island), on the other hand, the residential area was transferred. At the time of the *Periplus*, when Adulis amounted to merely a "fair-sized village," it was on the coast opposite Dissei Island. The location, while conveniently near the port, had one grave drawback—lack of water. So long as the settlement remained but a "fair-sized village" this was not fatal. However, as the kingdom of Axum increased

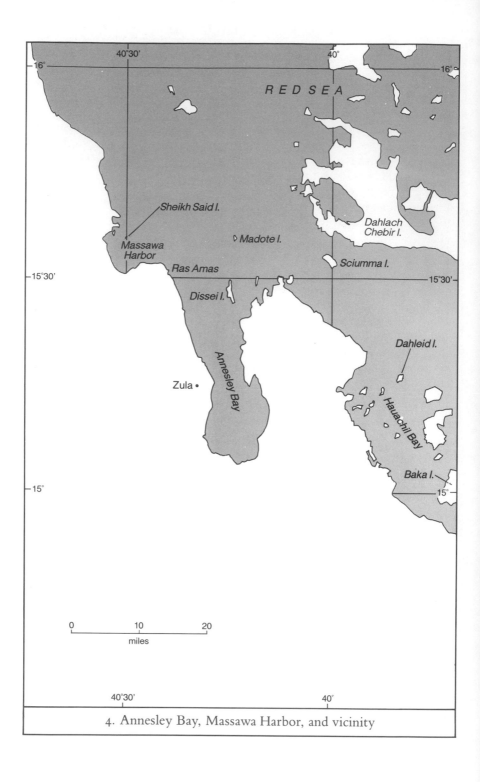

4. Annesley Bay, Massawa Harbor, and vicinity

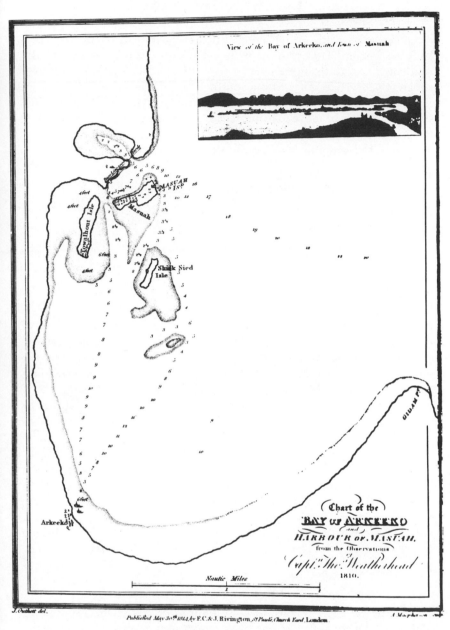

5. Massawa Harbor. Reproduced from H. Salt, *Voyage to Abyssinia*
(London, 1814)

in power and wealth, Adulis inevitably increased in size until the draw-back did become fatal; at some point the decision was taken to shift the residential area to the nearest settlement where water was available, by a stream twenty-five miles to the south. A good parallel is furnished by Basra: founded in A.D. 635 as a military camp, centuries later circumstances caused it to move to its present location, a dozen miles away from the original (cf. *Encyclopaedia of Islam* s.v. 1086–87 [1960²]). For a full discussion of the question, see Casson 1981 = Casson 1984.199–210.

4:1.20   a legally limited port of trade

See App. 1.

4:2.6   Koloê

Ptolemy (4.7.25) lists Koloê but places it considerably south of Axum, which does not at all suit the location indicated by the *Periplus*. At Ko-haito, a spacious plateau (2600 meters above sea level) on the road between Massawa and Adua just north of Adi Caieh, there are extensive ruins dating from the late Axumite period: remains of churches, tombs, and an impressive dam made of ashlar blocks and measuring sixty-seven meters in length and three high in the central portion, for impounding water (F. Anfray in Mokhtar 368–69). J. Bent was the first to suggest the identification with Koloê: "it is exactly where it should be, according to the description in the '*Periplus*,' three days from Adulis and five from Aksum, and on a mountain, immediately below which the ancient trade route into Ethiopia passed" (*The Sacred City of the Ethiopians* [London, 1893], 223). The identification has been almost universally accepted; see Schoff, Huntingford, Conti Rossini (115), Anfray (in Mokhtar 364). Y. Kobishchanov (*Axum* [University Park, Pa., 1979], 57, 141, 170, 171, 177, 185, 187) assumes that Matara, where Axumite ruins have also been found (Anfray in Mokhtar 367–68), is Koloê without ever discussing the merits of the case. It certainly does not fit the *Periplus's* travel time as well.

4:2.8   Axômitês

This is the earliest reference to the kingdom of Axum that, some two centuries later, qualified as one of the most important in its part of the world. At its height, from the second half of the third to the seventh century, it embraced a rectangular area that stretched east-west from the Red Sea to about longitude 30° and north-south from latitude 17° to 13° (F. Anfray in Mokhtar 363). Here, sometime around the middle of the first millennium B.C., a civilization arose consisting of a mix of native Ethiopic elements and Semitic elements from south Arabia (H. de Contenson in Mokhtar 341–59; P. Shinnie in *CHA* ii 262 [1978]). The *Periplus* is evidence that, by the first century A.D., in at least the coastal area, Hellenization had already begun, a Hellenization that is clearly evident during the kingdom's flourishing period. When, in the third century A.D., the Axumites began to mint their own coins, these bore legends in Greek, and Axumite inscriptions were carved in Greek as well as Sabaean and Ethiopic (E. Littmann in *RE* Suppl. 7.77–78 [1940]). Impressive ruins have been uncovered at Axum: remains of temples, palaces, tombs, and giant stelae; see Littmann 76 and, on the more recent excavations, H. de Contenson in *JA* (1960): 85–91, 92–93 (summary) and N. Chittick in *Azania* 9 (1974): 159–205. As to other Axumite sites—Zula, Kohaito, Matara—these date mostly from the nation's great period (Anfray in Mokhtar 364–69), the fourth century A.D. and after, and are thus considerably later than the *Periplus*.

4:2.9–10   from beyond the Nile through what is called Kyêneion

Schoff, assuming that the author referred to the river we know by that name, identified Kyêneion as Sennar, just across the Blue Nile some 350 airline miles west of Axum, and he has been followed by Huntingford and others (e.g., S. Hable-Selassie, *Beziehungen Äthiopiens zur griechisch-römischen Welt* [Bonn, 1964], 74; S. Munro-Hay in *Azania* 17 [1982]: 109). Yet elephants were to be hunted much nearer than that; at the beginning of this century, for example, they were still plentiful in Walkeit, the region beyond the Tekazze River, a mere seventy-five miles west of Axum (A. Wylde, *Modern Abyssinia* [London, 1901], 489). Moreover, there is no reason to assume that "Nile" here refers to the actual Nile; the ancients were understandably hazy about its upper waters, and it seems that they took various rivers in Ethiopia to be part of it (cf. M. Cary and E. Warmington, *The Ancient Explorers* [Penguin, 1963²], 210, 214). In the second inscription on the Monumentum Adulitanum (Cosmas Indicopleustes 2.104D Winstedt), a king of Axum boasts of conquests "beyond the Nile," and he almost certainly means beyond the Tekazze (cf. J. McCrindle, *The Christian Topography of Cosmas, an Egyptian Monk* Hakluyt Society No. 98 [London, 1897], 61; Conti Rossini 123). The same confusion could very well be true here; Kyêneion, then, would be Walkeit. Another possibility is that the Mareb rather than the Tekazze is meant; that would bring Kyêneion even closer, some twenty-five miles from Axum and to the north rather than the west (see Conti Rossini 115, who suggests equating Kyêneion with Cohain [when Eritrea was an Italian colony, Cohain was the administrative district embracing the area within the loop of the Mareb due north of Axum]). Around the headwaters of the Baraka, somewhat north of Cohain, elephants were seen during the last century (W. Gowers in *African Affairs* 47 [1948]: 178).

4:2.11   elephants

On elephants in general, see H. Scullard, *The Elephant in the Greek and Roman World* (Ithaca, N.Y., 1974). It was believed in antiquity that the African elephant was smaller than the Indian (Scullard 60), although we know today that the reverse is true. Very probably the beasts that were captured and trained for use in the elephant corps of the Ptolemaic army (cf. Scullard 124–37, 143) were forest elephants (*Loxodonta africana cyclotis*), which rarely grow taller than eight feet to the shoulder, and not bush elephants (*Loxodonta africana africana*), which generally do (Scullard 60–63). The forest elephant, now found only as far east as the Nile Valley, in ancient times no doubt reached up to the Red Sea although, as the *Periplus* itself makes clear, it was already being hunted out of existence there. During the third and second centuries B.C. the forest elephant was both captured for the army and slaughtered for its ivory, and the slaughtering continued throughout antiquity. Ptolemy XII, in 54 B.C., donated to the temple of Apollo at Didyma thirty-four tusks weighing a total of 24 talents, 20 mnas (T. Wiegand, *Didyma. Zweiter Teil: Die Inschriften*, von A. Rehm [Berlin, 1958] 240), an average per tusk of ca. forty-two pounds or one-fifth less, depending upon whether the Attic or Ptolemaic talent is meant; whichever it is, the tusks must have been from the smaller, forest elephant (Gowers [op. cit. under 4:2.9–10] 178). No doubt hunters brought down whatever prey they came across, and this may explain what the author intends by "Adulis (ivory)" (3:1.17); it would be from the smaller tusks of the forest elephant, which was found around Adulis, as against those of the bush elephant, which had to be sought inland. For a picture of an elephant tusk uncovered at Adulis, see F. Anfray in Mokhtar 380.

4:2.14   Alalaiu

Cf. under 4:1.19–2.15. These are islets of the Dahlach group just opposite Massawa; cf. Vincent 105, Müller, Schoff, Littmann in *RE* Suppl. 7.1 (1940).

5:2.16–18   very deep, bay . . . obsidian is found

This, without question, is Hauachil Bay (Baia di Ouachil), for Salt tells how he sailed into it, landed on the shore of the recess at 15°12′N (15°9′ on his chart opposite p. 453), walked to a hill in the vicinity, and "was delighted with the sight of a great many pieces of a black substance, bearing a very high polish, much resembling glass, that lay scattered about on the ground at a short distance from the sea; and I collected nearly a hundred specimens of it, most of which were two, three or four inches in diameter. . . . This substance has been analyzed since my return to England, and proves to be the true opsian, or obsidian, stone" (192). The actual distance from Massawa (or Zula) to the bay is nearer 500 stades than 800, as Salt was aware (cf. 194). On the chart, Hauachil Bay is a shallower indentation than Annesley, although the author describes it as deeper; perhaps he was thinking in terms of the distance from northwest to southeast, from inside Dahleid Island (15°17′N, 40°10′E) to below Baka Island (14°57′N, 40°18′E).

5:2.19–20   The ruler of these regions . . . is Zôskalês

Most commentators hold that Zôskalês was the king of Axum, the earliest known: see Conti Rossini 119; E. Littmann in *RE* suppl. 7.76 (1940); F. Gisinger in *RE* s.v. *Zoskales* (1972); F. Altheim and R. Stiehl, "Die Anfänge des Königreiches Aksūm," in E. Haberland, M. Schuster, and H. Straube, eds., *Festschrift für Ad. E. Jensen* (Munich, 1964), 3, 11; H. de Contenson, "Les premiers rois d'Axoum d'après les découvertes recentes," *JA* (1960): 75–95 at 77; Kobishchanov (op. cit. under 4:2.6) 54–59; F. Anfray in Mokhtar 362; P. Shinnie in *CHA* ii 264 (1978). Kobishchanov (54–59; in Mokhtar 381) is convinced that Zôskalês is to be identified with the Za-Haqâlê of the Abyssinian king list, but this list is late and most unreliable (cf. Huntingford 149). From the third century on, the sequence of kings is fairly sure, thanks to the evidence of their coins; see S. Munro-Hay in *Azania* 14 (1979): 26–27 and 19 (1984): 136 for an updated list.

A number of commentators hold that he was but a local ruler, in charge of the coastal area as subordinate of the king of Axum: see Huntingford 147–50; N. Chittick in *Azania* 16 (1981): 186; E. Gray in *Classical Review* 95 (1981): 276; J. Rougé in *Index. Quaderni camerti di studi romanistici* 15 (1987): 408; M. Rodinson, *Annuaire de l'École pratique des Hautes Études*, ive Section, Sciences historiques et philologiques (1974–75), 217, straddles the fence. But this view overlooks the fact that the author of the *Periplus* calls such subordinates *tyrannoi* (see under B 2:1.9–10), whereas he clearly refers to Zôskalês as a king (5:2.19: *basileuei*, "rules as king"; 6:2.33: "for [the] king").

There is a third possibility—that Zôskalês was king not of Axum but of an independent realm centered on Adulis and embracing the coastal areas to the north and south. In a paper presented at the *Colloque de Strasbourg, 24–27 juin 1987: L'Arabie préislamique*, G. Fiaccadori, on the basis of the later history of Adulis and its environs, argued that the area previously must have been independent; it follows that Zôskalês would have been its ruler at the time the *Periplus* was written. Epiphanius of Constantia (4th century A.D.), in a list of peoples living along the African shore of the Red Sea in the third century A.D., includes *Azomitorum cum ⟨A⟩dulitibus*, "the Axumites along with the Adulitans" (*Corpus Scriptorum Ecclesiasticorum Latinorum* 35, p. 478; cf. Desanges 346); this would indicate not only that Axum and Adulis were separate but that they long remained so.

Zôskalês' sway, we are told, extended as far as the border shared with the Moschophagoi and that shared with the "rest of Barbaria." This means that, to the north, it included Ptolemais Thêrôn which, being below the territory of the Moschophagoi (3:1.12–14), must have fallen within the embrace of Zôskalês' territory and, to the south, it reached as far as the Straits of Bab el Mandeb; the "rest of Barbaria" was the "farside" Barbaria (cf. under 7:3.10–11), that which lay on and beyond the straits as against the Barbaria that reached from below Berenicê to the northern border of Zôskalês' kingdom. Perhaps his realm took in some of the mountainous country inland from the coast. The list of items "for the king" includes (6:2.35) *kaunakai*, which are heavy cloaks. They would hardly be needed along the littoral, where in February, the coldest month of the year, the temperature averages 79° and does not go below 71°, but could well be useful in the highlands.

6:2.23–3.3   there is a market for . . . lac dye

The long and detailed list of imports attests to Adulis's commercial importance. Conformably, Pliny (6.173) calls it "the biggest port of the Troglodytes and, indeed, of the Ethiopians." He too lists ivory, tortoise shell, and rhinoceros horn as its exports, along with several others.

6:2.23–24   articles of clothing for the Barbaroi, unused, the kind produced in Egypt

These must have been garments of the kind worn by the Barbaroi that were manufactured in Egypt for sale to them. *P. Oxy.* 1684 (4th century A.D.), a list of clothing, includes (lines 5, 9) the term *barbarikion*, which must be an item of such clothing; cf. U. Wilcken in *Archiv für Papyrusforschung* 7 (1924): 98. On "unused," see under B 6:2.23a. At certain smaller ports traders were able to sell used clothing to the Barbaroi, e.g., at Avalitês garments that had been cleaned by fulling (7:3.17), at Malaô cloaks that had been cleaned and dyed (8:3.27–28).

6:2.24   wraps from Arsinoe

Arsinoe, an important town in the Fayum and a provincial capital, was noted for its textiles. See *Archiv für Papyrusforschung* 5 (1913): 388–89 for mention of "tunics of Arsinoe" and "clothing of Arsinoe." The "wraps from Arsinoe" may well have been of linen; the town boasted a special quarter given over to linen weavers (*ESAR* ii 332; Raschke 904, n. 1000). In 8:3.27 cloaks (*sagoi*) of Arsinoe are among the items exported to Malaô.

6:2.24a   *abollai*

Abollai were cloaks that ranged in quality from the common, heavy types worn by peasants or soldiers to those elegant enough for a king (Suetonius, *Cal.* 35); see R. Murri in *Aegyptus* 23 (1943): 106–10. They came in various colors (cf. *Stud. Pal.* 20.46.20, 2d–3d century A.D. [dark brown]; Martial 8.48.1 and Suetonius, loc. cit. [purple]), the kind obviously preferred by buyers at Adulis, as well as in plain white (cf. *SB* 9834 b 5, 3d century A.D.; *Stud. Pal.* 20.15.9, 2d century A.D.).

6:2.24b   of printed fabric

See under B 6:2.24–25.

6:2.25   double-fringed items

Cf. under B 6:2.25. The items might have been anything from small kerchiefs to large spreads; cf., e.g., Y. Yadin, *The Finds from the Bar Kokhba Period in the Cave of Letters* (Jerusalem, 1963), 241–44 (double-fringed kerchiefs), 245–46 (double-fringed spreads), 246–47 (double-fringed scarves).

6:2.25–26   glass stones and also of millefiori glass

"Glass stones" occurs as well among the items imported by Avalitês (7:3.16) and by Rhapta and the Azanian ports (17:6.15–16). The Greek word translated "stones" is *lithia*, which was commonly used as a generic term for precious stones (see under B 10:4.9). Here it must refer to glass imitations of such stones, "trifles of glass," as M. Trowbridge suggests ("Philological Studies in Ancient Glass," *University of Illinois Studies in Language and Literature* 13 [1928]: 231–436 at 251). The Greek word translated "millefiori glass" is *myrrhinê,* "myrrhine [glass]." It cannot here refer to true "myrrhine vessels" *(vasa myrrhina [murrea]),* for these were imported by the Roman West, not exported from it, and commanded astronomical prices; to own one was the hallmark of great wealth. This was because they were carved out of some valuable stone, although precisely what stone is a matter of controversy; for a review of the problem, see Trowbridge 313–24. Current opinion favors fluorspar: see S. Ball, *A Roman Book on Precious Stones* (Los Angeles, 1950), 217–19; A. Loewental and D. Harden, "Vasa Murrina," *Journal of Roman Studies* 39 (1949): 31–37. The *myrrhinê* listed here, an Egyptian export to minor settlements on the African coast, must be imitations in glass of true *vasa myrrhina* (cf. Ball 220, Loewental-Harden 33, Warmington 378), probably the type now called millefiori, a highly ornamental kind resulting from the manipulation of colored rods to produce composite canes and the slicing of these to form multitudinous flowerlike designs that are then embedded in a glass body. Fragments of such glass have been found at Heis, almost certainly the site of the *Periplus's* Mundu (see under 9:4.1).

6:2.26   Diospolis

Diospolis, the translation into Greek of *No-Ammon* (H. Kees, *RE* s.v. *Thebai* 1556 [1934]), was the common name for Thebes during the Ptolemaic and Roman periods. See Daris (op. cit. under 1:1.2–4) ii, fasc. 2 s.v.

6:2.26a   brass

Oreichalkos (the variant spelling in the text also occurs in the Greek papyri from Egypt; cf. *P. Giss.* 47.6 and Frisk 41–42), literally "mountain copper," originally referred to some kind of copper but by the end of the first century A.D. was used of brass. Brass was produced by alloying copper with zinc-bearing ore (zinc as a metal was unknown in ancient times); see R. Forbes, *Studies in Ancient Technology* 8 (Leiden, 1964), 265–75 and, on the nomenclature, 275–76.

6:2.32   resident foreigners

Presumably merchants from Roman Egypt who had settled in Adulis to carry on business there.

6:2.32–33   wine of Laodicea and Italy

Laodicea on the Syrian coast (modern Latakia) was the major supplier of wine to Alexandria (Strabo 16.752). Several ostraca found at Koptos record shipments that went up the Nile to Koptos and from there were transported overland to Myos Hormos (*O. Tait.* i P241 [A.D. 35], P289 [A.D. 60–61], P290 [A.D. 62]). Other ostraca attest shipments of the fine Italian wine, Aminaean, that went via Koptos to Berenicê (*O. Tait* i P224 [A.D. 6] and P240 [A.D. 34]; Aminaean came from a grape that Pliny [14.21] rates as the very best and was so costly that it was once subjected to price regulation [14.95 and cf. *ESAR* i 284–85]). The quantities listed on the ostraca are so small as to suggest that these shipments were for local consumption rather than export; see Introduction: Trade in the Indian Ocean, n. 11.

6:2.33–35   For the king . . . in price

Cf. under 24:8.7–9. The author notes (5:2.20–21) that Zôskalês is a hard man when it comes to possessions, and this may explain why the items for his court—goldware and silverware fashioned in the local manner and clothing of no great value—are fewer and much less extravagant than those listed for other courts (cf. 24:8.7–9, 28:9.16–18, 49:16.25–28).

6:2.35   *kaunakai*

The *kaunakês* was a type of heavy cloak developed by the Babylonians which proved so useful that it was adopted from India (cf. 6:3.3) to Italy (see J. Przylusky in *JRAS* [1931]: 343, 347). B. Hemmerdinger (*Glotta* 48 [1970]: 50–51) derives the name from a late Babylonian word *gunnaku*, Przylusky (347) from an Iranian **gaunaka*. The earliest *kaunakai* were made of fur or sheepskin or the like, but these later came to be copied in wool with a deep pile (cf. Hesychius s.v.). The *kaunakai* here presumably were of wool.

6:2.35a   with no adornment

See under B 6:2.34–35.

6:3.1   Ariakê

Part of northwestern India; see under 41:14.2–3.

6:3.1a   Indian iron and steel

"Indian iron" (*ferrum Indicum*) apparently was of high enough quality to justify importation by the West. It is included among the oriental imports subject to customs duty under Marcus Aurelius and Commodus (*Dig.* 39.4.16). Ctesias (*Ind.* 4) was given a pair of swords by the Persian king and the queen mother; these, presumably of fine quality, were of iron from India. Indians presented Alexander with a gift of 100 talents (almost 6000 pounds) of "white iron" (*ferrum candidum*; Quintus Curtius 9.8.1). Pliny states (34.145) that the very best iron is "Chinese iron" (*Sericum ferrum*), but this could well be iron from India which the Romans attributed to China; cf. R. Forbes in C. Singer, ed., *A History of Technology* ii (New York, 1956), 57. Chinese sources themselves refer to steel as coming from India or Persia; see S. Laufer, *Sino-Iranica*, Field Museum of Natural History, Publication 201, Anthropological Series xv.3 (Chicago, 1919), 515.

6:3.1–2   cotton cloth . . . *sagmatogênê*

Literally "Indian cloth," on which see App. 4. On *monachê* and *sagmatogênê*, see under B 6:3.2 and B 14:5.11–12.

6:3.3   garments of *molochinon*

Probably cotton garments of some sort; see under B 6:3.3.

6:3.3a   garments of cotton

See App. 4.

6:3.3b   lac dye

See Watt ii 409–12, s.v. *Coccus lacca*. Lac is "the resinous incrustation formed on the bark of the twigs [of certain trees], through the action of the lac insect." The red dye made from it has been used by "the natives of India from remote times . . . not only for textile purposes but as a pigment."

6:3.4   rhinoceros horn

Rhinoceros horn was made into oil flasks for the wealthy; see Juvenal 7.130.

6:3.6   from Tybi to Thoth

On the use of Egyptian month names, see Introduction: Text and Author, The Author and His Work.

6:3.6–7   the best time for departure from Egypt is around the month of September

See App. 3, n. 15.

7:3.8   trends eastward

Cf., two lines below, "on an eastward heading." Following the coast, the course from Ptolemais Thêrôn to Adulis would have been roughly south-southeast. From Adulis to Avalitês it would have been southeast, in other words, not due east but merely a little more easterly.

7:3.9   4000 stades

The total distance from Adulis, including the 800 stades from there to Hauachil Bay (see under 5:2.16–18), was 4800; on this figure, see App. 2 and under 7:3.13–14.

7:3.10–11   the rest of the ports of trade of the Barbaroi, those called "far-side," lying in a row

The "far-side" ports were the African ports on the far side of the Straits of Bab el Mandeb, namely Malaô, Mundu, Mosyllon, the Spice Port, and Opônê, most of which do indeed lie in a row. They were not part of a state; each was independent, ruled by its own chief (14:5.14–16). Ptolemy's list (4.7.10) of ports of trade beyond the straits in what he calls the Gulf of Avalitês (= Gulf of Aden) includes Avalitês (see under 7:3.13–14), Malaô, Mundu, Mosylon [sic], Kobê (presumably founded after the time of the Periplus), Akannai (see under 11:4.17–18), Spice Port. Since Ptolemy is writing a geography and not a manual for traders, he places (4.7.11) Opônê in his next area, what he calls the Gulf of Barbarikê (= western Indian Ocean).

7:3.13–14   The first is called Avalitês; at it the crossing from Arabia to the other side is shortest

Ptolemy (4.7.10) places Avalitês beyond the straits but the Periplus thrice unequivocally locates it in the straits: first here; then a few lines below

(7:3.19–20), where we are told that Avalitês' exports go "to Okêlis and Muza on the opposite shore"; and last in 25:8.13–15, where the Straits of Bab el Mandeb are described as being where "the Arabian mainland and the country of Barbaria across the water in the vicinity of Avalitês converge." Despite this, translators and commentators insist on placing Avalitês where Zeila now stands, on the southwestern shore of the Gulf of Aden (11°22′N, 43°28′E). They favor Zeila because it was a center of trade in later centuries (cf. *Encyclopaedia of Islam* s.v. *Zaila* [1934]), Avalitês' modest harbor fits Zeila's as described by travelers (cf., e.g., R. Burton, *First Footsteps in East Africa* [Memorial Edition, London, 1894], i 11), and it suits the distances given in the *Periplus* for Avalitês—4800 stades from Adulis (see App. 2), 800 from Malaô (= Berbera; see under 8:3.24)—better than any other possibility, being some 3500 stades from the first and 1000 from the second. Yet it is nowhere near the Straits of Bab el Mandeb, where "the crossing from Arabia is . . . shortest." Glaser (ii 195), tacitly rejecting Zeila, was certain that Avalitês lay on the north shore of the Gulf of Tadjoura, near Obock or Tadjoura, and some commentators agree (e.g., G. Mathew in Oliver-Mathew [op. cit. under 2:1.7–10] 94); this puts it considerably closer to the straits than Zeila but still well south of them.

The candidate that best fits the author's words, as L. Kirwan has suggested (*GJ* 147 [1981]: 83), is Assab on the African side just north of the straits (13°00′N, 42°44′E): it is more or less opposite Muza and just above the point where the sea so narrows that the shores are but some sixteen nautical miles apart (Zeila is a good eighty miles across the water from the nearest point on the Arabian coast). It has a usable harbor.

There is yet another possibility, one raised by Strabo's description of Bab el Mandeb. Right where the straits proper are, at the narrowest point between the two shores, he locates (16.769) on the African side a promontory named Deirê with a native town of the same name nearby and, on the Arabian side, what he calls Akila, the Okêlis of the *Periplus*. Very likely the native town was eventually Hellenized to become what Pliny (6.170) calls *Berenice Epidires* "Berenicê on Deirê." J. Desanges, on the basis of an exhaustive analysis of all the relevant texts ("Le littoral africain du Bab el-Mandeb d'après les sources grecques et latines," *Annales d'Ethiopie* 11 [1978]: 83–101), demonstrates that Strabo's promontory Deirê is most likely Ras Siyan (12°29′N, 43°19′E), which lies just under fifteen nautical miles across from Ras Bab el Mandeb on the other side. Deirê thus fits the *Periplus's* description of Avalitês even more exactly than Assab—but it would leave Avalitês with a very poor harbor indeed.

The *Periplus's* figure of 4800 stades from Adulis to Avalitês may seem to favor Zeila since Assab is but 2500 stades away, Ras Siyan about 3000, and Zeila 3700, but only at first sight. The figure the author gives for the run from Berenicê to Muza (see App. 2), just across the water from Ava-litês, reveals how greatly he can overestimate distance in these parts.

More of a problem is the 800 stades he gives for the run from Avalitês to Malaô (8:3.23–24). Malaô is almost certainly Berbera (see under 8:3.24); Assab is some 2100 stades away from Berbera, Ras Siyan 1600, Zeila 1000. Müller, who identified Avalitês with Zeila, was troubled by even the relatively small discrepancy between the *Periplus's* 800 and the actual distance of 1000, and suggested that perhaps a scribe had erred in copying the figure; such an explanation would take care of 2100 just as well as 1000. In any event, it is safer to rely on the author's unambiguous description of the location rather than his figures for distance, which can never be more than rough estimates (see App. 2).

Yet another ghost that haunts the locating of Avalitês is a mysterious modern village named Abalit. McCrindle mentions (55), without further comment, the existence of one such on the north shore of the Gulf of Tadjoura forty-three statute miles from the straits and twenty-seven from the town of Tadjoura; this would place it ca. 11°58′N, 43°14′E, some four miles west of Obock. Schoff states explicitly what McCrindle presum-ably had in mind, that Avalitês' "ancient name is preserved by the village Abalit," and this Abalit stubbornly turns up in the footnotes of those who deal with Avalitês (e.g., R. Mauny in the *Journal de la Société des Africa-nistes* 38 [1968]: 25, n. 1; Desanges 334, n. 166). There is certainly no settlement of any kind on that spot right now, and the nineteenth-century descriptions of the region make no mention of any (e.g., P. Barre in *Re-vue de géographie* 46 [1900]: 459–60 lists for the north shore of the Gulf of Tadjoura only Ambabo, Sagallo, Tadjoura, Obock). Even if an Abalit did exist there, why use it as evidence to support an identification with Zeila? Zeila is on the opposite coast, forty nautical miles distant over open water. N. Chittick reports (*Azania* 16 [1981]: 187) that he "was told of a hamlet along the coast to east of Zaila with a name resembling Abalit"; this would not answer to the location in the *Periplus* any more than Zeila itself.

By characterizing Avalitês as "first," the author cannot mean that it was the first of the far-side ports since, by his own description, it lay on the straits and not on the far side of them. Nor did it lie in a row with the others (cf. under 7:3.10–11). He just means it was the first port ships came to after the 4000-stade sail, the first in the next homogeneous trading area.

7:3.15   rafts

The use of rafts is mentioned again a few lines below (7:3.19). If, as seems likely, the rafts used in the straits were the same as those used along the

South Arabian coast, they were buoyed rafts; see under 27:9.9. Strabo, quoting Artemidorus (16.778), refers to the use of "leather boats" for crossing the straits, and Agatharchides to the Sabaeans' use on the Red Sea of "leather conveyances" (101, *GGM* i 189); strictly speaking such terms should refer to coracles (cf. *SSAW* 5–7) but, in view of the context, they may well be loose expressions for buoyed rafts.

7:3.16–17   some of the unripe olives that come from Diospolis

See under B 7:3.16–17 and, on Diospolis, under 6:2.26.

7:3.17   cleaned by fulling

That is, used clothing, which apparently found a market in a backwater like Avalitês. Adulis, on the other hand, required new clothing; cf. under 6:2.23–24.

7:3.18   tin

Cf. Introduction: Trade in the Indian Ocean, The Trade in Metals. The tin may just possibly have come from Egypt itself. There are deposits there, though it is questionable whether they were exploited in ancient times; see Lucas-Harris (op. cit. under 1:1.2–4) 253. It seems more likely that Roman Egypt, in common with most of the Mediterranean lands, imported tin, probably from Spain or Brittany (J. Muhly, *Copper and Tin: The Distribution of Mineral Resources and the Nature of the Metals Trade in the Bronze Age*, Transactions of the Connecticut Academy of Arts and Sciences 43 [Hamden, Conn., 1973], 253–55), including some for export.

7:3.20   a minimal amount of myrrh

On myrrh in the ancient world, see A. Steier, *RE* s.v. *myrrha* (1935). The Egyptians used it in embalming, the Greeks and Romans as incense and deodorant and spice, in pomades and perfumes, and in medicines (Steier 1142–45; for the evidence of the Greek papyri, see I. Andorlini in *Atti e memorie dell'Accademia Toscana di Scienze e Lettere* 46 [1981]: 61–65). As a medicine it was particularly used for treating wounds (modern experiments confirm its effectiveness; see G. Majno, *The Healing Hand* [Cambridge, Mass., 1975], 215–19) and as an ingredient in prescriptions for eye trouble (Andorlini 64). According to Pliny (12.70), on the Roman market myrrh cost between 11 and 16½ denarii a Roman pound; this

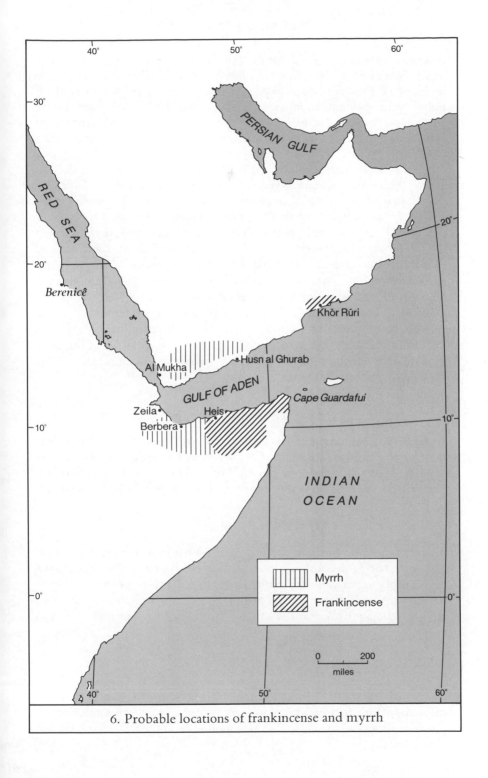

6. Probable locations of frankincense and myrrh

makes it expensive—over twice the price of the finest frankincense (6 denarii; see under 27:9.8–9) and four times that of bdellium (3 denarii; see under 37:12.20)—but far less expensive than the aromatics imported from India, such as cinnamon (see Casson 1984.230), nard (see under 39:13.10b), or malabathron (see under 65:21.21–22.6). Myrrh comes from *Commiphora myrrha* Nees, a scraggly, thorny tree found in Somalia and South Arabia. In Somalia it grows in the northwestern parts (see R. Drake-Brockman, *British Somaliland* [London, 1912], 302–5; G. Van Beek, "Frankincense and Myrrh in Ancient South Arabia," *JAOS* 78 [1958]: 141–52 at 143–44 [both of these writers use the older name for the tree, *Balsamodendron myrrha*]; N. Groom, *Frankincense and Myrrh* [London, 1981], 118–19) and has remained an important export right up to this century (see R. Pankhurst, "The Trade of the Gulf of Aden Ports of Africa in the Nineteenth and Early Twentieth Centuries," *Journal of Ethiopian Studies* 3.1 [1965]: 36–81 at 40–41 [Zeila], 45, 51, 56 [Berbera]). Since Avalitês was on the western edge of where the myrrh trees grew (Map 6), it handled only a "minimal amount"; cf. under 10:4.13. The ancients considered "Trogodytic myrrh," i.e., the myrrh from this area (cf. under 2:1.7–10), the very best (Pliny 12.69, Diosc. 1.64.1); this may explain why Arabia, which produced myrrh of its own (cf. 24:8.9–10), also imported from Somalia.

7:3.21   rather unruly

As late as the beginning of this century, visitors made the same observation about the locals of the area. Cf. Barre (op. cit. under 7:3.13–14) 459–60: along the north shore of the Gulf of Tadjoura, "les noirs Afars ou Danakils . . . sont sanguinaires et beaucoup tuent pour le plaisir de tuer."

8:3.24   Malaô

This is modern Berbera (10°27′N, 45°1′E). What makes the identification almost certain is the author's mention that the harbor is "sheltered by a promontory extending out from the east." There is precisely such a promontory at Berbera; see the map in Schoff (79) and cf. M. Schwabe, *RE* s.v. *Malao* (1930). For the distance from Avalitês, see under 7:3.13–14.

8:3.27   cloaks from Arsinoe

The word translated "cloaks" is *sagoi*. The *sagum*—to give it its Latin name, by which it is best known—was a wool cloak worn pinned at the shoulder. It was a particular favorite among both officers and men in the

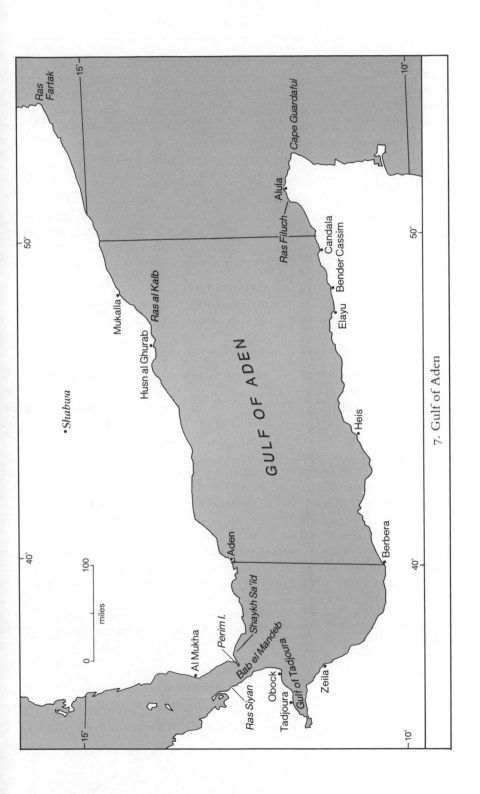

7. Gulf of Aden

Roman army; there were also cheap versions for rustics and the urban poor (see L. Wilson, *The Clothing of the Ancient Romans* [Baltimore, 1938], 104–9). Those shipped to Malaô were presumably a cheaper grade and secondhand at that (cf. under 7:3.17). On Arsinoe as a center for textiles, see under 6:2.24.

8:3.28–29 Roman money, in limited quantity, both gold and silver

Cf. 6:2.32, where the author lists a small amount of Roman money for dealings with resident Greco-Roman merchants. The limited quantity listed here is no doubt for the same purpose (and not, as has been claimed [Raschke 1010, n. 1483] for use as bullion).

8:3.30 myrrh

Cf. under 10:4.13.

8:3.30a a little "far-side" incense

For a comprehensive review of frankincense in the ancient world, its sources, nomenclature, production, uses, etc., see W. Müller, *RE* Suppl. 15 s.v. *Weihrauch* (1978). Like myrrh, frankincense came from Somalia and South Arabia; the "far-side" was Somalian, exported from the African ports on the "far side" of the Straits of Bab el Mandeb (cf. Müller 726). The trees in both areas are similar but distinct: the Somalian frankincense comes from *Boswellia frereana* and *Boswellia carteri* (Drake-Brockman [op. cit. under 7:3.20] 305–6), the Arabian from *Boswellia sacra* (N. Hepper, "Arabian and African Frankincense Trees," *JEA* 55 [1969]: 66–72, esp. 67, and cf. Müller 703). In Somalia the area producing frankincense lies more or less east of that producing myrrh, roughly from Berbera almost to Cape Guardafui (see Map 6 and cf. Van Beek [op. cit. under 7:3.20] 143). Like myrrh, frankincense was long a profitable export of the area; see Pankhurst (op. cit. under 7:3.20) 40 (Zeila), 48 and 53 (Berbera), 60 (Bender Cassim), 61 (Hafun).

Malaô was on the western edge of the frankincense region and hence its production was limited. For the price of frankincense see under 27:9.8–9.

8:3.30–13:5.4 cassia

On cassia in general, see "Cinnamon and Cassia in the Ancient World," Casson 1984.225–46. Cassia was available at most of the other "far-side" ports besides Malaô: Mundu (9:4.3, where it is presumably included among the "aforementioned"), Mosyllon (10:4.10), Spice Port (12:4.27), Opônê (13:5.4). Mosyllon is singled out as supplying by far the greatest quantity.

The author refers only to cassia, never cinnamon, although other ancient writers use both terms. The distinction was not, as today, botanical, but purely qualitative: cinnamon was the finer (Casson 227). Earlier writers, such as Herodotus and Theophrastus, were convinced that Arabia was the country of origin. Later writers, some of whom, such as Pliny, were aware that neither cinnamon nor cassia grew there, were convinced the source was the part of Africa known today as Ethiopia and Somalia (Casson 233). The author of the *Periplus* belongs to this school: as his language makes clear, he considered cassia a product of the area around the "far-side" ports, notably Mosyllon and Opônê.

What we call cinnamon comes from the bark of *Cinnamomum zeylanicum* Nees, and cassia from that of *Cinnamomum cassia* Blume, both of the laurel family (Casson 225). These trees do not grow in Arabia or Ethiopia or Somalia. Indeed, no member of the laurel family does grow there or could, for laurels require constant moisture; they could not possibly stand the periods of dryness that are part and parcel of the climate of the areas in question. It is pointless to suggest, as some commentators have, that the trees that supplied Greece and Rome once grew there but have since disappeared, the victims of disease or the like; the climate rules out such theorizing (Casson 233–36).

Strabo (16.782) and Philostratus (*VA* 3.4) mention India as a source, and in this they were close to the truth of the matter. For the cinnamon and cassia of the ancient world most likely came from mainland Southeast Asia and southern China. From there they were shipped to India, which forwarded to the West whatever was not needed locally. The best explanation for the West's ignorance about where cassia and cinnamon originated is that the forwarding was not done in Greek or Roman ships but in Arabian or Indian, whose owners and skippers, in order to maintain their hold on this lucrative trade, made a secret of the source and kept it so well that dealers from Egypt, picking up their supplies at the "far-side" ports, were convinced they were buying a local African product (Casson 233–39). As it happens, cinnamon and cassia were not the only Eastern products about whose source Western writers were mistaken. Pliny, for example, thought (12.28, 50) that ginger and cardamom came from Arabia.

For some reason the Arabs or Indians trading in cassia concentrated on Mosyllon as their principal disposal point, for the *Periplus* reports it as the place that shipped out the greatest quantity (10:4.9–10). Malaô could offer only one of the poor grades, a "rather harsh cassia"; on the ancients' various grades of cinnamon and cassia, see Casson 228–29 [at the bottom of 228 the following was inadvertently omitted: "Galen 14.73: The cassia called *gizi* (cf. 14.67: 'Called by dealers' "].

8:3.31   *duaka*

The word occurs nowhere else. It has been suggested (cf. F. Olck, *RE* s.v. *Casia* 1646 [1899]) that it derives from the Sanskrit *twak*, "bark," and that it is connected with *darka* or *dakar*, the name given by Dioscorides (1.13.2) to a cheap grade of cinnamon (cf. Casson 1984.229); if this linguistic association is correct, then the *duaka* shipped out of Malaô, like the cassia, unbeknownst to the author of the *Periplus*, was an import from India. On the other hand, Glaser (ii 197) connects it with the Arabic *duka*, the name of a variety of incense from Somaliland, while Watt (i 369) mentions "*dukh*, the Arabic name of the gum *Hotai*," and *Hotai* is the Somali name for the gum resin of *Commiphora playfairii*, a tree that is common on the maritime mountains south and southeast of Berbera (Drake-Brockman [op. cit. under 7:3.20] 310–11). If this association is correct, then *duaka* was no import but a local product.

8:3.31a   *kankamon*

Unlike *duaka*, which is unattested elsewhere, *kankamon* is described by several ancient writers. It appears to be a gum resin that is similar to myrrh. To cite Dioscorides (1.24), it is "the exudation of an Arabian wood, in a certain way resembling myrrh, . . . which is used as incense (*thymiama*) and also for fumigating clothes along with myrrh and storax"; he then lists its virtues as a medicament. Relying on what Dioscorides says, a number of commentators have sought to identify *kankamon* with one of the gum resins, of lesser value than myrrh, found in Arabia, particularly since there seems to be a connection with *kamkam*, the Arabic name for some aromatic gum or resin; see A. Grohmann, *Sudarabien als Wirtschaftsgebiet*, Osten und Orient. Erste Reihe: Forschungen, vierte Bd. (Vienna, 1922), 114–15, 119; Löw iii 32. However, Glaser (ii 196) rejects out of hand an Arabian origin. And Pliny (12.98) states that *cancamum*—to use his spelling—comes from the same place as cinnamon and cassia, which would mean eastern Africa (see under 8:3.30–13:5.4). Lastly there are those who reject both Arabia and Africa. Thus Schoff, followed by Warmington (201), identifies *kankamon* as India copal (i.e., white dammer) from *Valeria indica*, and Miller (39) as benzoin from *Styrax benzoin*, whose home is Southeast Asia. Schoff asserts, again followed by Warmington (178), that *kankamon* "is mentioned by Pliny as a dye," but Pliny says nothing of the sort; a connection with lac that has been offered goes back no earlier than Arab times (see J. Berendes, *Des Pedanios Dios-kurides aus Anabarzos Arzneimittellehre* [Stuttgart, 1902], 52).

Dioscorides' tree has been identified as *Commiphora kataf* (cf. A. Tschirch, *Handbuch der Pharmakognosie* [Leipzig, 1910] i.2 534 [where it is given the older name of *Amyris kataf*]; *LSJ* s.v. *kankamon* [where it is given yet another older name, *Balsamodendron kataf*]). Commiphora kataf grows only in Arabia. However, there is a tree found in Somalia, *Com-miphora erythraea*, which so resembles it that Watt (i 366) thought the two were the same. *Commiphora erythraea* produces a gum-resin, African bdellium (*habbak haddi* in Arabic, *bysabol* in Marathi; see Watt (i 366), Drake-Brockman [op. cit. under 7:3.20] 306–7), which, like certain other bdelliums, is so similar to myrrh that it has been called 'false myrrh' (Watt i 367). In other words, it both suits Dioscorides' description of *kankamon* and the Periplus' listing of it as an export from Somalia. As it happens, *Commiphora erythraea* grows in Arabia as well as Somalia (see O. Schwartz, *Flora des tropischen Arabien*, Mitteilungen aus dem Institut fur allgemeine Botanik in Hamburg 10 = Festschrift fur Hans Winkler [Hamburg, 1939], 128), which would justify Dioscorides' attributing it to that place.

The Periplus notes (8:3.31–32) that *kankamon* was exported to Arabia. Perhaps the 'false myrrh' from Somalia was superior to the kind from Arabia and hence commanded a market there just as Somalia's true myrrh did (cf. under 7:3.20).

As for the suggested identifications with India copal or benzoin, nei-ther fits the evidence as well as African bdellium.

8:3.31b *makeir*

Makeir is described by Pliny (*macir*, 12.32), Dioscorides (*makir*, 1.82), and Galen (*maker*, 12.66) and is listed in the botanical lexica of later centuries (M. Thomson, *Textes grecs inédits relatifs aux plantes* [Paris, 1955], 137; A. Delatte, *Anecdota Atheniensia et Alia* ii, Bibliothèque de la Faculté de Philosophie et Lettres de l'Université de Liége, fasc. 88 [Liége, 1939], 328.22, 335.21, 365.7, 380.18–19). Dioscorides says it is a bark from "the land of the Barbaroi" (cf. under 2:1.7–10, B 2:1.6–7), but both Pliny and Galen say from India. Pliny, Dioscorides, and Galen all mention its use-fulness in treating dysentery. Pliny adds two further details, that the med-icine was concocted from the root bark and that the root bark was reddish in color. He confesses to ignorance about the tree itself, and in like fashion both Dioscorides and Galen merely say "bark" without specifying of what tree.

Lassen (iii 31) suggested the bark of the tree "von den dortigen [the Malabar coast] Brahmanen *macre* genannten Baumes, dessen Rinde sehr geschätzt wird, der aber noch nicht genauer ermittelt ist," and his words are cited by Fabricius, who is cited by Löw (ii 60, n. 1). However, no such tree name appears in Watt's index. The main entry in *LSJ* defines *mak(e)ir* as "*muttee-pal*, the fragrant resin of *Ailanthus malabarica*"; this tree, to be sure, produces a medicine used for treating dysentery, but it is made from the bark and not the resin (Watt i 151–52) and, in any event, no ancient writer connects *mak(e)ir* with a resin. This may explain why in *LSJ* suppl. "*Ailanthus malabarica*" has been replaced by "*Myristica malabarica*," an identification that is repeated by Miller (60). However, Watt's discussion of *Myristica malabarica* (v 314–15) reveals that, though this tree too is the source of a medicine sometimes prescribed for treating dysentery, what is used are the seeds, not the bark. The most convincing identification is Schoff's: he suggests, seconded by Warmington (216), that *mak(e)ir* was from the common Indian tree *Holarrhena antidysenterica* Wall, of which Watt reports (iv 256) that "its root bark [is] reddish-brown" and (257) "alone is . . . the most powerful antidysenteric part of the plant." This fits the requirements perfectly. *Holarrhena antidysenterica* is still used today in parts of the Far East for treating dysentery; see L. Perry and J. Metzger, *Medicinal Plants of East and Southeast Asia* (Cambridge, Mass., 1980), 26.

Thus, like cassia (see under 8:3.30–13:5.4), *makeir* was an Asian product that traders from the West purchased in Africa. Dioscorides, as noted above, thought it actually came from there, though Pliny and Galen knew better.

8:3.31–32   which items are exported to Arabia

Arabia, to be sure, was itself a producer of myrrh and frankincense. In the nineteenth century, just as in the first, it imported both from Somalia (see Pankhurst [op. cit. under 7:3.20] 52, 53, 63; G. Mountnorris [Viscount Valentia], *Voyages and Travels to India, Ceylon, the Red Sea, Abyssinia, and Egypt in the Years 1802, 1803, 1804, 1805, and 1806* [London, 1811], ii 354, 356–57). The Arabian ports served as entrepôts, forwarding what came in to markets all over (Pankhurst 37, 49).

9:4.1   Mundu

Mundu must surely be Heis (10°53′N, 46°54′E), for Heis Island, lying one and one-quarter miles north-northeast, conforms nicely to the author's description. Moreover, sherds of Roman pottery and fragments of Roman glass dating from the 1st to the 5th century A.D. have been found in the area; see N. Chittick in *IJNA* 8 (1979): 274–75 (with an excellent photograph of Heis Island) and *Azania* 16 (1981): 187–88. The author gives the distance from Malaô to Mundu as two "runs" or 1000 stades (see App. 2). The distance from Berbera to Heis is ca. 120 nautical miles or 1200 stades. In his previous figures he had overestimated (see under 7:3.13–14); here he underestimates.

The Roman glass that has been discovered confirms the *Periplus's* mention of glass among the imports to the ports of this region (7:3.16 and presumably included among "the aforementioned" in 8:3.26–27, 9:4.3, 10:4.8). The finds include fragments of millefiori glass (cf. under 6:2.25–26); see E. Stern, "Early Roman Glass from Heis on the North Somali Coast," in *Annales du 10me Congrès de l'Association Internationale pour l'Histoire du Verre, Madrid 1985* (Amsterdam, 1987). Much of the glass found dates from the first half of the first A.D.

9:4.4   *mokrotu*

The word occurs only in the *Periplus*. Glaser (ii 196) and W. Müller (726–27) connect it with the Arabic *mghairot* aut sim. meaning "incense tree," and Müller cites a series of related dialectical forms used in southern Arabia, as well as borrowed forms used in Ethiopia and Somalia, all meaning "incense."

10:4.7   Mosyllon

There are no clues to the identification of this port other than the distances cited: two or three "runs" east of Mundu (Heis) and two "runs" west of a group of sites that includes Cape Elephas, which must be Ras Filuch (11°56′N, 50°38′E); the promontory has an unmistakable elephantlike shape, which explains its modern name (*fil* means "elephant") as well as its ancient. The small port of Bender Cassim (11°17′N, 49°11′E), lying ca. 135 nautical miles east of Heis and 90 west of Ras Filuch, suits rather well the distances given, though these are hardly a reliable criterion considering how much they vary from the actual in other instances (see, e.g., under 9:4.1). If Mosyllon lay nearer Mundu than Bender Cassim does, it could have been, say, at Elayu (11°14′N, 48°54′E); if nearer to Cape Elephas, then at Candala (11°28′N, 49°52′E). Mosyllon offered, we are told, no more than a beach with bad anchorage, and on this score all three, as well as some of their neighbors, qualify. What is certain is that Mosyllon was in this general area, within easy transport from one of Somalia's richest frankincense regions (see Map 6 and the map in Hepper [op. cit. under 8:3.30a above] pl. xv). In the days of the *Periplus* it shipped out frankincense, even as Bender Cassim and

Candala did centuries later (cf. Glaser ii 201; Pankhurst [op. cit. under 7:3.20] 60, 63).

10:4.9   precious stones

See under B 10:4.9. The author does not specify which kinds. Egypt has amethyst, beryl, chalcedony, carnelian, and others (cf. *ESAR* ii 241; Lucas-Harris [op. cit. under 1:1.2–4] 386–405) which could qualify for inclusion under this rubric.

10:4.10   bigger ships

Commentators assume that the author means "very large vessels" (cf. Raschke 853, n. 838), vessels as large as those used on the run to the Malabar coast (Warmington 81, 273, and cf. App. 3). Not at all; Mosyllon, with its lack of a proper harbor, was no place for such ships to frequent. As it happens, the African run, unlike the Indian, was open to quite small craft (App. 3); thus the "bigger ships" required here need not have been of any great size, merely bigger than those that normally served the ports of the area.

10:4.13   myrrh, but only on rare occasions

Mosyllon lay on the eastern edge of the myrrh-producing region (Map 6), just as Avalitês lay on the western (see under 7:3.20). This must be why, like Avalitês, it handled only small amounts. Malaô and Mundu, nearest the heart of the region, must have handled the most (8:3.30, 9:4.3–4, where myrrh presumably is included under "the aforementioned").

11:4.15–16   Neiloptolemaiu . . . a small laurel grove, Cape Elephas

These or similar place names occur in Strabo's account (16.774), based on Artemidorus (cf. 16.776), of this part of the coast. He lists, along with a number of others that do not appear in the *Periplus*, "a river land [*potamia*] called Neilos," "Laurel Harbor (*limên*)," and "Elephas, the mountain that juts into the sea," and he mentions that frankincense is one of the products that grow in the area. On Elephas, see under 10:4.7.

11:4.15–17   Cape Elephas, . . . called Elephas

The manuscript is defective at this point and some words have been lost; see under B 11:4.16–17.

11:4.17–18 a large laurel grove called Akannai

Laurels, as noted earlier (under 8:3.30–13:5.4), do not grow in Somalia. Quite possibly what the Greeks saw on this coast and called laurels were mangroves, which do grow there and have leaves that are not unlike those of the laurel; cf. H. Bretzl, *Botanische Forschungen des Alexanderzuges* (Leipzig, 1903), 112–13. Ten miles east of Ras Filuch is the port of Alula (11°58′N, 50°46′E), to the northeast of which lies a broad lagoon lined with mangroves. This could well be the "large laurel grove called Akannai"; cf. Bretzl 112 and N. Chittick in *Azania* 11 (1976): 124–25, 16 (1981): 188. Frankincense trees no longer grow in the area (Chittick 125, n. 7; cf. the map in Hepper [op. cit. under 8:3.30a] pl. xv), but as late as the last century Alula was still a source of excellent frankincense (Glaser ii 199). Alula lies about 100 nautical miles from Bender Cassim, which suits very well the *Periplus's* "two runs."

By Ptolemy's day a port had arisen at Akannai, for he lists it (4.7.10) as such.

12:4.20 trending to the south

After Alula (see under 11:4.17–18) the coast trends somewhat towards the south. The course along Somalia's northern shore up to Alula is by and large east, from Alula to Guardafui east-southeast.

12:4.20–21 The Spice Port and a promontory . . . Barbaroi

Cf. 30:10.2–3, where the promontory is called "the Promontory of Spices." Strabo (16.774), also describing it as "the last promontory of this coast," calls it "the Horn of the South." The promontory is unquestionably Cape Guardafui or Ras Asir as it is now called (11°50′N, 51°18′E), the eastern tip of Somalia and, as described, is steep. The Spice Port may well have been where the village of Damo now stands, some three miles west of the cape. Fragments of unglazed pottery were found here which seem "most likely to be of Roman origin" (N. Chittick in *Azania* 11 [1976]: 124 and 16 [1981]: 188; *IJNA* 8 [1979]: 275). The harbor is, as the author observes, exposed to the north, but it is well protected against winds from the south; see *RSP*, chap. 14.178.

12:4.25–26 the big promontory . . . called Tabai

The name is found only in the *Periplus*. Commentators assumed that the Spice Port and Tabai had to be fairly near each other so that ships, getting warning of a storm while at the first and hastening to take refuge at the other, would not have far to go. Most favored Ras Shenaghef, a big promontory no more than thirteen nautical miles away (McCrindle, Fabricius, Schoff, E. Warmington in *Cambridge History of the British Empire* viii [Cambridge, 1963²], 64), although it has dubious qualifications as a place of refuge (no anchorages are listed in its vicinity in *SDRS*, sector 10, p. 167). A graver objection is that it lies a good seventy-five nautical miles north of Opônê (= Hafun; see under 13:5.3), almost double the *Periplus's* figure of 400 stades. Fabricius solved this by assuming a lacuna in the text and filling it with an additional leg of 400 stades, an insertion that has made its way into a number of translations (Schoff, Warmington [op. cit. above], Mauny [op. cit. under 7.3.13–14] 26). Glaser (ii 201–2) located Tabai on Cape Guardafui itself, adopting Fabricius's insertion to take care of the distance. Huntingford put it at Tohen, roughly two-thirds of the way from Guardafui to Ras Shenaghef, without addressing himself to the problem of the distance. Guillain, whose experience in these waters was considerable and, like the ancients', done in sailing ships, conjectured (99–100) that Tabai must have been on the bay of Chori Hordio on the north side of the peninsula of Ras Hafun, pointing out that the run from there around the tip of the peninsula to Opônê on its southern shore was just about 400 stades. His conjecture has been confirmed by archaeology: excavation by N. Chittick in precisely the area mentioned (marked with a cross on Map 8) has brought to light ancient remains, including pottery that goes back to the third and second centuries B.C. (*Azania* 11 [1976]:121–23, *IJNA* 8 [1979]:275–77). The fact that Chori Hordio is almost a two-day sail from Cape Guardafui, far beyond what commentators reckoned feasible for a dash to safety, is no objection. They took the bit of weather lore given in the text as a sign of a storm that was soon to follow. It is rather the kind of sign that indicates a storm is brewing and will come in the next few days (cf. Theophrastus, *de Sign.* 10, 11, 12, where he lists signs indicating rain within three days). For a full discussion, see Casson 1986.

12:4.28   *gizeir, asyphê, arôma, magla, motô*

Gizeir, motô, and *asyphê* were, respectively, the best, second-best, and a cheap grade of cassia; see Casson 1980.496 and 1984.228–29. *Gizeir* is the Hellenization of some native term (cf. Galen 14.67: "called by those who trade in it after a two-syllable native [*barbarikos*] term, the first syllable of which is spelled *g* and *i* and the second *z* and *i*"); presumably *asyphê*, *magla*, and *motô* are as well.

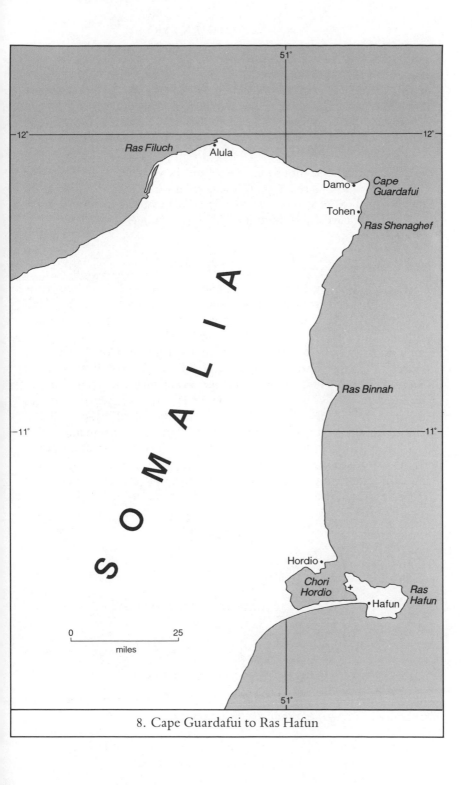

8. Cape Guardafui to Ras Hafun

12:4.28a   frankincense

Cf. Mountnorris (op. cit. under 8:3.31–32) 354: "The Frankincense [shipped to Mocha] is chiefly cultivated near to Cape Guardafui."

13:5.2   towards which, moreover, the current sets

During the northeast monsoon, the period in which the leg down the African coast took place (App. 3), the current in the area sets southward and westward (*SDRS*, sector 10, p. 167). This would draw a vessel that had rounded Guardafui right to Ras Hafun (= Opônê; see under 13:5.3).

13:5.3   Opônê

There is universal agreement that Opônê is Hafun—the modern name may be descended from the ancient—an excellent harbor on the south shore of Ras Hafun, the prominent peninsula some eighty-five miles south of Cape Guardafui (10°27′N, 51°24′E); Hafun was still serving the sailing ships of Arabia and Persia up to a few decades ago (on the phonetic connection of the names, see Glaser ii 202; F. Storbeck, *Mitteilungen des Seminars für orientalische Sprachen an den königlichen Friedrich-Wilhelms-Universität zu Berlin*, zweite Abteilung 17 [1914]: 123. On the port of Hafun, see A. Villiers, *Sons of Sinbad* [New York, 1940], 97–99). Recent archaeological investigation has brought to light ancient remains dating to the 2d and 3d centuries A.D. and perhaps later (N. Chittick in *Azania* 11 [1976]: 120–22 and *IJNA* 8 [1979]: 276). Some material produced a radiocarbon date of the 2d or 1st century B.C., but there is doubt about its validity (G. Mgomezulu in *Journal of African History* 22 [1981]:447).

13:5.4   cassia

Cf. under 8:30.30–13:5.4.

14:5.8   around the month of July

See App. 3.

14:5.9   from . . . Ariakê

The items listed as imports from Ariakê are conformably those the author lists later (41:14.5–6) as products of that region.

14:5.10   rice

Theophrastus (4.4.10) describes rice as a product of India, and its name in Greek, *oryza*, is probably derived from the Sanskrit *vrīhi*; see Hobson-Jobson s.v. *Rice*. India exported its rice to Socotra (31:10.22) as well as to the "far-side" ports.

14:5.11   ghee

The author uses the Greek word for "butter"; in the context, it can only be ghee. This, "the universal medium of cookery throughout India" (Hobson-Jobson s.v. *Ghee*), is made by heating butter "until the greater part of the moisture in it evaporates; the oil-like *ghi* then rises on the surface and the half-burnt refuse falls as a sediment" (Watt iii 491). It can keep for years and years without spoiling, and Watt cites examples of ghee over a century old used medically (for which purpose, the more it aged, the greater its properties were believed to be). In his day India exported ghee to Africa (iii 497), just as in the time of the *Periplus*.

14:5.11–12   cotton cloth, the *monachê* and the *sagmatogênê*

These were of ordinary quality; see under B 6:3.2 and B 14:5.11–12.

14:5.12–13   cane sugar

Literally "the cane honey called sakchari." The name comes from the Sanskrit *śarkarā* (Hobson-Jobson s.v. *Sugar*; L. Gopal, "Sugar-Making in Ancient India," *JESHO* 7 [1964]:57–72, esp. 57–66). India was the source of supply for the Greek and Roman world (Warmington 208–10). There it was used only in medical recipes, never for sweetening food, which was done with honey (Warmington 209). India used it both medically and as a sweetener (Gopal 58–66). In the Indian sources *śarkarā* generally means refined granulated sugar, although it can at times refer to the juice (Gopal 64–65). Judging by the author's expression, "cane honey," it would appear that what was imported was some form of cane juice to be used, as in India, for sweetening.

14:5.14   follow the coast . . . cargoes

This is the sole mention of ships that tramped; see Introduction: Trade in the Indian Ocean, The Lines and Objects of Trade.

14:5.14–16   The area is not ruled by a king . . . chief

See Introduction: Political Geography.

15:5.17–16:6.13   Beyond Opônê . . . the area
and its language

In 15 and 16 the author deals with Azania, i.e., the coast of Africa from
Ras Hafun south to Rhapta (see under 16:6.4). His description is summary and for good reason: this is a bare and desolate stretch of land that
offered as little then as now. He lists a number of landmarks, a few harbors, and just one port of trade, Rhapta, at the very end.

Cape Guardafui marked the limit of Strabo's or Pliny's knowledge of
eastern Africa (cf. Bunbury ii 63, 429, 451); the author's reaches as far as
Zanzibar (6°10'S, 39°11'E) or beyond (see under 16:6.4). By Ptolemy's
time more points along the coast were known; his list (4.7.11–12) runs as
follows: a village called Panôn, the port of Opônê, Cape Zingis, Mt.
Phalangis, the Bluff(s), Cape Southern Horn, the Small Beach, the Great
Beach, the port of Essina (see under B 15:5.25–26a), the harbor of Sarapiôn, the port of Tonikê, the metropolis of Rhapta. Six of these (Panôn,
Zingis, Phalangis, Cape Southern Horn, Essina, and Tonikê—unless this
is a variant of Nikôn) were not known to the author or not in existence
when he wrote, and Rhapta had not yet grown to the status of a metropolis. Of the islands, Ptolemy is unaware of the Pyralaoi group and is in-
consistent in the placing of Menuthias (4.8.2, 7.2.1; cf. J. Thomson, *History of Ancient Geography* [Cambridge, 1948], 274). But he has gained
some knowledge of the coast further south, perhaps as far as Delgado
(10°41'S, 40°38'E); cf. Bunbury ii 525–27, Thomson 275, Desanges 333.

The settlements along this coast today are of later date, most of much
later date than Greco-Roman times. Archaelogical surveys have turned
up nothing earlier than the 9th or 10th century A.D. (cf. Raschke 932;
Mgomezulu [op. cit. under 13:5.3] 447–48; N. Chittick in *Azania* 4
[1969]: 115–30 [Mogadiscio to Bircao] and 2 [1967]: 37–67 [the Lamu Ar-
chipelago]; P. Robertshaw in *Journal of African History* 25 [1984]: 385
[Lamu Archipelago]; H. Costa-Sanseverino in *Azania* 18 [1983]:151–64
[Bircao to the Kenya border]) with but a few insignificant exceptions.
Numerous finds of coins have been reported, but none are from securely
dated contexts; see G. Freeman-Grenville in *The Medieval History of the
Coast of Tanganyika* (London, 1962), 21–23, Chittick in *Azania* 4
(1969):130, A. Sheriff in Mokhtar 553–54, Desanges 335–37.

At the time the *Periplus* was written, Azania was under the domination
of an Arabian king, who administered the area through one of his sub-

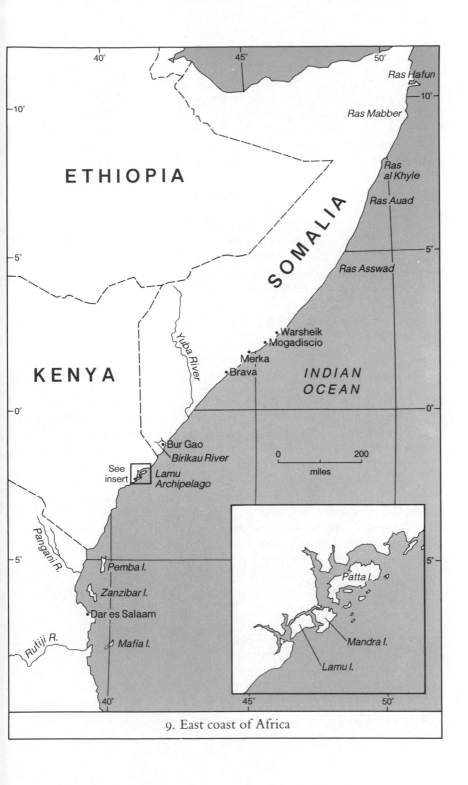

9. East coast of Africa

ordinates (cf. Introduction: Political Geography). Who were his subjects? The author supplies one possible clue: the natives of Rhapta, he reports, are "very big-bodied men." This, together with what scant linguistic and archaeological indications there are, has led most commentators to conclude that the inhabitants were Cushitic-speaking peoples; see R. Oliver in *Journal of African History* 7 (1966): 368, C. Ehret in *Nairobi Historical Studies* 3 (Nairobi, 1974): 28, R. Oliver and B. Fagan in *CHA* ii 373–74 (1978), B. Heine in *Sprache und Geschichte in Afrika* 1 (1979): 45 and 3 (1981): 169–70. A minority view holds that they were Bantus (Freeman-Grenville 27–28), but the Bantus most probably came to this region at a later date (N. Chittick and R. Rotberg, eds., *East Africa and the Orient* [New York, 1975], 8; Oliver-Fagan 369; E. Turton in *Journal of African History* 16 [1975]: 524–27; Huntingford 147). To complete the range of scholarly opinion, V. Grottanelli argues that perhaps neither Cushites nor Bantus were there at the time, that "the Asiatic merchants operating in the area of the Horn may have had to deal exclusively with hordes of hunters" (Chittick-Rotberg 71; cf. 20, where Chittick rightly asserts just the opposite).

15:5.18   Azania

Cf. Ptolemy 1.17.9 where, as here, the name is used of the land south of Opônê as far as Rhapta (although Ptolemy at one point [4.7.28] defines it more narrowly as the hinterland back of the coast). Pliny (6.172) mentions an "Azanian Sea," but this has scant relevance since he places it north of Adulis (cf. A. Dihle in *ANRW* ii 9.2 562–63 [1978]). He also mentions (6.176) a people called the Zangenae, whom H. von Wissmann, *RE* suppl. 11.1337–48 (1968), connects with Azania and locates in eastern Africa. The connection may well be right but not the location, which is based on highly speculative arguments (cf. Dihle 563, n. 58). Many commentators connect Azania with Zanj, the name that Arabic writers gave to this stretch of coast and that forms the first element in Zanzibar (e.g., Glaser 203–4; Dihle 564, n. 61; Freeman-Grenville [op. cit. under 15:5.17–16:6.13] 29; E. Turton, *Journal of African History* 16 [1975]: 525).

15:5.18–20   the Small and Great Bluffs . . . Small and Great Beaches

The accuracy of the author's summary description of this stretch of coast has long been recognized; cf. Bunbury ii 453. Guillain, who observed it from the deck of a sailing ship, states (100–101): "nous croyons pouvoir placer les grandes apocopes aux creux formés, dans la côte, par la projection de Ras-Mâabeur [Ras Mabber, 9°28'N, 50°51'E] et celle de Ras-el-Khil [Ras al Khyle, 7°44'N, 49°52'E]; les petites apocopes seraient alors représentées par les anses ou criques beaucoup moins profondes que forment les sinuosités du rivage compris entre ces deux caps." As regards the beaches, he points out (134) that "de Ras-el-Khil . . . à Ras-Aouad [Auad or Awath, 6°18'N, 49°5'E], la côte est très-basse; c'est, à proprement parler, une plage bordée çà et là de petites falaises rocheuses, ayant de 3 à 4 mètres de hauteur: ce caractère est uniforme dans toute son étendue et répond assez bien au nom *Sîf-et-Taouïl* (la longue plage), qui lui a été donné par les Arabes. Au contraire, à partir de Ras-Aouad (cap de la substitution), la côte s'élève graduellement, et, à 3 ou 4 lieues en arrière du rivage, elle est dominée par une terre beaucoup plus élevée, de hauteur uniforme. . . . On cesse d'apercevoir cette haute terre aux environs de Ras-Açoued [Asswad, 4°34'N, 48°1'E]; mais la côte conserve toujours une élévation de beaucoup supérieure à celle de la partie dite *Sîf-et-Taouïl*. Nous pensons, en conséquence, que c'est à cette disposition naturelle des lieux que sont dues les appellations de *petit* et *grand* rivage." Cf. 102: "Ce dernier [the Great Beach] se terminera ainsi un peu au nord de Ras-M'routi" (i.e., ca. one degree short of Warsheik [2°18'N, 45°48'E]).

N. Chittick, who traveled the area by land, states (*Azania* 11 [1976]:120): "From there [Hafun] southwards to El Fosc ('Eel Fosk), lat. 7°10'N, south of Ras al-Khayl, the coast is mostly exceedingly rocky and inhospitable, with steep cliffs plunging into the sea; these are the 'small and great bluffs of Azania' of the *Periplus* (sec. 15). At El Fosc begins a long stretch of almost straight coast, sandy and for the most part featureless. This is probably the 'small and great beach' of the *Periplus* (sec. 15). This region ends at around Warsheikh, where begins the Banadir, or coast of harbours."

Thus the two observers agree on the general area, differing only on where each stretch ends, and then by only one day's run or less: Guillain ends the bluffs around Ras al Khyle (7°44'N) and Chittick et El Fosc (7°10'N); he end the beaches one degree short of Warsheik, Chittick at Warsheik itself. The total distance from Hafun to Warsheik is just under 600 nautical miles, which is exactly equivalent to twelve runs (cf. App. 2). For whatever reason, the author's estimates of distance for this part of the coast of Africa work out better than those given for the parts described hitherto; cf. under 9:4.1 and 15:5.24.

15:5.21   the runs of Azania

The same expression is used by Marcianus (13 = *GGM* i 523).

15:5.22–24   Sarapiôn run; then the Nikôn . . . seven in all

Along the stretch of coast after the Great Beach, i.e., from Warsheik on, harbors are plentiful; indeed, the Arabic name for it is Banadir, "coast of harbors" (see Chittick cited under 15:5.18–20). Guillain, like Müller and others (e.g., Bunbury ii 452), takes the runs of Azania to be seven in all (see under B 15:5.23–24). Since the first two, Sarapiôn and Nikôn, cover the stretch almost to or right up to Merka (see under 15:5.22a), that leaves five to be distributed between there and the island of Patta (see under 15:5.24). Guillain (104) allocates them as follows: "la première, au port de Braoua [Brava, 1°5′N, 43°58′E]; la seconde, à un point intermédiaire entre ce port et l'embouchure du Djoub [Yuba River, 0°15′S, 42°38′E], par example Djora; la troisième, à cette embouchure; la quatrième, à Cheut-Bourgâo (la rivière Durnford des cartes) [Bircao; see under 15:5.22a]; la cinquième enfin, qui doit nous conduire aux îles Pyralāon . . . , nous fait arriver au groupe des îles Kouiyou, Patta, Mandra, Lâmou." The distance is some 320 nautical miles; thus each run would be ca. sixty-four, somewhat higher than normal (see App. 2). Guillain (96–97) attributes this to the increased velocity of the current south of Ras Asswad (4°34′N, 48°1′E), two to three knots as against one and one-half.

If, as a number of translators render the passage (McCrindle, Schoff, Huntingford), there were seven runs *beyond* Nikôn, each would be a little under fifty nautical miles, the normal figure. Huntingford offers a list of the various stops on this basis but, since he equates Nikôn with Brava and starts his seven runs from there, they work out to considerably less than normal: five of the seven are but forty nautical miles apart.

The rivers along this stretch of coast are hardly numerous, but there are at least two: the Yuba (0°15′S, 42°38′E), with an anchorage in Kisimayu Bay, some nine miles below its mouth, and the Birikau (1°13′S, 41°53′E), with an anchorage at its mouth (*SDA*, sec. 10–98 to 102).

15:5.22   Sarapiôn

This, the first of the "runs of Azania," is the first harbor on the barren stretch south of Ras Hafun that the author names—and the first harbor there worthy of the name is Warsheik (2°18′N, 45°48′E) according to Guillain (98: "Le premier havre, au sud de Hhafoun, est celui de Ouarcheikh"; 102–3: "à 20 lieues environ du point où nous avons placé la fin du grand rivage, se trouve [le premier de tout le littoral en venant du nord] le petit havre de Ouarcheikh, relâche sûre dont les bateaux qui venaient de parcourir cette longue côte inhospitalière ne devaient pas manquer de profiter").

15:5.22a   Nikôn

This, as the second of the "runs of Azania," should lie some fifty nautical miles down the coast beyond Warsheik; cf. Guillain 103: "[Nikôn] se trouvera . . . tomber sur l'un des points situés entre Moguedchou [Mogadiscio, 2°2′N, 45°21′E] et Meurka [Merka, 1°43′N, 44°47′E], peut-être à Gondeurscheikh [Gonderscia, 1°50′N, 44°58′E], havre plus grand que Ouarcheikh et bon mouillage pour les beateaux." Another possibility is Danane, just a few miles up the coast from Gonderscia, where an anchorage with good holding ground is reported (*SDA*, section 11–31). And Guillain (103, n. 4) does not rule out Merka itself. G. Mathew (in Chittick-Rotberg [op. cit. under 15:5.17–16:6.13] 155) and others (e.g., Wheeler 114, G. Freeman-Grenville in *Numismatic Chronicle* [1971]: 283, A. Sheriff in Mokhtar 562) place Nikôn at Bircao (Bur Gao, Port Durnford, 1°13′S, 41°53′E), but that is far enough south to be the next to the last of the runs of Azania; see under 15:5.22–24.

15:5.24   the Pyralaoi Islands and
what is called the Canal

On the form of the name, see under B 15:5.24. Commentators are agreed that these must be the islands of the Lamu Archipelago—Patta, Mandra, and Lamu—for the very good reason that they are the first encountered along the coast south of Ras Hafun that deserve to be called islands; the other possible candidates are merely reefs or islets. Moreover, they are separated from the mainland by what can aptly be termed a canal; Guillain (107–8) points out that, unlike the channels encountered up to this point,

> ce bras de mer étroit, dans lequel les bateaux peuvent mouvoir à la perche comme sur un de ces canaux qui servent de voies de communication intérieure; ce bras de mer, disons nous, justifie, on ne saurait le nier, l'appellation de canal bien autrement qu'un simple chenal, bordé, du côté du large, par des îlots s'élevant à peine au-dessus du niveau de la mer, ou même pas de simple hauts fonds ou récifs.

And last, the distance works out nicely: from Ras Hafun to the Lamu Archipelago is around 1000 nautical miles, or the equivalent of twenty runs—just about the number the author assigns (six for the Small and

Great Bluffs, six for the Small and Great Beaches, and seven or nine for the runs of Azania).

15:5.26   Menuthias

Some 170 nautical miles south of the Lamu Archipelago is the first of three large islands, Pemba. The other two, still further south, are Zanzibar and Mafia. Commentators have debated endlessly which of the three is to be identified with Menuthias. The distances given, considering the rough way the author reckoned these (cf. App. 2), could fit either Pemba or Zanzibar; they fit Mafia, the most distant, less well, and hence it is least favored. Archaeology throws no light since the remains are all late: on Zanzibar there is nothing before the ninth century and on Pemba nothing before 1100; see M. Horton and K. Clark in *Azania* 20 (1985): 169.

A key argument put forth for Zanzibar (Müller, Fabricius, Guillain 112) is that it alone boasts what can be called rivers (cf. 15:5.27). A key argument put forth for Pemba is that vessels must pass it to arrive at Zanzibar and, if Zanzibar is Menuthias, then the author inexplicably failed to mention Pemba (cf. B. Datoo in *Azania* 5 [1970]: 68, A. Sheriff in Mokhtar 562). Moreover, W. Ingrams, who lived for years in the area and knew it well, states that, "There is a good river in the north of Pemba" (*Zanzibar: Its History and Its People* [London, 1931], 63). Some (Müller, McCrindle 71, Bunbury ii 454) suggest that the author derived his information from hearsay and conflated reports about the two islands; see, however, Introduction: Text and Author, The Author and His Work, n. 14. In later ages, Pemba seems to have been as important or even more important than Zanzibar. On it are extensive ruins of mosques, imposing tombs, houses, etc., dating from the twelfth century and after; see F. Pearce, *Zanzibar: The Island Metropolis of Eastern Africa* (London, 1920), 343 (date), 350 (list of ruins), 363–97 (principal architectural remains).

In sum, Menuthias was either Pemba or Zanzibar, with the odds very slightly in favor of Pemba.

15:5.29   crocodiles

Neither Pemba nor Zanzibar has crocodiles. However, Zanzibar has a type of monitor (*Varanus niloticus*), a lizard that can attain a length of four feet; it could have been mistaken for a crocodile or, for lack of a more precise term, called such. It is, as the author states, harmless. See Ingrams (op. cit. under 15:5.26) 430; Pearce (op. cit. under 15:5.26) 338.

15:5.30   sewn boats

Sewn boats, i.e., craft whose planks are fastened together by some form of cord, are known from practically all times and places; see *SSAW* 9–10, 201, 447. Several types have been identified in the particular area the author is discussing; see N. Chittick in *IJNA* 9 (1980): 297–309.

15:6.1   baskets

Traps of basketry are commonly used along the East African coast for fishing; see Ingrams (op. cit. under 15:5.26) 299–300 and the illustration in Schoff 95. However, there is no mention of any used for catching sea turtles.

16:6.4   Rhapta

Rhapta lay, we are told, two runs (1000 stades or 100 nautical miles) beyond Menuthias, and so its location depends upon the identification of that island, whether it be Pemba or Zanzibar: if Pemba, then Rhapta lay in the vicinity of Dar es Salaam; if Zanzibar, it lay at the mouth of the Rufiji River. Ptolemy's locating of Menuthias and Rhapta presents difficulties; cf. B. Datoo, "Rhapta: The Location and Importance of East Africa's First Port," *Azania* 5 (1970): 65–75 at 68. Ptolemy (4.7.12) implies, for whatever the information is worth, that Rhapta was on or near a river. The only candidates are the mouth of the Pangani (5°26'S, 39°1'E) and the delta of the Rufiji (7°49'S, 39°27'E); cf. Datoo 69 and Raschke 933, n. 1139. The one would put Rhapta about one degree north of, and the other one degree south of, Dar es Salaam (6°49'S, 39°18'E). If we follow the *Periplus*, since the identification of Menuthias with Pemba is more likely than with Zanzibar (cf. under 15:5.26), Rhapta was at Dar es Salaam, and this is the location argued for by L. Kirwan ("Rhapta, Metropolis of Azania," *Azania* 21 [1986]: 99–104), who points out that Dar es Salaam boasts a good harbor.

The Arab geographer al-Huwārizmi (mid-10th century A.D.; see *Encyclopédie de l'Islam*, suppl. 68 [1936]), in his edition of Ptolemy's *Geography*, identifies Rhapta with a coastal city named Rafāṭā (cf. G. Ferrand in *JA* [1921]: 311; G. Fiaccadori in *Studi classici e orientali della Università degli Studi di Pisa* 34 [1984]: 298). However, Ibn Mājid (see App. 3, n. 4) assigns this Rafāṭā a latitude that works out to 19°43'S (Ferrand 311, Fiaccadori 298), much too far south for Rhapta.

Ptolemy lists Rhapta as a metropolis, and even in the days of the *Periplus* it must have been of considerable size in order to accommodate, as

Zanzibar did in later centuries (App. 3. nn. 11, 13), vessels and their crews as they awaited the shift of the monsoon.

16:6.6   Very big-bodied men

See under 15:5.17–16:6.13.

16:6.7–8   behave . . . like chiefs

The sentences that follow reveal that the area was under Arabian domination and was governed by a merchant oligarchy from the busy Arabian port of Muza. This would explain not only the absence of native chiefs exercising authority but also why the peasantry enjoyed such uninhibited independence: the merchant governors no doubt concentrated their attention on the port and its commerce and paid scant heed to the countryside.

16:6.8–9   under the rule of the governor of Mapharitis

See under 22:7.25 and cf. Introduction: Political Geography.

16:6.9   Arabia as first constituted

The kingdom referred to is that of the Sabaeans and Homerites since Mapharitis was a province within it; see Introduction: Political Geography. The author is indicating that the subjugation of the eastern African coast took place long ago; having no idea of how long ago, he leaves an ample spread of time by describing the subjugator as the kingdom that arose when Arabia first gave birth to states.

18:6.23–24   the parts of Ethiopia and Libya and Africa that turn away

I.e., the parts that turn away from the direction they have followed hitherto; cf. G. Giangrande in *Museum Philologum Londiniense* 5 (1981): 47–48. Up to Rhapta they ran north-south; below Rhapta they made a bend and ran east-west. The author, it is clear, follows the "theory adopted by Eratosthenes and Strabo concerning the deflection of the African coast to the westward. . . . It serves to show how strongly rooted was the belief in men's minds, before the time of Ptolemy, that the whole African continent was surrounded by the ocean" (Bunbury ii 454). The term Africa here has a rather special meaning. Used politically, it was the name of the province that the Romans fashioned from the conquered Carthaginian territory, a sense that manifestly does not fit the context here. Used geo-graphically, it often referred to the northern coast of Africa westward of Egypt, and sometimes, as today, to the whole continent, although that was ordinarily called Libya (see M. Besnier, *Lexique de géographie ancienne* [Paris, 1914], s.v. *Africa*). Here Libya apparently refers, as it sometimes can (cf. Bunbury ii 328), to the western area of the continent and Ethio-pia, as it usually does, to the southern; this leaves Africa to refer to the eastern, i.e., the area whose shore the author has just described.

18:6.25 western sea

Sc. the Atlantic Ocean.

19:6.26–28 To the left of Berenicê . . . Leukê Kômê

In the author's reckoning, Berenicê was the key Egyptian port for departure on the routes he describes; see under 1:1.2–4. Consequently he begins his account of the voyage to Arabia and India from there. However, in order to provide coverage of the whole of the Red Sea, including the portion north of the latitude of Berenicê with the very important port of Myos Hormos, he backtracks to there ("to the left of Berenicê") and describes a course beginning from that point ("from Myos Hormos . . ."). Such a course took a vessel past the mouth of the Gulf of Suez and Gulf of Aqaba to the coast in the vicinity of 'Aynūnah (28°2'N, 35°12'E), a voyage of some 100 nautical miles. This fits the words of the *Periplus* almost exactly: the course is roughly east-northeast; the "gulf lying alongside" is presumably the Gulf of Aqaba, since it is nearest the arrival point; and "two or three runs," 1000 or 1500 stades, would be 100 to 150 nautical miles. Wellsted, who went over the route in the days of sail, placed Leukê Kômê at 'Aynūnah; it offered what he considered a suitable, well-sheltered harbor and, what is more, had an abundant supply of good water nearby (ii 161–67). For some reason a host of authorities, including Müller, Fabricius, and Schoff, have preferred to locate it much further south at Haura (25°7'N, 37°13'E, according to Schoff), even though this does not at all suit what the *Periplus* says: it is south-southeast from Myos Hormos; on the run to it no "gulf lying alongside" is passed; and the distance, some 250 nautical miles, is a sail of five days, not two to three. The discrepancies were such that Schoff felt constrained to suggest a scribal error. Huntingford, without mentioning his grounds, puts it still further south, at Yanbu (24°6'N, 38°3'E), the port of Medina. H. von Wissman, too, puts it there and mentions his grounds (*RE* Suppl. 12.543 [1970])—that the *Periplus* reports Leukê Kômê as being "auf derselben

143

Breite ('gegenüber')" as Berenicê; the *Periplus* reports nothing of the sort. Recent commentators have returned to the identification with 'Aynūnah; see Beeston 356, L. Kirwan in *GJ* 147 (1981): 83 and *Studies in the History of Arabia*. ii, *Pre-Islamic Arabia* (Riyadh, 1984), 55–61; Sidebotham 124–26. Strabo (16.780–81), describing the invasion of Arabia in 26/25 B.C. or a year later (cf. Desanges 308–9) by the Roman commander Aelius Gallus, reports that the expedition landed at Leukê Kômê and departed from a port that seems to have been lower down (Egra = al Wajh, 26°13'N, 36°27'E); cf. G. Bowersock, *Roman Arabia* (Cambridge, Mass., 1983), 48–49. 'Aynūnah suits these entry and exit points better than any ports further south. And it suits, too, Strabo's remark (16.781) that Leukê Kômê was on a well-traveled caravan route to Petra (cf. under 19:6.28–29); as Beeston and Kirwan indicate, this can hardly be said of places as far south as Haura or Yanbu.

Identification with 'Aynūnah is supported as well by the findings of archaeologists who have surveyed the area. The port would have been not at 'Aynūnah itself, which is a short distance inland, but at the modern village of Khuraybah on the water. Between the two sites archaeologists have identified signs of extensive occupation that date to the early centuries A.D. or even before: remains of impressive building complexes, a necropolis with over one hundred tombs, an abundance of Nabataean-Roman pottery; see M. Ingraham and others in *Atlal* 5 (1981): 76–78.

19:6.28–29 through which there is a way inland up to Petra

On the words "a way inland," see under B 19:6.29. Strabo (16.781) remarks that large camel caravans regularly went back and forth between Leukê Kômê and Petra. If we assume the identification with 'Aynūnah (see under 19:6.26–28), the route would have followed the Wadi al Afal to Aqaba and, from there, the track that, in the next century, was to be utilized by the builders of the Via Nova Traiana; see Kirwan (op. cit. under 19.6.26–28) 83. Going by land to Aqaba was preferable to water because of the foul winds in the Gulf of Aqaba; cf. Wellsted ii 165. On Petra, the impressive Nabataean capital, see A. Negev in *ANRW* ii.8 588–604 (1977).

19:6.29 Malichus, king of the Nabataeans

To be identified with Malichus II, who ruled from A.D. 40 to 70; see Introduction: Text and Author, The Date. Of the impressive buildings at Petra, long dated to the second century A.D., at least some were put up by Malichus's predecessor, Aretas IV, in the first half of the first century A.D.; see Bowersock (op. cit. under 19:6.26–28) 59–62.

19:6.31–7.1   customs officer . . . centurion

A debate has raged over whether the customs officer and the centurion mentioned in this passage were Roman officials, and hence Leukê Kômê was an outpost of Roman authority, or whether they were Nabataean. For the extensive bibliography, see Raschke 982, n. 1350. Bowersock (op. cit. under 19:6.26–28, 70) properly points out that "with the great Nabataean settlement inland at Madā'in Ṣāliḥ, as well as other Nabataean installations in the Ḥejāz, it is inconceivable that the port of Leuke Kome was being administered by Roman officials." Both officials must have been Nabataeans (centurion was a rank in the Nabataean army as well as the Roman; see Bowersock 71). Rome might possibly have stationed its own personnel at some major commercial center where imperial interests could be involved but hardly at a place like Leukê Kômê. As the text plainly states, it was not much of a port of trade, and whatever facilities it offered were for small-scale merchants from Arabia, a point that is underscored by the absence of the author's usual list of imports and exports; here they were irrelevant to his readers. The facilities included a fort, a garrison, and, since Leukê Kômê was the first Nabataean port traders from Arabia came to, a customs office.

19:6.31   the (duty of a) fourth

The Ptolemies levied customs duties this high and even higher (cf. P. Fraser, *Ptolemaic Alexandria* [Oxford, 1972], i 149–50), and the papyrus in the Vienna collection (see Introduction: Trade in the Indian Ocean, Between Alexandria and the Red Sea) attests to a duty of one-fourth levied by Rome (in this case on goods imported from India). A Roman official with the title "collector of the fourth" (*tetartônês*) is attested at Palmyra in the mid-2d century A.D. (see H. Seyrig in *Syria* 22 [1941]: 263–66). According to Pliny (12.68), harvesters of Arabian myrrh paid a levy of one-fourth to the king of the Gebbanites.

20:7.4–6   a variety of tribes speaking languages that differ

Strabo (16.768) lists the four most important: "the Minaeans in the region towards the Red Sea, whose largest city is Karna or Karnana; next to them the Sabaeans, whose metropolis is Mariaba [Marib]; third the Kattabanians [inhabitants of Qataban] . . . ; and, farthest to the east, the

Chatramôtitae [inhabitants of the Hadramaut], whose city is Sabata."
Pliny (6.157–59) gives a long and detailed list of towns as well as tribes;
these have been identified with varying degrees of certainty (cf. H. von
Wissman, *RE* Suppl. 11.1323–35 [1968]).

The differences in language are amply attested by the inscriptions
found in Arabia. Those of the Nabataeans are in Aramaic, the language
they consistently used at this time to write in, those of other peoples in
Thamudic, Lihyanic, Sabaic, and other Semitic languages or dialects. See
H. Roschinski, "Sprachen, Schriften und Inschriften in Nordwestara-
bien," *Bonner Jahrbücher* 180 (1980): 155–87; R. Schmitt in *Bonner Jahrbücher*, Beihefte Bd. 40 (1980): 208–9; C. Rabin, s.v. '*Arabiyya* in *Encyclopaedia of Islam* (1960²).

20:7.6   similarly

I.e., as on the Egyptian side; see 2:1.7–8.

20:7.6a   mean huts of the Ichthyophagoi

See under 2:1.7–10 and 2:1.7–8.

20:7.8–9   they plunder . . . and they enslave

Agatharchides (ap. Diod. 3.43.5) and Strabo (16.777) tell of Nabataean
piracy in the Red Sea and its suppression by the Ptolemies (bibliography
in Raschke 939, n. 1152; cf. also Desanges 263–65, Bowersock [op. cit.
under 19:6.26–28] 20–21). Apparently, by the time the *Periplus* was written, there had been a recrudescence, carried on this time by the peoples to
the south of the Nabataeans. Pliny (6.101) remarks that ships on the India
run were assigned units of archers as guards because the waters were in-
fested with pirates but does not specify which waters, whether those of
the Red Sea or beyond.

20:7.11   Kanraitai

The name occurs nowhere else. Glaser (165–66) emended to "Karnaeitai,"
i.e., inhabitants of Karna, chief city of the Minaeans (cf. Strabo cited under 20:7.4–6), on the grounds that the people in the ports, from whom
the author got his information, knowing little about those who lived inland other than the name of their one big city, called them thus.

20:7.11–12   the coast of Arabia is altogether risky

Cf. the remarks of Alan Villiers who sailed northward along this coast from Mocha in an Arab coastal craft ("Sailing with the Arabs," *Mariners Mirror* 47 [1961]: 242–55). He notes in particular the ubiquitous reefs, more dangerous here than reefs elsewhere (250–52).

20:7.15–16   Katakekaumenê ["burnt"] Island

Ptolemy (6.7.44) places it almost opposite Muza (see under 21:7.19). Pliny, who calls it Exusta (6.175), places it somewhere on the course down the Red Sea (cf. Desanges 157, n. 39). Probably, as suggested by Müller, Schoff, and earlier commentators and more recently by Beeston (356), it is to be identified with Jabal at Ta'ir (15°33'N, 41°50'E), which has a volcano not yet completely dead ("sulphurous jets of steam appear at the summit of the island," *SDRS*, sector 3, p. 34) and, indeed, was active up to a few years before 1837 when Paul-Émile Botta paid a visit (*Relation d'un voyage dans l'Yémen* [Paris, 1880], 162). Skippers have continued to use the island as a reference point in the central passage of the Red Sea: cf. J. Bruce, *Travels to Discover the Source of the Nile* (Edinburgh, 1804²), ii 234 ("Jibbel Teir is the point from which all our ships, going to Jidda, take their departure, after sailing from Mocha"); *SDRS*, sector 3, p. 33 ("The central passage through the Red Sea from Madiq Jubal [27°40'N, 34°0'E] as far as Jabal at Ta'ir, about 830 miles SSE, is free from dangers").

20:7.16–17   peaceful inhabitants . . . camels

Below the latitude of Katakekaumenê Island the mainland along the coast was part of the realm of the Sabaeans, a rich and well-ordered kingdom (see under 23:7.27–29). The camels were no doubt in caravans.

21:7.19   Muza, a legally limited port of trade

On the expression "legally limited," see App. 1. Muza is identified by most authorities with Mocha (al Mukha, 13°19'N, 43°15'E). Further on (25:8.13–15), the author gives 300 stades as the distance from Muza to the strait. From Mocha to Bab el Mandeb is 40 nautical miles = 400 stades, but there is no harbor nearer than Mocha to the strait that could possibly serve as a candidate and, in any event, the author's figures for distance are never very accurate, particularly for courses far removed from Egypt (see App. 2). A village, Mauza, some twenty miles inland to the east from

Mocha, bears the ancient name. This may have been the residential area, with its port, bearing the same name, on the coast; cf. A. Grohmann, *RE* s.v. *Muza* 988 (1935) and Beeston 356.

21:7.21   12,000 stades

The actual distance is ca. 8000 stades. On the discrepancy, see App. 2.

21:7.21–23   The whole place . . . activity

On Muza's share in the trade with Africa and India, see Introduction: Trade in the Indian Ocean, The Lines and Objects of Trade.

21:7.23   across the water

Sc. the ports in Africa.

22:7.24–25   the city of the province

Apparently there was only one settlement in the province big enough to be called "city" (*polis*), the others being but towns or villages.

22:7.24   Sauê

Called Save by Pliny (6.104) and Sabê by Ptolemy (6.7.42). Its identification with Sawwā to the south of Ta'izz (13°34'N, 44°2'E), originally suggested by Glaser (cf. Grohmann, *RE* s.v. *Mapharitis* 1407–9 [1930]) has met with general approval; see J. Tkač, *RE* s.v. *Sabe* 2 1567 (1920); Beeston 356. Grohmann's map (1407) places it rather far east; H. von Wissman, who did the endpaper map in Grohmann's later *Arabien*, Handbuch der Altertumswissenschaft, Kulturgeschichte des Alten Orients 3.4 [Munich, 1963]), there locates it due south of Ta'izz and due east of Mocha, more or less in the vicinity of the modern village of Kuwayrah (13°19'N, 44°1'E); see too his map in *ANRW* ii 9.1375 (1976). The distance from Mocha to Ta'izz by the modern road is sixty-five miles. In 1763 Carsten Niebuhr covered it in four days (*Reisebeschreibung nach Arabien und andern umliegenden Ländern* [Copenhagen, 1774], i 373–76).

22:7.25   Mapharitis

Mapharitis has been identified with the Bilād al-Ma'āfir of the Arab geographers, a region in southwest Yemen with its center more or less where

Ta'izz (cf. under 22:7.24) now stands; see Grohmann, op. cit. under 22:7.24. By the time of the *Periplus* it had attained its greatest extent, reaching southwestward to include Okêlis (cf. under 25:8.19).

22:7.25–26   The governor, Cholaibos

On this name, corresponding to the Arabic Kulayb, see M. Rodinson, *Annuaire de l'École pratique des Hautes Études* ive Section, Sciences historiques et philologiques (1975–76): 205–6. The name is not attested as that of an official in any of the South Arabian sources. On his title, see under B 2:1.9–10 and, on his place in the administration, see Introduction: Political Geography.

23:7.27   Nine days further inland is Saphar

The manuscript reads "Aphar"; since both Pliny (6.104) and Ptolemy (6.7.41) have Sapphar, the restoration is certain. It has been identified with Zufar (14°13′N, 44°31′E), some twenty miles southeast of Yārim, where extensive ruins are visible (*Encyclopaedia of Islam* s.v. *Zafār* 1185 [1934]). Yārim (14°18′N, 44°23′E) is eighty miles from Ta'izz by the modern road, a distance which Niebuhr (op. cit. under 22:7.24, i 394–99) covered in six days. Since the distance from Sauê to Saphar appears to have been roughly the same, nine days seems excessive; cf. Grohmann (op. cit. under 22:7.24) 1406–7. Sprenger (184) suggested the road may have followed a roundabout route in order to take advantage of less hilly terrain.

23:7.27–29   Charibaêl, legitimate king of the two nations, the Homerite and the one, lying next to it, called the Sabaean

Of the two nations mentioned, the Sabaean for long was the more important. The Sabaeans make their appearance in history relatively early, being attested in Assyrian inscriptions as well as the Old Testament (cf. Grohmann, *Arabien* [op. cit. under 22:7.24] 24–25). Around the seventh century B.C. they had achieved a level of political organization and of prosperity that enabled them to carry out such large-scale public works as the temple and mighty dam at their chief city, Marib, impressive ruins of which still stand (see B. Doe, *Southern Arabia* [London, 1971], 76–78 and pls. 14, 15). A Greek geographer, writing about 100 B.C., remarks on the Sabaeans' wealth, pointing out that much of it came from the trade they carried on in aromatics, those imported from Africa (cf. 7:3.18–20 and 8:3.31–32) as well as their own (Artemidorus ap. Strabo 16.778). Aelius Gallus, the Roman commander who attempted to conquer Arabia (cf. under 19:6.26–28), was also impressed with the Sabaeans' wealth: of all the Arabian peoples they were, he stated (Pliny 6.161), "the richest, thanks to the fertility of their forests for producing aromatics, their gold mines, their well-watered fields."

The Sabaeans and the Himyarites—or Homerites, as Greek writers called them—are attested in numerous inscriptions found in South Arabia. The Himyarites, who occupied lands lying to the south of the Sabaeans, enter the stage of history long after their neighbors: the earliest inscription to name them dates from the end of the first century B.C. or the first century A.D. (cf. H. von Wissman, "Ḥimyar, Ancient History," *Le Muséon* 77 [1964]: 429–99 at 443–44). Aelius Gallus reckoned them the most populous of the nations of Arabia (Pliny 6.161). The inscriptions reveal that relations between Himyar and Saba were often hostile (cf. A. Beeston, "The Himyarite Problem," *Proceedings of the Eighth Seminar for Arabian Studies* [London, 1975], 1–7 at 4). However, at the time the *Periplus* was written, it would appear that the two were under a single ruler whose domain reached to the southwestern tip of the peninsula, so that the ports of Muza, Okêlis, and Eudaimôn Arabia all fell under his jurisdiction (see Introduction: Political Geography). How long this situation lasted, we cannot tell; all we can be sure of is that his reign was long enough to span the rule of at least two Roman emperors (see under 23:7.29–30).

Historians of South Arabia have long been convinced that the *Periplus's* characterization of Charibaêl as king of both the Sabaeans and Himyarites is the equivalent of a title frequently found in the inscriptions, "king of Sabaeans and dhū Raydān," and that therefore dhū Raydān must refer to Himyar. They then go further and infer that a union of the two must have taken place, one in which Himyar held the upper hand and so was able to shift the site of the court from Marib to Zufar (cf. J. Ryckmans, "Chronologie des rois de Saba et ḏū-Raydān," *Oriens Antiquus* 3 [1964]: 67–90 at 76–77; von Wissman 448–49, Grohmann 28). However, Beeston (2–4) has cast serious doubt on this reconstruction of events and, indeed, now informs me that evidence newly available indicates it should definitely be discarded. After the reign of Charibaêl, the two peoples must have been politically separate because they are often found in conflict with each other. Despite this, both sides use the title "king of Sabaeans and dhū Raydān" (cf. the instances cited by von Wissman in *ANRW* ii 9.1 436–37 [1976]). C. Robin, who has given particular attention to the anomaly, takes (J. Chelhod et al., eds., *L'Arabie du sud: Histoire et civilisation*. i, *Le peuple yemenite et ses racines* [Paris, 1984], 212) dhū Raydān to be "le nom de la confédération tribale dominée par les souverains himyarites" and suggests that "le double titre des rois sabéens résulte du fait qu'ils ne reconnaissent pas la légitimité des rois himyarites et revendiquent leur royaume. Les souverains himyarites reconnaissent bien les rois sabéens mais seulement comme 'rois de Saba' '; leur double titre s'explique certainement par des visées sur le haut-pays de Saba', c'est-à-dire la région de Sanaa."

Beeston's study of the inscriptions reveals that, about the time the *Periplus* was written, there is "the remarkable spectacle of two sets of coregents belonging to different family groups simultaneously claiming to be kings of Saba and Dhū Raydān" ("Kingship in Ancient South Arabia," *JESHO* 15 [1972]: 256–68 at 261). This may explain why Charibaêl is specifically referred to as "legitimate king"; it was the author's way of indicating which of those who used the title was, in his judgment, the actual ruler. Charibaêl—i.e., Krb'l—is a common royal name in inscriptions and on coins from South Arabia, occurring from the fifth century B.C. to the time of the *Periplus* and later (cf. Grohmann 26, von Wissman 498). Which is to be identified with the Charibaêl of the *Periplus* has been much debated; for a review of the various suggestions, see Rodinson (op. cit. under 22:7.25–26) 201–5.

23:7.29–30 a friend of the emperors, thanks to continuous embassies and gifts

A passage in Pliny (12.57) refers to such embassies and provides a clue to the nature of the gifts. Discussing how little is known about the frankincense tree, he remarks on "the embassies that came from Arabia in my lifetime" and then follows with mention of "the branches of incense that come to us," clearly implying a connection between the two, that the frankincense had been brought by the embassies. Pliny does not mention myrrh, since it was not relevant to his subject; Charibaêl, ruler of the area where myrrh grew (see under 24:8.9), no doubt would have sent myrrh. The plural "emperors" implies that his time on the throne spanned the reigns of at least two emperors.

24:7.31 though without a harbor

Cf. *SDRS*, sector 7, p. 118: "Al Mukha (13°19′N, 43°15′E) has an open roadstead exposed to all but E winds."

24:8.1   the anchorages with sandy bottom

When James Bruce visited Mocha he too was impressed by this feature (op. cit. under 20:7.15–16, ii 206): "The ground for anchorage is of the very best kind, sand without coral, which last chafes the cables all over the Red Sea."

24:8.2   Arab sleeved clothing

The sleeved tunic is often, as here, the mark of foreign garb; cf. Herodotus 7.61 (Persian), Strabo 4.196 (Gallic). However, it was also worn by Greeks and Romans, both men and women, particularly as a winter garment; cf. *P. Cairo Zen.* 59092 (= *Sel. Pap.* 182).10–11 (257 B.C.; part of Zenon's wardrobe), 59146.3 (256 B.C.), 59469.6 (mid-3d century B.C.); *P. Teb.* 46.34 (113 B.C.; a woman's tunic); Pliny, *Epist.* 3.5.15.

24:8.3   with checks

Or perhaps "tartan." The Greek is *skotulatos,* a transcription of the Latin *scutulatus;* on this term, see J. Wild, "The Textile Term *Scutulatus,*" *CQ* 14 (1964): 263–66. Wild cites several examples of ancient checked garments, silk as well as wool, that have been found; all, as it happens, come from northern Europe.

24:8.3a   saffron

The Greek is *krokos,* appearing in the *Periplus* only in this passage and to be identified here as *Crocus sativus* L., the source of saffron; see F. Orth, *RE* s.v. *Safran* (1920). Saffron was highly prized both for the yellow dye it yielded (Orth 1729) and its use in perfumery (1730). It was also used in medicines. Dioscorides (1.26), for example, recommends it for eye ailments, and it occurs in a prescription for eye salve found in Egypt (*O. Tait* 2181 [2d–3d century A.D.] and commentary by C. Préaux in *Chronique d'Égypte* 31 [1956]: 137–39) as well as in other prescriptions (see, e.g., under 28: 9.16a and cf. V. Gazza in *Aegyptus* 36 [1956]: 86). It is still used medicinally in parts of the Far East; see Perry and Metzger (op. cit. under 8:3.31b) 182. The best grew in various places in Asia Minor (Diosc. 1.26, Pliny 21.31–34), less prized varieties elsewhere, but none in Egypt; it must have been imports that merchants loaded at Myos Hormos and Berenicê to bring to Muza (cf. *P. Cairo Zen.* 59678.3 [mid-3d century B.C.], where saffron appears in a list of what the editor considers to be goods from abroad). Diocletian's Edict lists "Arabic saffron" (*Ed. Diocl.*

36.60); since saffron does not grow in Arabia (indeed, no member of the genus *Crocus* is listed in Schwartz [op. cit. under 8:3.31a] 1–393), this must be a trade term of some sort.

Löw (ii 8), mistakenly taking the *krokos* mentioned here to be an import from India, identified it as turmeric.

24:8.4   *cyperus*

Dioscorides (1.4) describes *kyperos* as a reed resembling a leek that serves various medicinal purposes, and the term appears in a number of prescriptions found in the Greek papyri from Egypt (*P. Ryl.* 531 verso col. ii 45, 3d–2d century B.C.; *PSI* 718.4, 4th–5th century A.D.; *P. Coll. Youtie* ii 87.15, 6th century A.D.). It is generally identified as *Cyperus rotondus* or *Cyperus longus* (Berendes [op. cit. under 8:3.31a] 27; Löw i 558–59), both of which grow in Egypt (V. Täckholm, *Students' Flora of Egypt* [Cairo, 1974²], 786–87). Watt (ii 686–87) identifies it specifically as *rotondus*, describing the plant's widespread use in India in perfumery as well as for medicines; he lists no uses whatever for *longus* (ii 685). Similarly, Täckholm notes (786) medicinal use in Egypt of *rotondus* but not of *longus*.

Why the plant was imported is puzzling, since it grows in Arabia, even in areas not too far from Muza; see Schwartz (op. cit. under 8:3.31a) 338.

24:8.4a   cloth

Either of linen or wool; see App. 4.

24:8.4b   *abollai*

See under 6:2.24a.

24:8.5   with shaded stripes

See under B 24:8.5.

24:8.5a   unguent

The unguents of perfumery came from a wide variety of plants; see Pliny 13.8–18 and, for those native to Egypt, *ESAR* ii 4. It was common, as here, merely to write "unguent" without specifying what kind; cf., e.g., *PSI* 4.333.6, 11 (mid-3d century B.C.), *SB* 9348, col. i.9 (A.D. 169/170), *BGU* 1.11 (3d century A.D.).

24:8.6   the region produces . . . wine

Wine is still produced there, particularly around San'a, where Niebuhr (op. cit. under 22:7.24, i 420) saw twenty different varieties available in the market. For the evidence for wine in South Arabia in ancient and medieval times, see Grohmann (op. cit. under 8:3.31a) 234–36. There is no need to speculate that the wine may have been palm wine (cf. Mc-Crindle 27) or date wine (cf. Warmington 265).

24:8.7   the king and the governor

That is, Charibaêl and Cholaibos; cf. Introduction: Political Geography.

24:8.7–9   the king and the governor are given . . . copperware

For the ports serving capitals the list of imports and exports usually includes a special group of costly goods identified as being "for the king" or, as here, the king and governor. See 6:2.33–35 (Adulis), 28:9.16–18 (Kanê), 49:16.25–28 (Barygaza), and, for the absence of such a listing at Barbarikon, see under 39:13.7–9, and at Muziris/Nelkynda see Introduction: Trade in the Indian Ocean, The Trade with India. Some take these to be gifts for obtaining royal favor (McCrindle 30, 39; Schoff 284–87; Warmington 262). It seems hard to believe that the merchants whom the author addresses could afford to give away so many high-priced things—from golden tableware to expensive clothing, from horses to beautiful slave girls (cf. M. Charlesworth, *Trade Routes and Commerce of the Roman Empire* [Cambridge, 1926²], 68). Moreover, when the author does deal with gifts for currying favor, he expressly describes them as such; see 17:6.17. It seems best to take the goods "for the king" as referring to what could be offered for sale to the court as against ordinary buyers.

In the passages dealing with Adulis, Kanê, and Barygaza, the author simply writes "for the king" and follows this with a list of goods. Only here is there the verb "are given." It could well be not the author's word, but some scribe's insertion.

24:8.9   myrrh

The myrrh of Arabia comes from the same tree as the Somalian (see under 7:3.20), *Commiphora myrrha* Nees, although Arabia has other myrrh-bearing trees as well (cf. Van Beek [op. cit. under 7:3.20] 143, Groom [op. cit. under 7:3.20] 118–20, Schwartz [op. cit. under 8:3.31a] 128–29).

They all grow only in Yemen and the westernmost part of the Hadramaut, in other words, west of the area that produces frankincense (Map 6). Pliny (12.69) states that Minaean myrrh, i.e., from northeastern Yemen (see under 24:8.10a) is inferior to Trogodytic, i.e., the myrrh of northwestern Somalia (see under 2:1.7–10, 7:3.20). This is strikingly confirmed by a schedule of tariffs found at Oxyrhynchus in Egypt (*WChrest* 273, 2d–3d century A.D.; cf. *ESAR* ii 607), which lists Minaean "unguent" at one-third the tariff for Trogodytic; the "unguent" must be myrrh, the only plant common to both regions that produced an unguent worth exporting (cf. W. Wilcken in *Archiv für Papyrusforschung* 3 [1906]: 187–88).

24:8.10   *stactê*

Stactê is oil of myrrh produced by crushing and pressing (Theophrastus, *de Odor*. 29, Diosc. 1.60, 1.64.1), which is rich and thick enough to serve as an unguent by itself (Diosc. 1.60, Pliny 13.17). It was a very choice form (Pliny 12.68) and costly (Diosc. 1.60); on the Roman market its price ranged from 13 to 40 denarii a Roman pound as against 11 to 16 for all other types (Pliny 12.70). Pliny (12.68) wrongly took *stactê* to be the natural exudation from the tree as against the exudation caused by gashing the bark; see Steier (op. cit. under 7:3.20) 1136.

24:8.10a   Abeirian (?) and Minaean

The manuscript reads "Abeirminaia." Since Minaean myrrh is well attested (Diosc. 1.64.2, Pliny 12.69, Galen 14.68, *WChrest* 273 [cf. under 24:8.9]), the text has been emended to "Abeir⟨ian and ⟩ Minaean."

On the Minaeans, see Doe (op. cit. under 23:7.27–29) 66–70; A. Beeston in *Encyclopaedia of Islam* s.v. *Maʿin* (1986²). They not only are mentioned by Greek and Roman writers (Strabo 16.768 [cf. under 20:7.4–6], 776; Pliny 6.157, 6.161, 12.54, 12.69) but appear in numerous inscriptions, including many from the region they inhabited, Maʿin, which is placed just above parallel 16° north and between meridians 44° and 46° east (see the endpaper map in Grohmann, op. cit. under 22:7.24). At the end of the last century this was still an important myrrh-producing region; see A. Deflers, *Voyage au Yemen: Journal d'une excursion botanique faite en 1887* (Paris, 1889), 120–21 (the district he refers to, ninety kilometers north-northeast of San'a, would fall within Maʿin). The Minaeans were a great trading people (cf. Raschke 964–65, n. 1251) who specialized in aromatics (Strabo 16.776, Pliny 12.54), including frankincense, which was grown totally outside their homeland; thus references to "Minaean frankincense" (*P. Cairo Zen* 59536.11, *PSI* 628.5; both mid-3d century B.C.) can only mean frankincense that they traded or transported (cf. W. Müller 725). Similarly, references to "Minaean myrrh" might be to myrrh from outside Ma'in, which they handled, as well as to their own production (cf. C. Préaux, *L'économie royale des Lagides* [Brussels, 1939], 362; A. Beeston in *Proceedings of the Fifth Seminar for Arabian Studies* [London, 1972], 5).

"Abeirian" myrrh is just possibly to be identified with the "Gabirean" mentioned by Dioscorides (1.64.1), as Sprenger (167) has argued; pointing to such alternate names of Arabian towns as Azza and Ghazza, Amorra and Gomorra, he takes "Abeir" as an alternative form of "Gabeir." Yet, even if this is so, nothing is known of "Gabirean myrrh" beyond the name.

24:8.10b   white marble

The Greek word is *lygdos*, which Pliny (36.62: *lygdinus* [sc. *lapis*]) describes as a stone of extraordinary whiteness that came in pieces big enough only for carving into plates or bowls and that he considered a close second to alabaster for making unguent jars; he notes that previously the sole source had been Arabia but now it was Paros. Numbers of stone boxes found on Paros and elsewhere are made of a Parian marble of exceptionably pure and even crystallinity, and this has been identified as the stone Pliny refers to; see O. Rubensohn, *RE* s.v. *Paros* 1794 (1949), and cf. L. Robert, *Hellenica* 11–12 (1960): 118–19, n. 7. A form of alabaster is quarried in the region some twenty miles east of San'a (*Western Arabia and the Red Sea* [Admiralty, Naval Intelligence Division, Geographical Handbooks, 1946], 527; cf. C. Millingen, "Notes of a Journey in Yemen," *Journal of the Royal Geographical Society* 44 [1874]: 118–26 at 121: "Gypsum, alabaster, and marble are found in the neighboring hills [sc. around San'a]").

24:8.10–11   all the aforementioned merchandise from Adulis across the water

Namely ivory, tortoise shell, and rhinoceros horn; see 6:3.4.

24:8.11-12   The best time for sailing to this place is around . . . September

See App. 3.

25:8.13   300-stade

See under 21:7.19.

25:8.15   a strait, not very long

The Straits of Bab el Mandeb.

25:8.15–16   that contracts the waters and closes them off into a narrow passage

The Large Strait, between Perim Island and the African shore, is about twelve miles wide and the Small Strait, between Perim and the Arabian shore, about one and one-half; cf. Desanges (op. cit. under 7:3.13–14) 84.

25:8.16   60 stades

This figure, which was the estimate of Timosthenes (Pliny 6.163), admiral under Ptolemy II (Pliny 6.183), was apparently the generally accepted one, for it appears in both Strabo (16.769) and Pliny (6.163: 7500 paces) as well as here. It is a grave underestimate: the total width is 16 nautical miles = 160 stades; the Large Strait alone is 12 = 120 stades (see Desanges 275 and op. cit. under 7:3.13–14, 84). The author may have taken the figure at secondhand, since he very likely never crossed the strait himself; his route to the ports of Africa went down the western shore, to those of Arabia and India down the eastern. Only locals made the crossing (7:3.15–16, 18–20).

25:8.17   Diodôros Island

Perim Island, which, as the author states, lies between the two shores.

25:8.17a   strong currents

There are two in the straits, the current caused by the wind and the tidal current. At times either may reach a velocity of three to four knots (*SDRS*, sector 5, p. 80).

25:8.19   Okêlis

It was first known as Akila (Strabo 16.769; cf. Dihle [op. cit. under 15:5.18] 561–62). Pliny, probably using information derived from late

Hellenistic sources, calls it Acila in one passage but Ocilia in another and seems to be unaware that they are the same place (6.151, 12.88; cf. Dihle 562). In a third passage, in which he deals with the monsoon voyages that ships made in his own day, like the author of the *Periplus* he calls it Ocelis (6.104). The *Periplus* characterizes Okêlis as a stopping point rather than a port of trade; by Ptolemy's time it had achieved that status (6.7.7: *Okêlis emporion*). The site has been identified as the lagoon called Shaykh Sa'īd or Khawr Ghurayrah (12°43'N, 43°28'E); see Sprenger 67, Glaser 169, Grohmann (*Mapharitis*, cit. under 22:7.24) 1409. This lagoon is probably the "small harbour" that Wellsted saw (ii 466). The French thought it useful enough to acquire rights to it, though they never exercised them; see Barre (op. cit. under 7:3.13–14) 375.

25:8.19a   belongs to the same province

I.e., Mapharitis; cf. Introduction: Political Geography.

25:8.20   watering station, and the first place to put in for those sailing on

See under B 25:8.20. The author has in mind vessels that went directly to India without intermediate stops at any of the ports in Arabia. Leaving from Myos Hormos or Berenicê and taking the central passage down the Red Sea (cf. 20:7.14–16 and under 20:7.15–16), they made their first stop at Okêlis to attend to last-minute matters and take on water before the long haul over the open sea. Cf. Pliny 6.104: "It is most convenient for those sailing to India to take their departure from Ocelis."

26:8.21–22   the waters . . . open sea

The Gulf of Aden.

26:8.22–23   1200 stades distant is Eudaimôn Arabia

There is universal agreement that Eudaimôn Arabia was on the site of Aden; see Müller, McCrindle, Fabricius, Schoff, Warmington 9, Huntingford. The figure of 1200 stades is somewhat high; Shaykh Sa'īd is about ninety-five nautical miles from Aden.

The name the author gives the port is the same as that which the Romans gave to the kingdom of the Sabaeans, Arabia Felix in Latin (cf. Bowersock [op. cit. under 19:6.26–28] 2). Ptolemy (6.7.9) calls it *Arabia emporion*. However, a dedicatory inscription found at Koptos, dated A.D.

70, reveals that the name Aden was also in use at this time: the dedicator refers to himself as *Adaneitês*, "citizen of Adanê" (published by G. Wagner in *Bulletin de l'Institut français d'archéologie orientale* 76 [1976]: 278). Philostorgius, writing in the first quarter of the fifth century A.D., calls it Adanê (*Hist. Eccl.* 3.4); thereafter no other names appear.

26:8.23–24   the same kingdom, Charibaêl

Cf. Introduction: Political Geography.

26:8.24–25   sources of water much sweeter

The sources must have been reservoirs for storing rain water such as Aden has had to use throughout the centuries. Ibn Battuta (cf. Yule-Cordier ii 440) remarked on the city's lack of fresh water and its use of reservoirs, and there are impressive remains of some fifty still to be seen (Yule-Cordier ii 440, O. Löfgren in *Encyclopaedia of Islam* s.v. '*Adan* [1960²]).

26:8.27–30   in earlier days . . .
the cargoes of both

On the nature of trade with India before the discovery by Greek seamen of the monsoon winds, see Introduction: Trade in the Indian Ocean, The Setting. Since Aden at this time was no longer required as an entrepôt and since Muza, also a port of Charibaêl's realm, was presumably handling all the country's trade, Aden was experiencing a period of neglect; moreover, it had to recover from an attack it had suffered recently (cf. under 26:8.31–32). But the place boasts a powerful and useful location and snug inner harbor (see Wellsted ii 385–86), so its period of neglect need not have been very long. Ptolemy's listing of the port (cf. under 26:8.23) would indicate that by his day it was once again active. A remark dropped by Philostorgius (*Hist. Eccles.* 3.4) reveals that in the mid-fourth century A.D. Roman ships regularly stopped there. And Idrisi (trans. P. Jaubert in *Recueil de voyages et de mémoires publié par la Société de Géographie* v [Paris, 1836], 51), writing in the mid-twelfth century, describes it as the point of departure for vessels en route to China and India, while Marco Polo (3.36), at the end of the thirteenth, notes the great volume of traffic from India that came to it. As in the time of the *Periplus*, however, there were certain periods when, for one reason or another, Aden went into eclipse; see Löfgren (op. cit. under 26:8.24–25).

26:8.31–32   not long before our time,
Caesar sacked it

The only Roman attack upon South Arabia that is known is the expedition led by Aelius Gallus (cf. under 19:6.26–28), and that ground to a halt long before reaching the vicinity of Aden. Thus this brief sentence presents a puzzle, one that has bred an abundant literature. Earlier commentators and translators cut the Gordian knot by emending "Caesar" out of the text and replacing with the name of a local ruler, Elisar (Müller, Fabricius) or Charibaêl (Glaser ii 171, Schoff). Subsequent commentators have been less drastic. One school of thought, using vague remarks in Pliny plus arguments based on presumed imperial foreign policy towards the Orient, holds that there must have been a Roman attack upon the town, but there is total disagreement as to which Caesar was responsible and consequently when the attack took place; Augustus, Gaius, Claudius, Nero, Trajan, and Septimius Severus all have their supporters (references in Raschke 872, nn. 909–12). Another school holds that the *Periplus's* words can only refer to Gallus's expedition but reflect a misapprehension about it: Gallus led his men into the region called Eudaimôn Arabia but, by the time the *Periplus* was written, perhaps a century later, memories had grown hazy and it was assumed that the expedition had marched into the town of the same name (first suggested by J. Mordtmann in *Zeitschrift der deutschen morgenländischen Gesellschaft* 44 [1890]: 180; cf. J. Anderson in *CAH* x 883 [1934] and, for the fullest presentation, K. Wellesley, "The Fable of a Roman Attack on Aden," *La Parola del Passato* 9 [1954]: 401–5). For a convenient survey of the various views, see Rodinson (op. cit. under 5:2.19–20) 233–37.

Clearly, at the time of the *Periplus*, the town was in a more or less abandoned state. The basic cause, as the author states (26:8.27–31), was the total loss of the trade it had enjoyed as an entrepôt before the shippers of Roman Egypt began to sail directly to India; how much further downhill military attack pushed it must remain an open question. However, by the mid-fourth century A.D., it had reasserted itself (see under 26:8.27–30).

27:9.1–2   a long coast . . . 2000 stades or more

From Aden to just short of Husn al Ghurab (= Kanê; see under 27:9.3–4) the coast is, by and large, low and sandy with few indentations, capes, or other irregularities; these start at Ras al Usaydah (13°57′N, 48°10′E), nine or so nautical miles before Husn al Ghurab. See *SDRS*, sector 9, pp. 127–29. On the figure of 2000 stades, see under 27:9.3–4.

27:9.3–4   beyond the projecting headland . . . Kanê

The placing of Kanê in the area of the prominent cape of Husn al Ghurab (13°59'N, 48°19'E), suggested over a century ago (Müller, Glaser 174–75), is certain: the site is some 205 nautical miles from Aden, which nicely suits the author's estimate of 2000 or more stades; an inscription found there attests to the name Qn', or Qana' as it is usually expanded (see G. Mathew in Chittick-Rothberg [op. cit. under 15:5.7–16:6.13] 159–60, W. Müller 712); and ancient ruins have been found precisely where the author locates the port, just beyond the cape (see Doe [op. cit. under 23:7.27–29] 182–86, with a plan [183] and excellent photographs of the site [pls. 81, 82]).

27:9.4   the kingdom of Eleazos

See Introduction: Political Geography. Eleazos is the Greek transcription of 'L'z, or 'Īl'azz as it is generally expanded, a name that occurs frequently in the South Arabic inscriptions. It was borne by at least two kings but, though arguments have been put forth to identify one of these with the Eleazos mentioned here (cf. Raschke 984, n. 1358; H. von Wissmann, *RE* Suppl. 11.1346–47 [1968] and 12.542 [1970]), too little is known of the early history of the Hadramaut to permit certainty; cf. Rodinson, op. cit. under 5:2.19–20, 237–38 and op. cit. under 22:7.25–26, 201.

27:9.5–6   two barren islands, one called Orneôn ["of birds"] and the other Trullas

The most likely candidate for Orneôn, the "Isle of Birds," is Sikha (13°55'N, 48°23'E) and for Trullas Barraqah (13°59'N, 48°28'E); though both are nearer Husn al Ghurab than the distances the author gives, other islands in the vicinity are even more so. Sikha lies some six and one-half nautical miles to the southeast, Barraqah some eight to the east; both rise to peaks that are white with guano, a feature that explains such a name as "Isle of Birds." See *SDRS*, sector 9, pp. 129–30. Müller identifies Trullas with Hillaniyah; that island, lying just off the coast, suits a distance of 120 stades far less well than Barraqah (cf. Beeston 356).

Ptolemy (6.7.10) lists a Trulla Limên (Port Trulla) which he places a sixth of a degree south of Kanê. He makes no mention of the Isle of Birds.

27:9.7   Saubatha

This is the Sabata of Strabo (16.768), the Sabota of Pliny (6.155, 12.52), and the Sabbatha of Ptolemy (6.7.38) which, like Saubatha, are transcriptions of Šabwat or Shabwa, as it is usually spelled, the ancient capital of the Hadramaut. Its importance is attested by inscriptions (cf. Doe [op. cit. under 23:7.27–29] 233–35), Pliny's statement (6.155) that it boasted sixty temples within the embrace of its walls and was a collection point for frankincense (12.63), and Ptolemy's according it the status of a metropolis. The site is marked by the remains of town walls with bastions, an impressive complex with column bases that probably was a temple, and structures with windowless rooms or vaults that may have served as storerooms for incense. See B. Doe, *Monuments of South Arabia* (Naples, 1983, 136–41) and J. Breton, "Shabwa, Capitale antique du Hadramawt," *JA* 275 (1987): 13–34.

27:9.8 All the frankincense grown in the land is brought into Kanê

A few lines above (27:9.4–5), the author had identified Eleazos's kingdom as the "frankincense-bearing land," and here he identifies Kanê as the port from which the frankincense was shipped out. Actually Eleazos's sway, extending from Shabwa to that point past the Isles of Zênobios where Persis' sway began (33:11.11–12), i.e., past ca. 56°20′E (see under 33:11.10–11), included an area west of what is now the frankincense-bearing region. The Arabian frankincense tree (*Boswellia sacra*; cf. under 8:3.30a) today grows mainly in the Dhufar plain of Oman, more or less from 53° east to a little beyond 55° east—in other words, from a point a good deal east of Kanê (48°19′E) to just short of the eastern border of Eleazos's realm; see Hepper (op. cit. under 8:3.30a) 66–67 and Map 6. This agrees with the reports of ancient writers: Strabo (16.782) had been told that the source of the best frankincense was the area nearest Persis; Pliny states (12.52) that from Sabota to the land of frankincense was an eight-day journey, presumably to the east; and our author places the "frankincense-bearing land" along the gulf east of Kanê (29:9.23–24), whence the frankincense was brought to Kanê by both land and water (cf. W. Müller 711–14, Van Beek [op. cit. under 7:3.20] 142). It was brought there because Kanê was the major port of call on the South Arabian coast and a point of departure for ships making the direct crossing to India (see App. 3).

According to Pliny (12.65), the best grade of Arabian frankincense sold on the Roman market for 6 denarii a Roman pound, the next best for 5, and the poorest for 3. Such prices put frankincense among the cheapest of the imported aromatics: see under 7:3.20 and cf. *ESAR* v 285.

27:9.9 rafts of a local type

These were buoyed rafts, consisting of a platform held up by inflated skins, a well-known type of primitive water transport that is found in many parts of the world; see J. Hornell, *Water Transport* (Cambridge, 1946), 20–34, esp. 30–31. Pliny (6.176) tells how certain Arab pirates who haunted this part of the coast (cf. Sprenger 98–99, 313–14) made rafts "by spreading a plank over a pair of ox bladders"; in the 1830s Wellsted saw rafts of exactly this description off the coast of Oman: he reports that the local Beduins would come out to his boat "on two inflated skins with a board placed across" (*Travels to the City of the Caliphs* [London, 1840], ii 123).

27:9.11   Barygaza, Skythia, Omana

The ports are listed from furthest to nearest. On the location of Skythia see under 38:12.23, and of Omana under 36:12.3–4. On the nature of their trade, see Introduction: Trade in the Indian Ocean, The Lines and Objects of Trade.

27:9.12   Persis

See under 33:11.12.

28:9.16   coral

Coral was exported to India as well as Arabia; cf. 39:13.8, 49:16.21, 56:18.19. Red Sea coral, to be had all along the western coast of Arabia, hardly required importation via shippers from Egypt; moreover, it was considered of inferior quality (Pliny 32.21). The coral referred to here must have come from the Mediterranean, which produced prized varieties (cf. under 39:13.8b).

28:9.16a   storax

Storax is an aromatic resin that the Greeks and Romans used as incense and medicament; see A. Steier, *RE* s.v. *Storax* (1932) and cf. *P. Vindob. Worp* 20 (1st–3d century A.D.; prescription consisting of storax, alum, saffron, galbanum). D. Hanbury, in an authoritative study of its source in antiquity ("On Storax" and "Additional Observations on Storax" in his *Scientific Papers* [London, 1876], 129–50), concluded that ancient storax must have been the so-called solid storax, which is derived from *Styrax officinalis* L., a small tree found in parts of southern Europe, Asia Minor, and the Levant (129, 148), and not the so-called liquid storax, which comes from *Liquidambar orientalis* Miller, a lofty umbrageous tree found only in southwestern Asia Minor (139). Dioscorides (1.66) and Pliny (12.124–25) state that the tree that produces storax resembles the quince and that it grows, according to Dioscorides in southeastern Asia Minor and northern Syria, according to Pliny in northern Syria, Phoenicia, Cyprus, and Crete. Their words thus suit *Styrax officinalis* very well but *Liquidambar orientalis* not at all, and so most commentators, like Hanbury, take ancient storax to have been the solid variety; see Berendes (op. cit. under 8:3.31a) 82, Löw iii 394, Laufer (op. cit. under 6:3.1a) 456, J. André in *Lexique des termes de botanique en Latin* (Paris, 1956) s.v. Solid storax has always been rare and, in the course of time, ceased to be an article of commerce (Hanbury 145); thus Hanbury was never able to secure samples for proper analysis (cf. 132). Moreover, he was unable to derive the resin from trees he examined (128, 148) because all, as a result of repeated cutting for fuel, had been reduced to little more than shrubs.

Liquid storax, on the other hand, is not at all rare; exported from Asia Minor, it long figured in the drug trade (Hanbury 141–42). A number of commentators hold that this, and not the solid, is the storax of the ancients (see F. Flückiger and D. Hanbury, *Pharmacographia* [London, 1879²], 272; Schoff followed by Warmington [265–66]; V. Gazza in *Aegyptus* 36 [1956]: 98). Their view perforce assumes that Dioscorides and Pliny wrongly identified the source. This Hanbury (148) denies and argues that *styrax officinalis*, if left to grow to proper height, would certainly produce resin.

28:9.17   money (?)

Cf. under B 28:9.17.

28:9.17a   for the king

Cf. under 24:8.7–9.

28:9.19   aloe

Dioscorides (3.22.1–5) and Pliny (27.14–22) both devote long sections to the aloe, pointing out its usefulness in treating skin irritations, boils, wounds, constipation. There is evidence that the plant entered Roman pharmacy relatively late, not earlier than the reign of Augustus; see J. Scarborough, "Roman Pharmacy and the Eastern Drug Trade: Some Problems as Illustrated by the Example of Aloe," *Pharmacy in History* 24 (1982): 135–43 at 138, 140. Though a variety of aloe, *Aloe vera*, is found in southern Arabia (Scarborough 139; Schwartz [op. cit. under 8:3.31a] 350), the aloe of this passage may be the type native to Socotra, *Aloe perryi* Baker, brought over from the island in local craft for shipment from Kanê; the Socotrine seems to be the variety Dioscorides describes (Scarborough 138), and it was highly prized in the Middle Ages and later (Scarborough 139; cf. Idrisi [op. cit. under 26:8.27–30] 47). However, the author does not include aloes in his list of Socotra's products; he mentions only tortoise shell and dragon's blood (30:10.11–17, 24).

28:9.19a the rest of its exports are through its connections with the other ports of trade

Kanê, one of the jumping-off points for the voyage to India (57:19.7), was well suited to serve as transshipment port for cargoes headed there (cf. 27:9.10–11). The author lists copper, tin, coral, and storax among the items imported both at Kanê (28:9.15–16) and at Barygaza (49:16.21, 23); some of what arrived at Kanê could well have been transferred to Arab or Indian craft for forwarding to Barygaza, as Schoff (127) and Warmington (387, n. 21) suggest.

28:9.20–21 The time to set sail for this place is about the same as for Muza, but earlier

Cf. 24:8.11–12 and App. 3.

29:9.22 After Kanê

No figure in stades or "runs" is given for the distance—some 250 nautical miles—from Kanê to the next reference point, Syagros (30:9.33, 32:10.26), either through an oversight on the author's part or a defect in the text.

29:9.22–23 with the shoreline receding further, there next come another bay . . . called Sachalitês

At Ras Mijdaha (13°59′N, 48°28′E), just past Barraqah (cf. under 27:9.5–6), the coast recedes somewhat to the north and then sharply to the north a little further on at Ras al Kalb (14°2′N, 48°41′E); from there it runs northeast for thirty-eight nautical miles to Mukalla (14°32′N, 49°8′E). Sachalitês is the Greek transcription of the name Sa'kalan (S'kln and S'klhn in the inscriptions; cf. W. Müller 712, Beeston 357 and *Journal of Oman Studies* 2 [1976]: 39). Here Sachalitês is used of the body of water stretching from the point of coastal recession just described up to Syagros (Ras Fartak; see under 30:9.32–33). In 32:10.30 it is used of the region around Moscha Limên. Ancient geographers were of two minds about the name: to Marinus it was, as here, the body of water west of Syagros; to Ptolemy, as in 32:10.30, it lay east of Syagros (Ptolemy 1.17.2–3 and cf. Müller's note to *Periplus* 29). To the writer of the *Periplus* it was the whole area from east of Kanê to at least Moscha Limên (cf. Glaser 177), more or less the region that produced frankincense (cf. under 27:9.8).

29:9.26   The frankincense-bearing trees are neither very large nor tall

Other writers remark on the smallness or lowness of the tree; cf. W. Müller 715. In height it runs but six to nine feet and, with its branches starting close to the ground, has the appearance more of a shrub than a tree (W. Müller 702).

29:9.28   gum

The reference is to the gum arabic produced by Egypt's acacia trees, either the common *Acacia nilotica* or the rare *Acacia arabica*; see Lucas-Harris (op. cit. under 1:1.2–4) 5–6; Täckholm (op. cit. under 24:8.4) 290.

29:9.29   the districts are terribly unhealthy

The author may well be repeating propaganda put out by Arab traders anxious to discourage competitors (cf. Müller; W. Müller 717); the area where incense grows is no more unhealthy than any other part of southern Arabia. Scary tales about the incense lands go back at least to the time of Herodotus, who reports (3.107) that the trees were guarded by hosts of winged serpents which could be driven off only by the burning of storax.

30:9.32–33   On this bay is a mighty headland, facing the east, called Syagros

Cf. Pliny 6.100 and Ptolemy 1.17.2–3; both, like the author of the *Periplus*, treat Syagros as a prominent landmark. The headland in question can only be Ras Fartak (15°39′N, 52°16′E), "the highest and most prominent headland on the Hadhramaut coast. Here the coastline makes a great northward bend into Qamr bay, and for 8 miles north of the cape precipitous cliffs nearly 2,000 feet high rise sheer from the water." (*Western Arabia* [op. cit. under 24:8.10b] 152). Indeed, it is the second highest and largest promontory along the entire coast (*RSP*, chap. 12.134); Ras Sajir (16°45′N, 53°35′E), 103 nautical miles further, is taller but does not face east.

30:9.33–10.1   at which there are a fortress . . . a harbor, and a storehouse

The harbor could not have been on the eastern face of Ras Fartak; the eight miles of precipitous cliffs (see under 30:9.32–33) effectively preclude this. Possibly it was at the base of the high land on the western side; Khaisat (15°37′N, 52°15′E), the modern port there, offers anchorage to coastal craft and handles a considerable amount of trade (*RSP*, chap. 12.133).

30:10.3   Dioscuridês

This is Socotra, the large island (seventy miles long) that lies 126 nautical miles east of Guardafui and 193 south and a little east of Ras Fartak. It is mentioned by Ptolemy (6.7.45, 8.22.17) and by Pliny (6.153), who estimates its distance from Syagros (= Ras Fartak; see under 30:9.32–33) as 280 Roman miles, a figure that is not too far off. The author, on the other hand, mistakenly takes the island to be nearer the Arabian coast than the African; very likely he sailed by it only from Arabia and never from Africa, since he includes it in his Egypt-Arabia-India route but not in his Egypt-Africa route.

30:10.4   rivers

The northern part of Socotra is well watered and has two rivers that end in bays where vessels can find anchorage (see P. Shinnie, "Socotra," *Antiquity* 34 [1960]: 100–110 at 101; *RSP*, chap. 15.24–25).

30:10.5   crocodiles, a great many vipers, and huge lizards

Cf. H. Forbes, *The Natural History of Sokotra and Abd-el-Kuri* (London, 1903), 83: " 'lizards of enormous size, of which the flesh serves for food, while the grease is melted down and used as a substitute for oil,' can hardly apply to any other than a species of *Varanus*. I have seen the Malayan Monitors applied by the natives to both the uses here stated. . . . The species would probably be either the *Varanus griseus* (Daud.), which is distributed over Northern Africa, South-West Asia, from Arabia to the Caspian Sea and North-West India, or *V. niloticus* (Linn.). Its extinction in Sokotra may be due to the fact of its being used as food and medicine in an island where both are scarce." Of the crocodiles he observes that (93) "the species one would expect to have found would be *Crocodilus niloticus*." All the creatures mentioned in the *Periplus* are no longer to be found on the island. The sole wild animal there today is the civet cat (*RSP*, chap. 15.25).

30:10.7–9 The inhabitants, few in number, live on one side of the island, that to the north

The population of Socotra has always been concentrated in the northern and western parts because these are watered (cf. under 30:10.4). Here extensive ruins have been found; see B. Doe, *Socotra: An Archaeological Reconnaissance in 1967* (Miami, 1970), xviii. Doe assumes (152) that at least some of these go back to the time of the *Periplus*, although no pottery dating earlier than the tenth century A.D. (152) was found. Nor is there any evidence of prehistoric occupation (151).

30:10.11–13 tortoise shell . . . thick shell

For the "genuine," "land," and "light-colored" tortoise shell, see under 3:1.15–16. The "oversize mountain variety with an extremely thick shell" could well have come from *Geochelone pardalis babcocki*, the leopard tortoise. There are no tortoises on Socotra today and only two genera in the area of Africa nearest it. Of these one species is the leopard tortoise, which grows to more than two feet in length and so favors mountainous areas that some call it the mountain tortoise. Presumably it existed on Socotra in Roman times. For a full description see Loveridge-Williams (op. cit. under 3:1.15–16) 235–51. I have handled the shields of a specimen; they are distinctly thicker than those of the hawksbill turtle.

30.10.14 [sc. regular] cutting

The Romans used tortoise shell above all for veneering large objects (see under 3:1.15–16) and hence were particularly interested in securing big pieces.

30:10.17 so-called Indian cinnabar

This is dragon's blood, the resin secreted at the base of the leaves of *Dracaena cinnabari* (see *Western Arabia* [op. cit. under 24:8.10b] 208, Watt ii 18), which was used as a pigment and a drug. The tree is native to Socotra, and the islanders have exported its product for centuries (Watt ii 18, Wellsted [op. cit. under 27:9.9] ii 286–88). Pliny (33.115–16) refers to cinnabar as the name given to dragon's blood by the Indians. It would appear that the term "Indian cinnabar" was used of the vegetable pigment as against the mineral (red mercuric sulphide). Perhaps this was because another form of dragon's blood, very similar to that from *Dracaena*, did come, if not from India at least by way of India, namely, the resin of a palm, *Calamus draco* Willd., which grows in Malay and the East Indies and is the source of the dragon's blood of modern commerce (Watt ii 17). This could well have been called "Indian" in the West because it arrived there through Indian merchants or on Indian ships.

31:10.19–20   just as Azania is to Charibaêl and the governor of Mapharitis

See Introduction: Political Geography.

31:10.20   The island is subject to the aforementioned king of the frankincense-bearing land

Dependence upon the mainland opposite has been the rule through much of Socotra's history. When the Portuguese seized the island in 1507 parts were under some sovereign in South Arabia and, when they left shortly after, he resumed his sway. In the nineteenth century it was under the Mahri sultan of Qishn, whose territory more or less faced the northern coast of Socotra. Since 1967 it has been under Southern Yemen.

31:10.21   Limyrikê

The Malabar coast; see under 51:17.15.

31:10.24–25   At the present time the kings have leased out the island, and it is under guard

The author's description of Dioscuridês seems to have been designed to discourage the merchants and shippers of Roman Egypt from bothering with the island: its chief product was tortoise shell—but not the desirable kind, only what was useful for small objects; dragon's blood was available, but the author makes no mention of its export; the only traders who frequented the place were Arabs from Muza plus occasional Indians who chanced upon it; and, to cap it all, the island not only has been leased out, which would permit the lessee to ban landing there, but is under guard, which would ensure that the ban be respected.

Who held the lease? Some have argued (cf. *CAH* x 881) that it was Roman traders from Egypt, but this makes no sense; the whole point of the *Periplus*'s remarks is to emphasize that the local products were not for them. More likely it was an Arab merchant or consortium of Arab merchants from the "frankincense-bearing land" to which the island was subject. And, if we assume that they not only harvested what grew there—dragon's blood, aloes (see under 28:9.19), and incense (see Doe [op. cit. under 30:10.7–9] 153–54)—but themselves took care of shipping out the goods for sale abroad, we have an explanation of why the author omits listing these as exports.

Presumably by the plural "kings" the author means the predecessors of the present sovereign as well as the present sovereign.

32:10.26–29   a bay . . . Omana, 600 stades across the mouth; after it, high mountains . . . for another 500

At Ras Fartak (= Syagros) the coastline "makes a great northward bend into Qamr bay" (see under 30:9.32–33); Omana, thus, is Qamar Bay. The mountains are the Jabal Qamar, which rise to between 3000 and 4000 feet and approach the coast at Ras Sajir (16°45′N, 53°35′E), then, running eastward, again come close to the coast at Mirbat (16°59′N, 54°44′E), a little beyond Khōr Rūri (= Moscha Limên; see under 32:10.30a). The distance from Ras Fartak to Khōr Rūri is some 170 nautical miles, considerably more than the author's estimate of 1100 stades (600 + 500).

32:10.28–29   where men live in caves

Cf. *RSP*, chap. 13.34: "The inhabitants [of the coast around Khōr Rūri] for the most part dwell in caves, some of which are large; as these caves are usually situated on precipices facing the sea, their positions may sometimes be distinguished at night by their lights."

32:10.30   designated

See App. 1.

32:10.30a   Moscha Limên

Schoff placed Moscha Limên on the inlet of Khōr Rūri (17°2′N, 54°26′E), and recent discoveries have vindicated his choice. For excavation has not only laid bare there the remains of a strongly fortified town (see Doe [op. cit. under 27:9.7] 147–50) but unearthed inscriptions that reveal that it had been founded by a group of colonists sent out under a leader from Shabwa—in other words, by order of the king of Hadramaut (see J. Pirenne, "The Incense Port of Moscha (Khor Rori) in Dhofar," *Journal of*

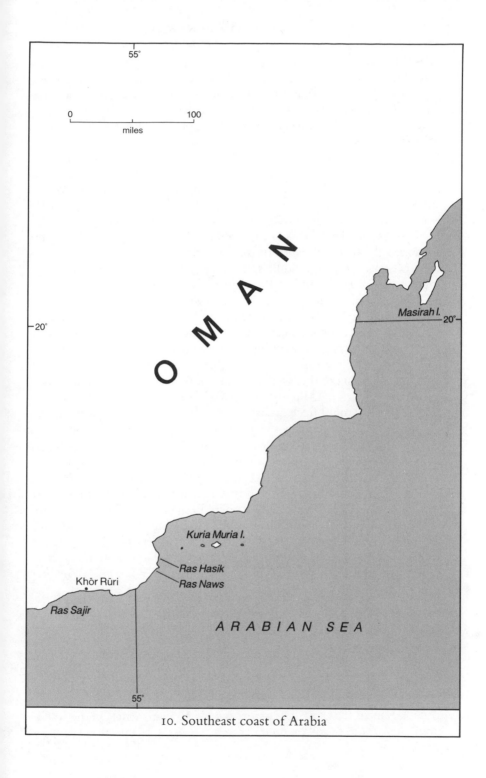

10. Southeast coast of Arabia

Oman Studies 1 [1975]: 81–96 and A. Beeston, "The Settlement at Khor Rori," ibid. 2 [1976]: 39–42). Furthermore, in the debris of the earliest occupation level were found four fragments of Roman ceramic ware dating to the end of the first century B.C. or the beginning of the first century A.D., later rather than earlier (see H. Comfort in *Bulletin of the American Schools of Oriental Research* 160 [1960]: 15–20).

One objection that can be raised against the identification is that Khōr Rūri does not suit the figures the author gives for the location of Moscha Limên: 1100 stades from Syagros (32:10.26–27, 29) and 1500 on to Asichôn (33:11.8–9). Since the actual distance from Ras Fartak to Khōr Rūri is 170 nautical miles (see under 32:10.26–29) and from Khōr Rūri to Ras Hasik 60 (see under 33:11.8–9), it would appear that he seriously underestimated the first and overestimated the second. According to his figures, Moscha Limên should lie sixty or so miles west of Khōr Rūri, i.e., somewhere in the vicinity of Ras Sajir (16°45'N, 53°35'E). Yet there are no likely candidates in this area. The nearest would be Zafar, which was a famed port in the Middle Ages. However, Zafar is little improvement so far as location is concerned since it is but fifteen or so miles further west than Khōr Rūri (it lies within modern Salalah [17°1'N, 54°6'E]) and, what is more, excavation has shown that its origins go back no earlier than the beginning of the twelfth century A.D. (see P. Costa, "The Study of the City of Zafâr (al-Balîd)," *Journal of Oman Studies* 5 [1979]: 111–50, esp. 146). Thus, until fresh archaeological examination reveals new possibilities, Khōr Rūri remains the most likely site for Moscha Limên.

As noted above, the *Periplus* places Moscha Limên well east—some 1100 stades—of Syagros. Ptolemy, who locates the Bay of Sachalitês east of Syagros (see under 29:9.22–23), i.e., the reverse of where the *Periplus* puts it, also reverses (6.7.10) the position of Moscha Limên: the *Periplus* puts it east of Syagros, Ptolemy west of it. Quite possibly both the author of the *Periplus* and Ptolemy misplaced Moscha Limên because they had no access to reliable information. It was a port solely for the use of the king's shippers, and the only foreigners ever found in it were Indian seamen who had been forced to winter there (see under 32:11.1–3); neither were likely sources of information for Westerners.

32:11.1–3   Some vessels are customarily sent to it from Kanê; in addition, those sailing by from Limyrikê or Barygaza that passed the winter [sc. at Moscha] because of the season being late . . . cargo of frankincense

Moscha Limên, thus, was not a port serving foreign vessels in the frankincense trade; these took on their cargoes at Kanê, the collection point for all Arabian frankincense (27:9.8–10), some of which was brought there by water and some by land (27:9.9–10). Moscha Limên was situated in the heart of the region called Sachalitês (as against the bay of that name; cf. under 29:9.22–23), that is, in the Dhufar Plain, the region par excellence of the frankincense tree (see under 27:9.8). It served as a subsidiary collection point into which was gathered whatever was to go on to Kanê by water. And what was gathered there was safe, since Moscha was a "designated harbor," one that enjoyed special security (App. 1).

The only foreign bottoms to be seen in the harbor were accidental arrivals, namely Indian ships that, passing by Moscha, discovered it was too late to catch the last of the southwest monsoon for home and had to lay over until its reappearance the following spring; by special arrangement with the local royal agents they were allowed to exchange what they had on board for a cargo of frankincense. Commentators have assumed that these ships were Arab craft returning from Limyrikê or Barygaza; see Schoff (who even translates the word that means "sailing by" as "returning"), Warmington (342, n. 34), Wheeler 117, Van Beek (op. cit. under 7:3.20) 148, W. Müller 727. But there was no reason for returning Arab craft to stop and winter at Moscha; winter was precisely the time when they did return from India, not only to Arabia but to anywhere west of it; see App. 3. Müller's idea that they were vessels which "serius enavigaverant quam ut secundo etesiarum flatu in Africae oram deferri possent" is wrong for the same reason: the winter was the best time for sailing from Arabia to Africa.

There is archaeological confirmation of Moscha's relations with India, namely the discovery at Khōr Rūri of a bronze Indian statuette that probably dates from the second century A.D. (*Archaeology* 7 [1954]: 254).

32:11.3   cotton cloth and grain and oil

All three were products of the region around Barygaza; see 41:14.4–6. As that pasage shows, the oil was sesame oil.

33:11.8–9   another 1500 stades . . . Asichôn

Asichôn must be Ras Hasik (17°23′N, 55°20′E), for it not only preserves the ancient name but answers the geographical requirements: it is the point in front of which lie the Kuria Muria Islands (the Isles of Zênobios; see under 33:11.10–11); indeed, the island nearest to it is called Hasikiyah. The author gives the distance from Moscha Limên to Asichôn as 1500 stades; having underestimated the previous stage (Syagros to Moscha Limên; see under 32:10.26–29), he grossly overestimates this: from Khōr Rūri to Ras Hasik, sixty nautical miles, is less than half that.

33:11.9   mountain range (?)

If the restoration is correct (cf. under B 33:11.9–10), the mountains would be the Jabal Samhan, a range that extends for seventy-three miles from a point thirty-three miles northeastward of Ras Sajir (16°45′N, 53°35′E) to Ras Naws (17°15′N, 55°19′E).

33:11.10–11   called the Isles of Zênobios

These are undoubtedly the Kuria Muria Islands, running from Al Hasikiyah (17°27′N, 55°37′E) to Al Jabaylah (17°30′N, 56°20′E), with As Sawda, Al Hallaniyah, and Qarzawit in between. There are but five, though Ptolemy (6.7.46) as well as the *Periplus* says seven. The name is preserved in the name of an important tribe inhabiting parts of the mainland opposite and still found on the islands, the Bani Janabah; see S. Miles, *The Countries and Tribes of the Persian Gulf* (London, 1919), 429, 475, 485–86, 488–89, 493; J. Anthony, *Historical and Cultural Dictionary of the Sultanate of Oman* (Metuchen, N.J., 1976), 50–51; H. Treidler, *RE* s.v. Ζηνοβίου ἑπτὰ νησία (1972). For a description of the islands, see *Western Arabia* (op. cit. under 24:8.10b) 616–18, Doe (op. cit. under 30:10.7-9) 137–39.

33:11.12   Persis

Persis was originally a district of the Persian empire that embraced the lands along the eastern shore of the Persian Gulf; see W. Hinz, *RE* Suppl. 12 s.v. *Persis* (1970). During the centuries when a Parthian dynasty ruled in Persia (ca. 248 B.C. to A.D. 226), the district became virtually an independent kingdom, with its own rulers and coinage, acknowledging vassalage to Parthian overlords only when these were strong enough to insist on it (cf. Raschke 815, n. 719). To judge from the statements in the *Periplus*, at the time of writing Persis controlled a broad expanse of territory, from a point on the Arabian coast opposite the Kuria Muria Islands to past Omana on the Makran coast (see under 36:12.3–4). It controlled as well the head of the Persian Gulf (cf. 36:12.5–6).

33:11.12a   over open water

I.e., from the Isles of Zênobios to the Isle of Sarapis the course did not follow the coast but cut straight across.

33:11.13   Isle of Sarapis

Ptolemy (6.7.46) calls it Sarapias. The identification with Masirah is certain, since it is the sole island along this stretch of the coast that corresponds in any way to the specifications the author supplies. From its southern tip, Ras Abu Rasas (20°10′N, 58°39′E), to Ras Hasik is about 250 nautical miles and to the westernmost of the Kuria Muria Islands is some fifteen miles less; neither is too far off from the author's estimate of 2000 stades. Masirah lies eight to twelve miles off the coast, and this suits very nicely his 120 stades. And he has more or less gotten the proportions of the island's length to breadth right even though his figures are double the actual: it is 35 by 10 miles (= 350 by 100 stades rather than 600 by 200).

33:11.15–16   three villages and by holy men of the Ichthyophagoi

Ptolemy (6.7.46) mentions that the island has a sanctuary. The holy men presumably lived there and not in the villages. Cf. under B 33:11.16.

33:11.16–17   use the Arabic tongue and wear loincloths of palm leaves

The primitive peoples whom the Greeks lumped together under the name Ichthyophagoi (cf. under 2:1.7–10) no doubt spoke various native languages that were incomprehensible to Greeks (e.g., Herodotus [3.19] indicates that some living near Elephantine spoke an "Ethiopian tongue"), and many went about naked (Agatharchides 31 = Diod. 3.15.2 [*GGM* i 130]). The author is emphasizing that those on Sarapis were less primitive: they spoke a known language, Arabic, and wore loincloths. Glaser's suggestion (187) that the author is emphasizing the use of Arabic on the island as against a different language on the mainland not only is far-fetched but misses the point. The leaves were no doubt of the doum palm (cf. Löw ii 303), which still grows in some coastal parts of Arabia (see F. Hepper and J. Wood in *Proceedings of the Seminar for Arabian Studies* 9 [1979]: 65).

33:11.17   tortoise shell

Cf. *RSP*, chap. 13.89: "In the spring, at night, very large numbers of turtles come ashore to lay their eggs."

34:11.20   coasting due north along the next stretch of the shore

Cf. under B 34:11.20. From the Kuria Muria Islands to Masirah the course had been over open water (33:11.12); at this point it returns to follow the coast. From Masirah to Ras al Hadd (22°33′N, 59°48′E), the southeast corner of Arabia, the course is actually north-northeast rather than due north, and, from Ras al Hadd to the mouth of the Persian Gulf, northwest by north.

34:11.21–23   in the vicinity . . . of . . . the Persian Gulf, you meet numerous islands, called the Isles of Kalaios, strung out along the coast for almost 2000 stades

Bunbury (ii 460) aptly remarks that the description of the part of the Arabian coast leading up to the Straits of Hormuz is among the least satisfactory portions of the *Periplus*. At the straits themselves, at least as early as the late fourth century B.C., there was a port that handled overseas products destined for Mesopotamia (Arrian, *Indica* 32.7), and in later ages the coast to the south boasted such famed ports as Muscat and Sur. Yet the *Periplus* lists no stopping places at all, and what geographical information it vouchsafes is hard to identify. Between Masirah and the mouth of the Persian Gulf there is only one group of islands, the Jazair Daymaniyat (23°50′N, 58°4′E), just west of Muscat. They are thus the sole candidate for the Isles of Kalaios. Yet they are by no means "around the entrance to the Persian Gulf" but a good 170 nautical miles away, and they by no means stretch "for almost 2000 stades" (200 nautical miles) but a mere twelve miles, the equivalent of 120 stades. Schoff was convinced that there was a connection between the name Kalaios and the town of Qalhat (22°42′N, 59°23′E), which Ibn Batuta (eds. C. Defrémery and B. Sanguinetti, ii 225 [1854]) noted was important in the India trade, but Qalhat is nowhere near the Jazair Daymaniyat and even farther away than they from the entrance to the Persian Gulf.

34:11.23–24   The men who populate them are rascals who do not do much looking during the daytime

The passage has puzzled commentators. Müller suggested emending it, Fabricius inevitably did, and Schoff translated his version. As Frisk (113) properly points out, no emendation is called for. He, followed by Huntingford, took it that the author was describing eye trouble of some sort. But, as W. Schmid argues (*Philologische Wochenschrift* [1928]: 791–92), the

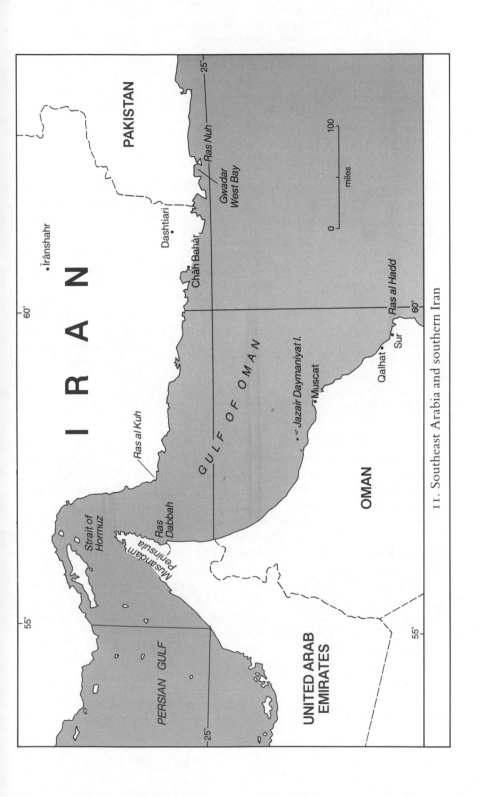

11. Southeast Arabia and southern Iran

nature of the phraseology suggests that he was writing with tongue in cheek: these barren and waterless islands were inhabited by the sort of people who used their eyes at nighttime, pirates or smugglers or others of the ilk that prefers to carry on its unsavory doings under cover of darkness. For another example of the author's dry humor, see 38:13.3–4.

35:11.26 Kalon Oros

Presumably this is a distinctive peak of the Ruus al Jibal chain near its end in the Musandam Peninsula. There are a number of likely candidates; see the mountain landmarks noted on the sketches of the shoreline in *SDRS*, sector 13, p. 211.

35:11.26–27 much diving for pearl oysters

The so-called Great Pearl Bank stretches along the southern bight of the Persian Gulf roughly between Dubai and Qatar; see *SDRS*, sector 15, p. 255. Wellsted (op. cit. under 27:9.9, i 114–23) describes in detail the extensive activity carried on there at the time of his visit. Cf. also Warmington 167–68.

35:11.27–29 mouth of the Persian Gulf . . . Asabô . . . Mt. Semiramis

The author reports that the left side of the mouth of the Persian Gulf is marked by a mighty mountain range, the Asabô (cf. under B 35:11.28); that the right side is marked by a mountain, round and high, which was visible directly across, Mt. Semiramis; and that the distance across the mouth is 600 stades (60 nautical miles). As it happens, along the Arabian shore—the left side, in the author's terminology—starting at Ras Dabbah (25°36′N, 56°22′E) and running forty-eight miles north to end in the Musandam Peninsula, there is a chain of mountains, the Ruus al Jibal, which has peaks reaching 6000 and 7000 feet (*SDRS*, sector 13, p. 209) and thus could well merit the description "mighty" and hence correspond to the author's Asabô (cf. Sprenger 108–9); Miles (op. cit. under 33:11.10–11, 10) suggested a connection with Khasab, in his day "a hamlet in a small valley, probably the residence in former times of a tribe so called," but today an important town on the tip of the Musandam Peninsula. Ptolemy notes the same mountain landmarks on either side of the straits, the Asabô on the Arabian (6.7.12) and Mt. Semiramis, which he also characterizes as round, on the Persian (6.8.11). Now, the route the *Periplus* is describing, from Egypt to India, does not include the Persian Gulf but "sails by" (36:12.3) it (many commentators have misunderstood the text in this regard; see under 36:12.3–4). On such a course, a vessel, after leaving the Arabian coast, would steer for Ras al Kuh (25°48′N, 57°18′E), the cape where the Iranian coast, which runs south from the Straits of Hormuz, makes a sharp bend to go eastward towards India. It was probably at Ras al Kuh that the fleet under Alexander's admiral Nearchus, under orders to explore the route from India to the Persian Gulf, "no longer continued to sail west [from India] but rather set their prows midway between west and north" (Arrian, *Indica* 32.3). From Ras al Kuh to the Arabian shore opposite is some sixty nautical miles, exactly the author's estimate of 600 stades, whereas the distance at the actual straits narrows to half that. And, just three miles north of Ras al Kuh and a mile in from the coast stands a remarkable rock, Kuh-e Mobarak (25°51′N, 57°19′E); this is generally identified as Mt. Semiramis, since it is perfectly cylindrical and so distinctive that it has for centuries served as a landmark and still does (cf. Sprenger 108; W. Tomaschek, "Topographische Erläuterung der Küstenfahrt Nearchs vom Indus bis zum Euphrat," *Sitzungsberichte der phil.-hist. Kl. der kaiserlichen Akademie der Wissenschaften, Wien* 121 [1890], Heft 8, 37; *SDRS*, sector 13, p. 222). The identification is attractive but by no means certain, for there are difficulties. Kuh-e Mobarak, though appropriately round, is only 330 feet high; indeed, it is not even a mountain but a rock. More serious, the author's language strongly suggests that Mt. Semiramis stood at the straits proper and was visible from the Arabian side, i.e., presumably from some point on the Musandam Peninsula; Kuh-e Mobarak is much too far south to satisfy such requirements. This is why commentators, though putting it forth as first choice, offer as alternatives several mountains that are far higher and more aptly located (cf., e.g., Tomaschek 39; F. Weissbach, *RE* s.v. Σεμιράμιδος ὄρος [1923]). However, none of these are either round or distinctive landmarks (cf. *SDRS*, sector 13, pp. 222–23).

35:11.32–12.1   a legally limited port of trade called Apologos, lying near Charax Spasinu

On "legally limited" ports of trade, see App. 1. The name Apologos is not attested elsewhere. Strabo (16.765) mentions only a Terêdôn at the head of the gulf. Pliny (6.145) mentions a Forat as well as Terêdôn and (6.139–40) discusses Charax at length. Forat, the Furāt Maisān of the early Islamic period, was probably located about twenty airline miles northwest of Basra (J. Hansman, "Charax and the Karkheh," *Iranica Antiqua* 7 [1967]: 21–58 at 26, 47, 51–52). Assyrian records of the eighth and seventh centuries B.C. list among the peoples in the area an Aramaean tribe called the Ubulu (D. Luckenbill, *Ancient Records of Assyria and Babylonia* [Chicago 1926–27] index s.v.); perhaps Apologos is a Hellenizing of that name (cf. M. Streck, *RE* Suppl. 1.111 [1903]). Apologos itself seems to have survived in the name Ubulla, the town that served as port for medieval Basra; it was located on the site of al 'Ashār, the district of modern Basra that lies along the Shatt al Arab (cf. Streck, *Encyclopaedia of Islam* s.v. *Maisān* 152 [1936]). Charax Spasinu (or Pasinu, as it is spelled in Ptolemy 6.3.2 as well as here) was originally one of Alexander the Great's many foundations called Alexandria; destroyed by flood, it was rebuilt as Antiocheia by Antiochus IV (175–164 B.C.) and then given a great antiflood embankment by his governor there, Hyspaosines, and renamed "Charax ['palisade'] of Hyspaosines"; see S. Nodelman, "A Preliminary History of Characene," *Berytus* 13 (1960): 83–121 at 90–91. It has been identified with a site marked by remains of an impressive set of embankments some thirty airline miles northwest of Basra (Hansman 38–39).

Apologos at this time was part of the kingdom of Persis (36:12.5–6 and see under 33:11.12).

36:12.3–4 After sailing by the mouth of the gulf, six runs further . . . Omana

Here the name is spelled Ommana but in all other places Omana (27:9.11; 36:12.7, 8, and cf. 13). If the six runs (3000 stades) are reckoned from the Straits of Hormuz, Omana could well be either Chāh Bahār at the mouth of a small bay (25°17'N, 60°38'E), as a number of commentators have suggested (Müller; Bunbury ii 461; Fabricius; R. Boucharlat and J.-F. Salles in *Proceedings of the Seminar for Arabian Studies* 11 [London, 1981]: 67), or Tiz at the bottom of the bay. Chāh Bahār has a good harbor (*SDRS*, sector 12, p. 200), while Tiz was a flourishing port during the early Middle Ages (T. Holdich, *The Gates of India* [London, 1910], 298–301; Sir Aurel Stein, *Archaeological Reconnaissances in North-Western India and South-Eastern Iran* [London, 1937], 87–93; see also under 36:12.10–12). If the six runs are reckoned from Kuh-e Mobarak (cf. under 35:11.27–29), Omana might lie further eastward, perhaps on Gwadar West Bay (25°10'N, 62°16'E) or Pasni (25°15'N, 63°28'E); remains of Harappan port sites have been found near both (see S. Ratnagar, *Encounters: The Westerly Trade of the Harappan Civilization* [Delhi, 1981], 51). The author's figures for distance can never be pressed too closely and particularly so when he is dealing with distant waters and reckons in runs rather than stades.

Some commentators have placed Omana inside the Persian Gulf

(Glaser ii 189–90; Schoff; Warmington 54, 263) or at the straits (Tarn 481; F. Altheim and R. Stiehl, *Der Araber in der alten Welt* i [Berlin, 1964], 108; C. Brunner, *CHI* iii.2 [1983], 756, 772). In either case they have disregarded the explicit words of the text (cf. A. Herrmann, *RE* s.v. *Omana*; Salles in *Proceedings of the Seminar for Arabian Studies* 10 [London, 1980]: 103–4).

36:12.6   copper

On the problem presented by this instance of copper from India, see Introduction: Trade in the Indian Ocean, The Trade in Metals.

36:12.7   sissoo

See under B 36:12.7. Sissoo wood was being imported by Persia from India as early as the sixth century B.C.; see K. Maxwell-Hyslop, "*Dalbergia Sissoo* Roxburgh," *Anatolian Studies* 33 (1983): 67–72 at 71.

36:12.8–9   sewn boats, the kind called *madarate*

On African sewn boats, see under 15:5.30. Marco Polo (1.19) reports on the sewn boats he saw at Hormuz, i.e., at the western end of the coast on which Omana lay. Indeed, sewing planks together instead of nailing them or using joinery was widely practiced by Arab shipwrights right up to the present century (Procopius, *Bell. Pers.* 1.19.23 [cf. *SSAW* 209]; Yule-Cordier i 117; Hornell [op. cit. under 27:9.9] 234–35). Glaser (190) sought to derive the name *madarate* from Arabic. Remarking that it "hat ein so augesprochen arabisches Gepräge, dass man schwer an eine andere als eine arabische Werft denken kann," he connected it with *muddarra'at*, a formation from the verb *dara'a*, "mit einem Panzer bekleiden." Though *muddarra'at* means "things that are armored," Glaser, by a tortured line of reasoning, convinced himself that it could mean "bastgebundene," and commentators have consistently repeated this; cf. Schoff 154 ("*muddarra'at*, 'fastened with palm fiber' "), Frisk 114 ("*muddara'at* [*sic*], 'attaché avec des fibres de palme' "), Huntingford 162, Hornell 234. If *madarate* is indeed derived from *muddarra'at*, the craft must have been so called not because they were sewn—as the text indicates, they were but one type of such boats—but because they differed from the others by virtue of somehow being "armored," a feature so desirable that seamen of the Arabian peninsula went to the trouble and, presumably, expense of importing these vessels that boasted it.

36:12.10–12   pearls . . . slaves

All the exports listed in this passage could have come from Apologos alone, located as it was at the end of the great routes that reached down through Mesopotamia, and very likely the pearls (cf. under 35:11.26–27) and purple (cf. Warmington 263) did. But Omana was not unimportant; in 27:9.11, for example, it is linked with Skythia and Barygaza as the overseas points with which Kanê maintained trade relations. Assuming it lay in the area of Chāh Bahār or Tiz (see under 36:12.3–4), it could well have supplied the clothing, dates, slaves, and gold. Chāh Bahār and Tiz are but forty-five miles or so from the Dashtiari Plain, "the most fertile part of Persian Baluchistan" (J. Harrison in *GJ* 97 [1941]: 14), where dates are an important crop. Two roads lead from Chāh Bahār north to Īrān-shahr, a major road leads from there to Zāhedān (see map in *CHI* i 82 [1968]), and Zāhedān is the junction for important routes in all directions, including one that passes through the Jīroft district, 120 miles south-southeast of Kerman, where gold has been found (*CHI* i 515–16). Certainly Tiz was once a flourishing center: Al-Maqdisi, writing in the tenth century, talks of its beautiful mosque and large crowded inns (B. Spooner, "Notes on the Toponymy of the Persian Makran," *Iran and Islam: In Memory of the Late Vladimir Minorsky* [Edinburgh, 1971], 517–33 at 518).

37:12.13–14   the country of the Parsidai,
part of another kingdom

See under B 37:12.13. The "other kingdom" would be that of the Indo-Parthians (38:13.3–4 and note ad loc.).

37:12.14–16   Gulf of the Terabdoi . . . Hôraia

Neither a Gulf of the Terabdoi nor a port of trade called Hôraia are attested elsewhere. Müller and all subsequent commentators have taken the gulf to be a huge body of water reaching from Ras Muari (Cape Monze, 24°50′N, 66°40′E) as far west as Ras Nuh (25°5′N, 62°24′E), in other words, embracing practically the whole of the Makran coast. And, in its western part, they sought to identify a "headland that juts out" (e.g., Schoff concluded that it must be Ras Ormāra [25°10′N, 64°36′E]). But the stretch of coast included in their gulf is more or less straight; it lacks the curves or indentations that form bays (Schoff at least was aware of this; cf. 161). The first indentation that could properly be called a bay, the only one east of Ras Nuh formally identified as such (see *SDRS*, sector 12), is Sonmiani Bay, and it extends no further west than Ras Kachari

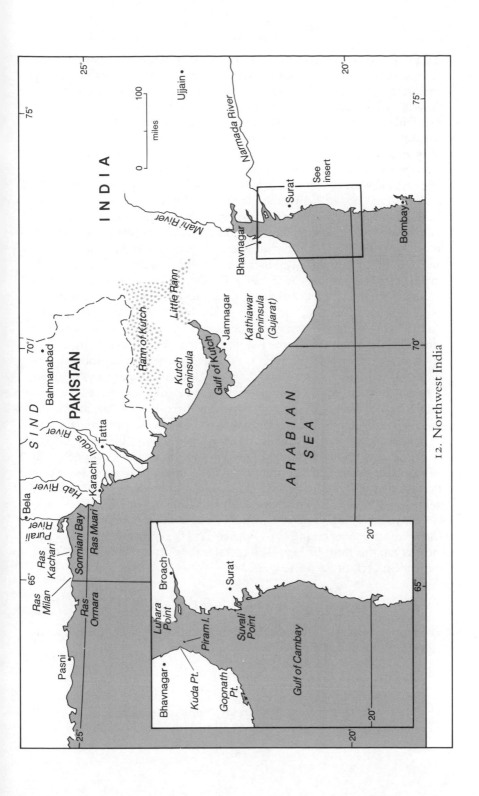

12. Northwest India

(25°22′N, 65°44′E). And the "headland" that the commentators have been so concerned with is an insertion by Müller, not the reading of the manuscript (see under B 37:12.15). The best clue to the location of both the gulf and Hôraia is the author's mention (37:12.17–19) that seven days' travel inland from the coast, presumably from the point on it where Hôraia stood, is a region capable of producing rich crops. This can only be Welpat, roughly the modern district of Las Bela, at the north of the spreading plain of the Purali River, a plain that is roughly triangular in shape, with Welpat at the apex and the coast of Sonmiani Bay forming the base. For one, at Welpat the Purali's flood waters can be trapped and there are, in addition, permanent springs, two features that enable this area alone of the region to enjoy successful agriculture (see Sir Aurel Stein in *GJ* 102 [1943]: 196–97). For another, Welpat is the right distance from the coast (cf. H. Lambrick, *Sind: A General Introduction* [Hyderabad, 1975²], 136: "six ordinary marches"). It follows that the Gulf of the Terabdoi is Sonmiani Bay; a vessel, after rounding Ras Muari, which marks its eastern end, comes to the region of the Indus Delta, precisely as the author states in the next chapter (38:12.21–24). And the river at whose mouth Hôraia lies would be the Purali, which now empties into the marsh of Miani Hor but in ancient times would have reached the bay more or less about the midpoint of its coast (cf. Lambrick 144 and accompanying map).

Hôraia is surely connected with the Hôritai, as they are called by Quintus Curtius (9.10.6, 19), or Ôreitai, as they are called by Arrian, for the town lay right in the area where they lived. Their eastern boundary was formed by the Arabis River (Arrian, *Indica* 21.8, 22.10), the modern Hab (Stein 213), whose mouth lies a few miles northeast (24°55′N, 66°40′E) of Ras Muari; their western boundary was Malana (Arrian, *Indica* 25.1–2), which still bears that name (Ras Milan, 25°19′N, 65°12′E), about thirty miles west of Ras Kachari. O. Stein (*RE* s.v. *Ori* [1942]) connects Hôraia with the Ori, a people who dwelt near the mouth of the Persian Gulf, explicitly rejecting (*RE* s.v. *Oreitai* 947 [1942]) any connection with the Ôreitai; this must be because he locates the port of Omana within the Persian Gulf (cf. under 36:12.3–4).

37:12.15   around the middle of which . . . bulges

The word for the geographical feature being described has dropped out of the text; see under B 37:12.15.

37:12.17–18   an inland city . . . called . . .

The name of the city was inadvertently omitted. Arrian (*Anab.* 6.21.5) mentions a Rhambakia as the largest village of the Ôreitai and relates how impressed Alexander was with its site: it could support, he felt, a large and prosperous city. Rhambakia thus must have been in Welpat (see under 37:12.14–16), probably in the vicinity of the modern town of Bela (26°14′N, 66°19′E), as Stein suggests (op. cit. under 37:12.14–16, 215). The anonymous city probably was either Rhambakia or whatever settlement had supplanted it.

37:12.18   site of a royal palace

The area was under the rule of Indo-Parthian kings (cf. under 37:12.13–14 and 38:13.3–4), whose capital was at Minnagar (38:13.3). The royal palace here must have been a residence for their local administrator, or for their use during visits, or both.

37:12.19   rice

Rice is grown in Welpat today; see Lambrick (op. cit. under 37:12.14–16) 144.

37:12.20   bdellium

The author notes the export of bdellium from Sind (39:13.10, shipped out of Barbarikon) and northwestern India (48:16.19 and 49:16.28, shipped out of Barygaza) as well as from this part of the Makran coast. Bdellium is described in detail by Dioscorides (1.67) and Pliny (12.35–36); Pliny lists several varieties, including an Indian, and gives the price on the Roman market, namely 3 denarii a Roman pound, which puts it on a par with the cheapest frankincense (see *ESAR* v 285). There is general agreement that bdellium is the resin of *Commiphora* (*Balsamodendron* in older writers) *mukul* Hooker, or gugul to give it its Indian name (Watt i 366; Hobson-Jobson s.v. *Bdellium*; Berendes [op. cit. under 8:3.31a] 83; Löw i 304–5; C. Joret, *Les plantes dans l'antiquité et au Moyen Age* [Paris, 1897–1904] ii 654; Groom [op. cit. under 7:3.20] 124). The tree grows in the drier parts of western India and Pakistan, including the region referred to in this passage. Indeed, the region exported gugul in the nineteenth century just as it had in ancient times; see Hobson-Jobson s.v. *Googul* ("It is imported [by India] from the Beyla territory, west of Sind," i.e., Welpat [cf. under 37:12.17–18]). Alexander's army on its march through the Gedrosian Desert saw "myrrh" trees whose resin the Phoenician camp followers eagerly collected (Arrian, *Anab.* 6.22.4); very likely these were *Commiphora mukul* (cf. Bretzl [op. cit. under 11:4.17–18] 282–83). Dioscorides and Pliny give a long list of medicinal uses for bdellium. It is still used medicinally in India (Watt i 366–67).

38:12.21–22   the coast by now curving like a horn

This is the stretch of coast a ship passes after doubling Ras Muari (cf. under 37:12.14–16), what is today the area around Karachi. The coast the author saw can bear little resemblance to what exists today, since the shoreline has advanced enormously in the intervening centuries; places once on the sea are now far inland (cf. Smith 109, n. 1; Schoff 165).

38:12.23   Skythia

This is the name the author gives to what Ptolemy (7.1.55) calls Indos-kythia, more or less the region of Sind, the alluvial plain of the Indus. At the time the *Periplus* was written it was under Parthian domination (38:13.3–4) but still bore the name it had under its previous rulers, the Iranian-speaking nomads whom the Indians and Greeks both called Sakas but the Greeks at times also called Scyths (cf. Tarn 79). The Sakas, orig-inally from Central Asia, moved southward until, by the closing decades of the second century B.C., they had established themselves in Sind (Tarn 232–33; A. Bivar in *CHI* iii.1 192–94 [1983]). The first king of this India-based realm was Maues, whose capital was at Taxila; he held the throne sometime around the beginning of the first century B.C. (Bivar 194–95; G. Fussman, *JA* 275 [1987]: 338). The last was Azes II, whose rule ex-tended into the beginning of the Christian Era (Bivar 196–97). The Sakas had long been in conflict with the Parthians (cf. Tarn 223–24, 291–92), and during Azes' reign these invaded and took over the area (see under 38:13.3–4).

Skythia extended eastward as far as the Gulf of Kutch, the Rann of Kutch, and the Little Rann; beyond its eastern border lay India proper and an area where a Saka dynasty still held sway (see under 41:14.2).

38:12.23a   very flat

The alluvial plain of the Indus reaches far inland from the coast.

38:12.24   the Sinthos

The name in Sanskrit is *Sindhu*. Greek writers called it the *Indos*, Romans the *Indus*, whence the modern name. Pliny (6.71) observes that it was "called Sindus by the natives." The *Periplus's* spelling is even more accu-rate.

38:12.27–28 snakes that emerge from the depths
to meet them

As late as the eighteenth century, mariners heading for the west coast of India, low and flat and hence hard to make out, relied upon the sighting of clusters of sea snakes as a signal that they were approaching land. Thus Carsten Niebuhr, writing of his voyage in 1763, reports (op. cit. under 22:7.24, i 452) that his approach to India's west coast was carried out with the greatest safety thanks to "viele kleine Schlangen, 12 bis 18 Zoll lang, auf der Oberfläche der See. . . . Wir sahen die Wasserschlangen zum erstenmal am 9ten September gegend Abend. Wir hatten auch um 1 Uhr nach Mitternacht Grund auf 53 Faden, und die Tiefe ward immer weniger, je mehr wir uns der Küste näherten." Similarly, L. de Grandpré reports (*A Voyage in the Indian Ocean and to Bengal Undertaken in the Years 1789 and 1790*, translated from the French [London, 1803], i 25–26) that between the Maldives and the Malabar coast he saw "on the surface of the water a great number of living serpents. . . . They begin to appear as soon as we get within the Maldives; but they are not very numerous till we arrive at about eight or ten leagues from the coast, and their numbers increase as we approach."

The author reports such snakes off the Indus Delta (38:12.28), the Persian coast (38:12.28–29), the Gulf of Kutch (40:13.30), the Gulf of Cambay (40:13.31–32), and the Malabar coast (55:18.12–15). Those off Kutch were "huge and black," off Cambay "smaller and yellow and golden in color," and off the Malabar coast also black but "shorter and with dragon-shaped head and blood-red eyes."

For details on the sea snakes of the waters in question, see M. Smith, *The Fauna of British India: Reptilia and Amphibia*. iii, *Serpentes* (London, 1943), 439–77; color illustrations of many of them can be found in B. Halstead, *Poisonous and Venemous Marine Animals of the World* iii (Washington, 1970). All are more or less varicolored, marked with bars or spots or stripes; as a consequence, the two types described in the *Periplus* as black are hard to identify. *Praescutata* (or *Thalassophis*) *viperina*, specimens of which can be grey above, or grey with dark spots or bars (Smith 448; Halstead, chap. viii, pl. xii.2) may possibly be one of them, probably the shorter type found off the Malabar coast, for it runs under a meter in length whereas truly large sea snakes are double that. *Praescutata viperina*, to be sure, does not have a "dragon-shaped head and blood-red eyes"— but neither does any other known sea snake. The "huge and black" type found off the Gulf of Kutch is a puzzle. There are several sea snakes inhabiting those or nearby waters that, since they run from a meter and one-half to two or more in length, can well be characterized as "huge," namely *Astrotia stokesi* (Smith 471–72), *Hydrophis spiralis* (453), and *Hydrophis cyanocinctus* (454–56), but all have distinctive coloration. A possibility is *Enhydrina schistosa*; over a meter in length, it is larger than *Praescutata viperina* but, like it, is grey above (Smith 450; but cf. Halstead, chap. viii, pl. vii. 1 picturing a specimen with yellow bands).

Two of the very large types just mentioned, *Hydrophis spiralis* and *Hydrophis cyanocinctus*, are plausible candidates for the "yellow and golden" snakes off the Gulf of Cambay, for both have a good deal of yellow in their coloration (Smith 453, 455; Halstead, chap. viii, pls. xi. 1 and viii. 1).

38:12.28–29   in the places around Persis mentioned above, the snakes called *graai*

Praescutata viperina, *Enhydrina schistosa*, *Hydrophis spiralis*, and *Hydrophis cyanocinctus* (cf. under 38:12.27–28) are all found in the Persian Gulf and other waters around Persia as well as around India. Other types found there are: *Hydrophis ornatus* (Smith [op. cit. under 38:12.27–28] 460–61), *Hydrophis lapemoides* (461–62), *Lapemis curtus* (470–71), *Microcephalophis gracilis* (472–74).

Graai very likely is the Sanskrit *grāha*, used of any large fish or marine animal, such as crocodiles, sharks, serpents, etc. (cf. McCrindle).

38:12.29–30   seven mouths

Ptolemy (7.1.2) gives the same figure. Strabo (15.700, 701), following Aristobulus, who accompanied Alexander, says it has but two. Both figures can be right since the river has frequently changed its course, at times drastically. Strabo (15.693) reports one shift that caused the abandonment of a thousand cities. A change documented in 1758 moved the channel twelve or fifteen miles from its former location (H. Cousens, *The Antiquities of Sind*, Archaeological Survey of India 46 [Calcutta, 1929], 6).

38:13.2   Barbarikon

A few lines below (39:13.5), the name is spelled Barbarikê. Ptolemy (7.1.59) lists a Barbara, but locates it far inland. A plethora of locations have been offered for the port, no two alike: cf., e.g., Müller, Fabricius, Schoff, W. Tomaschek (*RE* s.v. *Barbarei* [1896]), Warmington (55), A. Cunningham (*Ancient Geography of India* [1871], ed. S. Majumdar Sastri [Calcutta, 1924], 294–95). Smith (245) prudently observes that "the extensive changes which have occurred in the rivers of Sind during the course of eighteen centuries preclude the possibility of satisfactory identifications of either of these towns [Barbarikon and Minnagar]."

38:13.3   Minnagar

The name means "Saka-town" (cf. McCrindle 109, Tarn 235). Ptolemy (7.1.61) lists a Binagara in the general area, which is probably the same place. Cunningham (op. cit. under 38:13.2, 289) thought Minnagar was at or near modern Tatta (24°45′N, 67°55′E), "as the position [of Tatta] at the head of the inferior Delta commanded the whole traffic of the river." McCrindle cites three other identifications, all different. More recent authorities show a very slight tendency to favor Bahmanabad; cf. A. Herrmann (*RE* s.v. *Minnagar* 1854 [1932]), Warmington 55. Smith (107) locates Bahmanabad at 25°52′N, 68°52′E, ca. six miles west of Mansuriya; he himself does not support the identification and indeed abstains from attempting any (see his words cited under 38:13.2). Tarn (235) guardedly places Minnagar "somewhere eastward of the Indus Delta."

38:13.3–4   in the hands of Parthians

The Parthian invasion of Sind ended Saka rule there (cf. under 38:12.23), and Gondophares, first of the Indo-Parthian kings (so called to distinguish them from the rulers of the Parthian Kingdom, Rome's great rival), replaced Azes II. Gondophares is fairly securely dated—he reigned from A.D. 20 to 46 (Bivar [op. cit. under 38:12.23] 197; cf. G. Fussman, *JA* 275 [1987]: 338)—and better known than others of his line, for he is named in Christian legend as the king who received the Apostle Thomas at his court (see the discussion in Smith 245–50). The sequence and connections of the Indo-Parthian rulers who came after Gondophares are obscure (Bivar 197). In any event, the line ended when the Kushans (see under 47:16.5–6) extended their penetration of India to take in the plain of the Indus. The founder of the Kushan dynasty in India, Kujula Kadphises, began his reign sometime in the opening decades of the first century A.D. (Bivar 198–200; conformably, Fussman [338] dates Vima Kadphises, the third member of the line [339], ca. A.D. 50). When the *Periplus* was written the Kushans had not yet taken over Skythia; Indo-Parthian rulers were still holding sway there although, to judge from the author's observation that they were "constantly chasing each other off" the throne, in no very stable fashion.

39:13.7–9   there is a market for . . . wine, limited quantity

No goods are listed "for the king" as at the other ports that served capitals, namely Adulis (6:2.33–35), Muza (24:8.7–9), Kanê (28:9.16–18), Barygaza (49:16.25–28). This is because the king received everything that was unloaded (39:13.5–6), including presumably those items specifically intended for him and his court. The silverware, for example, must have been one such, since its other occurrences are only in the lists of goods "for the king" (see the passages cited in the first sentence).

39:13.8   multicolored textiles

Cf. under B 39:13.8. These were a specialty of Egypt: cf. Pliny 8.196 (where he claims that the art of weaving them was invented at Alexandria), Martial 14.150. They were used for garments as well as hangings, carpets, and the like; see H. Blümner, *Die römischen Privataltertümer*, Müllers Handbuch der klassischen Altertumswissenschaft 4.2.2 (Munich, 1911³), 253. Apparently they were much in demand in India, since Muziris and Nelkynda imported them (56:18.19) as well as Barbarikon, while Barygaza imported one particular type (49:16.22–23).

39:13.8a   peridot (?)

The Greek word is *chrysolithon*, "golden stone"; see under B 39:13.8a. Pliny includes the term in his discussion of gems (37.126); there he remarks that the Indian variety was highly regarded, and this has prompted the suggestion (see D. Eichholtz's note to his translation of the passage [Loeb ed., 1962]) that the stone was yellow sapphire, found in the East Indies (Watt vi.ii 474). Whether Pliny's *chrysolithon* is actually yellow sapphire or some other yellow stone from India, it cannot be what the author of the *Periplus* has in mind, for he is referring to a stone imported by India and hence not obtainable there. Since India in Roman times was the gem-producing land par excellence (see Pliny 37.200 and, for details, Warmington 235–56), the *Periplus's chrysolithon* must have been one of the few India lacked and, to judge from the fact that it was imported at Barygaza (49:16.22) and Muziris and Nelkynda (56:18.18) as well as Barbarikon, was widely in demand. As it happens, there is a desirable stone not found in India which the shippers of Roman Egypt had at their very doorstep, so to speak, namely peridot. The sole source of peridot in ancient times was St. John's Island in the Red Sea (cf. under 1:1.2–4), only a few miles away from Berenicê, and the stone was so prized that it served as gifts to royalty (Pliny 37.108) and the kings of Egypt maintained a guard over the quarries (Strabo 16.770). Both Strabo and Pliny (37.107) call the stone *topazos*, but since they name the island as the source, there can be no doubt that they are referring to peridot (cf. Warmington 253; Eichholtz's note to his translation of Pliny 37.108). Peridot, the gem grade of olivine, is green rather than "golden," but there seems to have been some confusion about the color; whereas Pliny properly says that it has "its own greenish nature," Strabo describes it as being "like gold."

39:13.8b   coral

The author lists coral as an import at Barygaza (49:16.21) and at Muziris and Nelkynda (56:18.19) as well as here. According to Pliny (32.21), the Indians prized coral as highly as the Romans did pearls. They have continued to prize it: Watt (ii 532) reports that fine pieces of red coral from the Mediterranean were worth twenty times their weight in gold. The coral exported to India in ancient times must have come from the Mediterranean (cf. under 28:9.16). Indeed, so much was exported from there that by Pliny's day supplies had become scarce (Pliny 32.23 and cf. Warmington 263–64).

39:13.8c   frankincense

This is an object of trade that merchants from Roman Egypt could not have brought with them from home but must have picked up en route. They could have taken on their supplies at Kanê, which was the collection point for incense (27:9.8–10) and the departure point from which vessels commonly began the direct sail to India (57:19.7).

39:13.9   glassware

Excavations at Begram in Afghanistan, some forty-five miles north of Kabul, have brought to light, in what once was probably a palace, remains of glass vessels imported from the West, including some that almost certainly came from Alexandria (Wheeler 162–65, H. Seyrig in *Syria* 22 [1941]: 262). Like the glassware mentioned in this passage, it could well have been unloaded at Barbarikon in order to travel up to its destination by way of the Indus Valley; cf. Seyrig 262.

39:13.10   costus

The word is derived from the Sanskrit *kushtha*. The author reveals later (48:16.16–18) that costus originated in "the upper areas." These must have been in Kashmir, for costus is the fragrant root of *Saussurea lappa*, "a tall, very stout herb . . . indigenous to the moist, open slopes, surrounding the valley of Kashmir, at an elevation of 8,000 to 9,000 feet" (Watt vi.ii 481; cf. Laufer [op. cit. under 6:3.1a] 462–64). Dioscorides (1.16), who notes an Arabian and Syrian costus as well as an Indian, lists its manifold virtues as a medicine. It was comparatively cheap: its price at Rome, 5½ denarii a pound, was in the lowest level of prices for the plant products from Arabia and India (see *ESAR* v 285–86; the cheapest nard, for example, cost 40 [see under 39:13.10b]). It is attested frequently in the

Greek papyri from Egypt as a component of medical or magical prescriptions (*BGU* 953, 3d–4th century A.D.; *P. Coll. Youtie* ii 86, 3d–4th century A.D.; *P. Oxy.* 1384, 5th century A.D., where it is in company with such modest ingredients as cumin, fennel, parsley, pennyroyal, and the like) as well as in other contexts (*P. Oxy.* 2570 iii 6, A.D. 329; *PSI* 1264.19, 4th century A.D.; *SB* 9834 b 22, 4th century A.D.).

39:13.10a *lykion*

There have been found a number of containers inscribed with the word *lykion*, sometimes accompanied by the name of a druggist: see E. Sjöqvist, "Morgantina: Hellenistic Medicine Bottles," *American Journal of Archaeology* 64 (1960): 78–83 and pl. 19; Majno (op. cit. under 7:3.20) 377; Y. Calvet, "Pharmacopée antique: Un pot à lykion de Beyrouth," *Archéologie au Levant: Recueil à la mémoire de Roger Saidah* (Paris, 1982), 281–86. They are juglets, mostly of clay but a few of lead, which have turned up in Sicily, southern Italy, and Athens; a taller type measures ca. 5–5.5 centimeters in height with a maximum circumference slightly less than the height, a shorter measures ca. 2.5–3 centimeters in height with maximum circumference slightly more than the height, and the interior cavity is small in comparison with the exterior size (Sjöqvist 79–81). Dioscorides (1.100.1; cf. Sjöqvist 81) describes *lykion* as a drug made from a variety of buckthorn native to Lycia—whence, no doubt, the name—and Cappadocia. However, he also mentions (1.100.2, 4; cf. Pliny 12.31) what must correspond to the *lykion* of this passage, a variety from India, which he praises as the most effective. J. Forbes Royle, the authority on India's flora, identified it as what the Indians call *rasout, rusot,* aut sim. (cf. Watt i 445, Sjöqvist 81), an extract from the wood or root of certain barberries found in the western Himalayas, *Berberis lycium* Royle or *Berberis aristata* D.C. or *Berberis asiatica* Roxb. (Watt i 442–46), an identification that has been widely accepted: see Watt i 445, Flückiger-Hanbury (op. cit. under 28:9.16a) 34–36, Berendes (op. cit. under 8:3.31a) 118, McCrindle, Schoff. Others hold that it was what the Indians call cutch, an extract from the wood of *Acacia catechu* Willd., which grows in most parts of India and Burma (Watt i 27–30); see H. Lenz, *Botanik der alten Griechen und Römer* (Gotha, 1859), 737, Lassen iii 31, *Oxford Latin Dictionary* s.v. *Lycium* (*LSJ* reserves judgment), André (op. cit. under 28:9.16a) s.v. *lycium* (although subsequently, in his commentary to Pliny 24.125 in the Budé edition [1972], he reserved judgment). Professor John Scarborough, specialist in ancient pharmacology, who kindly reviewed the evidence for me, favors this identification, emphasizing that the properties of an extract from *Acacia catechu* would better suit the uses for which Greek and Roman medical writings prescribe *lykion*.

The inscribed juglets and frequent mention of *lykion* in medical writings attest to the drug's widespread use. For some reason it has so far made scant appearance in the many medical prescriptions found in the Greek papyri from Egypt. None is listed in V. Gazza, "Prescrizioni mediche nei papiri dell'Egitto greco-romano" ii, *Aegyptus* 36 (1956): 73–114 or in M. Marganne's much fuller *Inventaire analytique des papyrus grecs de médecine* (Geneva, 1981); L. Youtie, *Bulletin of the American Society of Papyrologists* 22 (1985): 367, lists one occurrence (*Mitteilungen aus der Papyrussammlung der Nationalbibliothek in Wien*, Neue Serie xiii [1981]: 3.9, where *lykion* and not *krokos* is to be read).

39:13.10b   nard

The Greek term *nardos* was used of the oils from certain fragrant grasses (cf. *LSJ* s.v.) as well as of true nard or spikenard, to give it its full name, the oil derived from *Nardostachys jatamansi* D.C., a perennial herb growing in the remote and mountainous regions of India at heights of up to 17,000 feet; cf. Watt v 339–40, Laufer (op. cit. under 6:3.1a) 428, Löw iii 482–83, and see under 48:16.16–18 for the several types named according to locality. There is a good discussion of nard, with full documentation, in Warmington 194–97. Famed as an unguent, it was also used in drugs and cooking. The Romans imported both the leaves and the rootstock, the "spike," and the prices that Pliny cites (12.43, 44), 40 to 75 denarii per pound for the leaves and 100 for the spike, give nard the distinction of being among the costliest of the imported plant products. It appears frequently in the Greek papyri of Egypt, usually, as one would expect, in company with the other imported drugs or aromatics which, though less costly, were still expensive: *SB* 6775 (257 B.C.), record of a delivery that includes five sealed pouches of nard along with three of incense and three of myrrh; *PSI* 628 (mid-3d century B.C.), a list that includes 2 mnas (ca. two pounds) of nard, 5 of myrrh, 1 of incense, and a phial of oil of cinnamon; *SB* 9860a (3d century B.C.), a medical prescription among whose ingredients are nard, myrrh, and cinnamon; *O. Tait* 2153 (4th century A.D.), a list that includes nard along with malabathron and myrrh. *P. Oxy.* 1088, col. iii (1st century A.D.) contains a series of prescriptions for liver complaint that include nard together with far more modest ingredients, but the amount of nard is minuscule, under one gram in one prescription and in another, touted as particularly strong, still under five.

39:13.10c   turquoise

The Greek, *kalleanos lithos*, means literally "blue-green stone." It corresponds to what Pliny (37.110) calls *callaina*, which his description (37.110, 112) makes clear is green turquoise; cf. Warmington 255–56. Pliny gives the source as the mountains to the north of India; it was, rather, those to the northwest, for the principal turquoise mines in the world are at Ma'dan, some thirty miles from Nishapur in Iran (Watt vi.iv 204, Schoff).

39:13.11   lapis lazuli

The Greek word is *sappheiros*, which means lapis lazuli rather than sapphire, as Pliny's description makes clear (37.120; see D. Eichholtz's note to his translation in the Loeb edition [1962] and cf. *Theophrastos on Stones*, ed. E. Caley and J. Richards [Columbus, 1956], 136–37). The finds in Egypt show that lapis had made its way there very early (cf. Lucas-Harris [op. cit. under 1.1.2–4] 398–400). The chief source in ancient times were the famous mines at Badakshan in the northeast corner of Afghanistan, some 200 airline miles north-northeast of Kabul, which made Barbarikon a natural choice as point of export: shipments could go from Badakshan via Kabul to Peshawar and from there follow the Indus right down to its mouth.

39:13.11a   Chinese pelts, cloth, and yarn

See Introduction: Trade in the Indian Ocean, The Trade with India.

39:13.11–12   indigo

The Greek term is *indikon melan*, literally "Indian black." The same term is found in a Greek papyrus (*P. Holm.* 9.8, 4th century A.D.), which elsewhere uses such expressions as "Indian drug" (*indikon pharmakon*, 11.2 and 13.2), "Indian color" (*indikon chrôma*, 11.6), and simply "Indian" (13.35); all of these, the editor asserts (191), mean the same, namely indigo. The term corresponds to what Vitruvius (7.10.4) and Pliny (35.42–46), in discussing the materials available to painters to produce black or purple or blue, call *indicum*, which K. Bailey (*The Elder Pliny's Chapters on Chemical Subjects* i [London, 1929], 236) states "was unquestionably indigo." His conclusion is based on Pliny's description (35.46) of it as coming "from India, where it occurs as slime adhering to foam on the reeds. When first separated it is black, but, on treatment with water, it gives a wondrous blend of purple and blue" (trans. Bailey, ii [1932] 89).

The description provides as well an explanation of why indigo was called Indian "black" rather than blue; solid indigo, as Bailey notes (ii 219), "is very dark in colour."

The ancients used indigo not only as a coloring matter but also as a drug (Pliny 35.46), as the Indians do (cf. Watt iv 388), but not as a dye for fabrics since they lacked the requisite chemical knowledge (see Bailey i 236). Pliny in one passage (33.163) gives the price of indigo as 7 denarii to the pound, in another (35.46) as 20; the first falls in the lower range of prices paid for exotic plant products, the second in the middle range (cf. *ESAR* v. 285–86).

39:13.12–13 Those who sail with the Indian [sc. winds] leave around July

I.e., with the southwest monsoon; see App. 3.

39:13.13–14 The crossing with these is . . . favorable and shorter

See App. 3.

40:13.16–17 Eirinon, with the additional names Little and Big

This is the Rann of Kutch. 'Rann' comes from the Sanskrit *iriṇa*, "salt-swamp," "desert," or *araṇya*, "wilderness"; see Hobson-Jobson s.v. *Runn (of Cutch)*. The Greek name may well be derived from the same source. The Rann of Kutch is still viewed as consisting of two bodies, and one of these is still called "Little," as in the time of the *Periplus*; this is the part that lies to the northeast of the Gulf of Kutch, being connected with it by Hansthal Creek (22°50′N, 70°20′E). The other body lies to the north of the Gulf of Kutch, its center being more or less at the point where 24° north and 70° east intersect; see *WCIP*, chap. 8, p. 146. Today both are dry stretches of sand flat and salt waste that, during the southwest monsoon, are overrun by high tides or land floods; in antiquity they apparently were bodies of water (cf. Smith 109, n. 1), though too shallow for vessels of the size that made the voyage from Egypt.

40:13.20–22 a promontory . . . embraces the gulf called Barakê

Over the centuries changes have taken place in the coastline and these, coupled with the rather imprecise indications the author gives, make it hard to identify what he is describing except in a very general way. The consensus is that Barakê is the Gulf of Kutch; cf. Müller, McCrindle, Fabricius, Schoff, W. Tomaschek in *RE* s.v. *Barake* II (1896). Ptolemy calls the Gulf of Kutch Kanthi (7.1.2, 55) and reserves the name Barakê for one of the islands in it (7.1.94) but Ptolemy is particularly unreliable on this part of India's coast (cf. Tarn 233–34 and the map showing Ptolemy's conception in A. Berthelot, *L'Asie ancienne centrale et sud-orientale d'après Ptolémée* [Paris, 1930], opp. p. 312). Just below the southern entrance to the Gulf of Kutch is a town called Dwarka (22°15′N, 68°58′E), and this name, it has been suggested, is related to Barakê; see Hobson-Jobson s.v. *Dwarka*, S. Lévi in *JA* (1936): 72. The crooked promontory embracing Barakê could have been an arm projecting downward from the Kutch Peninsula that bounds the Gulf of Kutch on the north or upward from the Kathiawar Peninsula that bounds it on the south.

40:13.22–27   seven islands . . . violent whirlpools

Along the southern shore of the Gulf of Kutch, from the western tip extending as far east as Jamnagar (22°31′N, 70°2′E), there is a series of islands (cf. McCrindle 112, who traces them as far east as Navanagar). These are set amid dangerous shoals and bars (*WCIP*, chap. 8, pp. 138–44), and in places the tidal stream runs at a rate of four to six knots and creates heavy tide rips (p. 141). Thus the area, in location and the hazards its presents to the sailor, well fits the author's description.

40:13.28–29   anchors lying parallel . . . to withstand

A standard procedure today for securing a vessel in a tideway, called "mooring," is to set out anchors from both sides of the bow with an equal amount of cable to each; the vessel forms the apex, as it were, of an isosceles triangle, of which the anchors form the other two angles and the cables the sides. The words "anchors lying parallel" indicate that this is what the author has in mind: in "mooring," the anchors lie parallel with each other and more or less parallel with the vessel rather than straight ahead, as in the case of a single anchor. It is always good anchoring practice to give plenty of scope, to let out a long length of cable—and this is what the words "thrust out (cf. under B 40:13.28–29) to withstand [sc. the current]" must refer to. Giving plenty of scope allows the cable to lie flatter and thereby provides a better direction for the strain on the anchor. But a long cable inevitably lies for some of its length on the bottom, and, if this is rough and uneven, is exposed to the danger the author describes.

40:13.29   and some even get smashed

On a rocky and sharp bottom, even if an anchor escaped getting cut loose (see under 40:13.28–29), it ran the risk of getting smashed. This was because ancient anchors, unlike those of latter times, usually had arms and shank of wood (*SSAW* 253–55).

40:13.30   snakes

Cf. under 38:12.27–28.

41:14.1–2   the gulf of Barygaza and . . . Ariakê

The gulf of Barygaza is the modern Gulf of Cambay. The author's listing reverses the geographical order: Ariakê (see under 41:14.2–3) comes first and then the gulf of Barygaza.

41:14.2–3   Ariakê, the beginning both of Manbanos's realm and of all of India

Ariakê is mentioned thrice elsewhere: in 6:3.1 as a source of exports for Adulis, in 14:5.9 as a source of exports for the "far-side" ports, in 54:18.1 as an area that maintained trade relations with the Malabar coast. Here and in 6:3.1 the scribe wrote *Arabikê*, but the context renders the emendation certain. The border between Skythia (see under 38:12.23) and India seems to have been the Gulf of Kutch and the Little Rann; cf. Introduction: Political Geography. Ariakê extended from there south as far as Barygaza (= Broach; see under 41:14.9) and east into the interior at least as far as Minnagara (see under 41:14.8). According to S. Chattopadhyaya, *The Sakas in India* (Santiniketan, 1955), 37, the name may be connected with the Aryans, a Hellenized version of "Āryaka, the land of the Āryas or the Āryāvarta." S. Lévi, *JA* (1936): 73, suggests a derivation from a legendary figure Āryaka, who may "représente . . . le pays Ārya, enfin libéré de ses maîtres étrangers."

41:14.2   Manbanos's realm

Although the Sakas had been driven out of Sind (see under 38:13.3–4), they still held the area to the east and south, including the region called Ariakê with its great port of Barygaza (cf. under 41:14.2–3). Their realm embraced as well the northern Konkan at least as far south as Bombay or slightly beyond, up to the northern border of the Andhras, their neighbors to the south; cf. Introduction: Political Geography.

Manbanos is usually identified with a Saka ruler called Nahapāna. Nahapāna, whose name is attested on coins and his titles and deeds in inscriptions (see Raschke 754, n. 475), expanded Saka domination to the south, wresting from the Andhras control of Nasik, Junnar, and Karli (see D. Sircar in R. Majumdar, ed., *The History and Culture of the Indian People*. ii, *The Age of Imperial Unity* [Bombay, 1951], 180–81); these towns were particularly important since they commanded the passes through the western ghats that gave the ports of the northern Konkan access to the hinterland. A Boyer first suggested the identification, pointing out (*JA* [1897]: 137) that in transliteration into Greek Nahapāna would become "Nambanos," and this could easily have been altered by transposition to Manbanos. The identification has generally been accepted: cf. J. Fleet, *JRAS* (1912): 785; Smith 221; S. Lévi, *JA* (1936): 72; J. Banerjea in K. A. Nilakanta Sastri, ed., *A Comprehensive History of India*. ii, *The Mauryas and Satavahanas, 325 B.C.–A.D. 300* (Bombay, 1957), 275, 279; K. Gopalachari in Nilakanta Sastri 309; S. Chattopadhyaya, *Early History of North India* (Calcutta, 1968²), 83, 128–29; Raschke 755, n. 476. On Nahapāna's date, which has been much debated, see Raschke 631–32; as he points out, if Nahapāna is to be equated with Manbanos, the *Periplus* fixes the date for his reign rather than the reverse.

41:14.4   Abêria

The manuscript reads *Ibêria*, but the emendation is certain (cf. Ptolemy 7.1.55). Abêria is the land of the Ābhīras, a foreign people who appear in Indian legend (cf. R. Shafer, *Ethnography of Ancient India* [Wiesbaden, 1954], 119). In the second century B.C. they seem to have been in the Indus Delta (cf. Smith 290, Tarn 235–36) but sometime after that moved to the general area between Broach (Barygaza) and Ujjain (Ozênê), i.e., the easternmost part of Gujarat and westernmost of Madhya Pradesh (cf. Tarn 236, Sircar [op. cit. under 41:14.2] 221).

41:14.4a   Syrastrênê

Sanskrit Surāshtra, what is today the Kathiawar Peninsula; see Hobson-Jobson s.v. *Surath*. Ptolemy, whose conception of the coast east of the Indus Delta is askew (cf. under 40:13.20–22), places the district (7.1.2, 55) too far north; cf. Berthelot, op. cit. under 40:13.20–22.

41:14.4–6   The region, very fertile, . . . cotton

Presumably the author has in mind the eastern and southern parts, especially around Broach and Surat where the soil is rich and yields in particular fine cotton crops.

41:14.6   cotton, and the Indian cloths made from it

See App. 4. Marco Polo (3.26, 29) remarks on the cotton production of the area.

41:14.7–8   of very great size and dark skin color

Shafer (op. cit. under 41:14.4, 19–20) holds, on the basis of indications in Indian legend, that western India was early the home of a population created by the intermarriage of Iranian invaders with the natives they found there, the Bhils, "the only race in western India that could be called black" (Shafer 7). The tall, dark–skinned people referred to here, he suggests (20, 119) were their descendants.

41:14.8   The metropolis of the region is Minnagara

This is a second "Saka-town," to be distinguished from the Minnagar in Sind (38:13.3); the latter had been taken over by Parthians, but this was still a Saka center. Ptolemy (7.1.63) locates it between Barygaza (Broach) and Ozênê (Ujjain), which would put it north of the Narmada River (Ptolemy actually says "east" because he conceives of the river as running north-south at this point instead of its true direction, east-west; see Berthelot, op. cit. under 40:13.20–22). Either Indore (22°44′N, 75°52′E), as suggested by Müller and McCrindle, or Dohad (22°50′N, 74°15′E), as suggested by J. Fleet (*JRAS* [1912]: 788), fits the requirements. Baroda (22°18′N, 73°12′E) is another possibility; Roman remains have been found there (see C. Margabandhu in *JESHO* 8 [1965]: 319). Smith (221, n. 1) offers Mandasor (24°4′N, 75°4′E); lying well north of Ujjain (23°11′N, 75°46′E), it is less likely. As metropolis of the region, Minnagara was probably also the capital; cf. 4:2.8 (Axum), 23:7.27–28 (Saphar), 27:9.7–8 (Saubatha).

41:14.9   Barygaza

The spelling, following the usual Greek method of transcribing the sounds of Sanskrit, represents the Sanskrit name Bhārukaccha (see Shafer [op. cit. under 41:14.4] 114), modern Broach near the mouth of the Narmada River. Barygaza is far and away the most important of the foreign ports mentioned in the *Periplus*, occurring in nineteen of the sixty-six chapters. Tarn (260) argues that it was a key port as early as the mid-second century B.C.

41:14.9–10   signs of Alexander's expedition

Alexander got no further into India than the Hyphasis (Beiah) River (Arrian, *Anab.* 5.24.8), at some point where it flows east of Amritsar, and from there he backtracked to sail down the Indus; thus he came nowhere near the area described in this passage. Tarn (148) holds that the remains, though not Alexander's, were genuinely Greek, having been left by the expedition led by Apollodotus, who, acting on behalf of Demetrius, ruler of the Greek Bactrian kingdom, conquered this area some decades before the middle of the second century B.C. (Tarn 147–51). It is also possible that the remains had as little to do with Apollodotus as with Alexander, that they may have been, like so many similar identifications, manufactured by local guides to please tourists from the West.

41:14.12–13   the promontory near Astakapra across from Barygaza called Papikê

The location is defined more closely a few lines below ("the promontory in front of Astakapra," 43:14.26). The promontory Papikê "across from Barygaza," i.e., on the western shore of the Gulf of Cambay opposite Barygaza, is Kuda Point (21°38′N, 72°18′E), some four miles south-southeast of Gogha (cf. *WCIP* 129). The name Astakapra represents the Sanskrit Hastakavapra (cf. under B 41:14.12), a district that included the village of Kukkaṭa, which is the modern Kūkaḍ (21°29½′N, 72°13′E), twenty miles south of Bhavnagar; see H. Yule in *Indian Antiquary* 5 (1876): 314. Presumably the district reached at least twelve or so miles north of the village to encompass the area behind Kuda Point.

41:14.13   3000 stades

The distance is actually 4500 stades (450 nautical miles); see App. 2.

42:14.14–15   another gulf, on the inside of the waves, that forms an inlet directly to the north

The author divides the Gulf of Cambay horizontally into two segments. The lower, from the entrance up to a line running from Kuda Point on the western shore (cf. under 41:14.12–13) to the mouth of the Narmada on the eastern, he calls the gulf of Barygaza (41:14.1); the upper, from that line north to the head, he calls "another gulf" (cf. McCrindle 116). The upper gulf is "on the inside of the waves" in the sense that the waves are outside it—it lies up a deep inlet well removed from the open sea where waves are found; cf. under B 42:14.14.

42:14.15   Baiônês

Piram Island (21°36′N, 72°21′E), three miles southeast of Kuda Point (cf. under 41:14.12–13), so well suits the location given for Baiônês that there is universal agreement on the identification; see McCrindle, Fabricius, Schoff, Huntingford, W. Tomaschek in *RE* s.v. *Baione* (1896), Hobson-Jobson s.v. *Mahi*.

42:14.16   the Mais

Unquestionably the Mahi, the river that empties into the head of the Gulf of Cambay; see Müller, McCrindle, Fabricius, Schoff, Huntingford, Hobson-Jobson s.v. *Mahi*.

42:14.17   300 stades

The width of the Gulf of Cambay at the point the author is describing, abreast of the mouth of the Narmada or to be specific, from Kuda Point (21°38′N, 72°18′E) to Luhara Point (21°39′N, 72°33′E), is fifteen nautical miles, just half the author's figure. Only at its mouth, the span from Gopnath Point (21°12′N, 72°7′E) to Suvali Point (21°5′N, 72°38′E), does the gulf reach a width of 300 stades.

42:14.18   highest point is visible

A major difficulty in negotiating these waters was the lowness of the shores and the consequent dearth of landmarks; see 43:15.1–2. Baiônês fortunately had a point high enough to be discerned.

42:14.20   is called the Lamnaios

The text reads "is called the Lamnaios," but that clearly is an error. Broach, the ancient Barygaza, lies on the north bank of the Narmada, a name that is identical with the Sanskrit name (cf. O. Wecker, *RE* s.v. *Lamnaios* [1925]). In Ptolemy (7.1.5, 31, 62, 65) it appears as Namadês.

43:14.23   by the left-hand side is better

The center of the mouth of the Gulf of Cambay is dangerous because of the Malacca Banks, a series of parallel north-south reefs that force vessels, today as in the times of the *Periplus,* to stay close to one shore or the other (*WCIP* 126–27). And today, too, the approach by the left-hand shore, through the channel (Grant Channel) between the coast of Kathiawar and the westernmost of the Malacca Banks, is preferable (*WCIP* 126).

43:14.24–25   a rough and rock-strewn reef called Hêrônê

There is a series of offshore reefs extending from Suvali Point (21°5′N, 72°38′E) along the eastern shore of the Gulf of Cambay up to the mouth of the Narmada (*WCIP* 127); Hêrônê must have been one such.

43:14.25   Kammôni

This village must have been somewhere on the eastern shore of the Gulf of Cambay below the mouth of the Narmada. Ptolemy (7.1.5) calls it Kamani and places it three-quarters of a degree below the mouth.

43:14.27–28   because of the current around it and because the bottom, being rough and rocky

Sailors today are given the same warning. Cf. *WCIP* 128–29: "Mallock Reef lies near the E edge of foul ground extending from NE to SE from Kuda Point [see under 41:14.12–13]. . . . Caution. the narrow channel between Piram Island and Mallock Reef to the W should not be used without local knowledge as tides run through at a great rate and there is little slack water."

43:15.1   is hard to find

The visibility is so poor that even modern navigational aids are hard to find. E.g., describing the shore about ten miles below the mouth of the Narmada, the *WCIP* (127) remarks: "Bhagwa Creek Light (21°19′N, 72°37′E) is exhibited from a steel framework tower on the coast E of Bhagwa Channel; it has been reported that this light-structure cannot be distinguished from a distance of a few miles even in favourable conditions."

44:15.4–5 local fisherman . . . come out with crews [sc. of rowers] and long ships

I.e., with fully manned galleys; cf. under B 44:15.5. The author's emphasis on the rowing crews—he mentions them again a few lines below (44:15.8)—is deliberate. The galleys were manned by multiple oarsmen whose muscle made it possible to tow the ponderous sailing vessels Westerners used (cf. App. 3) through the turns and twists of the channels from the mouth of the Gulf of Cambay to Barygaza, almost seventy nautical miles.

44:15.5 *trappaga* and *kotymba*

A Jain text, probably of the fourth century A.D. but undoubtedly incorporating earlier material, devotes a section to various types of vessels, characterizing certain of them as large, others as middle-sized, still others as small; see Muni Shri Punyavijayaji, *Aṅgavijjā*, Prakrit Text Society Series 1 (Banaras, 1957), introd. p. 49. Among the middle-sized were *tappaka* and *koṭṭimba*; as the editor suggests, these must be the two types referred to here. The passage in the *Periplus* makes it clear that they were galleys (see under B 44:15.4–5), not war galleys but types used by the local fishermen (cf. 44:15.4–5).

44:15.12 300 stades

A good enough estimate. The actual distance from the mouth of the Narmada to Broach is about twenty-five nautical miles.

45:15.16 much more extreme in the area around Barygaza

The tides in the Gulf of Cambay are particularly great. At its head the spring tides—the maximum tides that occur around the new and the full moon—achieve a range of no less than twenty-nine and one-half feet (*WCIP* 21).

46:15.23–24 restraining anchors do not stay in place

I.e., they drag. For the text, see under B 46:15.23–24.

46:15.26 in the channels some craft

The channels must have been waterways that were wide or deep enough to be considered safe for waiting out the ebb tide. "Some craft" must refer to those that were sharp-built, i.e., with the sides of the hull sloping more or less sharply towards the keel; when the water level drops to a point where it no longer offers full support, such vessels lean to one side or the other. Flat-bottomed boats, on the other hand, would be unaffected; even if a channel ran dry, they would simply come to rest on the bottom and float off with the incoming flood tide.

47:16.3–5   Inland . . . numerous peoples . . . is located

The names are misspelled in the manuscript, but the restorations seem well founded. The peoples listed were indeed inland, well-nigh a thousand miles north or northwest of Barygaza. The Aratrioi were probably the Āraṭṭas, a people located in the Punjab (cf. Shafer [op. cit. under 41:14.4] 32–33; W. Tomaschek, *RE* s.v. *Aratrioi* [1896]). The Arachusioi presumably dwelled in the region of Arachosia, southern Afghanistan (cf. Tomaschek, *RE* s.v. *Arachosia* [1896]), and the Gandaraioi in Gandhara, the land around Peshawar and between the Kunar and Indus rivers in northeastern Pakistan (cf. Tarn 135). Ptolemy (7.1.44) lists Poklaeis (alternate reading: Proklais) as a city of Gandhara, and it has been identified with Chārsadda on the left bank of the Swat (34°9'N, 71°44'E); see H. Treidler, *RE* s.v. *Proklais* (1957). The author of the *Periplus*, as is clear from a subsequent mention of Proklais (48:16.16–17), considers it a region; this explains how he can include within it Bukephalos Alexandreia (Bucephala), which lay some 150 airline miles southeast of the city of Proklais (cf. Tarn 353, n. 3; Treidler).

47:16.5–6   And beyond these is a very warlike people, the Bactrians, under a king

The text of the rest of the sentence is garbled, and no convincing restoration has been offered (see under B 47:16.6).

The Bactrians referred to are the Kushans, an Iranian people who enter Indian history about the beginning of the first century A.D. This was when they crossed the Hindu Kush and created an empire that included lands on both sides of it; centered on Peshawar and Mathura, their domains reached as far as the basin of the Ganges. The founder of the empire was Kujula Kadphises, who ruled probably in the first half of the first century A.D.; its most famous king was Kanishka, noted for his patronage of Buddhism, who ruled probably in the early second century A.D.; and its end came when, in the early third, most of its territories were conquered by the Sasanians. See Bivar (op. cit. under 38:12.23) 192–93, 197–203; the dates have been much disputed, but those cited above, or others in that range, seem now to be generally accepted (cf. J. Cribb in *Numismatic Chronicle* 145 [1985]: 136–49, esp. 146; he dates Kanishka a few decades earlier). Tarn (148, n. 4), followed by Raschke (751, n. 461 and 800, n. 677), takes the *Periplus*'s words to mean that, at the time of writing, the Kushans had not yet crossed the Hindu Kush, but the language is too vague to support so exact an interpretation.

47:16.7   Alexander . . . penetrated as far as the Ganges

The fiction that Alexander, who barely reached the Punjab (see under 41:14.9–10), had gotten as far as the Ganges arose early. Strabo (15.702) cites a letter purportedly from Craterus, one of Alexander's generals, that not only tells of making it to the river but adds eyewitness details about its great size.

47:16.8   Limyrikê

The Malabar coast; see under 51:17.15.

47:16.9–11   there are to be found on the market . . . old drachmas . . . of Apollodotus and Menander

In the middle of the third century B.C., Diodotus, the Greek governor of Bactria (northern Afghanistan), till then part of the Seleucid Empire, set himself up as an independent ruler. The kingdom expanded into India when, in the early second century B.C., one of his successors, Demetrius, crossed the Hindu Kush and added the upper Indus Valley, parts of the Punjab, and perhaps even some areas further south. Under pressure from the Sakas (see under 38:12.23) and Kushans (see under 47:16.5–6), the area under Greek control steadily diminished, but a remnant was still in existence as late as the second half of the first century B.C. See Tarn, chap. iii–viii; A. Narain, *The Indo-Greeks* (Oxford, 1957). Menander held the throne ca. 150 B.C. (Tarn 225–26) and was the most famous of the Indo-Greek kings; his name even made its way into Indian legend (see Tarn 265–69). Apollodotus may have reigned about the beginning of the first century B.C. (Tarn 318–19). Coins of both have been found in northern India (see Raschke 814, n. 709 and 1030, n. 1556; for examples, see Narain, pls. ii.7, 8 [Menander] and iv.5, 6 [Apollodotus]). What is particularly significant is the discovery of a large hoard at Gogha, just across the Gulf of Cambay from Barygaza (cf. under 41:14.12–13), which includes coins of Apollodotus together with coins of Nahapāna (cf. under 41:14.2); the hoard, in other words, supplies concrete evidence of the author's statement (see J. Deyell, *Numismatic Chronicle* 144 [1984]: 115–27). For the Greek term translated "are found on the market," see under B 6:2.23. As Deyell points out (121, 125; cf. D. MacDowall and N. Wilson in *Numismatic Chronicle* 130 [1970]: 235–36), these old issues probably did not circulate as coin of the realm but were marketed as bullion.

48:16.12–13 towards the east a city called Ozênê, the former seat of the royal court

Ozênê is the modern Ujjain (cf. O. Stein, *RE* s.v. 'Οζήνη [1942]), 200 miles to the northeast of Broach (rather than the east). The court must have transferred from there to Minnagara; cf. under 41:14.8. Ptolemy's entry (7.1.63) reads: "Ozênê, seat of the court of Tiastanos"; obviously, by his time the court had returned. Tiastanos is usually identified as Caṣṭana, one of the successors to Nahapāna (see under 41:14.2), who ruled a decade or so before A.D. 150; see Chattopadhyaya (op. cit. under 41:14.2) 41–47, 51. For details concerning the road from Broach to Ujjain, see J. Vogel in *BSOAS* 13 (1949): 148; J. Deloche, *La circulation en Inde avant la révolution des transports*, Publications de l'École Française d'Extrême Orient 122 (Paris, 1980), i 50. Both favor a route that went by way of Barodā and Dohad.

48:16.15 agate (?)

The Greek word is *myrrhinê*. In 6:2.26, where it occurs in a list of Egyptian exports to Adulis, it is used of glass imitations of true "myrrhine vessels," vessels carved out of some valuable exotic stone, probably fluorspar; see under 6:2.25–26. Here it is not an item exported from Egypt but just the reverse, one that India exported to the West. It cannot, therefore, be glass, which was an Indian import (cf. 39:13.9, 49:16.23, 56:18.19), but must be the stone from which the true "myrrhine vessels" were made. D. Eichholtz (note to Pliny 37.21, Loeb edition [1962]) concludes that in this context it "should mean agate, which, like fluor-spar, was used for cups," and Ball (op. cit. under 6:2.25–26, 221) points out that "the well-known Cambay agate and onyx locality is near, and Broach [Barygaza] is still the most important trade center of the Indian agate industry."

48:16.15a garments of *molochinon*

Cf. under 6:3.3.

48:16.16–18   there is also brought down . . . Skythia

Thus the Ujjain region was the collecting point for nard, which originated in three areas—around Kabul and, probably, the Hindu Kush and Kashmir (see under B 48:16.17)—and arrived by way of two routes, one through the region of Proklais (see under 47:16.3–5) and the other through Skythia (see under 38:12.23).

The points of origin are, as we would expect, all in the Himalayas, for nard grows only at very great heights (see under 39:13.10b). From them it was funneled into the region of Proklais. The author conceives of this region as extending as far as Bucephala; if we assume it extended a little further east of Bucephala it would include Sialkot, through which passed major routes coming from the three points of origin (see Moti Chandra, *Trade and Trade Routes in Ancient India* [Delhi, 1977], 15, 20; Deloche [op. cit. under 48:16.12–13] i 34 and fig. iv opp. 40). And from Sialkot a main road led south to Mathura and Ujjain (Chandra 5, 15; Deloche, ibid.; cf. P. Eggermont in *JESHO* 9 [1966]: 262–65, who suggests it swung eastward after Mathura to follow the courses of the Yamuna and Betwa rivers [see his map on 259]).

The part of Skythia adjacent to the region of Barygaza and Ozênê must have been in what is today southern Rajasthan. Apparently a certain amount of nard, instead of following the route that passed through Mathura, went by a more westerly course, perhaps by way of Ajmer, through which ran important routes leading south (Chandra 25; Deloche, fig. viii opp. 60 and fig. ix opp. 62).

49:16.21   wine, principally Italian but also . . . Arabian

The Arabian wine very likely came from Muza; see 24:8.6 and note ad loc.

49:16.21a   copper, tin, and lead

See Introduction: Trade in the Indian Ocean, The Trade in Metals.

49:16.23   yellow sweet clover (?)

The Greek word is *melilôton*, an alternate form of *melilôtos*, both of which can refer to several varieties of clover. Presumably it refers here to the variety with medicinal properties described by Dioscorides (3:40; cf. Pliny 21.151); he notes that it is saffron-colored and aromatic, and most authorities agree in identifying it as *Melilôtos officinalis* L., yellow sweet clover (cf. Löw ii 465; A. Steier, *RE* s.v. *Lotos* 1531 [1927]). This does grow in India, but only in remote highlands (Watt v 224). Schoff (191), seconded by Warmington (266), offers the far-fetched idea that *melilôton* here is the ordinary sweet clover which was shipped to India to be made into chaplets for sending back to Rome.

49:16.23a   raw glass

For other instances of India's importation of glass, see under 48:16.15. The Greek term here means literally "unfinished glass." It was common practice to ship glass in such a state. A wreck of the fourteenth century B.C. found off Kaş on the southwestern coast of Asia Minor was carrying as part of its cargo over a dozen and one-half discoid ingots of glass, the largest of which were six inches in diameter and two to three inches thick; see G. Bass in *AJA* 90 (1986): 281–82. A wreck found in the same general region and dating two and one-half millennia later was carrying about three metric tons of raw and broken glass (*IJNA* 11 [1982]: 9).

49:16.23b   realgar

Realgar—red sulphide of arsenic—is the meaning commonly assigned to the Greek *sandarakê* (see *LSJ* s.v.; Caley-Richards [op. cit. under 39:13.11] 171); the item reappears among the imports at Muziris and Nelkynda (56:18.20). Realgar was used both medicinally (Diosc. 5.122, Pliny 34.177) and as a pigment (Pliny 35.30); samples of the pigment have been found in Greece (Caley-Richards 171–72) and Egypt (Lucas-Harris [op. cit. 1:1.2–4] 348). Strabo (12.562) describes a mountain called "Mt. Realgar-Pit" (*Sandarakurgion oros*) near Pompeiopolis southwest of Tarsus in Asia Minor, which had been rendered hollow by prolonged mining for the substance. Realgar, as it happens, occurs in India (Watt vi.i 399); presumably the deposits were unknown in ancient times or too costly to utilize.

49:16.23c   sulphide of antimony

This is the meaning commonly assigned to the Greek *stim(m)i* (see *LSJ* s.v.; Lucas-Harris [op. cit. under 1:1.2–4] 82; Bailey [op. cit. under 39:13.11–12] i 213), an item which, like realgar, reappears among the imports listed for Muziris and Nelkynda (56:18.19). Dioscorides (5.99) and Pliny (33.101–2) discuss *stim(m)i* in some detail. It was used particularly for the eyes, both as a cure for sores and as a cosmetic to apply to the lids and lashes. It derives from the Egyptian *msdmt*, meaning "kohl" (Lucas-Harris 82), but despite this is not the substance from which kohl was commonly made, though often said to be so (cf. Schoff 192, Huntingford 140). In earliest times kohl was made from malachite, in later from galena, while the modern version is made from soot [Lucas-Harris 80–82 and cf. 195–99]).

49:16.23–24 Roman money, gold and silver, which commands an exchange at some profit against the local currency

Müller, McCrindle, Fabricius, and Schoff all translate "profit" and Huntingford even "much profit," although the text distinctly qualifies it merely as "some profit." Nahapāna had a silver coinage and this may have been the currency against which the exchange was made, although his money seems to have had a very limited circulation; see Deyell (op. cit. under 47:16.9–11) 122–23. It has been suggested that the Roman coins were sold as bullion which ended up in the hands of Nahapāna's treasury officials, who melted it down for minting his own issues; see Warmington 290, MacDowell-Wilson (op. cit. under 47:16.9–11) 234–36. However, this overlooks the fact that the *Periplus* mentions the exchange of gold as well as silver, whereas Nahapāna coined only in silver (cf. Raschke 631). The favorable exchange, which we are told involved but a modest profit, could well have been nothing more than the result of temporary market conditions: at the time the author was writing, perhaps Western merchants came out somewhat ahead by using local currency to buy whatever Indian products they had to, or Indian merchants by using Roman currency to buy whatever Western products they had to, or both.

49:16.25 For the king

Cf. under 24:8.7–9.

49:16.25a in those times

Presumably when Ozênê was the capital (48:16.12–13). At the time of writing, the capital had been transferred to Minnagara (41:14.8), where, it would appear, life was more austere.

49:16.26 slave musicians, beautiful girls

Several centuries earlier the Greek adventurer Eudoxus, on his third trip to India, took along a supply of young slave musicians (Strabo 2.99).

Western slaves are mentioned in Indian literature (Warmington 261). There is evidence of their importation even further west, into China; cf. Ying-shih Yü, *Trade and Expansion in Han China* (Berkeley, 1967), 180.

49:16.29   agate (?)

See under B 49:16.29 and 48:16.15.

49:16.30   [sc. silk] cloth . . . yarn

See Introduction: Trade in the Indian Ocean, The Trade with India.

49:16.30a   long pepper

On long pepper (*Piper longum*), see Watt vi.i 258–60. It is the fruit of a perennial shrub native to many of the hotter parts of India. Today as a spice it is considered inferior to black pepper (see under 56:18.17) and is little used as such outside of the area where it is grown. Its principal use in Roman times was pharmaceutical (Warmington 182), and it is still so used in India (Watt 259–60). It commanded, at least in Pliny's day, a higher price than black pepper, 15 denarii to the pound as against 4 (*ESAR* v 285).

49:16.31–32   For those sailing . . . the month of July

See App. 3.

50:17.2   Dachinabadês, . . . *dachanos*

Cf. Hobson-Jobson s.v. *Deccan*: "Hind. *Dakhin, Dakkhin, Dakhan, Dakkhan; dakkhina*, the Prakr. form of Skt. *dakshina*, 'the South.' . . . In . . . Upper India the Deccan stands opposed to Hindūstān, i.e. roundly speaking, the country south of the Nerbudda to that north of it. The term frequently occurs in the Skt. books in the form *dakshiṇāpatha* ('Southern region,' whence the Greek form in our first quotation [*Periplus* 50])." The Nerbudda is another name for the Narmada (cf. under 42:14.20). At the time of the *Periplus* the area referred to corresponded to "the empire of the great Andhra emperors extending as far as the Ganges" (P. Srinivasa Iyengar, *Indian Historical Quarterly* 2 [1926]: 456).

50:17.6 enormous serpents

The Indian python can reach a length of ten meters (*Grzimek's Animal Life Encyclopedia* vi 372 [1975]), although exaggerated reports put it at much more. For a convenient review of the various statements by ancient authors, see J. McCrindle, *The Invasion of India by Alexander the Great* (London, 1893), 361–62.

50:17.6a hyenas

The Greek word is *krokottas*, described by Agatharchides (77 = *GGM* i 161–62) as a combination of wolf and dog with extremely powerful teeth and guts; the one can crush bones of any kind and the other boasts an indescribably effective digestive capability. This has led authorities to identify the animal as a hyena.

50:17.6b monkeys

The Greek word is *kynokephalos*, "dog-headed," which according to Agatharchides (74 = *GGM* i 160), is an animal with a body like an ungainly human body and a dog's face. It is usually taken (*LSJ* s.v.) to be a baboon, in particular *Papio hamadryas*, the sacred baboon of Egypt, and most translators (McCrindle, Schoff, Huntingford) have rendered it "baboon" in this passage. But baboons have not been found in India since the Ice Age (*Grzimek's Animal Life Encyclopedia* x 414 [1972]). As Müller remarks in his commentary to Agatharchides' description, the ancients seem to have used the term to refer to many types of monkeys.

51:17.9 Paithana, twenty days' travel to the south from Barygaza

Ptolemy (7.1.82) spells it Baithana. It is the modern Paithan (19°28'N, 75°23'E), some 240 miles southeast, rather than south, of Barygaza; see J. Fleet, *JRAS* (1901): 538–39. Fleet (547) estimates that twenty days, i.e., twelve miles a day, would be about right for laden carts. Ptolemy refers to the place as a royal seat, and indeed it seems for a time to have served as capital of the Andhran Empire; cf. G. Venket in G. Yazdani, *The Early History of the Deccan* (Oxford, 1960), 78–79.

51:17.10–11 another very large city, Tagara

Ptolemy too (7.1.82) couples Tagara with Paithana, listing the one right after the other. Fleet (op. cit. under 51:17.9, 541–42) suggested the iden-

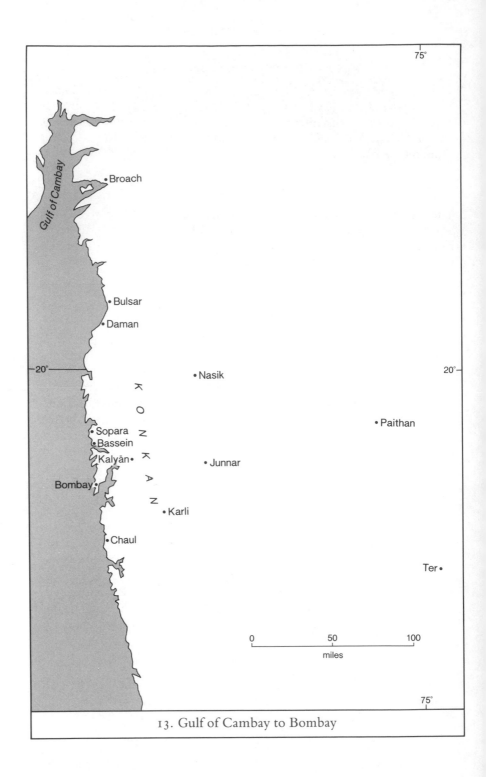

13. Gulf of Cambay to Bombay

tification with Tēr (Thair, 18°19′N, 76°9′E), and excavation has provided confirmation. There is abundant evidence of habitation during the Roman Imperial period including evidence for contact with the West (fragments of Roman pottery as well as of local imitations). See M. Despande, "Sátaváhana Coins from Ter," *The Indian Numismatic Chronicle* 3 (1964): 161–66; B. Chapekar, *Report on the Excavation at Ter (1958)* (Poona, 1969), iv–vi.

51:17.11   in wagons over very great roadless stretches

Paithana and Tagara were Andhran cities, whereas Barygaza belonged to the Sakas, a hostile nation; see Introduction: Political Geography. This explains why, although there was a well-defined route from Paithana to Barygaza (cf. J. Fleet, *JRAS* [1901]: 548 and [1912]: 790), the shipments went over back country where there were no roads at all: the Andhran authorities no doubt frowned upon trading with the enemy, and the wagoners had to follow routes that precluded meeting any of their agents; see Casson 1983.175–77 = Casson 1984.218–19. They might have tried to get their loads to Kalliena, a good port that, lying almost due west, was considerably closer, but at the time of the *Periplus*, no Greek ships were to be found there; see 52:17.19–21 and note ad loc.

51:17.14   from the coastal parts

I.e., the east coast, on the Bay of Bengal; cf. J. Fleet, *JRAS* (1901): 547–48. He suggests that a starting point was Masulipatam (see under 62:20.21–22) and that the route from there went by way of Hyderabad.

51:17.15   Limyrikê

This is the author's name for what in general corresponds to the Malabar coast. He begins it at Naura and Tyndis (53:17.26–27). Ptolemy (7.1.8; cf. 1.7.6, 7.1.85) also calls it Limyrikê—not "Dimirike," as Schoff (205) and Warmington (344, n. 65) report, nor "Damirike" as Huntingford (116)—and begins it at Tyndis; thus the two are in substantial agreement. It probably stopped short of Cape Comorin; cf. Ptolemy 7.1.9, who locates the cape in the next region. It so happens that the *Tabula Peutingeriana*, a Roman map probably drawn up in the fifth century A.D. but based on earlier sources, gives the name Dymirice to an area somewhat near the Malabar coast and the name Damirice to an area between the Himalayas and the Ganges (see section 4 of segment xi of the reproduction [photographed from the original] in A. and M. Levi, *Itineraria picta: Contributo allo studio della Tabula Peutingeriana* [Rome, 1967]; for the date, see pp. 172–74). In the last century the possible phonetic connection between *Damir-* and *Tamil* so impressed students of Indian languages (see Mc-Crindle 126) that they jumped to the conclusion that Damirice had to be right and that the Limyrikê of both the *Periplus* and Ptolemy reflected scribal blundering. This view has long enjoyed wide acceptance: see Hobson-Jobson s.v. *Malabar*, Smith 457, Schoff 205, Warmington 57 and 167, Wheeler 121, G. Mathew in *Proceedings of the Seminar for Arabian Studies* 1–3 (1970–73): 29, Huntingford 116. However, it is not even mentioned by O. Wecker, *RE* s.v. *Limyrike* (1926) and rightly so: the area marked Damirice on the *Tabula* is over a thousand miles away from the land of the Tamils. Schoff went so far as to use "Damirica" in the text of his translation, and this has led the unwary into automatic acceptance of it (e.g., K. Sivaraja Pillai, *The Chronology of the Early Tamils* [Madras, 1932], 176; K. Nilakanta Sastri, *Foreign Notices of South India from Megasthenes to Ma Huan* [Madras, 1972], 57; Chandra [op. cit. under 48:16.16–18] 116).

51:17.15a   7000 stades

This is an underestimate; see App. 2.

51:17.16   most vessels continue on to the Strand

I.e., to Palk Bay between the northern tip of Ceylon and India; see under 59:19.25–20.1. The Strand, it would seem, was normally the end of the run for Western vessels; cf. Introduction: Trade in the Indian Ocean, The Trade with India.

52:17.17   Akabaru

Unidentified. Cf. under B 52:17.17.

52:17.17a   Suppara

Also mentioned by Ptolemy (7.1.6). Its name in Sanskrit was Sūrpāraka, it is attested in Indian inscriptions and literature, and it is listed among the ports of the area by Arab geographers. It stood near the modern town of Bassein (19°21′N, 72°48′E), just north of Bombay. See Hobson-Jobson s.v. *Supara*.

52:17.18   Kalliena

The city still bears the same name, Kalyān. It lies thirty-three miles northeast of Bombay, up the Ulhās River. See Hobson-Jobson s.v. *Calyan*.

52:17.18a   Saraganos

There is general agreement that this represents a Greek's attempt at reproducing Sātakarṇi, a name borne by a number of Andhran kings; see Casson 1983.169 = Casson 1984.214–15. In the days when he was in charge, the city of Kalliena was still in Andhran hands; see under 52:17.19–21.

52:17.19–21   after Sandanês . . . under guard to Barygaza

For a detailed discussion of the historical context that explains this passage, the struggle between the Sakas and Andhras, see Casson 1983 (= Casson 1984.211–24). At the time the *Periplus* was written, the Sakas had succeeded in wresting from the Andhras the cities of Nāsik, Junnar, and Karli, all three important because they controlled the passes through the western ghats down to Suppara, Kalliena, and the other ports of the northern Konkan. And the Sakas succeeded as well in taking over Kalliena; Sandanês must have been the official they put in charge of this newly acquired possession. The "hindrance" to trade that ensued can only have been caused by the Andhras: the highlands east of the ghats were still in their hands, and the rulers must have instituted an embargo that prohibited Andhran goods from going to ports now in the hands of the enemy (cf. under 51:17.11). Thus, if Greek ships by chance entered any of them, they found no goods to load aboard, and so the Saka authorities forwarded the vessels to Barygaza, the great Saka port, where there were plenty. The forwarding of them under guard no doubt was a precaution taken to thwart possible attacks from Andhran warships out to disrupt Sakan maritime commerce.

53:17.22   Sêmylla

Coming after Kalyān, Sêmylla must have been either in the area of Bombay or just south of it. Ptolemy lists it (7.1.6) after Suppara and remarks (1.17.3–4) that the natives pronounced it "Timoula." It has been identified (Hobson-Jobson s.v. *Choul, Chaul*; Schoff) with the Saimur of the Arab geographers, the Chaul of later writers, which for long was an active port. The *Imperial Gazetteer of India* gives (x 184 [1908]) the coordinates of Chaul as 18°34′N, 72°55′E and places it thirty miles south of Bombay. O. Wecker, *RE* s.v. *Simylla* (1929), prefers a location north of Bombay, but offers no sound arguments in its favor.

53:17.22–27   Mandagora . . . Nelkynda

For the location of the sites listed in these lines, see App. 5.

53:17.22–23   Mandagora, Palaipatmai

Ptolemy reverses the order. He ends (7.1.6) the region he calls Ariakê with Baltipatna (= Palaipatmai) and begins (7.1.7) the region "of pirates" with Mandagara [*sic*].

53:17.23   Melizeigara

Commentators (Müller, McCrindle, Schoff, A. Herrmann in *RE* s.v. *Milizigeris* [1932]) equate this site with Ptolemy's Milizêgyris (7.1.95), although Ptolemy's coordinates reveal his site to be an island well off the coast (see App. 5, n. 3). They also equate it with Pliny's Zigerus (6.101), and this is more plausible, since Pliny refers to Zigerus as a "port of India" and the context makes clear it was on the west coast.

53:17.23a   Byzantion

The suggestion that, because of its name, this was a Greek colony is totally without validity, yet keeps cropping up; see the instances cited by Schoff, Warmington 68, Meile 119, G. Fiaccadori in *La Parola del Passato* 213 (1983): 444.

53:17.23b   Toparon

See under B 53:17.23–24 and App. 5, n. 1.

53:17.23–24   Tyrannosboas

For the various attempts at identification, see O. Stein in *RE* s.v. Τυραν-νοςβόας (1948).

53:17.25–26 around which places there are pirates

Presumably around the Sêsekreienai Islands, the Isle of the Aigidioi, and the Isle of the Kaineitoi. Ptolemy (7.1.7) includes in his region "of pirates" the coast from Mandagora to Tyndis, while according to Pliny (6.104) pirates operated as far south as Muziris. They were still plaguing the Malabar coast in Marco Polo's day; he reports (3.25) on the efficient methods they used, so efficient that they were able to blanket "something like an hundred miles of sea, and no merchant ship can escape them."

53:17.26 White Island

Also listed by Ptolemy (7.1.95). For the identification with Pigeon Island, see App. 5. Another name for Pigeon Island is Netrani, and this has led Schoff, followed by Warmington (57), to suggest that the Nitraiai listed by Ptolemy (7.1.7) and mentioned by Pliny (6.104) was yet another name for White Island. Ptolemy's Nitraiai, however, is no island but a port of trade right on the coast (on its identification, see App. 5, n. 14).

54:17.29 the kingdom of Kêprobotos

Very likely a miswriting for Kêrobotros (see Frisk's apparatus and cf. McCrindle's commentary), since Pliny (6.104) has Caelobothras and Ptolemy (7.1.86) Kêrobothros. Keralaputra appears in the inscriptions of Asoka (mid-3d century B.C.) as the name of the kingdom in the south called in Sanskrit Kerala and in Tamil Cēram or Chera, as historians commonly write it (see J. Filliozat's note to Pliny 6.104 in the Budé edition [1980]; Smith 464–65). A form Cheraputra seems to lie behind the version in the Western writers; see O. Wecker, *RE* s.v. *India* 1281 (1916). The author of the *Periplus*, in naming the king of this land Kêprobotos, was following the Indian practice of calling a ruler by the name of his country or capital (see Strabo 15.702, where he explains how "King Palibothros" is named after his capital at Palibothra; for other examples see Tarn 150). Kerala—or Chera; the two are used interchangeably (Smith 465)—was one of the three great kingdoms of the south, the others being Pandya and Chola (Smith 464). The *Periplus* reveals that at the time of writing Kerala's southern boundary lay between Muziris and Nelkynda. The northern boundary, at least during most periods, was at the Chandragiri River (12°29'N); see Smith 466. For a summary of the little that is known of the history of the Chera kingdom, see Smith 476–80. Its capital was at "Vanji, Vanchi, or Karūr, now represented by the deserted village Tiru-

Karūr, high up on the Periyar, about 28 miles ENE. of Cochin" (Smith 477). Cochin's coordinates are 9°58′N, 76°14′E.

54:17.29–30   Tyndis, a well-known village on the coast

By the time Ptolemy wrote, Tyndis had grown large enough for him to call it (7.1.8) a city (*polis*). The Tamil poems that mention it reflect Ptolemy's age or later, for it appears there as a sizable and important center (see App. 5, n. 9).

54:18.2   on a river

The Periyār; see App. 5.

54:18.2–3   by river and sea

The coastline has changed so much that it is impossible to try to identify what river is meant. The extensive backwaters in the area today may not have existed at the time of the *Periplus*; see K. Padmanabha Menon in the *Indian Antiquary* 31 (1902): 339.

54:18.5   likewise by river and sea

See under 54:18.2–3.

54:18.5–6   another kingdom, Pandiôn's

Sailing south along the coast, after the Chera kingdom one came to the second of the three great realms of southern India, the Pandya kingdom. Pliny (6.105) and Ptolemy (7.1.89) also refer to it as "Pandiôn's" (for the naming of a king after his country, see under 54:17.29) and agree with the *Periplus* in setting its upper boundary north of Nelkynda. It was the southernmost of the three, stretching right to Cape Comorin. On its east it extended to the Coromandel coast. The capital in early days was Korkai, or Kolchoi, as the *Periplus* (59:19.22) calls it; see Smith 468–69. Then there was a shift, for both Pliny and Ptolemy report it to be Modura = Madura (9°56′N, 78°7′E). The Greek world became aware of the existence of the Pandya kingdom at least as early as the beginning of the third century B.C. since Megasthenes, the ambassador sent in 302 B.C. by Seleucus I to the court of Chandragupta, included in his report on India a discussion (Arrian, *Indica* 8) of its legendary origins. Among the numerous legations that Augustus states (*Res Gestae* xxxi.v.50–51) came to him

from India, one was from a ruler of the Pandya kingdom (Strabo 15.686).
For a résumé of Pandyan history, see Smith 468–76.

54:18.6   on a river

The Pāmbiyār; see App. 5. Ptolemy (7.1.8) preserves its ancient name,
Baris.

55:18.8   Bakarê

The manuscript reads "Bararê." The correction is based on the form of
the name in Ptolemy (Bakarê, 7.1.8) and Pliny (Becare, 6.105). Ptolemy
agrees with the *Periplus* in placing it at the mouth of a river.

55:18.9–10   to which vessels drop downriver . . . that are shoal

Vessels, it would appear, arrived so lightly loaded that they could float
over the sandbanks and shoals of the river. But the return cargoes—no
doubt chiefly pepper; cf. 56:18.16–17—if taken on board would have set
them too deep in the water to repeat the process going downstream.
Hence the cargoes were barged down to the mouth and put aboard there.

55:18.11–12   The kings themselves of both ports of trade dwell in the interior

That is, the kings of the Chera kingdom, to which Muziris belonged, and
the Pandya kingdom, to which Nelkynda belonged. For the location of
their capitals, see under 54:17.29 and 54:18.5–6.

55:18.13   snakes

See under 38:12.27–28.

55:18.13–14   these are also black

I.e., like those found off the Gulf of Kutch (40:13.30).

56:18.16   these ports of trade

I.e., Muziris and Nelkynda. For a discussion of these ports, see Introduction: Trade in the Indian Ocean, The Trade with India.

56:18.17   pepper

Black pepper comes from the berries of a climbing plant that "has been extensively cultivated on the Western Coast of Southern India for many centuries" (Watt vi.i 261). On pepper and its uses in the Roman world, see Warmington 181–84. The *Periplus* does not specify black pepper at this point, but it certainly was the type favored in the West in later ages (cf. W. Heyd, *Histoire du commerce du Levant au Moyen-Âge* [Leipzig, 1936], ii 658–59) and unquestionably made up the bulk of Rome's shipments, although no doubt there was some white as well (cf. Warmington 181). So much of the black was sold to the West that, in Pliny's day at least, it was almost the cheapest Indian spice, costing but 4 denarii a pound, a fraction of the price of an expensive spice such as nard (see *ESAR* v 285). In addition to its use in cooking, it appears as an ingredient in medicines (Warmington 182; Raschke 1013, n. 1495; cf. Watt vi.i 263 for its use in Indian medicines).

The fruit is plucked in October or November and laid out in the sun to dry. After a few days it turns black and is ready for sale: see A. Das Gupta, *Malabar in Asian Trade* (Cambridge, 1967), 21. Thus vessels from the West were able to take on a cargo and set sail for home any time after that, the very best time for the westbound voyage (see App. 3).

Pepper was certainly in common use in the West as a condiment (cf. Warmington 182–84 and, for the Middle Ages, Heyd 664). However, the very large amounts the West imported may reflect its common use also as a preservative; see J. Needham, *Science and Civilisation in China* iv.3 520–21 (1971).

56:18.17a   malabathron

This is a variety of cinnamon leaf from trees that grow in northeastern India; see under 65:21.21–22.6. Muziris/Nelkynda served merely as transshipment points. Transport from the region of origin to the Malabar coast, like that of Gangetic nard (see under 56:18.25), no doubt was by boat from the mouth of the Ganges.

56:18.18   a great amount of money

See Introduction: Trade in the Indian Ocean, Barter and Purchase.

56:18.20   wine, in limited quantity, as much as goes to Barygaza

A passage in a Tamil poem mentions (Meile 103) "the wine, with its sweet bouquet, brought by the fine vessels of the Yavanas [Westerners]."

At Barygaza wine headed the list of imports, and there was no indication that what arrived there was limited in quantity (49:16.20–21). Meile (104–5) suggests that at Muziris/Nelkynda the amount was "in limited quantity" in comparison with other, bulkier imports such as metals.

56:18.21   orpiment

Orpiment—yellow sulphide of arsenic—is the meaning commonly assigned to the Greek *arsenikon*; see *LSJ* s.v. and Caley-Richards (op. cit. under 39:13.11) 171. It was used medicinally (Diosc. 5.104.2, Pliny 34.178), as a depilatory (Diosc. and Pliny, ibid.; the ancient Hindus used it extensively for the very same purpose [Watt v 497]), and as a pigment (Vitruvius 7.7.5). In Egypt it has been identified as a pigment on objects and in mural paintings, and a small quantity of the mineral in its natural state was found in a linen bag in the tomb of Tutankhamen; see Lucas-Harris (op. cit. under 1:1.2–4) 350. Some was also found in a Greek grave (Caley-Richards 172). It came from various parts of Asia Minor (*ESAR* iv 623). As it happens, orpiment is found in India, in the northwestern parts (Watt v 497); this may explain why none was imported at Barygaza.

56:18.21–22   grain in sufficient amount . . . because the [sc. local] merchants do not use it

The grain was for the resident foreigners as against the local merchants; see Introduction: Trade in the Indian Ocean, The Trade with India.

56:18.23   Kottanarikê

This is the same as the Cottonara that Pliny (6.105) locates near Bakarê and describes as pepper country, as the "Kottiara a metropolis" that Ptolemy (7.1.9) lists south of "Melkynda" (= Nelkynda), and as the Cotiara that the *Tabula Peutingeriana* (see under 51:17.15) places south of Muziris. The consensus is that all are versions of Kuṭṭanāḍu, a place name found in ancient Tamil literature and still in use for the area that includes the valley of the Pāmbiyār, noted for its fine pepper; both Nelkynda and Bakarê very likely stood on the Pāmbiyār (see App. 5). See Pillai (op. cit. under 51:17.15) 176; P. Thomas, "Roman Trade Centers on the Malabar Coast," *The Journal of the Madras Geographical Association* (= *Indian Geographical Journal*) 6 (1931): 230–40 at 238; A. Sreedhara Menon, *A Survey of Kerala History* (Kottayam, 1967), 60.

56:18.24   pearls

Very likely from the Gulf of Mannar; see under 59:19.22–23.

56:18.24a   ivory

The papyrus from the Vienna collection (see Introduction: Trade in the Indian Ocean, Between Alexandria and the Red Sea) mentions ivory shipped out of Muziris (Harrauer-Sijpesteijn 132, verso col. ii.4–15; the recto deals with a shipment originating in Muziris, and the verso probably concerns the same shipment [cf. Harrauer-Sijpesteijn 150]).

56:18.24b   Chinese [i.e., silk] cloth

Brought by ship from the mouth of the Ganges; cf. 64:21.13–15 and Introduction: Trade in the Indian Ocean, The Trade with India.

56:18.25   Gangetic nard

This must have been nard that originated in the mountains north of the Ganges and was brought down the river to the port at its mouth; cf. 63:21.5. No doubt it traveled from there by sea to Muziris/Nelkynda. Gangetic nard shipped out of Muziris is mentioned in the Vienna papyrus (see under 56:18.24a). The amount listed, sixty containers (Harrauer-Sijpesteijn 132, verso col. ii.1), cost 45 talents = 67,500 denarii. The prices Pliny cites for nard (see under 39:13.10b) run from 40 to 100 denarii a pound. Since prices did not advance to any great extent between Pliny's day and the date of the papyrus, the mid-2d century A.D. (cf. *ESAR* ii 434–36), this permits a conjecture about the size of the shipment: it was not inconsiderable, at least some 700 or so pounds and possibly as much as 1700, depending upon the quality.

56:18.26   all kinds of transparent gems

Schoff takes it that beryls are meant, chiefly because beryls are mined in quantity in the Coimbatore district nearby. No doubt Coimbatore beryls were sold for export to Rome; it has been suggested that this may account, at least in part, for the many hoards of Roman coins found in the Coimbatore area (Warmington 251, Wheeler 145). Warmington prefers to include among these "transparent gems" certain types of garnet (252 and cf. 250–51 on beryls).

56:18.26a   diamonds

The Greek is *adamas*, "adamant," used as the name of extremely hard metals as well as stones. Pliny (37.56) describes various types of *adamas* that originate in India, and the details he furnishes make it certain that he is talking about diamonds; see Warmington 236; Ball (op. cit. under 6:2.25–26) 242–56 (an exhaustive discussion); D. Eichholz's note to Pliny 37.56 in the Loeb edition; A. Barb in J. Bibauw, ed., *Hommages à Marcel Renard* i (Brussels, 1969), 66–82, esp. 78–79 (Barb argues that *adamas* originally meant hematite but, by Pliny's day, was used of diamonds as well as other hard stones, such as corundum). Indeed, at the time of the *Periplus*, probably all the diamonds that came to Rome were from India (Warmington 236, Ball 249). The source of diamonds nearest to Muziris/Nelkynda would be the fields around Madras (Watt iii 97–98).

56:18.26b   sapphires

According to Ball (op. cit. under 6:2.25–26, 294–95) Ceylon, where sapphires are abundant, was the principal source in ancient times. Warmington (248) suggests that those shipped from Muziris/Nelkynda may have come from areas in southern India as well. Sapphires have been found, for example, around Salem and the valley of the Kāveri (Cauvery) River in Tamil Nadu, east of Muziris/Nelkynda (Watt vi.2 474).

56:18.26–28   tortoise shell, both the kind from Chrysê Island and the kind caught around the islands lying off Limyrikê itself

Chrysê ("golden") Island was somewhere east of India; see under 63:21.1. The islands "lying off Limyrikê" can only be the Laccadive (Lakshadweep) Islands, a cluster of nineteen lying two hundred miles west of the Malabar coast. The tortoise shell involved in this passage is the fine variety from the hawksbill turtle (see under 3:1.15–16). Watt reports (vi.1 431) that "the finest tortoise shell is obtained from the Eastern Archipelago, but it is also exported from the southern coasts of the Indian continent." The first could well include the author's "Chrysê Island" variety, later (63:21.10) described as the very best to be found, and the second the variety from the islands off Limyrikê.

56:18.28–29   For those sailing . . . the month of July

See App. 3.

57:18.30–19.12   The whole coastal route . . . aforementioned bays

Cf. under B 57:18.30–19.12.

57:19.5–7   a southwesterly . . . called after the name of the one who first discovered the way across

On the monsoons and their use by Greek and Roman seamen, see Tarn 366–70; R. Böker, *RE* s.v. *Monsunschiffahrt nach Indien*, Suppl. 9 (1962); Raschke 660–63. There is no question that Arab and Indian seamen had exploited the monsoons for voyaging between their countries long before any Westerners (cf. McCrindle 135, Tarn 367). The first Westerner to use the southwest monsoon to reach India, as our author states categorically, was the ship captain Hippalos, who was honored for this feat by having the wind named after him (cf. Pliny 6.100) as well as the sea he had crossed (cf. Ptolemy 4.7.41). However, a long account in Strabo (2.98–99) of the voyages of Eudoxus of Cyzicus gives the credit to him: an Indian, sole survivor of the wreck of his vessel, was brought to Alexandria, and Eudoxus, by virtue of this man's help, led two expeditions from the Red Sea to India under the auspices of Ptolemy VIII shortly before and after 116 B.C.; the help almost certainly consisted of divulging to Eudoxus the convenient nature of the monsoon winds (see the exhaustive study by J. Thiel, *Eudoxus of Cyzicus*, Historische Studies uitgegeven van-wege het Instituut voor Geschiedenis der Rijksuniversiteit te Utrecht 23 [Groningen, 1966]). One solution is to connect Hippalos with Eudoxus, as his pilot or navigating officer or the like (Thiel 18, Raschke 661, Desanges 158–59, Dihle [op. cit. under 15:5.18] 548, L. Mooren in *Ancient Society* 3 [1972]: 133). In any event, Hippalos certainly dates from Eudoxus's time or shortly afterward (cf. Dihle 548–49) and not the time of Augustus or later, as some think (cited by Raschke 969, n. 1272). And there is no reason at all to believe with Rodinson (op. cit. under 22:7.25–26, 208–9) that Hippalos "n'est qu'une fiction, une personification [of the southwest monsoon]"; that is pure guesswork.

58:19.13–16   Red Mountain . . . Balita

On these place names, see App. 5.

58:19.18–21   Komar, where there is . . . perform ablutions

This is Cape Comorin, the southernmost tip of the peninsula. At the time of the *Periplus*, there was but a harbor there; when Ptolemy wrote much

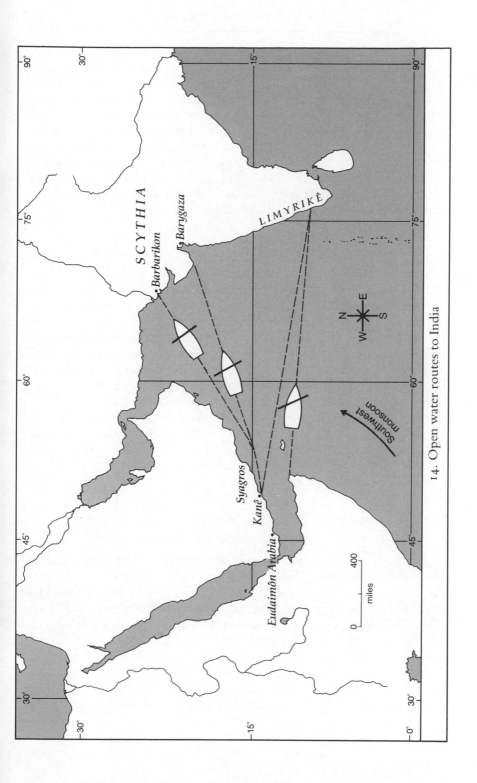

14. Open water routes to India

growth must have taken place, for he refers to it (7.1.9) as "a cape and city (*polis*)." He calls it Komaria, and the *Periplus* itself a few lines later (59:19.22) calls it Komarei, which is more accurate, for the name is derived from the Sanskrit *Kumārī*, "young girl," specifically the goddess Durga, the presiding deity of the area; see McCrindle and Hobson-Jobson s.v. *Comorin, Cape*. McCrindle remarks that "the monthly bathing in honor of the goddess Durgâ is still continued at Cape Comorin, but is not practised to the same extent as in ancient times." It has been suggested (see Iyengar [op. cit. under 50:17.2] 458) that the community of holy celibates were *sannyāsīs*, men who had forsaken the everyday world to lead an austere retired life (cf. Hobson-Jobson s.v. *Sunyasee*).

59:19.22–23   Kolchoi, where diving for pearls goes on

The name appears in Tamil literature as Korkei (= Korkai); there, as in the *Periplus*, it is referred to as a port of the Pandya kingdom (59:19.24) celebrated for its pearls; see Meile 96–97. Ptolemy (7.1.10) lists it as a port on the "Gulf of Kolchoi, where there is pearl fishing." It was situated at the mouth of the Tāmraparni River, which empties into the Gulf of Mannar, site of India's finest pearl-fishing grounds (Watt vi.1 120). As the river silted up and the coast retreated, Korkei lost its usefulness and a new settlement on the coast, Kayal, supplanted it. This was the port that Marco Polo visited and calls Cail (3.21). According to the note to the passage in Yule-Cordier, Kayal is a mile and one-half from the river's mouth and the site of Korkei two or three miles further upstream (8°39′N, 78°7′E; see the map facing p. 374). Exploratory archaeological excavation there has brought to light some fragments of "imported" ceramics; see V. Begley in *AJA* 87 (1983): 471.

59:19.25–20.1   the Strand, bordering a bay with, inland,
a region named Argaru

See under B 59:20.1. Argaru is most often identified with Uraiyur, now part of Trichinopoly (Tiruchirāppalli; 10°49′N, 78°41′E); see Schoff, Warmington 61, Iyengar (op. cit. under 50:17.2) 459. Uraiyur was the capital of the third great kingdom of southern India in ancient times, the Chola (see under 54:17.29). The Sanskritized name was Uragapuram (Pillai [op. cit. under 51:17.15] 175, n. 1; Iyengar 459). Meile (98) equates Uraiyur with Ptolemy's Orthura (7.1.91), while K. Nilakanta Sastri (*The Cōḷas* [Madras, 1955²], 22) equates it with both Argaru and Orthura, although in a subsequent publication (op. cit. under 51:17.15, 59), he opts for Argaru alone. Uraiyur was certainly in touch with the West, for frag-

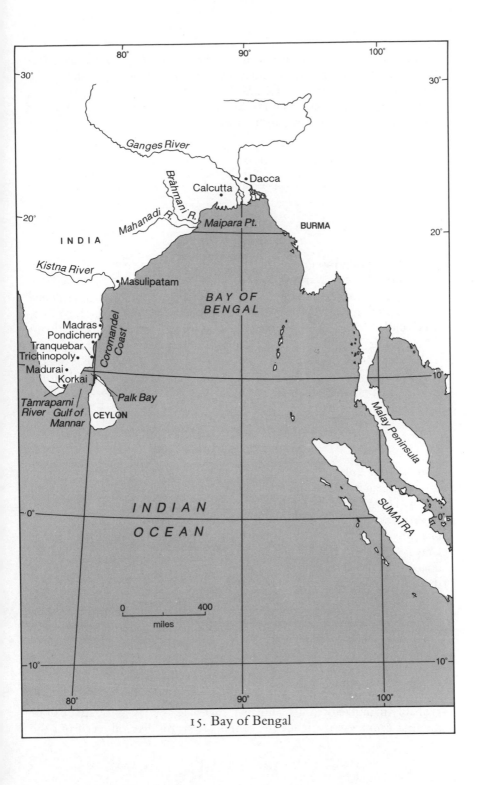

15. Bay of Bengal

ments of Roman pottery have been found there (see *Indian Archaeology: A Review* [1964–65]: 25; K. Ramachandran, *Archaeology of South India: Tamil Nadu* [Delhi, 1980], 119, 125).

If Argaru = Uraiyur, then the Strand was the shore of Palk Bay, the body of water that separates India from Ceylon.

60:20.5   from . . . the north

E.g., from the mouth of the Ganges; cf. 64:21.13–15 (silk from there shipped to Limyrikê).

60:20.6   Kamara

This place name cannot be identified unless, as many argue (Müller, McCrindle, Schoff, Warmington 61, Wheeler 123; A. Herrmann, *RE* s.v. *Kamara* [1919], reserves judgment), it is the same as the *Chabêris emporion* listed by Ptolemy (7.1.13). Chabêris is surely to be identified (cf. Müller, McCrindle, Schoff, Warmington 61, Wheeler 123) with Kāvirippaṭṭinam ("Port Kāviri"; cf. Meile 97) at the mouth of the Kāveri (Cauvery) River, a place described in Tamil literature as a flourishing port where Westerners (Yavanas) were to be seen (Meile 113). A fishing village at latitude 11°9′N, just north of Tranquebar (11°2′N, 79°51′E), still bears the name (Meile 98, n. 1).

60:20.6a   Podukê

Listed, with but a minor variation in spelling (Pôdukê), by Ptolemy (7.1.14). The identification with Pondicherry (from Tamil Puduchchēri, "New Town"; cf. Wheeler 123) has been strengthened by the discovery at Arikamedu, two miles to the south, of a site where excavation unearthed Roman remains—pottery, fragments of amphorae, glass, lamps—extensive enough to indicate the existence there of a foreigners' quarter (cf. Wheeler 145–50, esp. 147). Wheeler (148) dates the entry of the port into foreign trade about the beginning of the Christian Era and its main development about the middle of the first century A.D. However, a comprehensive new review of the pottery indicates that the port was in contact with the West as early as the second century B.C. and that its "Roman period" can be dated back to the beginning of the first century A.D.; see V. Begley, "Arikamedu Reconsidered," *AJA* 87 (1983): 461–81, esp. 470, 475, 480. Moreover, a careful restudy of the amphora fragments reveals that, of some one hundred pieces, about half are from wine jars, probably manufactured in Campania, that date as early as the first half of the first century B.C., while the others are from olive oil jars from the northern Adriatic area and garum jars from Spain, both dating to the early first century A.D. (E. L. Will in *AJA* 91 [1987]: 293 and cf. Begley in *AJA* 92 [1988]: 439, n. 55). The wine no doubt was for both the foreign colony and the local population (fragments of Roman wine jars have been found at numerous inland Indian sites), the olive oil and garum probably for the foreign colony.

Arikamedu continued as a port in contact with the West until ca. 200 A.D. (Wheeler 148, Begley 480).

60:20.6b   Sôpatma

The identification is unsure. Müller, followed by Schoff, conjectured Madras (13°5′N, 80°17′E), and Wheeler (123) Marakkānam, a little to the south of Madras (12°12′N, 79°57′E), where a harbor once existed (see C. Maloney in B. Stein, *Essays on South India*, Asian Studies at Hawaii 15 [1975], 31). Pillai (op. cit. under 51:17.15, 177) equated it with "Sōpaṭṭinam, a fortified town also known as Eyil-paṭṭinam, the sea-port of Nalliyakkōḍan," but Meile (98) rejects this on the grounds that the place name Sōpaṭṭinam is not attested in Tamil literature.

60:20.7   local boats

These must have been, like the *sangara* (see under 60:20.8), small maneuverable vessels of scant draft that could thread the shallow channels between the southern tip of India and the northern tip of Ceylon and thereby avoid the long haul around Ceylon. For examples of the native craft used for negotiating the waters of the strait, see Hornell (op. cit. under 27:9.9) 262–63.

60:20.8   others, called *sangara*, that are very big dugout canoes held together by a yoke

The Greek word translated "dugout" is *monoxylon*, on which see *SSAW* 8, n. 21. The Jain text referred to earlier (under 44:15.5) includes in its listing of middle-sized boats *saṃghāḍa*, and this is doubtless the source of the author's *sangara*. The form in Tamil is *shangāḍam*, which was borrowed by Portuguese as *jangar* or *jangada*, "raft" (Hobson-Jobson s.v. *Jangar*). *Jangar* was also specifically used of "a double platform canoe made by placing a floor of boards across two boats" (Hobson-Jobson, ibid.).

60:20.9   Chrysê

See under 63:21.1.

60:20.9–10   the very big *kolandiophônta*

See A. Christie in *BSOAS* 19 (1957): 345–53 and Needham (op. cit. under 56:18.17) 459–60. Christie (347) points out that Chinese sources mention *po* as the name of large seagoing craft, while *k'un-lun* is a Chinese term for "various littoral peoples of South East Asia" (348). Thus *kolandiophônta* are "large ocean-going ships of South-east Asia, . . . a corrupted Greek form of *Khun-lun po*" (Needham 460). Other explanations that have been offered (reviewed by Christie 346; see also K. Zvelebil in *Archiv Orientalní* 22 [1954]: 587) are less satisfactory.

60:20.10–13   There is a market . . . along this coast

By "all the trade goods imported by Limyrikê" the author means specifically goods imported from the West (see under B 60:20.10–11). Thus the distinction he is making here is between these, for which Limyrikê was just a transshipment point, and Indian goods from Limyrikê's environs and nearby coastal areas, for which it was the point of export. He is also making a distinction between the times the east coast ports received the two types of goods; indeed, this second chronological distinction is what gives the first its importance. As it happens, the arrival of what came from the West was strictly determined by the behavior of the monsoon winds: ships left the Red Sea in July and reached Barygaza or Limyrikê in September; thereafter there were no new arrivals until the following September (see App. 3). But vessels working the coastal route between Limyrikê and the east coast ports, particularly the small craft the author reports were used on this run (60:20.7–8), had no such limitation; they could leave at any time. Thus the share of money that these ports received from the merchants of Roman Egypt (sc. in exchange for purchase of east coast products) came in all year round and so did the goods originating from Limyrikê (sc. and not just at certain times like the transshipped Western goods).

61:20.15–19   there projects due west into the ocean an island now called Palaisimundu, but by its ancient [? inhabitants] Taprobanê. . . . It extends almost up to the part of Azania that lies opposite to it

Ceylon, knowledge of which first came to the Greeks as a result of Alexander's expedition (see Bunbury i 645–46), was always called by them Taprobanê (Strabo 15.691, Pliny 6.81, Ptolemy 7.4.1), although they were aware of other names including Palaisimundu. Pliny, for example, cites (6.85) Palaesimundum as the name of the island's capital and mentions (6.86) a Palaesimundus River. Ptolemy, breaking it into *palai* and *Simundu*, states (7.4.1) that the island "long ago (*palai*) was called *Simundu* but now Salikê," which Marcianus (1.8 [*GGM* i 521]) refashions to "formerly was called Palaisimundu but now Salikê." The text is defective at this point, but what can be read seems to say the reverse of what Ptolemy says, seems to indicate that the author takes Taprobanê to be the older designation.

There has long been speculation about the origin of Ceylon's various names. For some earlier conjectures, see Yule-Cordier's note to Marco Polo 3.14. Most commentators agree that Taprobanê derives from the Sanskrit Tāmbraparṇī, probably, as suggested by J. Filliozat (in the Budé edition of Pliny, vol. vi.2, pages 150–51 [1980]), by way of the Tamil form Tāmpirapanni. Simundu has been connected by some with the Sanskrit *samudra*, "ocean" (cf. F. Schwartz in *Der kleine Pauly* s.v. *Taprobane* [1975]) but Filliozat (151) offers cogent arguments against.

In stating that Ceylon was oriented east-west and that it was large enough almost to reach the coast of Africa, the author repeats common misconceptions of his time (cf. Bunbury i 645–46; ii 63–64, 422); in particular, Ceylon's size was greatly exaggerated, not only by Greek and Roman writers but by Hindu and Arab as well (cf. J. Tennent, *Ceylon* [London, 1860⁵], i 6, 9). Clearly the author had no access to firsthand information; in his day Ceylon must have been outside the routes followed by traders from the West. Though the earliest Roman coins found there date from the reign of Nero, significant quantities do not begin to turn up until the fourth century A.D. when the island finally came within the orbit of trade with the West; cf. Dihle (op. cit. under 15:5.18) 571–73, and for literature on the early contacts between Ceylon and Rome, Sidebotham 33, n. 57.

61:20.19–20   pearls, transparent gems, cotton garments, and tortoise shell

There are rich beds of pearl oysters on the Ceylon side of the Gulf of Mannar (Watt vi.i 120), and the hawksbill turtle (cf. under 3:1.15–16) is plentiful in the waters about the island (Tennent [op. cit. under 61:20.15–19] i 190; cf. Pliny 6.91, where he reports that turtle hunting was a favored local practice and tells tall tales of the size of the creatures that were caught). "Transparent gems" may be garnets (cf. under 56:18.26), and garnets are found on Ceylon (Tennent i 37, Watt ii 154). The inhabitants early learned to become efficient weavers (Tennent i 451–52), but only the *Periplus* mentions textiles among the local products; Ptolemy (7.4.1) lists rice, honey, ginger, gems, and metals, while Cosmas Indicopleustes (xi 445D–448B, Winstedt) dwells chiefly on the island's transit trade.

62:20.21   Around this area

Sc. the area of Sôpatma. The author, after his digression on the island of Taprobanê, returns to the coast.

62:20.21–22   lies the region of Masalia, extending far inland; a great many cotton garments are produced there

Just south of the "Gangetic Gulf," i.e., in the northern part of the Bay of Bengal, Ptolemy (7.1.15) locates a region called Masôlia which reached inland far enough to encompass five towns including a metropolis (7.1.93). The consensus is that this is the same as the *Periplus's* Masalia and that the modern Masulipatam (16°10′N, 81°8′E) reflects the ancient name; so Müller, McCrindle, Fabricius, Schoff, Hobson-Jobson s.v. *Masulipatam*, Warmington 63, A. Herrmann in *RE* s.v. *Maisolia* (1928). The seventeenth-century traveler Jean Baptiste Tavernier considered Masulipatam the finest port on the Bay of Bengal and noted that it was the point of departure for major ports to the east and west (*Les six voyages*, 2d pt. bk. 1, chap. xi). Marco Polo (3.19) mentions the "most delicate buckrams" (i.e., fine cottons; see Yule-Cordier's note) that were produced in the region. Masulipatam is still "famous for the manufacture of excellent cotton stuffs" (Watt iv 44).

62:20.22–23   go due east from it across the bay that lies alongside

Presumably across the mouth of the small bay on which Masulipatam is located, i.e., heading towards Narasapur Point (16°18′N, 81°42′E). The course would actually be somewhat north of east.

62:20.23–24   the Dêsarênê region

Ptolemy lists (7.1.40) a Dôsarôn River that he conceives of (7.1.17) as flowing eastward to empty into the "Gangetic Gulf" (cf. under 62:20.21–22). It is generally agreed that the region this river passed through is the same as the *Periplus's* Dêsarênê and that it corresponds to what is today Orissa; see Müller, Fabricius (who actually altered the text to read *Dôsarênê*), Schoff (who introduced Fabricius's fabrication into his translation), Warmington 63 (who followed Schoff), W. Tomaschek in *RE* s.v. *Dosara*

(1905), R. Heine-Geldern in H. Mžik, ed., *Beiträge zur historischen Geographie, Kulturgeographie, Ethnographie und Kartographie, vornehmlich des Orients* (Leipzig, 1929), 158–59. The equating of the Dêsarênê region with Orissa is plausible. However, confusion has been caused by a name Daśārṇa which appears in Sanskrit writings as the name of both a river and a people. McCrindle (*Ancient India as described by Ptolemy* [Calcutta, 1885], 71) equated this with Ptolemy's Dôsarôn and Schoff with his own so-called "Dosarene." Schoff went further: to suit the geographical requirements, he stated (253) that "the Sanscrit *Dasarna*" was "the modern Orissa." It was nothing of the sort: it lay far to the west of Orissa, encompassing Chanderi (24°43′N, 78°8′E), part of the Betwa River, the central part of the valley of the Narmada (cf. Tomaschek; Eggermont [op. cit. under 48:16.16–18] 268; Heine-Geldern 159–61; D. Sircar, *Studies in the Geography of Ancient and Medieval India* [Delhi, 1960], 49, n. 3). If Ptolemy's Dôsarôn River is to be connected with the Daśārṇa River—and phonetically this is perfectly possible (cf. Shafer [op. cit. under 41:14.4] 114)—he blundered in thinking it flowed eastward into the Bay of Bengal (cf. McCrindle, *Ancient India* 80, Eggermont 265). More likely, as was early suggested (see R. Mitra, *The Antiquities of Orissa* i [Calcutta, 1875], 6; Tomaschek), his Dôsarôn has nothing to do with the Sanskrit Daśārṇa but refers to some river in Orissa (the Brāhmani according to Mitra, the Mahānadī according to others) whose ancient name has disappeared without trace (cf. Tomaschek).

62:20.24 Bôsarê

If Dêsarênê was in or about Orissa (see under 62:20.23–24), the type of elephant referred to here might possibly be, as has been suggested (Hobson-Jobson s.v. *Kling*), that described by the seventh-century Buddhist pilgrim Hsüan-tsang: "the kingdom of Kielingkia [i.e., Kalinga, roughly the coast between the mouths of the Kistna and Mahānadī rivers; see Hobson-Jobson 488] . . . produces wild elephants of a black colour, which are much valued in the neighbouring realms." The area appears in Indian literature as a source of superior elephants; see T. Trautmann, "Elephants and the Mauryas," in S. Mukherjee, ed., *India: History and Thought, Essays in Honour of A. L. Basham* (Subarnarekha, 1982), 254–81 at 273–74.

62:20.25 numerous barbaric peoples

As the rest of the sentence reveals, this section describes the hinterland rather than the coast.

62:20.26   Kirradai

These are the people Pliny (7.25) calls *Scyrites* and Aelian (*NA* 16.22) *Skiratai*. Ptolemy does not mention them (unless the *Tiladai* of 7.2.15 refers to them; cf. S. Lévi in *École Française d'Extrême-Orient: Études asiatiques publiées à l'occasion du vingt-cinquième anniversaire* ii [Paris, 1925], 24–25, Heine-Geldern [op. cit. under 62:20.23–24] 166). However, he does mention (7.2.16) the region they inhabited, Kirradia. It has long been recognized (cf. McCrindle, Schoff, O. Wecker in *RE* s.v. Σκιρᾶται [1929]) that these names are to be connected with the Kirātas, a people well attested in Indian literature (see Heine-Geldern 166–67, Shafer [op. cit. under 41:14.4] 124–25). There, as in the *Periplus*, they are characterized as barbaric in their ways and Mongoloid in appearance (Shafer 124). From the widespread area in which the literary sources place the Kirātas Heine-Geldern (167) concludes that the name was a general designation for all the Mongoloid peoples of the north and east. Shafer (124), on the basis of the nomenclature of their kings, concludes that they spoke a Tibeto-Burmic language and were the predecessors of the Kirantis now living in the easternmost province of Nepal. In his map 1 ("Ethnographic-Linguistic") he places a western branch of the Kirātas just northwest of Katmandu and an eastern branch just southeast of it.

62:20.26a   Bargysoi

These are to be identified with the Bhargas mentioned in the Vishnu Purana; see J. Taylor in *Journal of the Royal Asiatic Society of Bengal* 16 (1847): 12. According to Shafer (op. cit. under 41:14.4, 141), the Bhargas were Manavas, a people of Iranian origin, specifically part of an eastern branch that had fled east and was linked with Tibet in traditional stories (Shafer 17, 44). In his map 1 he places them south of the eastern branch of the Kirātas (see under 62:20.26), on the north side of the Ganges somewhat east of Patna.

62:20.27–28   Horse Faces, who are said to be cannibals

Reports of "horse-faced" peoples are found in Indian literature as well; see Taylor (op. cit. under 62:20.26a) 12. Tales of Indian cannibalism had reached the West early: Herodotus (3.99) had heard of its being practiced by peoples in eastern India, and Megasthenes (cited by Strabo 15.710) by Indian mountain tribes. And, in the folklore of the Santals living in the inner parts of Orissa, there figures a race of horse-faced or horse-nosed people who mint their own silver coins to buy humans to eat (see Heine-Geldern [op. cit. under 62:20.23–24] 171).

63:20.29–30   heading east with the ocean on the right,
and sailing outside past the remaining parts to the left,
you reach the Gangês

Apparently, at Maipara Point off the mouth of the Brāhmani (20°43′N, 87°2′E), the course did not follow the curve of the bay but went over open water straight to the Ganges Delta, a run of a day and one-half, either more or less depending upon what point along the coast of the delta was the destination. The course was not actually east but, again depending upon the destination, either somewhat to the north or the south of north-east.

63:20.30–21.4   Gangês

In these lines the author uses the name in three different ways: for a region, for the river, and for a port on the river.

63:21.1   Chrysê

For mention of Chrysê, "the golden [sc. region]" in Greek and Roman writings, see G. Coedès, *Textes d'auteurs grecs et latins relatifs à l'Extrême-Orient* (Paris, 1910) index s.v. Chrysê. Pomponius Mela (3.70 = Coedès 12) and Pliny 6.54, 80 = Coedès 14–15) talk in vague terms of Chrysê and a companion island Argyrê, "the silver," as places that were far off to the east (cf. Coedès xv). To the author of the *Periplus*, however, Chrysê was no vague land but an established trading area that happened to lie as far east as current geographical knowledge extended; on land there was a Chrysê region that marked the eastern edge of the continent, and in the sea there was a Chrysê Island (63:21.8–10) that marked the eastern edge of the inhabited world. By Ptolemy's time geographical knowledge had expanded: he knows of a Chrysê region (7.2.17 = Coedès 57), Chrysê Peninsula (7.1.15; 7.2.5, 12, 25 = Coedès 51, 53, 56, 60), and lands beyond both (cf. Coedès xxiii). The same distinction between a "golden region" and a "golden island" appears in Indian writings; cf. R. Majumdar, *Ancient Indian Colonies in the Far East*. ii, *Suvarnadvipa*. 1, *Political History*, Punjab Oriental Series, No. 16, P. 2 (Dacca, 1937), 37: "Suvarṇabhūni (gold-land) and Suvarṇadvīpa (gold-island), as names of oversea countries, were familiar to the Indians from a very early period." It is generally agreed that the region refers to Burma and the peninsula to Malay or Sumatra: cf. Coedès 172 (references to older literature); Bunbury ii 475, 605–6; Majumdar 46–47, 49–50 (where he suggests that Chrysê Island may be Sumatra, Argyrê being Java); Thomson (op. cit. under 15:5.17–16:6.13) 314–15; P. Wheatley, *The Golden Khersonese* (Kuala

Lumpur, 1961), 144–59, a detailed argument for equating Chrysê Peninsula with Malay; W. van der Meulen, "Suvarṇadvîpa and the Chrysê Chersonêsos," *Indonesia* 18 (October 1974): 1–40, who argues that most of the places and features ascribed by Ptolemy to the Chrysê Peninsula are to be found in Sumatra; and Filliozat (op. cit. under 61:20.15–19, note to 6.69 and app. 146–48), who also argues for identifying the peninsula with Sumatra.

63:21.3   a rise and fall

A number of Greek and Roman writers note this phenomenon; cf. E. Kiessling in *RE* s.v. *Ganges* 706 (1910).

63:21.4   a port of trade with the same name as the river, Gangês

Ptolemy (7.1.81) gives the name as Gangê, notes that it is a royal seat, and places it in the Ganges Delta. It has been suggested that this Gangê(s) was on the site later occupied by Tāmralipti (modern Tamluk), on the Hooghly River some thirty miles southwest of Calcutta, a town that appears in Indian epics and inscriptions, as well as in the accounts of Chinese Buddhist pilgrims, as an important trading center and point of departure for voyages to the east; see Schoff, Warmington 63, Iyengar (op. cit. under 50.17.2) 459, P. Chakravarti in R. Majumdar, ed., *History of Bengal* i (Dacca, 1943), 661. Excavation at Tamluk has brought to light a group of pots of Egyptian provenance, no doubt of the Greco-Roman period; see J. Vogel, *BSOAS* 14 (1952): 82. There are some, however, who link Tāmralipti not with Ptolemy's Gangê but with his Tamalitês (7.1.73); see O. Wecker in *RE* s.v. *India* 1285 (1916); F. Monahan, *The Early History of Bengal* (Oxford, 1925), 14; H. Raychaudhuri in Majumdar 29–30; Vogel 82; B. Law, *Historical Geography of Ancient India* (Paris, 1954), 263. But Tamalitês, judging from Ptolemy's coordinates, lay too far inland to serve as a port (cf. Raychaudhuri 14, who suggests that Ptolemy was misinformed about the location, and Vogel 82, who disregards the coordinates).

63:21.5   Gangetic nard

A "Gangetic nard" is included by Dioscorides (1.7.2) in his discussion of the various nards: "One kind of Indian nard is called Gangetic from a river, the Ganges, that flows by the mountain where it grows [i.e., the Himalayas, source of the other nards; see under 48:16.16–18]. It is weaker in its properties because it is found in damp places; it is longer, with numerous spikes from the same root bearing clusters and interlaced; and it has a rank odor." Pliny (12.42) adds the information that the Gangetic nard is "totally condemned and given the name 'the foul-smelling' [*ozaenitis*, from the Greek noun *ozaina*, 'a foul polyp in the nose']; the odor is fetid." Warmington thinks (196) that what is here described is not true nard but one of the oil-yielding grasses that the Greeks and Romans loosely called nards, the lemon grasses or ginger grasses. Yet Dioscorides (1.17–18) and Pliny (12.104–6) deal with these under separate headings— and with no mention of any variety that has a disagreeable smell. Miller is unaware that he contradicts himself when he classifies (90) Pliny's *ozaenitis* as "probably ginger-grass" and then, in his discussion of ginger grass (94–96), repeatedly notes its fragrance and cites Pliny (96) to the effect that the worst variety was odorless.

A "Gangetic nard" that was valuable enough to be one of India's exports, indeed to be lumped together with pearls and the finest muslins, must be different from the rank product to which Dioscorides and Pliny apply the name. It must be a form of true nard that could well have been called Gangetic by traders because all they knew about it was where it was shipped from, and that was the Ganges area (cf. Warmington 195). In the Middle Ages products were commonly referred to by place of purchase rather than of origin (Heyd [op. cit. under 56:18.17] ii 613).

63:21.5a   pearls

Cf. Taylor (op. cit. under 62:20.26a) 23–24: "The pearls that passed through the Gangetic mart appear to have been obtained from the rivers of the eastern part of Bengal. . . . They are found in a species of muscle in the rivers and marshes of the Dacca, Tipperah, and Mymensing districts. . . . The pearls found in the present day are small, of a reddish colour, and generally of little worth." Dacca (23°43′N, 90°25′E) is northeast of Calcutta; the Mymensingh district is just north of Dacca and the Tippera district southeast of it. The pearls were probably for local markets; buyers from Roman Egypt could find far better quality elsewhere (see under 59:19.22–23).

63:21.5–6   cotton garments of the very finest quality, the so-called Gangetic

Cf. R. Majumdar, *History of Mediaeval Bengal* (Calcutta, 1973), 177: "Bengal muslin was prized all over the world. . . . The principal centre of the manufacture of the most delicate muslin was Dacca [see under 63:21.5a], from where large quantities of the stuff were exported. . . .

Muslin of the best quality was so fine indeed that 20 yards of it could be put into a snuff box."

63:21.6–7   It is said that there are also gold mines in the area

Gold has been found in the Chota Nāgpur region west of Calcutta, especially in the area between 22° and 24° north, 83° and 88° east; see Watt iii 524–25. However, it is not mined but panned from the various rivers and streams. The author remarks on the presence of gold by way of explaining the use in this region of gold coin; see under 63:21.7.

63:21.7   *kaltis*

The earliest gold coins so far found in India, whose attribution is certain, were issued by Vima Kadphises, a king of the Kushans (see under 47:16.5–6) who probably ruled in the middle or end of the first half of the second century A.D. (cf. Bivar [op. cit. under 38:12.23] 200–3). The mention here of the *kaltis* indicates that he was not the first to mint gold (cf. Raschke 671). It also indicates that at this time native gold coins were still rare enough to be singled out for comment.

63:21.10   the finest tortoise shell

The tortoise shell ended up at Muziris and Nelkynda (see 56:18.26–27), almost certainly by way of the port of Gangês which shipped numerous products to those cities (cf. under 56:18.17a and 56:18.25).

64:21.13   Thina

This is the earliest occurrence of the name. Ptolemy speaks at one point (7.3.6) of "Sinai or Thinai, the metropolis," but elsewhere reserves Sinai for the name of the country (e.g., 7.3.1). Both forms apparently derive, by way of Sanskrit, from Ch'in, the name of the great dynasty (221–206 B.C.) that unified China; see J. Needham, *Science and Civilisation in China* i (Cambridge, 1954), 168–69.

64:21.13–14   silk floss, yarn, and cloth

Similarly, Chinese records of the gifts various emperors made to the Huns list three types of silk—floss, yarn, and cloth; see, e.g., B. Watson, *Records of the Grand Historian of China Translated from the Shih chi of Ssu-ma*

Ch'ien (New York, 1961), ii 174: reference (162 B.C.) to an annual gift that would include "silk cloth, thread, floss." The Greek term rendered "floss" means literally "wool." It unquestionably corresponds to what the translators of the Chinese render "floss," and "floss" better describes what is referred to, namely the tangled mass of miscellaneous lengths of fiber that is today called silk waste. After the filaments of proper quality have been drawn from the cocoons, there are left those that are not up to that quality—the threads from the extreme outside and inside of cocoons or from cocoons pierced as a result of the moths' emergence, uneven threads, threads broken in the reeling process, and so on. Some of this can be reclaimed by being hand combed and then spun the way other kinds of fibers are spun, by means of a distaff and wheel. To judge from the figures appearing in the Chinese records, "silk floss" was no unimportant aspect of silk production. Between 51 and 1 B.C., for example, various emperors made gifts totalling no less than 43,000 pounds. In one particular year the amount given was 16,125 pounds. See H. Bielenstein in *Bulletin of the Museum of Far Eastern Antiquities, Stockholm* 39.2 (1967): 91–92.

64:21.13–15   silk floss . . . via Bactria . . . and via the Ganges

See Introduction: Trade in the Indian Ocean, The Trade with India.

64:21.15   back to Limyrikê

The silk products shipped via Bactria to Barygaza, traveling overland, went first westward from the point of departure in China and then southward to Barygaza. Those shipped via the Ganges to Limyrikê first went eastward downriver to the port at the mouth; from there, traveling by ship, they had to go back westward around the tip of the peninsula to get to Limyrikê.

64:21.17–20   The area lies . . . into the ocean

The passage reflects the way contemporary geographers conceived of the configuration of the northeastern corner of Asia; see, e.g., Map 16a. In this view Asia was bounded by the ocean on the north as well as the east: the ocean swung around to wash both shores. The author locates Thina in the northernmost part, the part "right under Ursa Minor" (64:21.17). He then repeats a rumor (64:21.18: "it is said") to the effect that China's western border was contiguous with the coast of the Caspian and the

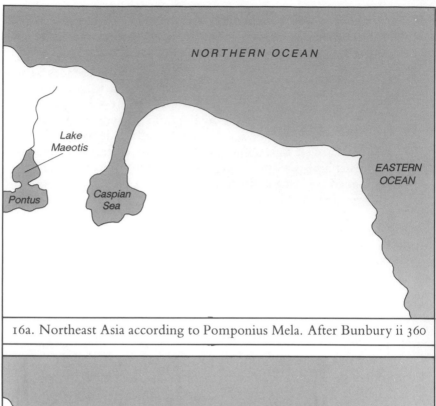

16a. Northeast Asia according to Pomponius Mela. After Bunbury ii 360

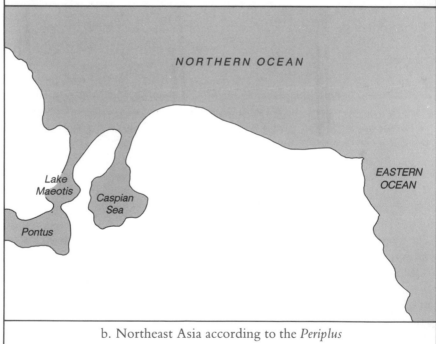

b. Northeast Asia according to the *Periplus*

Pontus (Black Sea) where "these parts turn off [sc. from the east-west direction of the northern shore of the continent] near where Lake Maeotis [Sea of Azov], which lies parallel [sc. to the Caspian Sea], along with [it] empties into the ocean." The geographers conceived of the Caspian as a gulf with a long narrow neck to the northern ocean (Bunbury ii 363; Thomson [op. cit. under 15:5.17–16:6.13] 293–94), and this is the view that the author follows. However, as Giangrande (op. cit. under 18:6.23– 24, 47–49) has shown, he conceives of the Pontus, with Lake Maeotis forming a sort of northern extension to it, as lying immediately parallel to the Caspian and, like it, stretching northward to empty into the ocean (Map 16b). In this he parts company with the geographers, who conceived of Lake Maeotis as being closed off on the north by the lands through which the Tanais (Don) River flowed.

65:21.21–22.6   Every year there turns up . . . who make them

The chapter describes the source of supply of malabathron. This is the leaf of certain cinnamon trees, notably the *Cinnamomum tamala* Nees and *Cinnamomum obtusifolium* Nees, both of which grow in the Himalayas all across the northern border of India but most commonly in the eastern portion (Hobson-Jobson s.v. *Malabathrum*, Watt ii 319–20; on the argument, based on doubtful evidence, that malabathron is patchouli, see Casson 1984.245–46, n. 57). The name is a Hellenization of the Sanskrit word for the leaf, *tāmalapattra*, the *ta* being mistaken for the Greek definite article (cf. A. Steier in *RE* s.v. *Malabathron* 818 [1928], Casson 1984.238).

Neither Dioscorides nor Pliny, nor even the author of the *Periplus*, was aware of the connection between malabathron and cinnamon or cassia, that one was the leaf and the other the bark of similar trees. They no doubt failed to make the connection because the two products were offered for sale in such widely separated places, malabathron at the mouth of the Ganges or on the Malabar coast (63:21.4–5, 56:18.25), cinnamon and cassia in Arabian and African ports (see under 8:3.30–13:5.4; Casson 1984.233–35).

Malabathron, it would seem, came to the Western world rather late; the earliest mention dates from the time of Augustus (Steier 819), and it does not appear in the Greek papyri from Egypt until the second century A.D. (*SB* 9826), while most occurrences are even later (*BGU* 93 [2d–3d century]; *BGU* 953 [3d–4th century]; *P. Ant.* 32, *P. Oxy.* 2570, *PSI* 1264, *O. Tait 2153, SB* 9834b [4th century]; *P. Genova* 1 [5th–6th century]). The ancients used it for a multitude of purposes: in medicines, unguents, cooking, as a breath sweetener, to repel moths from clothing (Steier 819).

Under the name *folium Indicum* or Indian leaf, it remained in the pharmacopoeia up to modern times (Hobson-Jobson s.v. *Malabathrum*, Watt ii 321–22), and in India was used as a spice until at least the last century (Watt ii 320, 322).

Dioscorides (1.12) was aware that malabathron came from India but thought it grew in swamps like duckweed (cf. Berendes [op. cit. under 8:3.31a] 34, n. 1). Pliny (12.129) repeats the statement about its growing in swamps but adds that malabathron came from Syria and Egypt as well as India. Perhaps, as Warmington (189) suggests, it was processed in those two lands before being exported to Rome, and Pliny assumed that it also grew there. He gives 60 denarii a pound for the price of malabathron oil, which makes it a fairly expensive item (cf. the list of prices in *ESAR* v 285; the prices cited there and in Warmington 189 and 228 for the oil and the leaves have been transposed; this is based on a willful emendation in Pliny 12.129 that modern editors reject). The variation in price of the leaves was "prodigious," to use his figure of speech; it ran the gamut from 1 denarius a pound to 300. The figure of 300, which must be for the unadulterated finest grade, makes malabathron India's costliest plant product, three times the price of the best-quality nard (cf. under 39:13.10b). The grades that sold at the lowermost range were very likely massively adulterated with the cheapest possible ingredients.

The locale that the author's vague indications point to, the border region between India and China, falls within the area where the trees bearing malabathron are found. Schoff (279), who is followed by Warmington (188–89), boldly identifies it with great precision, but Coedès (op. cit. under 63:21.1, xviii) is properly cautious: "dans les pays montagneux qui bordent la Chine au sud-ouest, quelque part entre l'Assam et le Se-tchouen." Ptolemy (7.2.16) remarks that the best malabathron grows in Kirradia; this could well be the same area (cf. under 62:20.26).

Several key elements in the account of the curious way in which the transfer of the leaves took place are conjectural because of uncertainties in the text (cf. under B 65:21.22–23, B 65:21.24–25). "They hold a festival," for example, is the translation not of a word in the manuscript but of a substitution—albeit a plausible one—for what stands there. And the name of the people who picked up the leaves left behind by the departing Sêsatai is missing; that it was the local inhabitants is simply an inference.

65:21.23   Sêsatai

Ptolemy (7.2.15) calls them Saêsadai and describes them more fully: they are not only short and flat-faced, as in the *Periplus*, but shaggy and white-skinned. Some of the manuscripts of Ptolemy read Bêsadai; see P. Eggermont in *Acta Orientalia* 19 (1943): 284, n. 1. Eggermont prefers this reading and offers (284–88) an interesting argument in its favor. The Greek merchants and sailors who traveled to India came from Roman Egypt. There one of their favorite deities was Bes, a god with the very characteristics listed above: he was dwarfish in stature, flat-faced, and shaggy. "Besadai," Eggermont argues, was not an attempt by these Egyptian Greeks to reproduce a native name but a nickname coined by them, "sons of Bes."

The characteristics themselves indicate that the Sêsatai were a people similar to the Kirradai (see under 62:20.26), and their access to the border with China indicates that they lived, as Coedès suggests (cf. under 65:21.21–22.6), "dans les pays montagneux qui bordent la Chine au sud-ouest, quelque part entre l'Assam et le Se-tchouen."

65:22.1–2   lightly doubling over the leaves and rolling them into ball-like shapes, they string them on the fibers

Dioscorides (1.12) explains that the stringing was done to dry the leaves; according to him, a linen cord was used. He makes no mention of doubling and rolling; this obviously had to be done with the fresh leaves, while they were still malleable.

66:22.7–8   extremes of storm, bitter cold, and difficult terrain

Presumably the forbidding regions of the Himalayas and beyond.

COMMENTARY B

(TEXTUAL, LEXICOGRAPHICAL,

GRAMMATICAL)

1:1.3 ἐν δεξιᾷ

On the use of ἐν for εἰς, see Frisk 76.

2:1.6–7 ἡ βαρβαρικὴ χώρα

Cf. Desanges 357, n. 301, where he takes Pliny's *baccar . . . barbaricam* (21.29) not as "exotic" aut sim. but in a geographical sense, sc. "native to the land of the Barbaroi." Similarly Galen (14.64) talks of cinnamon shipped ἐκ τῆς βαρβάρου, which in the context should be translated "from the land of the Barbaroi" (not "barbarian" as rendered in Casson 1984.232).

2:1.7 μάνδραις, "mean huts"

The word means basically "pen," "stable" (cf. Pollux 7.151, *Gloss.*), i.e., housing for animals. This was extended to housing, presumably of similar lowly quality, for humans; cf. *P. Oxy.* 984 (1st century A.D.), *P. Lond.* 1694.23 (6th century A.D.).

2:1.9 Μοσχοφάγων

Eaters of *moschoi*, "tender shoots," "tender stalks," rather than of "calves," as *LSJ* s.v. takes it; see Müller's note.

2:1.9–10   τυραννίδα, "chiefdom"

Frisk (96) states that *tyrannos* in the *Periplus* means "gouverneur subordonné." The term is wider than that, meaning "local ruler." He may be an independent chief ruling over a single port of trade (14:5.15) or as here, presumably, ruling over a tribe or group of tribes (cf. 16:6.7–8, where the landholders of Rhapta are said to be "like *tyrannoi*"). Or he may be, as in Frisk's definition, a governor ruling a province as subordinate of the head of the realm to which it belongs. In most instances of this use in the *Periplus*, the *tyrannos* involved happens to be the governor of Ma ʿafir in southwestern Arabia (16:6.9, 22:7.25, 24:8.7, 25:8.19 [*tyrannis*], 31:10.19–20); he resided at Sauê (22:7.25–26) and was the appointee of the "king of the Homerites [Himyarites] and Sabaeans" resident at Safar (23; cf. 20:7.10, a reference to the "governors and kings of Arabia"). Cf. W. Dittenberger, *Orientis Graeci Inscriptiones Selectae* (Leipzig, 1903–5), 654.7, where the *tyrannos* was a subordinate appointed by Cornelius Gallus, prefect of Egypt in 30 B.C.

3:1.13   τὸ πέρας τῆς ἀνακομιδῆς

These words, grammatically unsound, are probably an intrusive gloss (cf. Frisk 104) to supply the starting point of the distance of 4000 stades. For ἀνακομιδή here must mean "return" (cf. Schmid [op. cit. under 34:11.23–24] 790), and the "end of the return" would be Berenicê.

4:2.2   ἐξώτατον

The manuscript reads ἐσώτατον; for the emendation, see Casson 1980.495.

6:2.23   προχωρεῖ

The term is businessman's jargon meaning "find a market," "there is a market for"; we use "go" in much the same sense. Thus, in *P. Amh.* 133.18 (2d century A.D.), οὐ προχωρεῖ ὁ πυρός, εἰ μὴ ἐκ δραχμῶν ἑπτά means "there is no market for wheat (wheat won't go) except at seven drachmas"; cf. *SB* 9025.12–13 (2d century A.D.): δύναται προχωρῆσαι τοῦ στατῆρος μέτρου ἑνὸς ἡμίσους "[grain] can go for one stater per one and one-half *metra*." In a few passages the author introduces the imports of a place with εἰσφέρεται (17:6.14) or εἰσάγεται (28:9.13), the antonym of his words for "export" (ἐκφέρεται [8:3.29, 9:4.3, 17:6.18] or simply φέρεται [6:3.4, 7:3.18, 49:16.28, 56:18.22]; ἐξάγεται [10:4.9, 24:8.9,

28:9.18]). However, he prefers προχωρεῖ; see 6:2.30, 7:3.16, 8:3.26, 9:4.3, 10:4.8, 12:4.26, 13:5.3, 24:8.1, 39:13.7, 49:16.20, 56:18.17, 60:20.10.

6:2.23a ἱμάτια . . . ἄγναφα

For ἱμάτια, "articles of clothing," see *Ed. Diocl.* 7.48, 51 where the Latin for ἱμάτιον is *vestis*; *Stud. Pal.* 20.15.18 (A.D. 190) or *P. Oxy.* 1273.12 = *Sel. Pap.* 5 (A.D. 260) where, in the detailing of a dowry, the rubric ἱμάτια introduces a list of the bride's various garments. For ἄγναφος, literally "unfulled," used in the sense of "new," see Matt. 9.16 (also Mark 2.21, Luke 5.36): "No man putteth a piece of new (ἀγνάφου) cloth unto an old garment"; cf. *Gloss.* ii 175.30, 47 and iii 369.45, where the Latin for ἄγναφος is *rudis*, and *Ed. Diocl.* 7.58, 60, 62 and 22.1a, 2, 4–10, where the Greek for *rudis* is καινός. Clothing that is ἄγναφος is frequently mentioned in the Greek papyri from Egypt: see Preisigke, *WB* s.v. and *P. Merton* 2.71.10–11, 14–15 (A.D. 160–63); *P. Oxy.* 3060.5 (2d century A.D.); *SB* 9834b.5, 10–12, 14, 15 (4th century A.D.). A garment that had been to the fuller once, i.e., was almost new, was πρωτόγναφος; cf. *P. Micha.* 18 A, col. ii 3 and note (3d century A.D.).

6:2.24–25 ἀβόλλαι νόθοι χρωμάτινοι

The term νόθος occurs four times in the *Periplus* (here and in 28:9.15, 39:13.7, 49:16.22), always in connection with clothing and always mentioned along with garments described as ἁπλοῦς, "unadorned," i.e., lacking embroidery, appliqué, fringe, or the like (see under B 6:2.34–35). By an easy transfer from its literal sense of "bastard," "illegitimate," it came to mean "supposititious," "counterfeit." All commentators and translators have assumed that this is the sense in the *Periplus*, that it refers to garments inferior in quality or "made in imitation of a better quality" (Huntingford 60). It follows from the implied contrast with ἁπλοῦς that the inferior quality, or the imitating of a better quality, must have something to do with adornment. There is a type of garment that answers perfectly to this description, the garment made of printed cloth, i.e., cloth adorned with designs dyed into it rather than woven into it. In the Middle Ages and later, printed fabrics that were copies of costly textiles with embroidered decoration were sold as inexpensive substitutes. The word νόθος is most likely trade jargon, the term used by merchants for a print, a "counterfeit" of the higher quality made with woven decoration. The printing of fabrics was known at least as early as the first century A.D. (Pliny 35.150; cf. H. Blümner, *Technologie und Terminologie der Ge-*

werbe und Künste bei Griechen und Römern i [Leipzig and Berlin, 1912²], 229–30). For a full discussion, see Casson 1983.199–202.

6:2.25   διϰρόσσια

The word occurs only here. Cf. ϰρόσσοι, "tassels" (Pollux 7.64; Hesychius) and δίϰροσσος, "double-fringed" (Pollux 7.72).

6:2.26   ἄλλης

For the translation "also," see R. Kühner and B. Gerth, *Ausführliche Grammatik der griechischen Sprache* ii.1 (Hanover, 1898), 275, n. 1b.

6:2.27   μελίεφθα χαλϰᾶ

What copper object can be used for both "cooking" and "cutting up" into adornments? Frisk (92) cautiously went no further than "sorte d'objet de métal, sens obscur." Müller suggested soft copper discs resembling honey cakes in shape, Fabricius honey-colored copper bars for "smelting" or "cutting up." *LSJ* offers "honey jar" and cites μελ⟨ι⟩έφθιον from *P. Lond.* 964.24 (3d century A.D.) as the diminutive, a term which Preisigke, *WB* prefers to translate "in Honig gekochte Speise." That the word has something to do with the cooking or heating of honey is indicated by *SB* 11003 (4th–5th century A.D.), a list of artisans, some quite specialized, and alongside calf slaughterers, weavers, shoemakers, etc., appear μελιεψοί, "heaters of honey." Could a μελίεφθον be a shallow panlike receptacle which those who wanted could use for its proper purpose but whose shape enabled it to be easily cut up?

6:2.34–35   ἀβόλλαι ϰαὶ γαυνάϰαι ἁπλοῖ

The term ἁπλοῦς, "single," like διπλοῦς, "double," when used of outer garments, normally refers to size, the "double" being an ample type that could be folded over to double the thickness of cloth and thereby provide more warmth. In the *Periplus*, however, ἁπλοῦς is used not only of outerwear, as here, but also of ordinary clothing, e.g., a sleeved garment (24:8.2), where the word manifestly cannot have such a meaning. From its basic sense of "single" ἁπλοῦς acquired the derived sense of "simple," "uncompounded," i.e., composed of a single rather than a variety of elements. This I take to be the meaning here: it is a trade term for a "simple" garment, i.e., one that is "unadorned"—not with reference to color but to patterns or figures in the weave, embroidery, appliqué, and the like, elements that are commonly added to, compounded with, as it were, the simple fabric of a garment. This is confirmed by an illuminating use in a papyrus document (*BGU* 1564, A.D. 138), an order to a group of weavers to produce a blanket whose size is carefully spelled out (6 by 4 cubits) and which is to be a λώδικος λευκῆς ἁπλῆς a "plain white blanket," as N. Lewis renders it (*Life in Egypt under Roman Rule* [Oxford, 1983], 175). See Casson 1983.194–99 for a full discussion.

6:3.1   στόμωμα

This is the technical term for "steel" in both Greek and Latin; see H. Blümner, *RE* s.v. *Eisen* 2147 (1905). In *P. Cairo Zen.* 782a (3d century B.C.) it appears throughout as the material from which cutting edges were fashioned, which could then be welded to blades of ordinary iron. Sickles, mattocks, axes, etc., were made in this way; see the editor's note to line 6.

6:3.2   ἡ λεγομένη μοναχὴ καὶ σαγματογῆναι

Almost the same words recur in 14:5.11–12. Some commentators took μοναχή to mean "of first quality" (Vincent, cited in Müller's note; Warmington 211), but the word is found nowhere else with that meaning, and, as noted below, the quality here is just the reverse. Perhaps *monachê* cloth was so called because it was broader than the normal width and hence a single piece of it sufficed for making the ordinary articles of clothing. Garments characterized as μοναχός are attested in the Greek papyri from Egypt: *P. Hamb.* 10.26–27 (2d century A.D.): ἱμάτιον μοναχόν, *P. Oxy.* 1273.13–14 = *Sel. Pap.* 5 (A.D. 260): χιτώνιον μοναχόν. Preisigke, *WB* s.v. took the word in these passages to mean "unlined," but this would imply that the garments involved were regularly made with lining, and there is no evidence for that. Here too the meaning could well be that they were made out of a single piece of cloth rather than two or more stitched together.

The word σαγματογήνη occurs only here and in 14:5.12. Many commentators connect it with σάττω, "to stuff," and take it to refer to an inferior grade of cotton for stuffing pillows, cushions, and the like (Müller, McCrindle, Warmington 211). But the context both here and in 14:5.11–12 makes clear that it refers not to raw cotton but, like the *monachê* it is coupled with, to a type of cotton cloth. And, as the other passage makes equally clear, both are types of cloth of run-of-the-mill quality; see under B 14:5.11–12.

248

6:3.3   μολόχινα

Garments called μολόχινα, literally "of mallow" (μολόχη), are coupled with *sindones* (garments of cotton; see App. 4) in 48:16.15 and 51:17.13 as well as here, and cloth "of mallow" with cloth of cotton and of silk in 49:16.29–30. There are also allusions to *molochina* in Plautus (*Aulularia* 514) and other writers of Latin comedy. In both Plautus and the *Periplus* the garments are manifestly of high quality, fit for a rich woman's wardrobe in the one case and, like *sindones* and silk, worth importing all the way from India to Egypt in the other. Even in ancient times exactly what they were was unclear. Nonius (548.16–20, Lindsay 879) thought that their name referred to their color ("mallow-colored garments"), Isidore of Seville (*Orig.* 19.22.12) to their material ("garments of mallow fibers"). Among modern commentators, a few have followed Nonius but most have been aware of the difficulty in referring the word to color, aware that the mallow flower is but an undistinguished red. The majority have followed Isidore, even though there is just as much difficulty in referring the word to material. Mallow fiber, as it happens, is extremely coarse, and there is no record of its ever having been used for cloth anywhere.

I. Löw, specialist on the botany of the Near East, long ago presented evidence that μολόχη was also used of jute, and he took the passages in the *Periplus* to refer to garments of jute (ii 248, republication of a note that first appeared in 1899). This is possible but unlikely, for jute, although widely used for cloth, produces a grade of very low quality—in the last century, for example, most of India's poor were clad in homespun jute—and that hardly suits the context in the *Periplus*. It seems best to take *molochina* as cotton garments of fine quality, enough like *sindones* to be coupled with them but sufficiently different to have their own name. For a full discussion, see Casson 1983.202–7.

7:3.16–17   Διοπολιτικῆς ὄμφακος

Müller inserted χυλὸς before Διοπολιτικῆς, and this was retained by Frisk; it is unnecessary, since the genitive can be taken as partitive; see Giangrande 1976.155. ὄμφαξ means either unripe grape or olive; the singular here is used in a collective sense (cf. λόγχη in 17:6.15). Giangrande assumes that olives are meant and he is surely right, for the climate of the area rules out the transportation of grapes. Presumably the olives were imported to be pressed into ὀμφάκιον (L. *omphacium*), as the juice of unripe olives or grapes was called. Olive *omphakion* was used medicinally: according to Dioscorides (1.30) and Pliny (23.79), it was good for the gums and the teeth and effective as a febrifuge.

7:3.19   διαφερόντων

Frisk emended to διαπερώντων, which is unnecessary; cf. A. Roos in *Gnomon* 8 (1932):504, Schmid (op. cit. under 34:11.23–24) 790.

10:4.9   λιθία

The word means either fine building stone, such as marble, or used generically, precious stones; see *LSJ* s.v. Diodorus (1.46.4), for example, tells of Persian invaders stripping a temple at Thebes of "the costliness due to its ivory and precious stones (λιθεία)." Müller, Fabricius, McCrindle, and Schoff all render it here as "glass" or "glassware," presumably taking it as a shortened expression for the ὑαλῆ λιθία of 7:3.16, while Trowbridge (op. cit. under 6:2.25–26, 251) specifically characterizes it as such. But the author includes glass under his words "the aforementioned" (8:3.26–27, 9:4.3, 10:4.8); moreover, when listing ὑαλῆ λιθία he is always careful to note its miscellaneous nature (cf. 6:2.25, 7:3.16, 17:6.15–16). The λιθία here, like the silverware and ironware with which it is coupled, is a new item of import, one not in the previous lists. Apparently there were residents in Mosyllon wealthy enough to afford not only silverware but precious stones.

10:4.10   διὸ καί

The author throughout uses διό in combination with καί (19:6.31, 20:7.9–10, 20:7.14, 25:8.17, 46:15.21, 46:15.24, 50:17.2). The combination is very frequent, both in the Greek papyri from Egypt (cf. E. Mayser, *Grammatik der griechischen Papyri aus der Ptolemäerzeit* ii.3 [Berlin, 1934], 135) and in literature (cf., e.g., Diodorus, who uses it hundreds of times).

10:4.11   ἄλλα εὐοδια

Müller emended to ἄλλη εὐωδία, which Frisk retained. Note the omission of the accent; this was the scribe's way of dealing with words he found incomprehensible (cf. Frisk 33, 46). Fabricius emended to εὔοσμα, but even closer to the manuscript's reading would be εὔοδμα; for the use of this form in technical prose, cf. Theophrastus, *HP* 9.7.3, 9.13.1; *CP* 6.19.1. Müller himself translated this ("alia odorifera") rather than his own text, and others have followed suit ("other fragrant products," McCrindle; "fragrant gums," Schoff and Huntingford).

10:4.11a χελωνάρια, "low-quality tortoise shell"

The suffix -αριος, borrowed from Latin, properly denoted agent but acquired the function of "denoting bad physical or mental qualities" (L. Palmer, *A Grammar of the Post-Ptolemaic Papyri* i.1 [London, 1946], 48).

11:4.16–17 Ἐλέφας . . . τὸν λεγόμενον

It seems best, as Frisk (108–9) suggests, to take all the intervening words ("From Opônê the coast trends south, then southwest. It has rivers.") as an intrusive gloss and to retain the manuscript's ποταμούς. The gloss actually applies to a later passage (15:5.17). What governed the accusatives that follow has been irretrievably lost.

12:4.22 ἐπίσαλος

The manuscript reads ἐπι σαλι. Frisk emended to ἐπί σάλῳ, but the simplest solution is to read ἐπίσαλος as in the parallel passage in 8:3.25.

13:5.4 δουλικὰ

For the adjective used as substantive, frequent in the Greek papyri from Egypt, see Preisigke, *WB* s.v.

14:5.11–12 μοναχὴ καὶ ἡ σαγματογῆνη

The same pair of terms occurs in 6:3.2, a listing of Indian exports to Adulis. From a comparison of 14:5.10–12 with 41:14.5–6 it can be deduced that they are the names of types of cotton cloth of run-of-the-mill quality. 14:5.10–12 lists what the "far-side" ports imported from the Indian district of Ariakê, namely grain, rice, ghee, sesame oil, and "cloth, both *monachê* and *sagmatogênê*." 41:14.5–6 lists what Ariakê exported, namely grain, rice, ghee, sesame oil, and "cotton, and the Indian cloths made from it, those of ordinary quality." It follows that *monachê* and *sagmatogênê* are Indian cottons of ordinary quality.

15:5.19 †διὰ ἀγκυροβολίων ποταμοὶ†

Müller suggested in his commentary the words he conceived to be missing at this point; these were inserted in the text by Fabricius, and from there made their way into numerous translations: McCrindle, Schoff, E. Warmington in the *Cambridge History of the British Empire* viii (Cambridge, 1963²), 64, Mauny (op. cit. under 7:3.13–14) 27. The words are, as Frisk (109) puts it, "des fantaisies assez libres." As he rightly observes, "si on supprime les mots mystérieux, enclavés dans le crux, le texte semble être parfait."

15:5.23–24   τοὺς πάντας ἑπτά

Müller in his commentary explains that the phrase "separated by daily stops and runs" applies to all the runs of Azania, including Sarapiôn and Nikôn. Thus there are but "seven in all" from Sarapiôn to the Pyralaoi Islands, and he conformably reckons the distance between these two points as "septies quingenta stadia." McCrindle, Schoff, and Huntingford take the phrase as applying solely to the runs after Nikôn, making these "seven in all" and the runs of Azania nine in all.

15:5.24   Πυραλάων νήσων

A marginal note in the manuscript reads Πυράλαοι νῆσοι.

15:5.25–26   μικρὸν ἐπάνω τοῦ λιβὸς . . . παρ' αὐτὴν τὴν δύσιν

The unusual use of ἐπάνω here, as Frisk points out (78–79), is probably sailor's jargon. Since he accepted Müller's dubious emendation of παρ' αὐτὴν τὴν δύσιν, which eliminates δύσιν from the text (see under B 15:5.25–26a), he took μικρὸν ἐπάνω τοῦ λιβὸς to mean "a little more to the south," which suits the actual geography of the course from the Lamu Archipelago to Pemba or Zanzibar (see under 15:5.26). But, if the reading of the manuscript is to be maintained, the phrase must mean rather "a little more to the west." Arab sailors, who for centuries have made the run down this coast, stick close to shore, never letting it out of sight (cf. Villiers [op. cit. under 13:5.3] 125). No doubt the ancients did the same, and the author misjudged the trend of the coast (it runs southwest rather than west). He certainly thought it ran west below Rhapta (see under 18:6.23–24).

15:5.25–26a   ειτενηδιων

The scribe left ειτενηδιων without breathing or accent, indicating that it was as incomprehensible to him as it is to us. The notes in Müller and Fabricius supply a rich selection of imaginative emendations offered by earlier editors and commentators. Müller himself suggested (*GGM* ii, page 506) παρ᾽ . . . Αὐσινείτην (or ᾽Ασσινείτην) ἠιόνα. Fabricius adopted it, Frisk followed Fabricius, and the emendation has become enshrined in translations (Schoff; G. Freeman-Grenville in *The East African Coast: Select Documents from the First to the Earlier Nineteenth Century* [Oxford, 1962], 1; Mauny [op. cit. under 7:3.13–14] 27; Huntingford) and discussions (e.g., R. Delbrueck in *Bonner Jahrbücher* 155 [1955]: 22; Raschke 656; A. Beeston in *BSOAS* 43 [1980]: 457, n. 18) and has even been elevated to an entry in *RE* (s.v. Αὐσινείτης ἠιών [1896]). The restoration is pure speculation, deriving ultimately from the mention in Ptolemy (1.17.11) of a port of trade named Ἔσσινα. Müller (*GGM* ii, page 506) connected this with a modern African place name Wassina and created "Αυσιν" or "Ασσιν" as its putative form in Greek. Schoff (94) then introduced a variation of his own: spelling Müller's "Αυσιν" in the form "Ausan," he connected it with a district of that name in South Arabia; his assumption was that the Arab overlords of Azania named this stretch of the coast after part of their homeland. This fanciful connection, too, has made its way into the literature (Huntingford 148, Raschke 656).

15:5.26   Μενουθ[εσ]ιὰς

The emendation makes the spelling conform to that in Ptolemy (4.8.2, 7.2.1).

16:6.7   ὁρατοὶ

This is the reading of the manuscript, with the rough breathing added by the second hand. The reading was retained by Müller, although in his commentary he queried it and offered two possible emendations, one of which, added almost as an afterthought, was πειραταὶ. Fabricius introduced the word into his text, and since then, though the reading has neither paleographical nor other grounds to recommend it, Rhapta's "pirates" have made their way into almost all translations (Fabricius; Schoff; Freeman-Grenville [op. cit. under B 15:5.25–26a] 2 [although elsewhere he rejects the emendation (op. cit. under 15:5.17–16:6.13, 26, n. 17)]; Mauny [op. cit. under 7:3.13–14] 28; Huntingford) and even into some histories (e.g., *CHA* ii 373 [1978], Desanges 334, n. 165). Giangrande (1975.293–94) proposes ἀρόται—i.e., the inhabitants were cultivators of the soil rather than pirates—which far better suits both the paleography and the context. O. Bucci's attack on the suggestion (*Apollinaris* 50 [1977]: 300–305) is not only worthless but a wretched piece of scholarship (he manages to misspell ἀρόται in fifteen of his twenty-one citations of the word); see Giangrande in *Corolla Londiniensis*, London Studies in Classical Philology 8 (Amsterdam, 1981), 49–53.

17:6.20   ναύπλιος

This, the reading of the manuscript, is to be retained; see Casson 1980.496–97.

19:6.29   Ναβαταίων, ⟨ἀνάβασις⟩

The manuscript reads ἀναβαταιως, corrected by the second hand to ναβαταίων. Exactly the same error occurs in a papyrus of the mid-3d century B.C., *PSI* 406, col. i, 21–22; cf. Bowersock (op. cit. under 19:6.26–28) 17, n. 19.

19:6.30   ἐξαρτιζομένοις

For the rendition "loaded with freight," cf. *SB* 8754.31 (49/48 B.C.), an order for shipment of grain in which the shipper is instructed to put aboard 2500 artabs ἵνα δὲ συντόμως ἐξαρτίσθη "so that it may be loaded quickly."

19:6.31–7.1   διὸ . . . ἑκατοντάρχης

The transposition introduced by Fabricius and retained by Frisk is unnecessary; cf. Roos (op. cit. under B 7:3.19) 505.

20:7.14–15   εἰς . . . χώραν

There is no need to bracket these words, as Frisk does; cf. Schmid (op. cit. under 34:11.23–24) 790–91.

20:7.17   ⟨χῶραι⟩

The scribe commits the same error, omission of the geographical feature involved, elsewhere; see 29:9.22, 33:11.9, 37:12.15.

21:7.23   ἐξαρτισμοῖς

For the plural in the sense of "fittings," cf. *P. Ryl.* 233.13 (2d century A.D.), which refers to the "fittings" of a house. Here it seems to be a businessman's term ("outfits") for vessels "outfitted" with freight (cf. under B 19:6.30).

24:8.5 σκιωταὶ

Both σκιά and σκιωτός are used of clothing (cf. *LSJ* s.vv.), referring, it would appear, to "shaded" stripes, i.e., stripes whose colors shade from one to the next, e.g., from red to red-orange to orange, etc. For an excellent example, see Yadin (op. cit under 6:2.25) 245–46 and pls. 60, 71. Other examples have been found at Qusayr al-Qadim on the Egyptian shore of the Red Sea (see Whitcomb-Johnson, op. cit. [1982] under 1:1.2–4, 285) and at Qasr Ibrim in Nubia (information courtesy of N. Adams, Associate Curator of the Museum of Anthropology of the University of Kentucky, in charge of publication of the textile finds).

25:8.20 τοῖς ἔσω διαίρουσιν

"Those sailing into [sc. the Gulf of Aden]" or, in other words, those sailing on; cf. E. Wistrand, *Nach innen oder nach aussen? Zum geographischen Sprachgebrauch der Römer*, Göteborgs Högskolas Årsskrift 52 (Göteborg, 1946), 20–21.

26:8.25 κρείσσον

Frisk adopted the emendation ⟨καὶ⟩ κρείσσον⟨α⟩, which is unnecessary; see Drakonaki-Kazantzaki 48–50.

26:8.26 Εὐδαίμων Ἀραβία εὐδαίμων δὲ ἐπεκλήθη

Frisk bracketed Εὐδαίμων Ἀραβία, which is unnecessary; see Giangrande (op. cit. under 18:6.23–24) 47.

26:8.28 τοὺς ἔσω τόπους

There is no need to emend to τοὺς ἔξω τόπους as Frisk, following Fabricius, has done. The phrase can be taken to mean "to the places within [sc. the open waters]"; see Wistrand (op. cit. under B 25:8.20) 21, Giangrande 1976.154–55.

28:9.17 χρήματα

This is the sole instance of money as an item for a ruler. Inasmuch as Charibaêl, king of the neighboring state, receives the same items as Eleazos but gets χρυσώματα as well as ἀργυρώματα (24:8.8), it is tempting to emend χρήματα here to χρυσώματα. In quite a few places in the manuscript there is what seems to be a thoughtless substitution of a word of similar sound for what must have been the proper reading (e.g., πλεῖσται for πλεῖται, 28:9.20; κόσμου for κόλπου, 30:9.32; παρ' ὁδὸν for Παρσιδῶν, 37:12.13; λύκον for λύκιον, 39:13.10; πέλαγος for πλάτος, 42:14.17; τέλος for ὕελος, 56:18.19).

29:9.22 ⟨γῆς⟩

For other instances of the omission of the geographical feature being described, see under B 20:7.17.

29:9.30 πάντοτε

For the meaning, see Drakonaki-Kazantzaki 51–54.

30:10.5–6 ὡς . . . σαυρῶν

The emending of ὡς to ὧν and the bracketing of τῶν σαυρῶν are unnecessary; see Giangrande 1976.157.

30:10.11 ἀληθεινὴν

This form, omitted in Frisk's apparatus criticus, is the reading of the manuscript. It should be retained; see Drakonaki-Kazantzaki 51.

30:10.14–16 μέρη μὲν . . . κατατέμνεται

The readings of the manuscript should be retained throughout; see Casson 1982.205.

31:10.20 αὐτῷ τῷ βασιλεῖ

On the use of αὐτὸς ὁ as demonstrative, see Frisk 65–66, and for the meaning "the aforementioned," see Mayser (op. cit. under B 10:4.10) ii.2 76–77.

31:10.23 διὰ σπάνιν

Frisk (76) argues that the accusative here is a substitution for the genitive, the phrase presumably being the equivalent of σπανίως as, e.g., διὰ τάχους is the equivalent of ταχέως. Such a substitution, however, as he admits, is rare, and there hardly is need to argue for it here.

32:11.4–7 παρ' ὅλον . . . δίχα

There is no need for any emendations; the text should read exactly as it is in the manuscript. See Giangrande 1976.156.

32:11.7–33:11.8 δαίμονος δίχα. ⟨Ἀπὸ δὲ Μόσχα⟩ λιμένος

Perhaps the examplar read δίχα λιμένος. Ἀπὸ δὲ Μόσχα λιμένος and the lacuna arose when the scribe's eye jumped from the first λιμένος to the second. For the "spirit of the harbor," cf. *P. Lond.* 7.2041 (mid-3d century B.C.): τῷ δαίμονι τοῦ χωρίου.

33:11.9–10 ἕως Ἀσίχωνος ἄχρι ⟨ὄρος⟩ . . . αὐτοῦ

On the scribe's tendency to omit the geographical feature being described, see under B 20:7.17. The emendations, even if not what the author wrote, reproduce its gist. Frisk (80) offers parallels to defend the linking of ἕως . . . ἄχρι, and Müller's insertion of ὄρος provides a suitable subject for παρατείνει, considering the nature of the region under discussion. However, since the mountains involved are a range (cf. under 33:11.9), we would expect ὄρη, as in 32:10.28, where the previous range is dealt with. αὐτοῦ must refer to Ἀσίχωνος, since the Isles of Zênobios (Kuria Muria Islands; cf. under 33:11.10–11) lie in front of its extremity and not in front of the extremity of the range; that is near Ras Naws (17°15′N, 55°19′E), eight miles to the south.

33:11.16 ἱεροῖς

P. Maxwell-Stuart points out (*Maia* n.s. 31 [1979]; 127) that Müller's suggested emendation πονηροῖς is unnecessary. He suggests instead ἠρεμαίοις—which is equally unnecessary.

33:11.19 ἐφόλκια

Epholkion, literally "for towing," is the technical term for a ship's boat. Such boats could be large enough to step their own mast and sail (cf. *SSAW* 248–49) and, as in this passage, be used as independent small craft.

34:11.20 περικολπίζοντι

The verb, which means literally "sail around a bay," is found only in the *Periplus*, where its sense is "follow the coastline" (cf. 57:19.1).

34:11.23 αὐτὰς

Frisk failed to note in his apparatus that this is an emendation. The manuscript reads αὐτὴν.

35:11.25 Καλαίου

The manuscript reads παπίου. The emendation seems justified, since no islands other than the Isles of Kalaios have been mentioned.

35:11.28 ⟨'Α⟩σαβῶ⟨ν⟩

The emendation is based on Ptolemy 6.7.12 where, under the heading "straits of the Persian Gulf," he lists Μέλανα ὄρη καλούμενα 'Ασαβῶν. Another possibility is 'Ασαβώ as in Marcianus of Heraclea 1.19 (although in 1.27 he has Πασαβώ); cf. Frisk 114. The marginal note in the manuscript of the *Periplus*, for what it is worth (according to Frisk [28–30], very little), reads Σαβαώ.

36:12.6 σαγαλίνων

See Casson 1982a. The manuscript reads σαγαλινο which Salmasius emended to σανταλίνων on the grounds that *santalina ligna* would be sandalwood, and sandalwood would be an obvious Indian export. All editors have retained the emendation. Yet the Greek word for sandalwood, borrowed from the Sanskrit *chandana*, is, as we would expect, τζανδάνα (Cosmas Indicopleustes 11.445D Winstedt). Long ago both Löw (iii 489–90) and Yule (Hobson-Jobson, s.v. *Teak*) recognized that σαγαλινο must be connected with the Sanskrit word for teak, *śāka*. Later forms show a change of *k* to *g*, as in the Hindustani word for teak, *sāgūn*, or the Marathi, *sāg*. There is even in Marathi an adjective *sāgalī*, "of teak." Thus the only emendation required is to ξύλων σαγαλίνων "teak wood."

36:12.6a κεράτων

The term κέρας may mean "sailyard" as well as "horn" (*SSAW* 232, n. 35). Greek sailyards were commonly made of two saplings or two long branches lashed together at their thicker ends (*SSAW* 232). It is easy to conceive of the word being taken over by merchants as a trade term for pieces of timber of that shape, like logs but more slender.

36:12.7 σασαμίνων

Editors have emended to σησαμ-, which is unnecessary. The author is referring to the wood of the *Dalbergia sissoo* which grows widely in India and produces fine timber for both construction and cabinet work (Watt iii. 13–15). In Hindustani and other major dialects it is called *sīsū, shīsham,* or the like. The name was borrowed by Arabic in the form *sāsam* and, it would appear, by Greek as well (Hobson-Jobson 842).

37:12.13 Παρσιδῶν

This is Müller's plausible conjecture for the manuscript's παρ' ὁδὸν. The Parsidai are attested in Ptolemy (6.21.4), who locates them along this portion of the coast. For other instances of the substitution of words of similar sound for what was the proper reading, see under B 28:9.17.

37:12.15 παρανατείνει. καὶ παρ' αὐτὸν

The verb lacks a subject; on the scribe's tendency to omit the geographical feature being described, see under B 20:7.17. Müller conjectured ⟨ἄκρα⟩ and expressed a preference for ἀνατείνει instead of παρανατείνει since he believed the feature involved to be a promontory (in the commentary he identified it as Ras Ormāra), both of which Frisk approved. But Müller's handling of the passage was based on a misconception of the topography; see under 37:12.14–16. A more suitable subject would be τόπος πολυφόρος aut sim. The παρ' of παρ' αὐτὸν may be connected with the behavior of the river: the Purali does not flow in a fixed channel but washes over the sprawling area of its bed all along the coast.

37:12.18 βασίλεια

This is Frisk's emendation of the manuscript's βασιλεία. There is no need to adopt Fabricius's conjecture, favored by Frisk (114), that the article was omitted.

39:13.8 πολύμιτα

Cf. *Gloss.* 5.524.34: *polimatus est textus multorum colorum;* 5.524.32: *polimita multicoloria,* i.e., any textile, such as brocade, woven with threads of different colors (not "damask," as in *LSJ*).

39:13.8a   χρυσόλιθον

The neuter form is exceptional; see Frisk 52–53. Elsewhere the word almost always occurs in the masculine, in both literature (*LSJ* s.v.) and papyri (*P. Lond.* 928.15 [2d century A.D.]; *P. Holm.* 9.1, 3 [4th century A.D.]), and so does its Latin equivalent (Pliny 37.126; Isidore, *Orig.* 16.15.2). The word means literally "golden stone," and the descriptions in Pliny and Isidore make clear that it was yellow in color; conformably, Propertius (2.16.44) refers to its "tawny luster" (*flavo lumine*). It is usually translated "topaz" (cf. McCrindle, Fabricius 150, Schoff, Huntingford 139, *LSJ* s.v.), sometimes "yellow sapphire" (D. Eichholtz, note to his translation of Pliny 37.126 in the Loeb edition [1962]), but in this passage it most likely means "peridot"; see under 39:13.8a

39:13.11   Σιρικὰ δέρματα καὶ ὀθόνιον καὶ νῆμα Σιρικὸν

Translators consistently take ὀθόνιον here to refer to cotton cloth. This would mean that, whereas silk cloth was brought down to Barygaza (49:16.30) and Muziris/Nelkynda (56:18.24), the other ports that handled Chinese products, to Barbarikon alone—which offered more varied Chinese products than any other port (it was the one place where Chinese pelts were available)—only silk yarn was brought down. The anomaly can be avoided by simply understanding an ellipsis of Σιρικὸν after ὀθόνιον: Barbarikon handled "Chinese pelts, (Chinese) cloth, Chinese yarn," i.e., silk cloth and silk yarn.

40:13.19–20   ἀπολλύμενα

Frisk follows Fabricius in emending to ἀπόλλυσθαι, which is unnecessary; see Giangrande 1976.155.

40:13.28–29   ἀποκοντουμένας

The rare word ἀποκοντῶ (it is found only here and in Procopius, *Secret History* 9.62) means "thrust out" and not "drop anchor," as Frisk thought; see Casson 1982.206.

40:13.29   συντριβομένας

Frisk emends to συντρίβεσθαι, which is unnecessary; see Giangrande 1976.155.

40:13.29a αὐτοῖν

This, the reading of the manuscript, is to be retained; see Giangrande 1976.155. On the author's occasional literary flourishes, see Introduction: Text and Author, The Author and His Work.

41:14.12 Ἀστακάπρα πέραν

The manuscript here reads ἄστα καὶ τραπεραν and in 41:14.26 ἀστακάνπρων. This is a transcription of the Sanskrit name Hastakavapra (see under 41:14.12–13). Properly it should be "αστακαοπρα," for the normal Greek transcription of the Sanskrit -va- is by omicron; see Shafer (op. cit. under 41:14.4) 115. Shafer characterizes this as a "most unexpected change"; it certainly seems to have been unexpected to the scribes involved in copying the *Periplus*.

42:14.14 ἔσω κυμάτων

Müller in his commentary suggested that ἔσω may have been an error for ἔξω, and Frisk introduced the suggestion into the text. But the manuscript reading can be retained; cf. Giangrande 1976.155. "On the inside of the waves" can be taken to mean on the side within the embrace of the land and consequently away from any waves. The gulf is, as it were, on the inside, and the open sea with its waves on the outside.

44:15.5–6 πληρώμασιν μακρῶν πλοίων . . . ἐξέρχονται

"[Fishermen] come out . . . with crews and long ships," i.e., with galleys and their complements of rowers. The "long ships," as the adjective implies (cf. νῆες μακραί, "war galleys" [*SSAW* 169]) and as their function as tugboats (see 44:15.8 and cf. *SSAW* 336–37) makes certain, were galleys.

46:15.23–24 οὐδὲν . . . ἄγκυραι

The manuscript reads οὐδὲν παριεμένης αἱ κατέχουσιν ἄγκυραι, which is manifestly corrupt. Frisk reproduces Müller's text, whose alterations go further than required. The translation is based on minimum emendation: παραμένουσιν for παριεμένης and κατέχουσαι for κατέχουσιν. Used of anchors, κατέχουσαι would mean "restraining (anchors)," i.e., either extras over and above the number normally used or anchors set out as described under 40:13.28–29. For a full discussion of this passage, see Casson 1982.206.

46:15.29 συμμηνίας

Müller emended to νεομηνίας, which was retained by Frisk. The change is impossible to justify paleographically and unnecessary on the grounds of sense. The author is describing the violence of the neap tides, the minimal tides that occur at the dark of the moon, leaving it to the reader to imagine what the spring tides at the new and full moon must be like.

47:16.3 ἐπίκειται . . . ἔθνη

The scribe wrote ἐπίκειται γὰρ κατὰ του [sic] τῇ Βαρυγάζῃ μεσογεία πλείονα ἔθνη and then to the last letter of τῇ Βαρυγάζῃ μεσογεία respectively he added a superscript letter which could be iota or sigma. Frisk took it to be iota but sigma is supported by the British Museum manuscript which reads κατὰ τοῦ τῆς Βαρυγάζης μεσογείου; its scribe, in other words, took the words to mean "inland Barygaza."

47:16.6 ὄντων . . . τόπον

This is a notorious crux. For the various emendations that have been suggested, see Raschke 751, n. 461 and 800, n. 677; Huntingford 69; P. Eggermont in *Orientalia Lovaniensia Analecta* 13 (1982) = *Studia Paulo Naster Oblata* ii, 67.

48:16.17 Καττυβουρίνη . . . Πατροπαπίγη

The two names are unattested elsewhere and cannot be connected directly with any known Sanskrit names, but both must refer to northern regions that boast mountains lofty enough to produce nard (cf. under 48:16.16–18). Müller suggested (cf. Frisk's apparatus) that the first was a miswriting of Κασπαπυρηνή, the second of Παροπανισηνή.

Κασπαπυρηνή is a presumed Greek transliteration of a presumed Sanskrit name, *Kaśyapapura* aut sim., for Kashmir (cf. Hobson-Jobson s.v. *Cashmere*; Nilakanta Sastri [op. cit. under 51:17.15] 55), but the Sanskrit form is not certain (cf. Smith 40, n. 1) and, in any event, some identify the name with Multan in Pakistan, well to the southwest of Kashmir (see A. Foucher and E. Bazin-Foucher, *La vieille route de l'Inde de Bactres à Taxila* [Paris, 1942], ii 193–94). Possibly the *Periplus's* Καττυβουρίνη is connected with Κασπειρία, which Ptolemy (7.1.42; cf. 7.1.47, 49) applies both to the upper valleys of the Jhelum, Chenab, and Ravi, an area usually identified with Kashmir (cf. Hobson-Jobson s.v. *Cashmere*, Tarn 238), and to the area that stretched from Kashmir southeast to beyond Mathura (cf. Eggermont [op. cit. under 48:16.16–18] 261).

Πατροπαπίγη could well be, as Müller thought, a miswriting of Παρο-πανισηνή. The Paropanisos (so Ptolemy 6.11.1, 6.17.1; other authors spell it slightly differently [see A. Herrmann, RE s.v. Paropamisus (1949)]) is the Hindu Kush.

49:16.29   σμύρνα

The manuscript reads ὀνυχίνη λιθία καὶ σμύρνα. Since ὀνυχίνη λιθία καὶ μουρρίνη in 48:16.14–15 are listed as products brought to Barygaza for export to the West, σμύρνα here seems like yet another example of substitution of a word of similar sound for what must have been the proper reading (cf. under B 28:9.17).

49:16.30   Σηρικὸν . . . νῆμα

The author's practice is to refer to silk cloth as ὀθόνιον Σηρικόν and not Σηρικόν alone; cf. 56:18.24, 64:21.14, and under B 39:13.11. Thus ὀθόνιον in 49:16.29 is to be taken with Σηρικὸν as well as παντοῖον: "(cotton) cloth of all kinds and Chinese (cloth)." And, since νῆμα is elsewhere identified as Chinese (39:13.11, 64:21.13), here there must be an ellipsis of Σηρικὸν after it. In other words, Muziris/Nelkynda exported both silk cloth and silk yarn.

52:17.17   ᾿Ακαβαρου

Frisk (117) suggests that the initial alpha may be intrusive, produced by the preceding κείμενα, and that "Kabaru" may be the same as "une ville Khabiroun" that Idrisi lists after "Soubara" (Suppara). But Idrisi unmistakably identifies his Khabiroun as a region, not a town; see Géographie d'Édrisi, trans. A. Jaubert, Recueil de voyages et de mémoires publié par la Société de Géographie 5 (Paris, 1836), 170.

53:17.23–24   †τοπαρον καὶ τύραννος βοας†

Müller took both as place names, although in his commentary he offered the alternative of emending τοπαρον to τὸ πάρος, "[Byzantion], formerly also [sc. called] Tyrannosboas." See also under 53:17.23–24.

54:17.30 ἔνσημος

LSJ s.v. brands the word here as a false reading for ἐπίσημος. See, however, Frisk 98.

55:18.11 ἄλματα

Müller emended to ἔρματα, which Frisk retained. The emendation is unnecessary, for in the context ἄλματα can mean "sand flats"; see Giangrande 1975.294–95.

56:18.16 μεστὰ

Editors have emended to μεγάλα, which is unnecessary; see Drakonaki-Kazantzaki 50–51. The translation follows her explication of the text.

56:18.20 σώζει . . . ἐν

There is no need to emend to ὡσεί. In the context σώζει can mean "goes"; see Giangrande 1975.295. For the rendering of ἐν as "into," cf. Frisk 76.

56:18.21 τοῖς περὶ τὸ ναυκλήριον

The word ναυκλήριον is rare, occurring less than a half-dozen times in all of Greek literature. It can sometimes have the concrete meaning of "vessel," the *naukleros's* distinguishing possession (see *P. Oxy.* 87.7, 20 [4th century A.D.] and cf. the similar concrete use of ναυκληρία [*LSJ* s.v. II]), and that is the sense that all translators have given it here, taking "those involved with the vessel" to be the crew. But the author is presenting a list of items that merchants can expect to sell at Muziris/Nelkynda, and crews' provisions have no place there. Furthermore, he contrasts οἱ περὶ τὸ ναυκλήριον with οἱ ἔμποροι. The latter must be native dealers, as is made clear by their food preference—they eschew grain for, sc., rice; cf. Introduction: Trade in the Indian Ocean, The Trade with India. It follows that the former, interested in the purchase of grain, sc., for making the food they are accustomed to, must be resident Western dealers, "those involved with shipping." For ναυκλήριον used in this sense, cf. Plutarch, *Mor.* 2.234f and Cicero, *Tusc. Disp.* 5.14(40): Plutarch cites a Spartan saying about a shipowner who was fabulously wealthy through ναυκλήρια πολλὰ ἔχων; this Cicero renders "glorianti . . . quod multas naves in omnem oram maritimam dimisisset," i.e., not "through having many ships" but "through having dispatched many ships to the shore of every sea," in other words, through having carried on widespread shipping.

57:18.30–19.12   τοῦτον δὲ ὅλον . . . κόλπους

On this chapter, whose sense has been misunderstood and whose text has been distorted by misdirected emendation, see Casson 1984b. The insertion and deletion in 57:19.5–7, introduced by Müller and approved by Frisk, are to be disregarded. The readings of the manuscript are to be retained except as follows:

in 19.1 insert πρότεροι aut sim., as in Frisk's text
in 19.3–4 delete ἀφ' οὗ ; see Casson 1984b.474
in 19.4 delete τῶν as in Frisk's text
in 19.6 read ἐξευρηκότος as in Frisk's text
in 19.9 read οἵ τε as in Frisk's text
in 19.11 read ἐκ τῆς χώρας ὑψηλοὶ as in the manuscript

The word τραχηλίζοντες in 19.9 has caused translators and commentators much trouble. It is a wrestling term meaning "getting a neck lock on." In a nautical context it occurs only here. Presumably, just as a wrestler gets a neck lock on an antagonist and thereby is enabled to twist him where he wants him, so a skipper "gets a neck lock on" the wind and thereby is enabled to twist it till he has it where he wants it, in this case on the starboard quarter (cf. Casson 1984b.476–77).

In 19.10 the corrupt παρεπιφέρον is perhaps to be read παρεπιφέρον⟨ται⟩ and καὶ inserted after δρόμον. In 19.11, though the text is corrupt, the sense is clear. As Müller aptly remarks, "certe mira est verborum redundantia in istis."

58:19.14   τη . . . . κης

The scribe left blank a space long enough to accommodate approximately thirteen letters.

58:19.14a   Παραλία

The manuscript reads παραδία. Frisk failed to note it in his apparatus. Müller noted it incorrectly, without the accent.

58:19.18 βριάριον

The emendation to φρούριον, first suggested by Stuck and retained by subsequent editors, is a guess pure and simple. The manuscript reading can be retained: see Drakonaki-Kazantzaki in *Museum Philologum Londiniense* 8 (1987): 31–43; she takes βριάριον as the diminutive of βρία "village," hence "little settlement."

58:19.19–20 γενέσθαι . . . αὐτοῦ

The manuscript reads γενέσθαι χῆροι μένουσιν αὐτοῦ. εκεῖ ἐρχόμενοι, which the translation renders. The British Museum manuscript, apparently reflecting an attempt to make the language less clumsy, has χῆροι μένουσιν. αὐτοῦ δὲ ἐρχόμενοι.

59:20.1 Ἀργαλου

This is the same as the Ἀργάρου πόλις of Ptolemy 7.1.11 (who also lists a κόλπος Ἀργαρικός). The author himself a line below (59:20.2) refers to the textiles of the place as Ἀργαρίτιδες (adopting Müller's plausible conjecture for the slightly different reading of the manuscript). On the interchange between rho and lambda, see Frisk 45.

59:20.1a ἐν ἑνὶ τόπῳ . . . ἠπιοδώρου

The text is too defective to permit plausible emendation.

60:20.8 ἀφῆς

Müller's emendation to ἀφαῖς, retained by Frisk, is unnecessary; see Giangrande 1975.293.

60:20.10–11 πάντα τὰ εἰς τὴν Λιμυρικὴν ἐργαζόμενα

The masculine form ἐργαζόμενοι is used in the specific sense of "traders" (Dem. 34.51, Paus. 3.23.3), just as the *Periplus* uses ἐργασία in the specific sense of "trade" (17:6.17, 21:7.23, 30:10.10). Conformably, here the neuter form (which is extremely rare, being attested only in this passage and in Plato, *Resp.* 35 C) means "that which is traded," and this is the way Müller took it, translating "quaecunque in Limyricen negotiandi causa mittuntur." Frisk (73) brands Müller's version as a "traduction un peu douteuse" and, pointing out that εἰς can be used in the sense of ἐν, expresses a preference for Fabricius's "alles das, was in Limyrike producirt wird." But such a translation makes the author draw a distinction that is unreal, a distinction between "all that is made in Limyrikê" and (see the next two lines) "all that Limyrikê exports"; as is clear from 56:18.22–28, what Limyrikê chiefly "made" was pepper, and this it exported. Müller, as it happens, was on the right track. If we make the very reasonable assumption that by τὰ ἐργαζόμενα the author has in mind what came to Limyrikê through her trade with the West, then a very real distinction appears: he is differentiating the products for which Limyrikê was merely an intermediary, namely those from the West, from the products of India, for which it was the point of export. In its commerce with the ports on the east coast it included shipments of all of the first but not all, only most, of the second.

60:20. 10–13   προχωρεῖ . . . φερομένων

On this passage, see Casson 1987. In the context τῷ παντὶ χρόνῳ means "all year round." The author is pointing out that, whereas shipments from the West to Limyrikê arrived only at certain times of year, those from Limyrikê to India's east coast had no such limitation; cf. under 60:20. 10–13.

60:20. 13   διὰ

For the meaning "along," cf. Herodotus 4.39; *Act. Ap.* 9.25; 2 *Ep. Cor.* 11.33.

61:20. 14   περὶ δὲ τῶν μετ' αὐτὴν χωρῶν

Müller's emendation to τὴν . . . χώραν, retained by Frisk, is unnecessary; see Schmid (op. cit. under 34:11.23–24) 793. αὐτὴν here has the same antecedent as αὐτῆς in 59:20.2, the region of Argaru; the intervening chapter 60 is, in effect, an excursus.

61:20. 16–18   παρὰ δὲ τοῖς . . . πλιονακιστινει

The text is too defective to permit plausible emendation.

62:20. 25   πλέοντος τοῦ πλοός

Emendation to ἀπονεύοντος is unnecessary. The manuscript reading, meaning "sailing a course" (to the north), is to be retained; see Drako-naki-Kazantzaki 54–55.

62:20.26   ἐϰτεθλιμμένων

As Frisk notes (120), Apollodorus, *Bibl.* 2.5.9.1, uses ἐϰθλίβω in the same sense.

62:20.27   Ἱππιοπϱοσώπων [Μαϰϱοπϱοσώπων]

Frisk properly brackets Μαϰϱοπϱοσώπων ("long faces") as an intrusive gloss.

63:21.9   ϰλειομένη

There is no need to emend to ϰαλουμένη; see Drakonaki-Kazantzaki 47–48. On the author's occasional literary flourishes, see Introduction: Text and Author, The Author and His Work.

65:21.22–23   εν μοι . . . ἡμέϱαις

The manuscript reads εν μοι εἰς τέλος τε αὐτοὺς λέγεσθαι σησάτας παϱομοιοῦσιν ἡμέϱαις, which is hopelessly corrupt. Instead of εν μοι the British Museum manuscript reads αἴσιμοι, a variant that is hardly helpful. Frisk (121–22) rejects Müller's emendation (which Fabricius had adopted) and suggests a rather complicated emendation of his own. Cf. also Schmid (op. cit. under 34:11.23–24) 793, who offers ἐνεοὶ for εν μοι. The one change all agree on is ἀνημέϱοις for ἡμέϱαις. ἡμέϱαις is clearly impossible, probably the substitution by the scribe of a word of similar sound for what must have been in the exemplar (cf. under B 28:9.17). Yet, for all we know, the correct emendation may be ἡμέϱοις rather than ἀνημέϱοις; the Sêsatai may have been, or seemed to be, not savages but a mild, well-behaved tribe.

65:21.24–25   βαστάζοντες φοϱτία μεγάλα ταϱπόναις ὠμαμπελίνων παϱαπλήσια

The manuscript reads τέϱπονας . . . παϱαπλήσια. ὠμαμπέλινος, though unattested elsewhere, must be the opposite of the well-attested ξηϱαμπέλινος, "characteristic of the vine when dry, bright red" (*LSJ* s.v.) and mean "characteristic of the vine when fresh, green." τέϱπονας is not only unattested but has no congeners that would suit the context; accordingly it has been emended to ταϱπόνας which, though equally unattested, can be connected with τάϱπη, "wicker basket" (cf. Frisk 39), and the context requires, if not a basket, at least something plaited. Moreover, the error of writing epsilon for alpha is paralleled: in 3:1.15 ἐνέβησαν is clearly a mistake for ἀνέβησαν.

There has been universal acceptance, too, of the emendation of παραπλήσια to παραπλησίας. With καὶ inserted after μεγάλα (Müller), or an apposition assumed (Frisk), the result was translated in various ways: "magnas portantes sarcinas et sirpeas viridis vitis foliis comparandas" (Müller); "carrying great packs and plaited baskets of what looks like green grape-leaves" (Schoff); "carrying great packs, plaited baskets full of ⟨what look like⟩ fresh vine-leaves" (Huntingford). But what follows shows plainly that ταρπόνας, though the word surely refers to plaited objects of some sort, cannot mean baskets, as the translators have taken it. The Sêsatai, we are told, spread the ταρπόνας under themselves. This is what one does with a mat, not a basket. Furthermore, there is no need to emend παραπλήσια since, taken with φορτία, it is a perfectly sound form. All that is required is a further adjustment to the manifestly defective τέρπονας. The simplest emendation would be ταρπόναις: the Sêsatai came "bearing great packs resembling mats of green leaves [literally, 'of ⟨leaves⟩ characteristic of the vine when fresh']." In the one other occurrence of παραπλήσιος in the *Periplus*, it is construed with the genitive (46:15.31); although this can be defended (see Frisk 55), the dative is normal. Moreover, the author at times does not discriminate between these two cases: he will use now the one and now the other in the same construction (cf. Frisk 64). Alternatively, the genitive can be introduced here too by emending to ταρπόνων.

65:21.29–22.1   καλάμους . . . πέτρους

There is a confusion here. The name the author gives to the reeds that furnish the fiber for stringing, πέτροι, must surely refer to the malabathron leaf itself, being the Hellenizaton of the Sanskrit *pattra*, "leaf"; cf. under 65:21.21–22.6.

65:22.4   τὸ μεσόσφαιρον

Both Müller and Frisk neglected to report that the article does not appear in the manuscript.

APPENDIX 1.

HARBORS AND PORTS

In six instances the author uses the term *limên*[1] and in thirteen *hormos*.[2] Though there can at times be a distinction between the two, both here and in the Greek papyri from Egypt they seem just about interchangeable.[3] I have translated *limên* "port" and *hormos* "harbor."

More frequent then either is *emporion*, occurring some fifty times. It refers to a port that not only served as a harbor proper, i.e., a place to moor but, more importantly, offered facilities for buying and selling goods. I translate it "port of trade."

In some passages the author characterizes in a special way a given *hormos* or *emporion*. Three *hormoi* are described as *apodedeigmenos*, "designated": Myos Hormos and Berenicê (1:1.1–4), the two major ports of Egypt on the Red Sea, whence all the trade routes the author deals with originated; and Moscha (32:10.30), a minor port on the southern coast of Arabia. Three *emporia* are described as *nomimos*, a term that usually means "legal": Adulis (4:1.20) on the lower western shore of the Red Sea; Muza (21:7.19), a thriving port on the eastern shore just above the Straits of Bab el Mandeb; and Apologos (35:11.32–12.1) at the head of the Persian Gulf. Last, Kalliena (52:17.18–19), one of the many ports on the west coast of India that handled local trade, had once been *enthesmos*, an adjective more or less synonymous with *nomimos*.

Early commentators distinguished between *apodedeigmenos* and *nomimos* or *enthesmos*. They took the first to refer to a port's general standing and the second to some special legal status. To Fabricius, for example, *apodedeigmenos* distinguished a port as "gewöhnlich oder doch vorzugsweise besucht" (114), while an *emporion nomimon* was "einen von der Regierung dafür erklärten Stapelplatz, der eben für die Aus- und Einfuhr zur See in dieser oder jener Gegend allein gestattet und bestimmt war"

---

[1] 1:1.2 and 1.4, 30:10.1, 32:10.30, 33:11.8, 58:19.18.

[2] 1:1.1 and 1.2, 7:3.12, 8:3.24, 12:4.22, 15:5.23, 19:6.26, 25:8.20, 26:8.24, 32:10.29, 44:15.10, 58:19.16, 60:20.4.

[3] Thus, in 32:10.30, a port named Μόσχα λιμήν is referred to as a ὅρμος ἀποδεδειγμένος.

(117–18).[4] In this century, however, the consensus has arisen that all the terms are more or less similar in meaning and reflect various ways in which rulers sought to control or direct commerce; indeed, to some commentators they are evidence of Rome's close official interest in her trade with East Africa, Arabia, and India.[5]

Hormos Apodedeigmenos

All recent commentators take this expression to reflect government regulation of trade by the "designating" of certain harbors as authorized points for import or export.[6]

None have observed that it is not *emporia* that are "designated" but *hormoi*, in other words, not ports in their function as places to trade but as places to moor.

Furthermore, none have taken into consideration the occurrence of the identical expression in the Greek papyri of Egypt. A contract for shipping freight on the Nile includes a clause to the effect that skippers are not to sail at night or during storms and that they are to moor "each day at the designated and safest harbors" (unpublished document from Oxyrhynchus cited in *P. Oxy.* 3111.12 note).[7] Other such contracts contain the same kind of clause save that, instead of "designated harbors (*hormoi*)" they use the words "designated places (*topoi*)," but the context makes perfectly clear that harbors are meant (*P. Ross. Georg.* 2.18.33, 133, 196 [A.D. 140]).

More important, still another papyrus reveals why certain harbors

[4] Fabricius's view of an *emporion nomimon* has been revived by Huntingford (83): "ports recognized as official marts for the hinterland they served."

[5] The first commentators to connect the expressions with government regulations made exaggerated claims for Rome's official interest in, and supervision of, her trade with the East; see Introduction: Trade in the Indian Ocean, A Roman Economic Policy? For later, less exaggerated views, cf. Warmington 53 (*emporia nomima* were "legal marts where foreign trade was allowed and dues levied"); M. Charlesworth, "Roman Trade with India: A Resurvey," in P. Coleman-Norton, ed., *Studies in Roman Economic and Social History in Honor of Allen Chester Johnson* (Princeton, 1951), 131–43, esp. 138–43, and his conclusion on 142 ("these all appear to be varying terms for what the nineteenth century would have called 'Treaty-Ports' "); Wheeler 116–17 ("Rome had established trading rights at the town [of Muza]"; "a treaty-port called Apologos").

[6] See Charlesworth cited in n. 5 above; Wheeler 115 ("designated . . . perhaps as the authorized channels for certain types of goods"); J. Palmer, "*Periplus Maris Erythraei*: ἐμπόριον νόμιμον and other expressions," *CQ* 45 (1951): 156–58 at 158 ("the prescribed ports from which export cargoes for the East might be shipped, and to which possibly, certain imports from the East were confined").

[7] For other occurrences of the term "designated harbors," see *P. Laur.* 6.5–6 (A.D. 97–117), *P. Lond.* 295.7–8 (A.D. 118), *P. Aberd.* 20.9 (2d century A.D.).

were "designated." *P. Hib.* 198 lists a series of royal ordinances in force around 245–240 B.C., one of which stipulates that royal transports are to moor only at "designated places"; if caught by storm and forced to put in elsewhere, skippers are to hurry to the nearest police post and report their position so that a guard can be sent out.[8] The places on the river, in other words, were "designated" because the government maintained guard stations there against pirates and bandits.[9] To be sure, all this dates three centuries before the *Periplus* was written and concerns only the Nile. Yet the conditions that inspired the measures were very much present on the Red Sea at the time of the *Periplus*: piracy had been a problem there long before the author sailed its waters, was a problem when he did, and was destined to remain so long after,[10] while attacks by bandits were a problem as well.[11] The analogy of the papyri would indicate that Myos Hormos and Berenicê were "designated" because guards were stationed there, just as along the Nile. This would explain why *apodedeigmenos* is used of *hormoi* and not *emporia*: it was not the bazaar in town where trading took place that was "designated" but the areas in the anchorage where vessels moored. The author's discussion of the "designated harbor" at Moscha makes clear that it was the merchandise on the quays as well as the boats moored there that needed protection: Moscha was one place where, unlike other harbors, precious incense could be left "unguarded," thanks to the unique supernatural security there (32:11.4–7).

In Roman times Myos Hormos and Berenicê were made as safe as could be against attack by land: the first was in effect a fortified town, and the second boasted one of the biggest forts in the eastern desert (see under

[8] *P. Hib.* 198.110–22 and cf. the editors' note. R. Bagnall, in *Bulletin of the American Society of Papyrologists* 6 (1969): 93–96, taking the passage to refer to ships coming from the open sea to the mouth of the Nile, restored the text so that it said (93): "let those sailing toward the river to anchor give notice during the day at the appointed places etc." This asks too much of the technology of communications in a prewireless age; the editors' version is to be retained. Cf. J. Vélissaropoulos, *Les nauclères grecs*, Centre de recherches d'histoire et de philologie de la IVᵉ section de l'École pratique des Hautes Études iii: Hautes études du monde gréco-romain 9 (Paris, 1980), 159, who considers the restoration questionable on other grounds.

[9] The editors mention only the danger of pirates, i.e., attack from the river. However, for a boat forced to put in at some isolated point along the shore there was just as much danger of attack from the land; cf. W. Ashburner, *The Rhodian Sea-Law* (Oxford, 1909), cxliv.

[10] See under 20:7.8–9.

[11] Numerous votives, dating from the third to the first century B.C., were found at the sanctuary of Pan at El-Kanaïs, a station on a major route between Berenicê and the Nile Valley, in which the donors thank the deity for "having saved them from the Trogodytes"; see under 2:1.7–10. The *Periplus* (4:2.1–4) reports that at Adulis, because of raids carried out by the local Barbaroi, the port had to be transferred from its original location to an island a safe distance away. See Ashburner, loc. cit. n. 9 above, for legal provisions arising from banditry.

1:1.2–4). The protection on the sea very likely took the form of patrol boats, a Red Sea coast guard, as it were.[12] Moscha had the best form of protection of all—the power of the gods who watched over the place.

Emporion Enthesmon

This expression occurs but once, used of Kalliena, a port on the west coast of India in the vicinity of Bombay (see under 52:17.18). To arrive at its meaning we must take into account the political situation in the region at the time of the *Periplus*.

Kalliena was a pawn in the struggle between the Sakas, who during the period in question held the west coast of India down to Bombay, and the Andhras, who held the coast south of it. The city had at one time been Andhran and, in those days, the author notes, had been an *emporion enthesmon*. Then Sandanês, who was a Saka ruler or official, took it over and "there has been much hinderance [sc. to trade]" (52:17.20) caused certainly by the hostile Andhrans. As a consequence of this, at the time of writing Kalliena had diminished to the status of a port dealing merely in local products. Thus *enthesmos*, defined "lawful" in *LSJ*, would seem to mean here "where everything went according to law," i.e., in the days of Andhran control the authorities in the place were able to see to it that foreign traders were insulated from interference, a state of affairs that ceased when the port passed into the hands of the Sakas.[13]

Emporion Nomimon

Thus, neither *apodedeigmenos* nor *enthesmos* has anything to do with government efforts to control or direct trade but rather with efforts to protect traders.

The third expression, *emporion nomimon*, has been the one most fre-

[12] The Ptolemies maintained a patrol fleet on the Nile that eventually came to include units of the royal navy; see M. Rostovtzeff, *Social and Economic History of the Hellenistic World* (Oxford, 1941), 715. They may have had one on the Red Sea in the third century B.C. (Rostovtzeff 387), and they certainly did have a guard of some sort there in the late second century (Strabo 2.98: "guards of the Arabian gulf" pick up a sailor from a wrecked Indian ship). Opinion on whether the practice was continued by Rome is divided; see the literature cited by Raschke 892, n. 957 (pro) and 958 (con), and the discussion—with no resolution—in Sidebotham 68–71. The meaning I offer for *apodedeigmenos* supports the suggestion of C. Starr (*The Roman Imperial Navy* [Cambridge, 1960²], 113) that at least a limited number of ships were kept on patrol in the Red Sea.

[13] For a detailed study of the passage in which Kalliena is mentioned and its historical context, see Casson 1983a = Casson 1984.211–24.

quently put forward as evidence of official regulation. The cautious took it to mean "a market-town established by law."[14] Some went further and took it to mean a port where foreign trade was officially allowed and taxed, while some went further still and took it to mean a port where Rome's government had made special arrangements for its merchants, the equivalent of what the nineteenth century would have called treaty ports.[15]

In a short but conclusive note J. Palmer revealed the weakness of this view. The *Periplus*, he pointed out, lists thirty-seven ports of trade, of which three alone are distinguished as *nomimos*; if only these were, so to speak, "legal," then all the others must have been illegal, or at least irregular, in some way.[16] If only these allowed foreign trade and taxed it, there were opportunities galore to avoid taxes; if only these were treaty ports, it follows that some of the most important entrepôts in Arabia and India, such as Kanê or Barygaza or Muziris, lay outside the sphere of Roman influence. Palmer then brought up another, secondary but well-attested, meaning of *nominos*, namely "law-abiding." This, he concluded, is what it means in the *Periplus*: an *emporion nomimon* was a "law-abiding mart," "a trading-place where law applies, where traders are protected by law"— an expression well applied to Adulis, Muza, and Apologos, two places on the barbarous coasts of Africa and Arabia and a third at the faraway head of the Persian Gulf; despite their location, merchants were assured there of proper enforcement of the law.[17]

Palmer was quite right to emphasize that *nomimos* is used of but three ports of trade out of thirty-seven—three disparate ones at that—and consequently cannot support the conclusions that have been based on it. Yet he failed to see that the very same charge could be made against his own explanation. If an *emporion nomimon* was a port of trade where a merchant enjoyed the protection of the law, why are there only three such? Were traders elsewhere at the mercy of whoever took the law in his own hands? Is it conceivable that there was no law enforcement at Rhapta, where ships willy-nilly had to lay over for eight months?[18] Or at India's great *emporion* of Barygaza, mentioned far more times—twenty-eight—than any other? Or at Muziris, where foreign vessels flocked to pick up precious cargoes of pepper?[19] Palmer was uncomfortably aware that not a single Indian port was classified as "law-abiding" and sought to explain

[14] G. Hourani, *Arab Seafaring* (Princeton, 1951), 32.
[15] See Warmington, Charlesworth, and Wheeler cited in n. 5 above.
[16] Palmer (n. 6 above) 156.
[17] Palmer (n. 6 above) 156–57.
[18] They had to await the turn of the monsoon winds; see App. 3.
[19] Or at Mosyllon, which exported cassia in considerable quantity (10:4.9–10), or Kanê, whose trade connections reached to Persia and India (27:9.10–12)?

the anomaly by arguing that there such protection was taken for granted or, conversely, was not needed.[20] Neither explanation sounds convincing.

I suggest that an *emporion nomimon* was a "legally limited" port, i.e., one whose ruler insisted that all trade pass through his hands or those of his agents, where there was no free bazaar but only an authorized office of trade.[21] The three *emporia nomima* in the *Periplus* were ideally located for this sort of trading, since there were no other ports that could offer opportunity for bypassing: Adulis was the sole port along a long stretch of coast and the only entry to the upland kingdom of Axum; Muza commanded all the trade around the vital straits of Bab el Mandeb now that a possible rival, Eudaimôn Arabia (modern Aden), had been eliminated;[22] and Apologos was the only port available at the head of the Persian Gulf. Of the rest of the thirty-four *emporia* mentioned in the *Periplus*, a certain number were too close to potential competitors for their rulers to think of establishing legal limitations, while certain others dealt chiefly in a single desirable product, which gave the local ruler automatic control.[23] And, finally, some of the ports must have been under rulers who, for one reason or another, were content with a policy of laissez faire.[24]

NATURAL FEATURES

For certain ports the author issues warnings on the poor anchorage they provided. Thus, Ptolemais Thêrôn has no proper harbor (3:1.18), Mosyllon is on a beach off which it is hard to moor (10:4.7–8), Avalitês is a port for simple native craft or for small boats (7:3.15–16), Malaô has an

[20] Palmer (n. 6 above) 157.

[21] Cf. the situation that Jean-Baptiste Labat came across in West Africa in 1698: "c'est une coutume établie chez ces peuples, que le Maître ou Seigneur du Village, avec trois ou quatre principaux Maîtres du chemins, c'est-à-dire les principaux Marchands qui vont traitter dans les pays éloignez, font le prix des marchandises, et que ce qu'ils ont arrêté, est une taxe et une regle que tous les autres suivent sans contestation" (*Nouvelle relation de l'Afrique Occidentale* [Paris, 1728], iii 337–38).

[22] See 26:8.31–32.

[23] E.g., Mosyllon, where the export par excellence was cassia (10:4.9–10), or Kanê or Moscha, where it was frankincense (27:9.8–9, 32:11.3).

[24] Rougé (op. cit. under 5:2.19–20, 409) concludes that an *emporion nomimon* was "l'emporion d'un état plus on moins organisé dont le souverain veille à la sauvegarde du commerce moyennant des dons obligatoires qui ne peuvent être considérés comme les taxes que l'on prélèverait *ad valorem* sur des objets de commerce transitant par un port marchand." To arrive at this conclusion, he must assume that items listed "for the king" aut sim. are gifts and not objects of trade (but cf. under 24:8.7–9) and overlook the fact that neither king nor gifts are mentioned in connection with Apologos, one of the three *emporia nomima*.

open roadstead (8:3.24–25), the Spice Port has an open roadstead that on occasion is dangerous (12:4.21–22), Mundu is merely "fairly safe" (9:4.1–2). Muza has no proper harbor but fortunately offers good mooring (24:7.31–8.1). He rarely notes good quality and then only for very minor ports: Eudaimôn Arabia, now but a third-rate place, offers suitable mooring (26:8.24); Balita, a village near the southern tip of India, has a good harbor (58:19.16–17). He says nothing whatsoever about the quality of the major ports, such as Barygaza or Muziris or Kanê; it apparently goes without saying that these, or any others whose disadvantages are not specifically noted, are safe.

As it happens, the poor ports are all on the African trade route; no port in Arabia or India is among their number. There is good reason for this: the ships they had to accommodate were not the big freighters of the wind-buffeted India run but the smaller, lighter craft of the African run; see App. 3.

IMPORTANCE

The importance of the various ports is automatically revealed by the number of times they receive mention and by the description of the objects of trade they dealt in. Barygaza, for example, mentioned twenty-eight times and handling a long list of imports and exports (49:16.20–31), is unmistakably of ranking importance.

There is yet another, indirect, way in which the author indicates the importance of a given port—by noting, for the benefit of skippers intending a round-trip there (App. 3, n. 15), the proper time for setting out. He does this for Adulis (6:3.4–7), Muza (24:8.11–12), Kanê (28:9.20–21), Barbarikon (39:13.12–13), Barygaza (49:16.31–32), Muziris and the nearby pepper ports (56:18.28–29).

APPENDIX 2.

DISTANCES

The author of the *Periplus* reckons distances between ports or prominent geographical features in stades for the waters nearer Egypt (e.g., down the Red Sea) or waters presumably well known to him (e.g., the south coast of Arabia) and in "runs" (*dromoi*) for those further away (e.g., along the coast of Africa approaching Cape Guardafui and south of it). A "run" is the distance sailed from morning to night, for he specifies (cf. 15:5.25) when he means "day and night."[1]

His figures usually vary, at times considerably, from the true. The reason is not far to seek. The ancients never actually measured distances at sea, for they lacked the means. They did the best they could, which was to make an estimate on the basis of the length of time it took to travel between given points.[2] Their rule of thumb was 1000 stades to a day-and-night run, 500 to a day's run.[3] Assuming the use of the most common stade, that of 600 or so feet,[4] approximately ten stades correspond to a nautical mile.

For short distances, around 2500 stades or less, the author's estimates are rather good, being either exact or at most twenty percent off.

[1] A "run" was limited to a day's sail since, on coasting voyages, particularly along dangerous shores such as those of the Red Sea, it was common practice to travel only during daylight hours and put up at any convenient point for the night. Cf., for example, the voyage of Carsten Niebuhr in 1762 (T. Hansen, *Arabia Felix: The Danish Expedition of 1761–1767* [New York, 1962], 209) and of Alan Villiers in 1938 (*Mariner's Mirror* 47 [1961]: 247). When not coasting vessels perforce sailed night and day. The *Periplus* (20:7.14–16) counsels sailing straight down the middle of the Red Sea to get to Muza, thereby avoiding the pirates as well as the natural hazards of the Arabian coast; that voyage surely was done without a stop.

[2] F. Hultsch, *Griechische und römische Metrologie* (Berlin, 1882), 50–51.

[3] Hultsch 51, n. 1. Cf. Bunbury ii 455, n. 3, where he reckons a thirty-day run as 15,000 stades.

[4] Cf. Bunbury i 546. D. Engels's article, "The Length of Eratosthenes' Stade," *American Journal of Philology* 106 (1985): 298–311, in effect repeats (298) Bunbury's conclusion.

AUTHOR'S DISTANCES FOR SHORT RUNS

Reference	Course	Author's Distance in Stades	Actual Distance in Nautical Miles
4:1.22	length of the gulf near Adulis (Gulf of Zula)	200	20
9:4.1, 10:4.7, 11:4.14–16	Malaô—Cape Elephas (Berbera-Ras Filuch)	3000–3500[5]	345
26:8.22–23	Okêlis-Eudaimôn Arabia (Bab el Mandeb-Aden)	1200	95
27:9.2	Eudaimôn Arabia-Kanê (Aden-Husn al-Ghurab)	2000	205
32:10.27–29, 33:11.8–9	Syagros-Asichôn (Ras Fartak-Ras Hasik)	2600 (600 + 500 + 1500)	230[6]
33:11.12–13	Isles of Zênobios-Isle of Sarapis (Kuria Muria I.-Masirah I.)	2000	235

For long distances around 5000 stades or more, his figures are high, from twenty-five percent to as much as fifty percent.

AUTHOR'S DISTANCES FOR LONG RUNS

Reference	Course	Author's Distance in Stades	Actual Distance in Nautical Miles
3:1.13, 4:1.19–20	Berenicê-Adulis (Foul Bay-Massawa)	7000 (4000 + 3000)	530
5:2.16, 7:3.9	Adulis-Avalitês (Massawa-Assab)	4800 (800 + 4000)[7]	250

[5] The total of 2 + 2 + 2 or 2 + 3 + 2 runs, reckoned at 500 stades each. Mundu-Mosyllon (10:4.6–7) is "two, perhaps three, runs"; this I take to mean two with a normal wind, three with a wind feebler than normal.

[6] Over- and underestimates balance out to yield a more or less correct total; see under 32:10.30a.

[7] The author reports (7:3.9–11) that "after about 4000 stades . . . come the rest of the ports of trade of the Barbaroi." Commentators take this to mean from Adulis; cf. Müller,

| 21:7.21 | Berenicê-Muza (Foul 12000[8] Bay-Mocha) | | 800 |

If we turn from the figures for individual courses to their cumulative totals, we find that for the African trade route, which began at Myos Hormos and ended at Rhapta, the author's under- and overestimates balance out to produce a remarkably accurate result.

AUTHOR'S DISTANCES FOR RUNS
ON THE AFRICAN ROUTE

Reference	Course	Stades	Runs
1:1.3	Myos Hormos-Berenicê	1800	
3:1.13	Berenicê-Ptolemais Thêrôn	4000	
4:1.19–20	Ptolemais Thêrôn-Adulis	3000	
5:2.16	Adulis-a deep bay	800	
7:3.9	a deep bay-Avalitês	4000	
8:3.24	Avalitês-Malaô	800	
9:4.1	Malaô-Mundu		2
10:4.7	Mundu-Mosyllon		2
11:4.14	Mosyllon-Cape Elephas		2
	Cape Elephas-Tabai	not given	
13:5.1	Tabai-Opônê	400	
15:5.19	Opônê-Small and Great Bluffs		6
20	Small and Great Bluffs-Small and Great Beaches		6
23–24	Great Beach-Pyralaoi Islands		7
25	Pyralaoi Islands-Menuthias Island		4[9]
16:6.3	Menuthias Island-Rhapta		2
		14800	31 = 15500

To the above must be added a figure for the stretch for which the author neglected to provide one, from Cape Elephas around the Cape of Spices to Tabai (from Ras Filuch around Cape Guardafui to Ras Hafun, some 120 nautical miles), namely 1200 stades. This would bring the grand total up to 31,500 stades (14800 + 15500 + 1200). The actual distance from Myos Hormos to Rhapta (Abu Sha'r to the vicinity of Dar es

---

McCrindle, Fabricius. Yet the last mention of distance was the 800 stades from Adulis to Hauachil Bay (5:2.16).

[8] The author specifies that the figure is for the direct sail, not along the coast; cf. Bunbury ii 455, n. 3.

[9] Two day-and-night runs = four ordinary runs.

Salaam or to the Rufiji River some seventy-five miles further south) is ca. 3000 nautical miles. This is a mere five percent less.

For the other major trade route, to Arabia and India, the author does not do as well. For the first part of the route to India he supplies a half-dozen figures.

AUTHOR'S DISTANCES FOR THE RUN
FROM BERENICÊ TO SARAPIS

Reference	Course	Stades
21:7.21	Berenicê-Muza	12000
25:8.13	Muza-Okêlis	300
26:8.22–23	Okêlis-Eudaimôn Arabia	1200
27:9.2	Eudaimôn Arabia-Kanê	2000
	Kanê-Syagros	not given
32:10.27–29,	Syagros-Asichôn	2600
33.11.8–9		
33:11.12–13	Isles of Zênobios-Isle of Sarapis	2000
		20,100

If we add in a figure for the stretch he has omitted, Kanê to Sygros (Husn al Ghurab-Ras Fartak, some 250 nautical miles), namely 2500 stades, the grand total comes out to 22,600. The actual distance from Berenicê to the Isle of Sarapis (Foul Bay to Masirah Island) is approximately 1850 nautical miles. As in the case of the African route, he overestimates, but this time by a greater amount, some twenty percent.

Between the Isle of Sarapis (Masirah Island) and the port of Barbarikon (somewhere on the Indus Delta), the author provides (36:12.3–4) but one figure, for the stretch from the mouth of the Persian Gulf to Omana, and this he gives only in runs; he provides nothing for Sarapis to the Persian Gulf or Omana to Barbarikon. For Indian waters, however, he again offers figures and in stades; either he knew these better or, what is more likely, was able to talk with knowledgeable informants, such as resident Western merchants (see Introduction: Trade in the Indian Ocean, The Trade with India). His figures are quite good, considering the length of the distances involved. He states (41:14.11–13) that it is 3000 stades from Barbarikon to Astakapra, i.e., from the mouth of the Indus around the Kathiawar Peninsula and up the Gulf of Cambay to a point opposite Broach. The distance is actually some 450 nautical miles, one-half of his figure greater. He estimates 7000 stades presumably from Astakapra to the end of Limyrikê (51:17.15 and cf. Frisk 79). This is less of an underestimate, since the actual distance from Astakapra to the very tip of the peninsula, Cape Comorin, is some 900 nautical miles, and there is reason to believe (cf. under 51:17.15) that Limyrikê stopped short of the cape. For short distances, in one instance (the width of the Gulf of Cambay; see under 42:14.17) his reckoning is badly off, in another (from the mouth of the Narmada River to Barygaza; see under 44:15.12) pretty accurate.

In a word, when one considers the means he had at his disposal, the author's performance is impressive.[10]

[10] Bunbury was, if anything, overimpressed. He concludes (ii 455, n. 3) that the author's "statements as to distances are generally very correct."

APPENDIX 3.

THE VOYAGES TO AFRICA,

ARABIA, AND INDIA

The *Periplus* deals with two major trade routes originating from the Red Sea ports of Egypt. The first, the African, ran down the Red Sea, through the Straights of Bab el Mandeb, along the African coast of the Gulf of Aden and the Arabian Sea and then along the eastern coast of Africa to Rhapta, which was somewhere in the vicinity of Dar es Salaam (cf. under 16:6.4). The second, the Arabian and Indian, also went down the Red Sea and through the straits but either there or somewhat further along split into two: one branch followed the southern coast of Arabia and then crossed the Arabian Sea to head for the ports of northwest India; the other immediately beyond the straits or soon thereafter took off over open water for the ports of southwest India.

What made both routes possible were the monsoons, the winds of the Arabian Sea and western Indian Ocean that blow from the northeast during the winter months and then conveniently switch to the southwest during the summer. However, the division between the two is not clean and sharp. There are transition periods in spring and autumn as one monsoon comes to a close and the other begins; at such times the wind ceases to be fixed and turns variable until the new monsoon takes hold. Even more important is the difference in nature between the two monsoons. The southwest monsoon is boisterous and stormy; to quote Alan Villiers, who wrote from extensive personal experience, "Rain falls heavily during its continuance, and the weather is usually so bad that the exposed ports on the Indian coast are closed and the smaller trading vessels take shelter. . . . The other monsoon—the northeast—is as gracious, as clear, and as balmy as a permanent trade, and it is this wind which wafts the great dhows—the argosies of Araby—on their long voyages from the Persian Gulf to Zanzibar and beyond, and which blows the Indian dhows from

283

Chart of Prevailing Winds from the Red Sea to East Africa and India

	A June to August	B September	C October	D November to December	E December to March	F April	G May
1 Red Sea south of 20° N	N, NW	N, NW shifting to variable	S, SE	S, SE			S,SE shifting to N, NE
2 Gulf of Aden	S, SW, W		variable, shifting to E, ENE	E, ENE			E, ENE also variables
3 East African Coast to Zanzibar	S, SW	S, SW shifting to NE with variables and calms		N, NE		NE shifting to S, SW	
4 North-western Coast of India	SW	W, SW with variables and calms	S, SW shifting to NE	N, NE		NW to SW	S, SW
5 South-western Coast of India	SW	W, SW shifting to W, NW	light northerlies	N, NE		NW to SW	S, SW

the Malabar coast to Mombasa and the Madagascar coast."[1] Last, the Red Sea, which had to be traversed going and coming, had its own wind pattern which does not totally coincide with the monsoons. The accompanying chart shows what the winds in general are, month by month, in the areas under consideration.[2]

Presumably the vessels that made these monsoon passages were the same types that plied the Mediterranean. This certainly must have been true for the passage to India since it involved the rough winds and waters of the southwest monsoon, and the Mediterranean seagoing freighters of the age were particularly well suited for such work. Not only were they big—the largest were well over 1,000 tons burden—but they boasted

---

[1] *Monsoon Seas* (New York, 1952), 7.

[2] For the monsoons, see U.S. Defense Mapping Agency, Hydrographic Center Pub. 61, *Sailing Directions for the Red Sea and Gulf of Aden* (5th ed. 1965, rev. 1976) section 1–26 to 28 (Red Sea), 1–29 to 31 (Gulf of Aden); Pub. 60, *Sailing Directions for the Southeast Coast of Africa* (5th ed. 1968, rev. 1975) section 1–23; Pub. 63, *Sailing Directions for the West Coast of India* (5th ed. 1967, rev. 1976) section 1–26 to 27.

massively strong hulls whose planking was held together by thousands of close-set mortise and tenon joints, a method of construction unique to Greek and Roman shipwrights. Their rig, too, made for safety, its major component being a vast broad square sail on a relatively short mainmast; it was, however, slow and only effective with a following wind.[3] The Arab dhows that sail to India today and have for centuries are less limited; with their lateen sails they can travel against the wind but, being much feebler in construction than ancient craft, only against a light one.[4]

Although the two trade routes were approximately the same length, some 3,000 nautical miles, and took place in roughly the same waters and with the same winds, because of other factors they were totally unlike. To India and back could be done within a year but involved considerable danger. To Africa and back took twice as long but was a sailor's dream.

THE VOYAGE TO AFRICA

Ships heading for Africa left Egypt in July (14:5.7–8). This enabled a skipper to travel from Egypt to the Gulf of Aden with the favorable northerlies (Chart 1 A) and through the Gulf of Aden with the favorable southwest monsoon (Chart 2 A).

In the Red Sea, because of its dangerous shoals, vessels that follow the coast sail only during the day, putting in towards nightfall at the nearest available anchorage.[5] Consequently, even if they traveled steadily, getting quickly in and out of the ports they stopped at, they still would have required over thirty days to reach Cape Guardafui.[6] In any event, there

---

[3] *SSAW* 183–90 (size of Mediterranean freighters), 201–8 (hull structure), 239–43 (rig).

[4] Thus Ibn Mājid, author of a treatise on navigation published towards the end of the 15th century, cautions that, in certain crossings from the south coast of Arabia to the island of Socotra, "they do not travel . . . unless the wind is light because they are travelling contrary to the Kaws [southwest wind]" (G. Tibbets, *Arab Navigation in the Indian Ocean before the Coming of the Portuguese*, Oriental Translation Fund, New Series xlii [London, 1971], 229). A few lines later he speaks of a " 'wind of two sails' also needing a light wind"; a "wind of two sails" was a course not even involving a head wind but just a wind on the beam, its name deriving from the fact that one would sail with it on one side and then, returning, on the other (Tibbets 369). Alan Villiers (op. cit. under 13:5.3, 26, 30, 48–49) describes a voyage in a dhow during which they beat for 500 miles along the south coast of Arabia; it was against breezes so mild that the ship often merely ghosted along and was frequently becalmed.

[5] App. 2, n. 1.

[6] Ancient ships could make between four and six knots with a fair wind (*SSAW* 288) and thus log roughly 50 nautical miles during a day's run, and indeed 500 stades, the equivalent of 50 nautical miles, was the ancients' standard figure for the length of a day's run (see App. 2). Guillain (i 96–97) estimated 48 for the first part of the journey down the east coast of

was no sense in arriving there before the onset of the northeast monsoon in October; a better time yet was mid-October or the beginning of November when it had definitely settled in (Chart 3 C/D).[7] Until then the southwest monsoon was still blowing, and even more efficient sailing craft than the ancients' square-riggers could not have beat down the coast of East Africa against it.[8] The *Periplus* mentions (14:5.13–14) that some ships tramped, selling and buying cargo at points along the way, while others made directly for the incense ports of the African horn. They all must have traveled leisurely, taking from seventy-five days (say, July 15 to October 1) to over one hundred (July 15 to November 1) to reach Cape Guardafui. Once there, as we shall see in a moment, there was no need whatsoever to hurry.

The next stage, from Guardafui southward, was not only smooth sailing but quick, with the northeast monsoon at a vessel's heels (Chart 3 D). The distance is some 1400 nautical miles and current is favorable as well as wind.[9] The voyage, during which vessels could sail day and night (cf. 15:5.25), might have lasted but two weeks, but we must, of course, allow for stops en route.

Thus arrival at Rhapta, in the vicinity of Dar es Salaam, would have taken place in November or December. Now, once there, a skipper was committed to spending no less than eight months in the area. The earliest he could possibly leave, and then only if he intended to dawdle on his way up the African coast, was August. For he had to time his voyage so that he would sail from Rhapta to Guardafui no later than September-October in order to catch the end of the southwest monsoon (Chart 3 B/C), reach Guardafui not before October in order to catch the early northeast monsoon that would provide favorable winds for traversing the Gulf of Aden

Africa and 60 for the second, the difference caused by variation in the strength of the current (cf. n. 9 below). The distance from Myos Hormos to Cape Guardafui is ca. 1600 nautical miles.

[7] As Ibn Mājid puts it (n. 4 above, 234), "Those who travel from Aden and Yemen to Zanj [the African coast off Zanzibar] should start on the 320th or the 330th day [8 or 18 October]." Cf. Guillain i 95: "La mousson de l'est se fait sentir [in the Gulf of Aden] dans la première quinzaine d'octobre, et les bateaux qui vont à l'est de ce cap [Guardafui] doivent avoir dépassé son méridien avant le 1ᵉʳ novembre."

[8] Cf. the rueful words of a British naval commander who in 1799 tried to sail a full-rigged ship against the even milder northeast monsoon: "Thus terminated one of the most perplexing and tedious Voyages ever made by any Ships. It is, I believe, the first Attempt ever made to beat up the *Coast of Africa* against the *Easterly Monsoon*, and it is to be hoped Nobody would ever attempt it again" (A. Bissell, *A Voyage from England to the Red-Sea and along the East Coast of Arabia to Bombay . . . 1798 and 1799* [London, 1806], 47).

[9] Cf. Guillain i 96: one and one-half knots of current as far as some sixty miles south of Ras Asswad (4°34′N), two to three from there on.

(Chart 2 C), and catch favorable winter southerlies in the Red Sea (Chart 1 C/D).[10]

If we allow for the sail from Guardafui to Egypt the same amount of time as on the outbound voyage, over thirty days, he would arrive home in November or December, a year and a half after his departure. This left six months or so to collect a cargo for another venture to the area the next July. In effect, two years were required for a round trip.

It was the dogleg into the Gulf of Aden that caused the trouble, the need, after sailing north to Cape Guardafui, to make an abrupt left turn and head west. Ships returning from the East African coast to the Persian Gulf or to India had a straight run and hence could depart with the on-coming of the monsoon in April, after a layover that might be as short as three months.[11] Today dhows bound for the Red Sea may leave with them, taking advantage of the fact that in May the winds of the Gulf of Aden are not yet firmly locked into the southwesterly direction they will have in June but offer some variation.[12] This option was not open to a skipper of an ancient craft with its square rig, slower and less flexible than a dhow's. He could not leave until mid-April or so[13] and, if the variables in the gulf held him up,[14] he might not reach the Straits of Bab el Mandeb

[10] This is the way the ship that carried Henry Salt from Zanzibar to Aden in 1809 did it; see Salt 94–99. The southwest monsoon carried them north to Cape Guardafui by 27 September, then a light wind typical of the transition period and adverse current prevented progress all of the 28th, after which the northeast monsoon wafted them to Aden by the 3d of October. Zanzibar was by no means the only place where the alternation of monsoons could cause long layovers. "Because of the Azyab [northeast monsoon] . . . he who is forced to moor in Yemen," states Ibn Mājid (Tibbets, n. 4 above, 227), "must stay there a whole year when bound for India" (from October, when the northeast monsoon sets in, until September of the following year, when the southwest monsoon has quieted down sufficiently to allow a safe passage and arrival [cf. n. 18 below]).

[11] Alan Villiers traveled on a dhow from the Persian Gulf that arrived at Zanzibar in February, which was late since others had arrived in January, and left on 15 April (op. cit. under 13:5.3, 206, 269). Arrival in January and departure in April is standard practice; cf. A. Prins, "The Persian Gulf Dhows," *Persica* 2 (1965–66): 1–18 at 5–6. Cf. Bissell (above, n. 8) 35: "The small *Trading Vessels* from Muscat, and the Red Sea, after discharging their Cargoes, which is chiefly *Dates*, always *dismantle*, and *move* into an *Inner Harbour*, at the *back* of the *town*, and wait the *return* of the [southwest] *Monsoon*."

[12] Cf. Datoo (op. cit. under 16:6.4) 67.

[13] Vessels could not leave Rhapta until the southwest monsoon had established itself, and this might be well into April; cf. Bissell (n. 8 above) 37: "They [the locals of Zanzibar] ridiculed the *Idea* of our going away, before the SW Monsoon set in, and said we should be plagued with *Calms* and *Variable Winds*, with *Southerly Currents* till the *Middle* of *April*."

[14] Dhows generally shun the Gulf of Aden during May precisely because the winds then cannot be trusted; cf. Ibn Mājid's statement quoted above, n. 10, and the observations of a naval officer who visited Berbera in 1848: "From April to the early part of October, the place was utterly deserted . . . ; but no sooner did the season change, than . . . small craft

until the end of May—just when the wind would turn against him in the Red Sea (Chart 1 G). Besides, even if he was lucky enough to have a fair passage all the way, he would arrive no earlier than June, and this would hardly leave time to unload, refit, and take on a new cargo for departure in July. By lingering in Rhapta until the closing days of the southwest monsoon, he would be assured of fair and moderate winds all the way and plenty of time to prepare for a new round trip.

Had the vessels that started from Myos Hormos or Berenicê gone only as far as Africa's horn, leaving the long leg to Rhapta to others, such as the Arab craft that traded with that port (16:6.10–12), they could easily have done the voyage within half a year, outbound in July-September (Chart 1 A/B, 2 A/B) and homebound in October-December (2 C/D, 1 C/D). And certain remarks that the author drops make it clear that not all ships left Egypt to go the African route to the very end. There unquestionably were some that went only as far as Adulis and then turned back.[15] So it is very likely that some skippers would take advantage of the conditions so favorable to a quick turn-around-and-return and schedule voyages only up to the horn. However, the fact that the author not only provides a detailed account of the voyage right down to Rhapta but treats Rhapta as a major port of trade, listing both its imports and exports, makes it clear that vessels from Roman Egypt regularly went this far.

Though the voyage was long for these vessels, it was easy, since all of it took place under ideal sailing conditions. Outward bound, the leg through the Gulf of Aden was done during the closing days of the southwest monsoon when it had lost much of its bite, and the leg down the

---

from the ports of Yemen . . . hastened across, followed, about a fortnight to three weeks later, by their larger brethren from Muscat, Soor, and Ras el Khyma. . . . By the end of March . . . , craft of all kinds . . . commence their homeward journey. By the first week of April the place is again deserted" (*Journal of the Royal Geographical Society* 19 [1849]: 54–55; also quoted by Richard Burton in his *First Footsteps in East Africa* [London, 1856], 225–26).

[15] The author remarks that most vessels heading for Adulis, the port on the west coast of the Red Sea, left Egypt between January and September, preferably in September (6:3.4–7). This makes sense only for the round trip, Egypt-Adulis-Egypt: ships sailed south with the last of the Red Sea northerlies (Chart 1 B) and thus were able to return with the first of the southerlies in October (1 C). Similarly, on the India route, skippers headed for Muza left in September (24:8.11–12), and those headed for the more distant Kanê a little earlier than September (28:9.20–21). These dates make sense only for the round trip, Egypt-Muza-Egypt and Egypt-Kanê-Egypt.

In the well-known papyrus document (*SB* 7169, early 2d century B.C.) involving a loan to finance a voyage to Somalia, the loan was for one year, which U. Wilcken, the editor, suggests, was suitable for the round trip (*Zeitschrift für aegyptische Sprache* 60 [1925]: 94; cf. R. Bogaert in *Chronique d'Égypte* 40 [1965]: 149). Indeed it was. The outbound voyage could have started anytime between June and August (Chart 1 A, 2 A) and the homebound voyage between November and March (Chart 2 D/E, 1 D/E).

coast of East Africa under the mild northeast monsoon. Homeward bound, the leg back up the coast took place during the closing days of the southwest monsoon and the traversing of the Gulf of Aden during the opening days of the northeast monsoon. Indeed, the voyage is so undemanding that till recently merchants entrusted their goods, and passengers their lives, to "almost incredibly small and decrepit" vessels that were so hopelessly overcrowded that they could not possibly have survived even the slightest storm at sea.[16]

The Voyage to India

Ships left Egypt for India, as for Africa, in July (39:13.12–13, 49:16.31–32, 56:18.28–29). They did so for the same reasons, to take advantage of the summer northerlies in the Red Sea (Chart 1 A) in order to get down to its exit at Bab el Mandeb and of the southwest monsoon (Chart 2 A) in order to get out of the Gulf of Aden. And, carried by the southwest monsoon, they sailed over open water either to the mouth of the Indus River or Barygaza (on the Gulf of Cambay) on India's northwest coast or to Muziris on the southwest coast (57:19.7–12).[17] The voyage from the straits to Muziris, in round numbers some 2000 nautical miles, should have taken about twenty days.[18]

The return was no problem: departure was in December-January (Pliny 6.106) and this meant that it took place during the benign northeast monsoon (Chart 4 D/E, 5 D/E). And, since this lasted from November to April, one could shove off even earlier or later. But there was no leeway for the outbound voyage; that had to be timed as carefully as the homebound voyage from Rhapta that we discussed a moment ago. So far as

[16] Villiers (op. cit. under 13:5.3) 141–42; see also 154–55, 282. Carsten Niebuhr describes the overcrowding and haphazard stowage of cargo on the ship that carried him from Suez to Jiddah in 1762 and remarks that travelers trusted themselves to such craft only because of the dependable weather in the Red Sea (op. cit. under 22:7.24, i 256–57).

[17] The direct sail to India could take off from Okêlis on the Straits of Bab el Mandeb (see under 25:8.20). Or it could take off further along, at Kanê (57:19.7) or Syagros (Pliny 6.101) or even at Cape Guardafui (57:19.8).

[18] Ships leaving in July would start their leg from the straits or other points in the Gulf of Aden in August and thus be carried along by the southwest monsoon just when that strong wind was blowing its hardest, averaging twenty or thirty knots or even more, in the waters between the horn of Africa and the southwest coast of India (*Sailing Directions for the . . . Gulf of Aden* [n. 2 above], section 1–31). With favorable winds ancient sailing craft were capable of four to six knots (n. 6 above). Dhows frequently make the voyage in twenty days (G. Van Beek in *JAOS* 80 [1960]: 139); though faster than ancient ships, they must sail when the winds are more moderate. Pliny's figure of forty days (6.104) is a palpable error; see Casson 1980a.32–33 (= Casson 1984.190–91).

winds were concerned, leaving the Red Sea ports in June might seem as good as July (Chart 1 A, 2 A, 4 A, 5 A). But there was more to be considered than the direction of the wind. Departure in June would bring a vessel to India's shores in August—and that was to be avoided at all cost. During most of the summer, sailing conditions on India's west coast are so dangerous that practically all maritime activity ceases. This is particularly true of the southwestern coast, where Muziris lay. At present in this area the marine insurance rates, which vary between one and one and three-quarters percent during the northeast monsoon, rise to twenty percent by the end of May when the southwest monsoon has set in, and during June, July, and August, marine insurance is simply not available at any price. By September it is again offered at the fairly reasonable rate of two and one-half percent.[19] It follows that ancient vessels must have left their Red Sea ports in July and not before in order to reach the coast of India no earlier than September, when the southwest monsoon was approaching its end and beginning to quiet down. Arrival anytime later, in October, was inadvisable since it would have exposed ships to the contrary winds of the northeast monsoon (Chart 4 C, 5 C).

Thus the skippers who plied between Roman Egypt and India were not foolhardy: by delaying their departure until July, they avoided India's coast when it was most dangerous. But they still had to carry out a good part of their ocean crossing during the time when the southwest monsoon was blowing its hardest, often stirring up violent storms. From the writings of Arab navigators of the late fifteenth and early sixteenth century we know that in that age Arab skippers also used the southwest monsoon, but delayed departure until the end of August and the beginning of September when it was beginning to slacken. They were able to do so since their ships were either fast enough to reach India before the coming of the northeast monsoon or, failing that, with their lateen rigs could sail against the feeble breezes of its early stages.[20] The ancients did not have this al-

[19] The 15th- and 16th-century Arab writers on navigation took it for granted that most of the ports on India's west coast were closed from May to July and practically all of them in June and July (Tibbetts, n. 4 above, 367–68). For closing during August and in places even later, see Deloche (op. cit. under 48:16.12–13) ii 215–16. On the marine insurance, see Deloche 215 and R. Bowen, "The Dhow Sailor," *The American Neptune* 11 (1951): 5–46 at 12.

[20] The Arab navigators recommend departing for India as follows (Tibbetts, n. 4 above, 365): from Zeila and Berbera on 24 or 25 August, from Aden between 24 and 29 August (although Ibn Mājid will allow up to 18 September), from Shihr or Mishqās or Zafar (on the south coast of Arabia roughly 300, 400, and 600 miles respectively east of Aden) on 3 September or 14 September or (Ibn Mājid again) 8 October. These are consistently later than the ancients' departure date. This is understandable. The later one left, the weaker were the winds of the southwest monsoon that were encountered and the safer the crossing, a

ternative. As the author of the *Periplus* puts it (39:13.13–14), "The crossing with these [southwest winds] is hard going but absolutely favorable and shorter."

In sum, the two areas of trade were totally different in the demands they made on both shipowners and merchants. A venture to Africa was safe, cheap, and involved only short coastal hauls. Consequently it was open to owners of craft of no great size, on which they had expended no great amount of money for upkeep, carriers that were the ancient equivalent of the "incredibly small and decrepit" dhows Alan Villiers saw making the very same run, whose scant cargo space might be divided up for charter to a clutch of small-time traders. The ports these vessels put in at, most of them with no proper harbor but just open roads,[21] not only are like those that the "small and decrepit" dhows use today but testify to the fact that ancient skippers were able to count on the same benign weather conditions that skippers of such dhows count on. Neither the owners of ships that plied the African route, nor the merchants whose goods were aboard, were much concerned about storms at sea. However, though the stakes were safe, for those who squeezed out all they could by going the whole way, two long years had to pass before there were any profits to pocket.

On the other hand, ventures to India—at least the ones our sources consider the most important, those that exploited the direct crossing over open water—were just the reverse. It took only a year for the capital invested to yield a return. But the amount of capital required was formidable, and there was a definite element of risk. Such trading opportunities were open only to the owners of powerful vessels able to endure the force of the southwest monsoon and to the merchants with the money to purchase enough of the costly goods India exported—spices, silks, and the like—to fill the capacious holds.[22] The India trade was for large-scale operators, whether shipowners or traders.

---

crucial consideration for Arab craft, whose mode of construction was far feebler than the Greco-Roman (cf. Hornell [op. cit. under 27:9.9] 234–35). The same departure dates prevail today; see Van Beek, n. 18 above, 139 (*pace* Raschke [937], who accuses him of not saying exactly what he does say).

[21] See App. 1, "Natural Features."

[22] The author counsels (20:7.11–16) ships headed for the south coast of Arabia or for India to avoid the shoals and pirates of the Arabian coast of the Red Sea by holding a course down its center—a straight run of almost 800 nautical miles. He surely has in mind the big merchantmen that sailed on to India with the southwest monsoon. On the value of the cargoes they carried, see Introduction: Trade in the Indian Ocean, The Traders: Africa versus India.

APPENDIX 4.

THE TERMS FOR CLOTH

AND CLOTHING

In the *Periplus othonion*, in the singular in ten instances and the plural in two, is used generically: "cloth," "types of cloth." In one case (24:8.4) *othonion* is included among various textiles and clothing imported by Arabia presumably from Egypt, and so must refer to cloth perhaps of wool but more probably of linen (cf. below). Twice (56:18.24, 64:21.14) it is qualified as *Sêrikon*, "Chinese," and so must refer to silk, and very likely it refers to silk in yet two other instances (see under B 39:13.11, B 49:16.30). In the remaining seven instances it appears among items exported from India, and in three of these is actually distinguished as "Indian cloth" (6:3.1, 31:10.23, 41:14.6). That "Indian cloth" is cotton is clear from 41:14.6, where the author remarks that Ariakê produces much "cotton (*karpasos*) and the Indian cloths made from it."

Most of the cotton cloth that India exported was of relatively cheap quality. In some cases this is specifically indicated: the cloth that came from Ariakê was the "ordinary" (*chydaios*) grade (41:14.6) and so was that brought from Ozênê (48:16.15–16) and Tagara (51:17.13) to Barygaza for export. So too must have been the "cloth, the *monachê* and *sagmatogênê*" imported by the "far-side" ports (14:5.11–12) and Adulis (6:3.1–2); it came from Ariakê and, as we have just noted, Ariakê's production was of a cheap grade (cf. under B 14:5.11–12). The *othonion* that Socotra imported (31:10.23) must have been the cheap grade as well, since the island was a poor, out-of-the-way place and its other imports from India—rice and grain—were merely staples. But India's export must have included some cotton of superior quality, since the author notes that Barygaza shipped out "cloth of all kinds" (49:16.29), and these kinds presumably included better grades along with the "ordinary" grades collected from Ozênê and Tagara.

The term *sindones*, always in the plural and always among the exports from India, are "garments of cotton" (6:3.3, 48:16.15, 51:17.13, 59:20.2, 61:20.19, 62:20.22, 63:21.5). In Egypt and elsewhere *sindôn* usually means a garment of linen rather than cotton. However, both Theophrastus (*H.P.* 4.7.7) and Strabo (15.693) use the word of garments of cotton and, in any event, linen was what Egypt exported to India (Pliny 19.7), not imported from there. As it happens, linen was not particularly favored for textiles in India (cf. L. Gopal, "Textiles in Ancient India," *JESHO* 4 [1961]: 53–69, esp. 56–58) whereas cotton was (Herodotus 3.106, 7.65; Gopal 60–61; D. Schlingloff, "Cotton-Manufacture in Ancient India," *JESHO* 17 [1974]: 81–90). Cotton, to be sure, grew in Egypt and Nubia and was spun into cloth locally (Lucas-Harris [op. cit. under 1:1.2–4] 147–48, Raschke 651) but the products from India were no doubt of better quality.[1]

The word *himatia* occurs twice, meaning "articles of clothing" ("articles of clothing for the Barbaroi" 6:2.23, 7:3.17). Much more frequent is *himatismos*, "clothing": "Arab sleeved clothing" 24:8.2; "expensive clothing" (for the king) 24:8.8, "Arab" 28:9.14; "with common adornment or no adornment or of printed fabric" 28:9.15; "fine-quality with no adornment" (for the king) 28:9.18; "native" 36:12.11; "with no adornment" and "of printed fabric" 39:13.7, 49:16.22; "expensive with no adornment" (for the king) 49:16.27; "with no adornment" 56:18.18.

With one exception the clothing was exported from Egypt. This means it was either of linen or wool, more likely linen in the light of Pliny's remark (19.7) that Egypt grew flax in order to import the products of Arabia and India. It included at least some items purposely manufactured for the export trade: "articles of clothing for the Barbaroi" (6:2.23, 7:3.17); "Arab clothing" (24:8.2, 28:9.14). The single exception is the "native clothing" of Apologos and Omana that was exported to Barygaza and Arabia (36:12.11).

---

[1] Two varieties of cotton were known in the Old World, *Gossypium arboreum* and *Gossypium herbaceum*, both of which grew in India. Warmington (210) asserts that the first produced a cotton useful only for padding. According to the manuals, however, there is no distinction in quality between the two; see A. Doberczak, St. Dowgielewicz, and W. Zurek, *Cotton, Bast and Wool Fibers* (Warsaw, 1964), 16.

APPENDIX 5.

INDIA'S WEST COAST,

FROM BOMBAY TO

CAPE COMORIN

For this stretch of coastline the author provides a list of seventeen, or perhaps eighteen, ports of trade or harbors.[1] Unfortunately, he supplies very little detail and, save for one place,[2] gives no indication of distance, so it is extremely difficult to identify them. Ptolemy is of scant help, since his sites often do not coincide and, in addition, he omits some of the *Periplus's* listings (or gives them different names) and shifts the position of others.[3] A further complication is that extensive changes have taken place in the coastline.[4]

---

[1] 53:17.22–27 (Sêmylla, Mandagora, Palaipatmai, Melizeigara, Byzantion, Toparon [?], Tyrannosboas, Sêsekreienai Islands, Isle of the Aigidioi, Isle of the Kaineitoi, White Island, Naura, Tyndis, Muziris, Nelkynda [-Bakarê]); 58:19.13–18 (Red Mountain, Balita, Komar). On the querying of Toparon, see under B 53:17.23–24; O. Stein, *RE* s.v. *Toparon* 2 (1937), taking it for a proper reading, locates it at Devgarh (16°23′).

[2] 54:18.2–5: Tyndis is 500 stades before Muziris and Nelkynda 500 after it.

[3] Ptolemy (7.1.7) immediately after Byzantion lists "the Peninsula," omitting all the names that the *Periplus* puts between the two. Perhaps some or all of the Sêsekreienai Islands, the Isle of the Aigidioi, and the Isle of the Kaineitoi are included under his entry Heptanêsia ("Seven Islands," 7.1.95), although the coordinates he gives for it would indicate otherwise (cf. the map in Berthelot [op. cit. under 40:13.20–22] opp. p. 312). He omits Red Mountain. He places (7.1.6–7) Balipatna (= Palaipatmai) before Mandagara (= Mandagora), and his coordinates (7.1.95) for Milizêgyris (= Melizeigara) make it an island twenty miles off the coast south of Sêmylla (cf. McCrindle [op. cit. under 62:20.23–24] 57). The *Periplus's* Balita is probably the same as his Bambala (7.1.9).

[4] Cf. K. Padmanabha Menon, "Discursive Notes on Malabar and its Place-Names," *Indian Antiquary* 31 (1902): 338–50 at 339–40; P. Thomas, "Roman Trade Centers on the Malabar Coast," *The Journal of the Madras Geographical Association* (= *Indian Geographical Journal*) 6 (1931): 230–40 at 239–40. For example, in 1341 an extraordinary flood, by silting up the

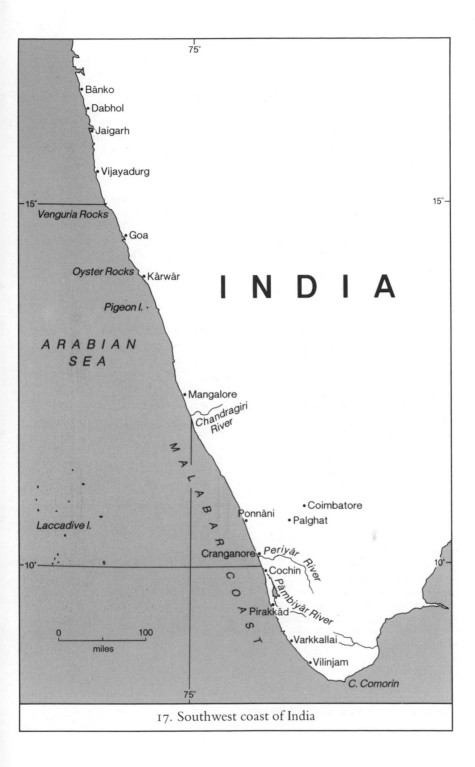

17. Southwest coast of India

Numerous suggestions have been offered for the location of the various sites.[5] Those in Table 1, except for the names in italics, are Schoff's, by and large the most plausible.

Five names—Sêmylla, Muziris, Bakarê, Red Mountain, Komar—can be identified with more confidence than the others. There is little doubt about the first site, Sêmylla (see under 53:17.22), and none about the last, Komar, which has to be Cape Comorin. Muziris, which shared with Nelkynda the distinction of being one of the two key ports of the Malabar coast,[6] is securely located, thanks to mention in Tamil literature: a poem that manifestly describes events of the early post-Christian centuries includes a passage which talks of

> the city where the beautiful vessels, the masterpieces of the Yavanas [Westerners], stir white foam on the Periyār, river of Kerala, arriving with gold and departing with pepper—when that Muçiri, brimming with prosperity, was besieged by the din of war.[7]

The poem not only names Muziris but conveniently locates it—at the mouth of the Periyār. This now empties into the sea at 10°11′N, but in ancient times its mouth was a little further north, where Crānganūr (Cranganore) stands.[8] Crānganūr, in other words, marks the site of ancient Muziris.

---

mouth of the Periyār River and opening an estuary at Cochin which made that city into a fine port, hastened the end of Cranganore's days as a major port and led to Cochin's rise; see Padmanabha Menon 339 and G. Woodcock, *Kerala* (London, 1967), 42.

[5] Not only in the commentaries of translators and editors but also in the various entries in *RE*. Since this voluminous work took almost a century to complete, the entries are the work of several scholars who unfortunately seem to have made no effort to coordinate their conclusions. For example, in connection with Muziris, A. Herrmann, s.v. *Musiris*, puts it at Cannamore; in the very same volume (16, 1935), O. Stein, s.v. *Nelkynda*, puts it at Cranganore. W. Tomaschek, s.v. Αἰγιδίων νῆσος (1894), puts that island at Goa, while Herrmann, s.v. Καινειτῶν νῆσος (1919), puts that at Goa. Stein, s.v. Νάουρα (1933), is dubious about its location, with some slight leaning in favor of Mangalore; H. Treidler, s.v. *Poduke* (1951), puts it at Honawar.

[6] Pliny (6.104) notes its importance, as does the *Periplus* (53:17.27–28). The *Tabula Peutingeriana* indicates the presence at Muziris of a temple to Augustus (see Levi, op. cit. under 51:17.15, section 5 of segment xi); this implies the existence of a sizeable permanent foreign colony (cf. Introduction: Trade in the Indian Ocean, The Trade with India).

[7] Meile 90–92. Although the term Yavanas can mean Westerners in general, in this context—Westerners who sail in with gold and leave with pepper—it can only refer to merchants from Roman Egypt (cf. Meile 102). The poems themselves—at least the earliest, from which the passages in question are drawn—date from the second to third century A.D.; see G. Hart in Stein (op. cit. under 60:20.6b) 41.

[8] Meile 95. On the change in the course of the river, see n. 4 above. A small excavation carried out at Koḍuṅgalūr (Cranganore) uncovered Chinese and Arab wares but no Roman; see C. Maloney in Stein (op. cit. under 60:20.6b) 28.

TABLE I
IDENTIFICATION OF THE PORTS
LISTED SOUTH OF BOMBAY

Name	Location	Latitude	Distance in Nautical Miles to the Next Port
Sêmylla	Chaul	18°34'	35
Mandagora	Bānkot	17°58'	24
Palaipatmai	Dābhol	17°36'	18
Melizeigara	Jaigarh	17°17'	50
Byzantion	Vijayadurg	16°34'	40 (to Sês. I.)
Toparon (?)			
Tyrannosboas			
Sêsekreienai Islands	Vengurla Rocks (also called Burnt I.)	15°52'	35
Isle of the Aigidioi	Goa	15°28'	40
Isle of the Kaineitoi (near "the Peninsula"	Oyster Rocks Kārwār	14°49' 14°48')	50
White Island	Pigeon I.	14°1'	75
Naura	*Mangalore*	12°52'	135
Tyndis	Ponnāni	10°46'	39
Muziris	Cranganore	10°13'	55
Nelkynda/Bakarê	*Niranom*-Pirakkād	9°21'	43
Red Mountain	Varkkallai	8°44'	27
Balita	*Vilinjam*	8°22'	40
Komar	Cape Comorin	8°5'	

The locating of Muziris provides clues for Tyndis and Nelkynda, since the first was 500 stades before it and the second 500 after. Schoff puts Tyndis at Ponnāni, which is somewhat short of 500 stades, while others put it at Kadalundi near Beypore (11°10'N), which is somewhat over; the odds are slightly in favor of Ponnāni.[9] Nelkynda, which is said to be on

[9] Tyndis is usually connected with Toṇḍi mentioned in Tamil literature as an important center (see Pillai [op. cit. under 51:17.15] 137, 157, 178; A. Sreedhara Menon, *A Survey of Kerala History* [Kottayam, 1967], 60, who cites an illuminating passage). The various attempts to locate the site of Tyndis/Toṇḍi are reviewed by O. Stein, *RE* s.v. Τύνδις 2 (1948), who cautiously reserves judgment. One factor in favor of Ponnāni is that it is the port nearest the great gap, twenty miles wide, through the ghats at Palghat which provides easy access to Coimbatore and across to the eastern coast. The route for traffic between the two sides of the peninsula, a route that eliminated the long sail around the tip, must have gone this way in ancient times as in modern. See W. Logan, *Malabar* (Madras, 1887), i 3, 77.

the river Baris, must be considered together with its harbor, Bakarê, which lay 120 stades downriver at the mouth.[10] Schoff identifies Nelkynda with Kottayam (9°35′N, 76°31′E) on the Minachil River and Bakarê with Pirakkād on the coast (9°21′N). But this puts them on two different streams, for the Pāmbiyār, and not the Minachil, flows past Pirakkād; moreover, Kottayam is a good deal further away from Pirakkād than 120 stades. The suggestion that Nelkynda was Niranom (Neranom), which is about 500 stades from Muziris and which is on the Pāmbiyār twelve miles east of Pirakkād, at least puts the port of trade and its harbor on the same stream and the proper distance from each other. Niranom was important enough to be one of the seven sites in southern India where, according to Indian tradition, the Apostle Thomas founded churches.[11] Another possibility is raised by the existence of at least two towns called Nilgunda,[12] a name that could easily have come out as Nelkynda on a foreigner's lips. Perhaps there was yet another whose name has survived only in this passage of the *Periplus*.

Another site fairly securely located is that which follows Bakarê, the Red Mountain. This surely refers to the red cliffs along the coast before and after Anjengo.[13]

Schoff placed Naura at Cannamore (11°52′N), with little to offer in support of his choice besides a vague similarity in name. A better argument can be made for connecting Naura with Naravu, the Tamil name for a town that seems to have been where Mangalore now stands (12°52′N).[14] He put Balita more or less by guesswork at Varkkallai

[10] The various attempts at identification are reviewed by O. Stein in *RE* s.v. *Nelkynda* (1935).

[11] For Nelkynda = Niranom, see Iyengār (op. cit. under 50:17.2) 458; Thomas (op. cit. n. 4 above) 236–38. For Niranom and St. Thomas, see P. Thoma, "The South Indian Tradition of the Apostle Thomas," *Centenary Supplement to the Journal of the Royal Asiatic Society of Great Britain and Ireland* (London, 1924), 213–23, at 216–17, 219. The town is not indicated on modern maps, even on that done on the scale of 1:250,000. Thomas (op. cit. n. 4 above, 238) describes it as being twelve miles east of Pirakkād, which would put it approximately 9°22′N, 76°32′E.

[12] One near Bombay and the other further south (14°44′N, 75°57′E); see *Epigraphia Indica* 12 (1913–14): 142, 148.

[13] See Hobson-Jobson, s.v. *Red Cliffs*: "The nautical name of the steep coast below Quilon [8°53′N]. This presents the only bluffs on the shore from Mt. Dely [Dilli, 12°1′N] to Cape Comorin, and is thus identified, by character and name, with the Πυῤῥὸν ὄρος of the *Periplus*." Cf. *WCIP* 85; describing the coast between Trivandrum (8°29′N) and Anjengo, it states: "Patches of red tableland, when seen from beyond about 7 miles, appear as red cliffs above the fringe of palms along this coast. . . . The coast N of Anjengo extends, with an aspect similar to that S of it, . . . to Tangasseri Point [8°53′]."

[14] See Pillai (op. cit. under 51:17.15) 137. Pillai further argues that Ptolemy's Nitraiai (7.1.7 = the Nitriae of Pliny 6.104), which the geographer lists just before Tyndis, is an-

(8°44′N), the very same location he gave to the Red Mountain. It is to be placed further south, at Vilinjam (8°22′N).[15]

In sum, there is fairly good evidence for locating Muziris near Cranganore, Tyndis near Ponnāni or Beypore, Bakarê near Pirakkād with Nelkynda some twelve miles inland, Red Mountain near Anjengo, and Balita near Vilinjam. The other identifications are little more than guesswork. In their favor is that they were all seaports of some account at one time or another and that they span the length of the coast in question with more or less plausible distances in between. There is but one exception: the run from Mangalore to Ponnāni, approximately 135 nautical miles, is almost double any other. However, any rearranging to close the gap would simply involve more guesswork.

---

other name for Naura, derived from Netrāvati, a later form of Naravu; Netrāvati is the name of the river at whose mouth Mangalore stands. O. Stein, *RE* s.v. Νάουρα (1933), rejects Schoff's suggestion of Cannamore and gives cautious and qualified approval to Pillai's identification.

[15] See Pillai (op. cit. under 51:17.15) 177: "Balita is 'Veḷiyam,' the older and non-nasalized form of Viḷiññam with the locative suffix *attu* added to it. 'Veḷiyattu' occurring in the early Tamil poems has been changed into 'Balita.' "

INDEX

INDEX OF CITATIONS